TIPPING POINTS IN INTERNATIONAL LAW

Addressing some of the most perilous, controversial issues in international law and governance, this volume brings together legal scholars from diverse geographic, personal and scholarly perspectives. They reflect on the pervasive feeling of crisis in the world today and share their views on the possibilities and limits of the international legal architecture and its expert communities in shaping the world of tomorrow. What exactly is this feeling that the contemporary international legal architecture is at a tipping point? What do these possible risks expose about the fragility and limits of our current conceptual and institutional order? What commitments drive our hopes and anxieties? Authors explore these questions across a wide range of possible tipping points and offer readers a unique snapshot of the lived experience of what it means to be an expert engaged right now in international law and governance. Each chapter covers both theory and practice in analysing a current problem.

Jean d'Aspremont is Professor of International Law at Sciences Po School of Law. He also holds a chair of Public International Law at the University of Manchester, where he founded the Manchester International Law Centre (MILC). He is a series editor of the Cambridge Studies in International and Comparative Law and Director of Oxford International Organizations (OXIO).

John Haskell is a Senior Lecturer at the University of Manchester Law School, serving as co-director of the Law and Technology Initiative and the Manchester International Law Centre. He is a junior faculty member of the Institute for Global Law and Policy at Harvard Law School and a board member of the Association for the Promotion of Political Economy and Law.

ASIL STUDIES IN INTERNATIONAL LEGAL THEORY

The purpose of the ASIL Studies in International Legal Theory series is to clarify and improve the theoretical foundations of international law. Too often the progressive development and implementation of international law has foundered on confusion about first principles. This series raises the level of public and scholarly discussion about the structure and purposes of the world legal order and how best to achieve global justice through law.

This series grows out of the International Legal Theory project of the American Society of International Law. The ASIL Studies in International Legal Theory series deepens this conversation by publishing scholarly monographs and edited volumes of essays considering subjects in international legal theory.

Books in the series

Tipping Points in International Law: Commitment and Critique
Edited by John D.Haskell and Jean d'Aspremont

Ethical Leadership in International Organizations: Concepts, Narratives, Judgment, and Assessment
Edited by Maria Varaki and Guilherme Vasconcelos Vilaca

International Law as Behavior
Edited by Harlan Grant Cohen and Timothy Meyer

Space and Fates of International Law: Between Leibniz and Hobbes
Ekaterina Yahyaoui Krivenko

Why Punish Perpetrators of Mass Atrocities?: Purposes of Punishment in International Criminal Law
Edited by Florian Jeßberger and Julia Geneuss

The Challenge of Inter-Legality
Edited by Jan Klabbers and Gianluigi Palombella

The Nature of International Law
Miodrag A. Jovanović

Reexamining Customary International Law
Edited by Brian D. Lepard

Theoretical Boundaries of Armed Conflict and Human Rights
Edited by Jens David Ohlin

Human Rights in Emergencies
Edited by Evan J. Criddle

The Theory of Self-Determination
Edited by Fernando R. Tesón

Negotiating State and Non-State Law: Global and Local Legal Pluralism
Edited by Michael A. Helfand

Jus Post Bellum and Transitional Justice
Edited by Larry May and Elizabeth Edenberg

Normative Pluralism and International Law: Exploring Global Governance
Edited by Jan Klabbers and Touko Piipaerinen

The Future of International Law: Global Government
Joel P. Trachtman

Morality, Jus Post Bellum, and International Law
Edited by Larry May and Andrew T. Forcehimes

Global Justice and International Economic Law: Opportunities and Prospects
Edited by Chios Carmody, Frank J. Garcia, and John Linarelli

Parochialism, Cosmopolitanism, and the Foundations of International Law
Edited by M. N. S. Sellers

The Role of Ethics in International Law
Edited by Donald Earl Childress III

The New Global Law Rafael Domingo

Customary International Law: A New Theory with Practical Applications
Brian D. Lepard

International Criminal Law and Philosophy
Edited by Larry May and Zachary Hoskins

Whither the West?: Concepts on International Law in Europe and the United States
Edited by Chiara Giorgetti and Guglielmo Verdirame

Tipping Points in International Law

COMMITMENT AND CRITIQUE

Edited by

JOHN D. HASKELL

University of Manchester

JEAN D'ASPREMONT

University of Manchester and Sciences Po Law School

CAMBRIDGE
UNIVERSITY PRESS

CAMBRIDGE
UNIVERSITY PRESS

University Printing House, Cambridge CB2 8BS, United Kingdom

One Liberty Plaza, 20th Floor, New York, NY 10006, USA

477 Williamstown Road, Port Melbourne, VIC 3207, Australia

314–321, 3rd Floor, Plot 3, Splendor Forum, Jasola District Centre, New Delhi – 110025, India

103 Penang Road, #05–06/07, Visioncrest Commercial, Singapore 238467

Cambridge University Press is part of the University of Cambridge.

It furthers the University's mission by disseminating knowledge in the pursuit of education, learning, and research at the highest international levels of excellence.

www.cambridge.org
Information on this title: www.cambridge.org/9781108845106
DOI: 10.1017/9781108954549

First published 2021

A catalogue record for this publication is available from the British Library.

ISBN 978-1-108-84510-6 Hardback

Contents

Contributors

JEAN D'ASPREMONT is Professor of International Law at Sciences Po Law School and holds a Chair in Public International Law at the University of Manchester Law School.

LARRY CATÁ BACKER is the W. Richard and Mary Eshelman Faculty Scholar and Professor of Law and International Affairs at Penn State University.

RAÚL CARRILLO is Associate Research Scholar, Yale Law School & Chair, Modern Money Network.

SARA DE VIDO is Associate Professor of International Law at Ca' Foscari University of Venice.

JUSTIN DESAUTELS-STEIN is Associate Professor of Law at the University of Colorado Boulder Law School.

DAVID J. GERBER is University Distinguished Professor of Law at Chicago-Kent College of Law, Illinois Institute of Technology.

ROHAN GREY is Assistant Professor of Law at Willamette University, the President of the Modern Money Network, and the Research Director of the Digital Fiat Currency Institute.

JOHN D. HASKELL is Senior Lecturer at the University of Manchester Law School.

MARK WESTON JANIS is William F. Starr Professor of Law, University of Connecticut and Visiting Professor of Law, Formerly Reader in Law, University of Oxford.

KISHAN KHODAY is Regional Team Leader for Nature, Climate and Energy with the United Nations Development Programme (UNDP).

BORIS N. MAMLYUK is Associate Professor of Law at the University of Memphis Cecil C. Humphreys School of Law.

RALF MICHAELS is Director at the Max Planck Institute for Comparative and International Private Law, Global Law Professor at Queen Mary, and Professor of Law at Hamburg University.

JAMEE K. MOUDUD is Professor of Economics at Sarah Lawrence College and Board Member of the Association for the Promotion of Political Economy and the Law (APPEAL).

USHA NATARAJAN is Edward W. Said Fellow at Columbia University, Global South Visiting Scholar at the University of British Columbia, and Senior Fellow at Melbourne Law School.

FRANK PASQUALE is Professor of Law at Brooklyn Law School.

ALBERTO RINALDI is a doctoral candidate at Sciences Po Law School.

CHRISTINE SCHWÖBEL-PATEL is Associate Professor of Law at the University of Warwick School of Law.

DAVID M. SCOTT is a doctoral candidate at the University of Manchester Law School and member of the Manchester International Law Center.

M. N. S. SELLERS is Regents Professor of the University System of Maryland and Director of the Center for International and Comparative Law at the University of Baltimore School of Law.

MARTIN WÄHLISCH is Political Affairs Officer at the Office of the United Nations Special Coordinator for Lebanon (UNSCOL) and Associate of the Berghof Foundation.

ADRIEN K. WING is Associate Dean for International and Comparative Law Programs and the Bessie Dutton Murray Professor of Law at the University of Iowa College of Law.

LUA KAMÁL YUILLE is Professor of Law at the University of Kansas School of Law.

Acknowledgments

We are very grateful for the financial support of the Humanities Strategic Investment Fund of the Faculty of Humanities at the University of Manchester. We also wish to express our gratitude to the American Society of International Law for allowing us to hold a seminar at the Tillar House and to the ASIL International Legal Theory Interest Group for their encouragement and collaboration throughout this journey. In this regard, our warmest thanks to Evan Criddle and Tim Sellers. The team at Cambridge University Press, especially Tom Randall, offered valued guidance and support. We are deeply grateful to the contributors who despite ever-growing constraints and burdens, shared their energy, time, and thoughts to create this volume together.

1

Experiencing Tipping Points in International Law

John D. Haskell

Things always have more than one beginning. It was one of those slightly cold days for my Californian blood, but this was northwest England and what would be described by locals as a pleasant afternoon in early 2017. The Manchester International Law Centre had arranged a two-day event, inviting colleagues to talk shop around formal panels and catch up on the latest professional gossip and personal updates over drinks and meals. Walking out from the sessions, Mortimer Sellers mentioned in conversation that the American Society of International Law (ASIL) Interest Group in International Legal Theory runs a series with Cambridge University Press. Maybe Jean and I would be interested to put together a proposal for an edited volume, and if we could land some funding, there might even be an occasion to host a workshop for authors at the ASIL Washington DC headquarters. In fact, we were just working to secure some seed money from the university to push international research and this seemed one of those fortuitous moments that life (or less romantically, our social status) occasionally arranges. But what to organise a volume around? Towards what ends? Over the coming months, Jean and I occasionally met up, usually over black coffee for an hour before catching a train or in between administrative meetings, and swapped ideas back and forth what might be interesting to do.

In hindsight, those months in spring feel an altogether more innocent time. Today, pandemic and protests rage in the streets while systemic ecological and economic collapse build on the horizon and digital technologists (or perhaps, the technologies themselves) dream up futures without the need for humanity. To enjoy a steady income working from home, to be writing from a quiet room, with food delivered to the doorstep and friends and family more or less immune from the immediate consequences of the unrest and violence, I cannot avoid the absolute reality that despite any complaint I may have day to day, that me and my cohorts are insanely privileged – and more troubling, that there is something intimately connected between our comfort and the precariat. If you had told Jean and I this in 2017, we would have of course agreed, each in our own ways. After all, wasn't the point to internalise the readings about the dark sides of our virtues, to begin to come to terms with the hard lessons of critical race studies, feminist approaches, political economy literature, queer theory and so forth, to personally and professionally not only check our status as white, Eurocentric/Anglo-American men of comfortable means, but act to some extent as traitors to our congregation in the name of real universal enfranchisement? Isn't a class traitor – on our best days – something to be? And was it not also in our own interests as well, at the level of pure survival instinct? Looking at the world, something felt terribly wrong. It was increasingly difficult not to pick up the bad vibrations. The 'establishment', the 'system', just didn't seem like it cared or knew how to address very visible problems. And yet there seemed so many good people of good will trying each in their own more or less quite competent ways to make things better. Whatever to do? We knew back in 2017 that so much was at stake, even as it often felt like not very much was actually at stake in our everyday lives. It was in the face of these contradictions that we sought to work harder, work better. Or so we told ourselves.

The two refrains that came out of shared sensibility was 'commitment/critique' and 'tipping point'. We were not exactly sure what we wanted to get at with these terms, but we had some ideas. We figured others also felt as if something was building – maybe reaching a 'tipping point' – though it was up for grabs what value to put on this momentum, or where it was located and how it might express itself, or exactly what one might hope could emerge. Our disciplinary training, personal affiliations, anecdotal backgrounds and professional obligations would undoubtedly reveal as much discord as shared sentiment. How are people, we wondered, experiencing the moment from their corner of the room? Could we steal away some time from the warp and woof of daily struggle and come together to reflect on the exact nature of what we felt troubled us regarding the nature of our critiques and the commitments that undergirded these critiques and pointed us towards certain normative inclinations? Maybe these commitments were internally at odds; maybe they didn't link up with our critiques. Maybe our critiques were more pedestrian than we imagined. Could we sidestep some of the suburban protocols of the professional lexicon that midwifed us into professional life? How much of what we were experiencing and doing was the stuff of (narcissistic) fantasy world-building; or could there be something meaningful to learn and say (beyond simple self-discovery, though nothing necessarily wrong with that)?

We felt, importantly, that this line of questioning could be fun, but that it also might be a serious intellectual project. Would the Interest Group and the publisher also think so? Were we right that there were colleagues interested to participate? Could they help us better understand the questions we were trying to ask? Would they be willing to actually reflect on their professed critiques and publicly speak about their personal and professional commitments? Would there be an audience for this sort of volume? We wrote multiple drafts and in mid-summer finally agreed to send the document off. The group was very supportive and not long afterwards the publisher also confirmed the project could have legs. The university provided just enough funding to reserve some hotel rooms near the Tillar House and cover meals for a cosy size cadre, but travel expenses and the like were off the table. Even then, Evan Criddle and Tim bent backwards to fill in gaps with the budget and the venues.

We put together a wish list of people that we would like to listen to in the volume. We tried to identify all the topics that we imagined might offer room for the experience of a 'tipping point' and then thought of people who might care to write on that theme. We tried to put more than one person down for each theme. The list was much longer than seats at the table in DC. Do we find some additional funding? We tried, but no dice. And we were on a timeline; we would have to send out the invitations sooner than later. Do we just slash the list of people and go with a smaller volume of contributors? But we had taken a long time putting the invitations together. We had even developed rules on the basis of what a fun party looks like: some unpredictability, a diverse set of folks, not everyone knowing each other ... That sort of thing. Here was a rule: the participants would be authors whom we had never yet published with together. In fact, neither of us had met a number of the possible invitees. Another rule: the cohort must include senior and emerging scholars, men and women, not everyone white (or, more accurately, a beige/pink hue), and not everyone traditionally situated within international law or even the legal discipline. The mirror is, after all, not usually the best place to know oneself. We learned things quickly about our own prejudices. Our list was almost exclusively divided down the middle between Anglo-American and European-based scholars. It privileged men and usually white people. There was definitely a wealth gap between our group and the general public. We were missing important topics. Why nuclear power/weapons but not agriculture/food? Why gender struggle but not refugees? Why development but not debt? We tried to fix some of these gaps – imperfectly. This was going to be difficult and time was running out.

We settled on an imperfect decision. Since the event was in the United States and we had just about as many seats as North American based colleagues on the list, they would be invited to the on-site event, and then the rest of our colleagues would be invited to contribute to the volume and we would try to create as many feedback loops and opportunities for communication and peer review as we could. Some folks did not reply. Others sent apologies. Others were tentatively interested but then dropped out. By some chance, we ended up with just about the exact equation of available seats for the workshop as colleagues in North America with resources to travel out and spend two days together, and we were able to match just about all our refurbished themes with an author. We held the event in May 2019. Tim, Evan and the ASIL community were very generous hosts. There were some slightly awkward moments trying to figure out how to talk to each other and some precious unscripted moments. I think folks had a good time. I know I did. The morning after, Jean and I met up for a late breakfast at an outdoor cafe not far from the hotel. We sat for hours, reflecting on the conversations from the previous day, looking through our notes, realising that in some ways we had to go back to the drawing board. How would we ever write an introduction to this set of themes? There were a lot of questions we needed to reflect on further. We would see each other the following month and see where we stood. Everyone unable to be in DC, we tried to keep close in the loop. The cohort was almost embarrassingly generous. Many people shared multiple drafts, showing real care in actually shifting direction or changing their overarching theme as they engaged with their chapters. A few people fell out due to life events, and their topics disappeared from the volume (e.g., gender, peace/war). Colleagues continued to offer suggestions that led us to rethink our own position towards the questions. The volume may be edited by two names, but we served merely as custodians to a group curating their own impromptu space and making sense of this only partially mediated congregation. Where we started was not where we ended up.

I remember speaking with Jean and a metaphor emerged to describe the document. We had all the session musicians in the studio and we were sharing with them the basic melody. And with any recording with an element of impromptu performance, wrong notes were expressions of soul – they weren't wrong notes at all, just the actual expression of what was going on. Here is what we sent around to the entire cohort – after the initial workshop in DC and subsequent email correspondence with a number of contributors – as what we were doing together:

The context: the feeling that international law is at a tipping point . . .

We feel, one again, that we live in a moment where international law looks on the precipice of foundational change – a perceived tipping point where what came before is about to change, or is already changing, and we are yet to understand this new environment or fully experience its effects.

This sense of impending change is a complex phenomenon. In the same instance, we may experience a type of modernist excitement and (at the very least, sublimated) existential dread, a feeling that so much is possible but also that we are being swept up by forces that scoff at resistance (e.g., global economic crisis), an experience that our actions matter and that we are only bit players in a much larger only somewhat human drama. What exactly might be newly possible and the exact nature of this looming dread is simply unclear. But what feels shared is the sense of crisis and the desire to escape our current situation.

This is, of course, not the first time we have collectively felt this way; within just the recent memory of Western oriented governance, other moments immediately come to mind, such as the build-up and immediate aftermath of the first and second world wars or when the Cold War came to a head. Conversely, what exactly is felt to be at stake and the institutional configuration of danger and possibility is distinct in its own historical particularity. Crisis comes in familiar guises but never actually returns the same. We are always faced with new challenges and constraints, and equally, new opportunities.

Even the 'we' referred to throughout the previous paragraph is itself always changing. Not too long ago, for instance, there would be no women, and certainly no women 'of colour' in an academic endeavour to think together and write about the crises of global governance. The feeling of profound crisis, however, warns against thinking this fact to reflect some progress narrative to the direction of history (as if it were a coherent, unified terrain of human experience writ large) nor that a particular tradition is responsible for whatever more inclusive communities we work (and possibly live) within. In so many almost countless respects, inequality functioning through the prism of race is manifest throughout the very structure of societies, impacting everyone albeit in different ways. The same could go for a number of other phenomena, often referred to under rubrics such as class, gender, human dignity, and so forth. And the interlocking configuration of dynamics that make up a given historical moment shape us differently where we almost feel our moment as different histories in the making and unmaking, and what is possible and should be possible along differing perceptions. We feel crisis but the nature and consequences of that crisis is ripe for miscommunication, confusion and despair.

To complicate matters further, even if we were of the same mind about the nature of crisis, how it is manifest and how it can be met changes depending on our chosen terrain of governance. We might agree that socio-economic inequality is a fundamental problem to a sustainable world order (at home or abroad), and that discrimination on the basis of race and gender is a stain on any individual or political order, but when it comes to tracing out the scope of the problem or fashioning solutions, our consensus rapidly breaks down. Or it may coalesce in one situation, but then diverge at the next stop. We are less a we, less in harmony, more at odds than we might have initially thought. What a strange reality to find ourselves within: people that feel themselves of good will, coming together in a spirit of camaraderie, willing to listen and to share, united around certain broad objectives, hopes and fears, and yet also finding ourselves in substantive disagreements without clear resolution. If this is so within our merry cohort, how much more so in the wider cultures we live within, at home, around the globe. If the crisis poses deep challenges, our solutions need to be equally bold and sweeping. If we cannot achieve consensus or a majority, do we still push forward? How does that impact the prospect of democracy, in terms of what it means and constituting a goal or metric of behaviour? What is it exactly, in short, that we stand for, at large and in a variety of specific contexts?

Whatever the specific personality of this crisis, this collective endeavour that brought us together to contribute to this volume is premised on the shared sense that there is indeed a crisis that confronts the architecture of global governance and which we feel with a sense of dread, which itself animates – or at least runs through the background of – our current thought and work . . .

Against the backdrop of the feeling that international law is at a tipping point, authors are asked to reflect on two mutually constitutive tasks.

First, there is the task of diagnosing what is currently troubling, wrong, being missed. However framed, this task is primarily about critique because it presupposes there is an unresolved problem. And this unresolved problem points to the world 'out there', but specifically to those cultures of expertise meant to confront these sorts of problems. Otherwise, if it was a problem that we had adequate answers for and which we were adequately addressing, then there would be no need to write further. It would already be something being taken care of, and so, on to the next thing. When we choose to research and write on a topic, it is always carried out with an at least implicit critique of the existing approaches among expert communities. This takes different tones (e.g., blind spots, class prejudices, intentional bad faith), but scholars are usually most comfortable in this mode of writing: pointing out problems, responding to what we believe other colleagues to be missing, and attempting to analyse the character of a given problem. In short, we are doing critique.

The second task is also always at work, though it is usually less pronounced in scholarship: *commitment*. By this, we mean to designate that normative orientation that motivates the critique and which points the way forward. Any critique, after all, is grounded on a standard, a metric of evaluation, of some form of commitment. Any stance (or attempt to not take a stance) is grounded on some commitment – or to put this a bit more simply, a belief. For a number of reasons, this is a far more difficult task for scholars generally to carry out.

It is true that we may find that we have multiple commitments functioning at once. For example, we might have a belief in the rule of law as a neutral process of adjudication that we feel necessary to uphold in the face of rising charismatic political authority, but at the same time, the issue in front of us seems to require we act perhaps slightly out of professional legal character to ensure a certain political outcome conforms to our broader understanding of truth, justice, the 'good'. One may identify at a Marxist and fight to uphold the legal 'reasoning' of the judge; one may call oneself a liberal committed to equality but side with the property rights of the few over the well-being of the many; one might be persuaded by deconstructionist literature but defend human rights legislation ... So we are faced with understanding a range of commitments and how these commitments are themselves part of an albeit loosely held broader commitment, however that might be characterised. Often, syncing critique and commitment means we expose ourselves to criticism of cognitive dissonance or being hypocritical. More often, we pass off any disconnect as being practical, noting that the world is complicated and constraining and that this is the best of the given situation as far as we can understand it – though, this itself is again, in a round about way, to speak to one's commitments without necessarily being explicit. To do so, would potentially mean a more uncomfortable situation: revealing that we actually believe something different to what we tend to think of ourselves, or simply that we don't care about following through on our beliefs, or facing that what we believe is different from what we tend to declare. Or, at the very least, that we haven't sufficiently thought through the hierarchy of our commitments or, if not a hierarchy, the relationship between our commitments, and in a variety of relatively common situations. So the task is extremely difficult to understand our commitments in relation to one another, how they make sense and operate in a variety of situations, and how our actions can be coordinated with our deliberate ideas and faiths.

At a more practical level, naming our commitments – let alone developing them in a programmatic fashion – is not common practice in scholarly circles, at least not in relation to law. We academics are most unassailable when we seek to 'analyse', 'clarify', 'diagnose', 'examine', 'investigate', 'study', 'test' ... We are in the business of ideas and understanding, not politics or making money – at least not in the first instance and perhaps such secondary interests are best kept to consultancy work for government or private industry. When we highlight a commitment or draw a conclusion it is almost always a general statement at the beginning of a paper that is not rigorously worked out in the text or occurs in the concluding passages of the text, pointing generally in some directions for others. The implicit assumption behind these tendencies is that the scholarship has shifted our thought in some way through its analytical clarity, and this will compel a change of mind among readers, which will somehow lead to reformed personal behaviour or institutional practices. Us scholars are part of a tradition – or perhaps more accurately, an industry – saturated by the belief that reason can guide thought and passion, and that ideas (the power and product of reason) shape deeds, and all of this subject to clarity and deliberation and wilful choice. The role of the scholar in this situation is to help clarify a given situation, to clear the way for reason to then chart our path forward. To concentrate on commitment raises the spectre of siding with individual passion and interest. And this is all the more the case with law-related scholarship and the humanities at large (and some social sciences): no more grand narratives or big explanatory pictures of the world or universal truths, at least not spelled out in substantive, specific terms.

All this amounts to an environment where academics tend to be distrustful of naming their faith. To do so is potentially bad form, bordering on the impolite, of saying that your tribe or club or belief is better than someone else's. It all feels a bit intolerant, a bit partisan, a bit out of step with the work of the scholar. And within the cultures of expertise surrounding global governance and the international legal architecture, not in keeping with being the counsellor, offering wise evaluation to the client, the elected officials, the prince . . .

To the extent that academics do take up this challenge, the suggestions suddenly look like a modified form of the tools and ideals that already exist, the argument that the promises of the international legal order have simply remained unfulfilled and need to be implemented with protestant zeal. The critics suddenly look not all too different from their mainstream counterparts, the difference largely the extent a given situation is liveable as it is, that it is a matter of complex practicalities that counsel cool passion and technocratic expertise, but not an existential emergency in need of profound revision.

Or perhaps it simply is a matter of following through on the promises embodied in the tradition of law. But even if we commit to a vision of dignity, equality, justice, or any other ideals, what exactly those ideals mean in our current historical configuration and how they specifically inform our critique in specific fields of law remains undeveloped within international legal theory. In short, while the discipline has become versed in critique and apology, it is less equipped examining the character of our commitments, of what a realised utopia looks like in practice.

. . . . .

No easy task to try and wrestle out. There could be any number of reasons for this, though perhaps most prominent in my mind is that the experiment embodied a contradiction. On the one hand, authors were called to adopt an almost confessional tone. With your tongue confess your heart! No more hiding behind your professed agnosticism and measured balancing posture! On the other hand, the legal discipline is fine with critiques and commitments, even with a bit of confession, so long as such gestures can plausibly be seen as going somewhere in the eyes of the practitioner, the policy maker or the judge. Thou shalt be useful! A confessional tone can easily get out of hand and relegate the author to amateur or outsider or quack status.

The real disquiet with a confessional tone is that the legal discipline is – for all its affinities and histories – not actually like religion (or therapy). Sure, you can plead guilty like the sinner in the confessional, but that is not why lawyers are trained. The advocate stops the police soliciting the confession, blocks incriminating evidence, contorts the documents and the facts to put their client in the most pleasing light before the judge and jury. In short, law is not about truth or justice – at least not in our practical training. It is a performance to an audience. When we write to an international law audience, we are being asked and perceived to perform. It can be impolite to say the quiet part loud, but anyone in the field can related to this. The author is also an actor; not necessarily dishonest but definitely putting on a show.

In an edited volume, the authors are catalogued into different types of roles and with different stakes – all of which are distinct from other types of publication medium. What is most striking about edited volumes, I think, is how rarely the chapters tend to become widely referenced sources within the genre. Not always the case, but book chapters are definitely lower on the totem pole than journal articles and monographs. The question then, why publish in an edited volume? For the love of the craft, for the opportunity to spend time with colleagues (edited volumes are often attached to in-person events), as a favour to this or that colleague . . . All these are undoubtedly true in many instances. At a formal level, for an emerging scholar, publishing in the volume is signalling that one is being invited into the club; for more established academics, that they are still important in the game and/or magnanimous to the community; for the editor, that there are a significant and well-respected cohort of colleagues to vouch for their credentials; perhaps to mount a collective assault on a certain professional sensibility that requires a show of numbers.

The edited volume also tends to follow certain conventions. One common trope that particularly impacts editors is that the introduction is expected to provide a short description of each chapter, which is usually situated within some claim about the overall new-ness or innovation of the volume and its potential impact on thinking in the field. The editor as curator of the artisan set pieces; the sum of the volume greater than its individual parts. This convention, however, seems categorically not the case in our volume and against the very spirit of the project. Ours was deliberately designed to make something together, to experiment in collaboration, and without a specific goal beyond trying to capture a snapshot of our current moment – of what felt to many of us, in different ways and for different reasons and with different anxieties and hopes, as a type of 'tipping point' that brought our commitments and critiques into sharp relief. If I were to characterise this time together, it was a conversation – sometimes with authors, regularly with my co-editor, Jean, and definitely with myself. Often it took the form of an internal dialogue, sitting alone over coffee, reflecting on what we talk about when we talk about 'tipping points'. To try and capture this mental back and forth, I feel, is somehow both confession and performance (or confession as a byproduct of performance). To personify this conversation that turns on itself, I tend to imagine the detectives that made a guest appearance in my first comic book as a young child, *Asterix in Belgium*: the incompetent twins, Thompson and Thomson . . .[1]

. . . . ..

Thompson: The text so far has already intimated a number of things that might be interesting to consider in relation to the discipline, though I imagine we may already be exhausting the reader's patience. Then again, perhaps that serves its purpose and they skip ahead, so long as they don't close the book instead. I have to admit I myself become wary whenever someone invokes language that we are undergoing some sea change. Is this taking place from within or outside the discipline and how are we really sure that something big is happening? I am not at all convinced that things 'out there' exist in advance of our professional lexicon, or if they do – as I guess things are happening all over the place all the time outside international law – I would wager it only registers on our radar to the extent it may be incorporated into our habits of thought and argument. The twentieth century dates that might spell big change for an international lawyer would gravitate around conflicts between major state powers: 1918, 1945, decolonisation and Cold War tensions, the Vietnam war, 9/11, and so on. These dates are attached to actors and organisations and ideas that seem to shape the narrative arc of how the world has come to be. If I was instead trained as an epidemiologist, however, I would have a very different sense of the drama of historical change: tracing outbreaks, looking at triggers that might spark new pandemics and getting into professional debates over how to stage and manage situations. The word

[1] In *Asterix in Belgium*, the twins appear with a specific legal-oriented mission. Thomson and Thompson disrupt a local brawl to announce that Julius Caesar has entered the territory.

'containment' means something very different to these two disciplinary cohorts and one is hard pressed to say which is more right than the other or if they necessarily line up or how to prioritise these lineages. If our language can account for any big change or if these changes can be largely missed out by other cadres of experts, then I just wonder to what extent it really is an actual 'tipping point' taking place or if we are talking about something less profound.

Thomson: Whether there really is something meaningful happening in the world outside our communities of people doing law stuff, I think that more often than not, the drama is felt and made real in the local politics of the discipline. In other words, the tremors intimate the possible reassembly of the discipline's vocabulary or moving around the deck chairs: which people in what organisations and cultural affiliations get to hold sway over things like academic promotion, consultancy, grants and prestigious publications, students and all the things that we might identify as a successful career.[2] There will be different priorities and styles of argument, to be sure, but it will all be somehow recognisable as 'doing international law'. I think you are right that this suggests the change is often something less than it is made out to be, that it is a type of rhetorical hyperbole to sustain the professional game. Saying that we are at a tipping point functions a lot like the move to pose a 'fundamental critique'; we are setting up for some renewed legitimation of a nook and cranny in the discipline. This is not to say that critique clears the way for our commitments to be made real or even known, but the substance and tone of the critique and whatever comes afterward offers insight into the commitments of the author – or for that matter, a view into the formal rhetorical economy of the discipline itself.

Thompson: And that commitment is not allowed as wide a range of political possibility as it is often characterised because its primary function is the furtherance of the discipline as an end in itself – what colleagues are getting at when they commonly speak to the 'progressive development of international law'. There is definitely something odd at work here: the discipline is a vessel that carries or embodies the ideological values of its constituency, but these commitments are themselves only legitimate to the extent they may give expression to the deepening and expansion of the discipline. What is lost is the possibility that there may be worthwhile commitments that run counter to the discipline, or at the very least, at odds with the expansion of the discipline. That the discipline may sometimes be part of the problem.[3]

2 See Thurman Arnold, *The Folklore of Capitalism* (Yale University Press 1937); Pierre Bourdieu, *Homo Academicus* (English translation, Stanford University Press 1988).

3 Note that this sort of claim, or critique, does not necessarily raise any fundamental critique of the profession. To the contrary, this style is an important outlet for dissent, failure and frustration by insiders and outsiders; it helps construct the 'spirit' of 'the law' across contexts.

Thomson: This begs the question, what then are the actual commitments, or politics, of the discipline? The discipline's immediate survival seems too easy an answer, because the discipline with all its argumentative protocols can only be sustained within a certain broader configuration of power among the institutions that make up the grist of everyday life. Up to this point we have emphasised the way the discursive structures and organisational roles shape the way participants can imagine the world, but it may equally be the other way around. The discipline expresses a commitment to a very specific way of ordering the world and assigning roles, and depending on the place and moment, different types of people gravitate to this encampment. International law is as much the outcome of a pre-existing cohort that bring with them a way of allocating resources as it is a machine that churns out initiates to 'think like a lawyer'. To get into what that politics might be is more tricky: partly because it is considered bad form to politicise the programme in broad strokes, partly because there will always be exceptions, and partly because it means going outside the autonomy of legal methodology and thereby losing one's legitimacy to be a trusted interpreter within the field. At the very least, one becomes associated with a particular school of thought or brand of ideology or seen as a methodological subgenre enthusiast – or on a bad day, all three at once, which smacks of being immodest if not downright unprofessional or even unsafe. But I think we can say that the profession operates with little deviation to ensure that mass democracy never fully seizes the reigns of state power. The people, or 'nation', may generate the fuel and justification for self-determination, for instance, but they are also one of the primary subjects to require restraint through international law. Reading through the canonical literature of the last century – for instance, the American Journal of International Law – this ambivalence towards mass democracy is expressed in a creative variety of ways: doctrinal arguments that sovereign immunity does not include property 'seizure', stretching the concept of global citizen to make the state only one of many stakeholders, rehearsing the historical threats of nationalist passion and isolationist tendencies, professing a cosmopolitan sensibility that transcends a country-specific society, the shift from attempting to educate the masses to struggling for authority with other experts and power-brokers, the concept of the human as a victim or consumer in the desert of politics and devoid of any collective agency making but entitled to fulfil their individual psychic-led desires in the marketplace of beliefs and experiences. What the discipline giveth, it also taketh away. And there are specific types of people that over time have gravitated to and away from this style of messaging.

Thompson: I agree and disagree. I would agree with you that international law both makes and is made by its constituencies and that it might be helpful to understand the discipline within a broader structural design of social organisations where factors outside the field of international law do a lot of work shaping its internal character. I also think you are probably right that whatever international law's reason *d'etat,* it leans conservative – after all, we are advocating the 'rule of law' at the end of the day.

Thomson: And it is exactly the bureaucracy that is the everyday messy world of struggle which makes up the 'rule of law' that is read out of the story. In some respects, suppressing the politics of the rule of law is the dynamo of the discipline. And what is the goal of a 'rule of law' if not a desire to harness the population.

Thompson: What social group doesn't decouple its administrative everyday from its more general knowledge production or outward facing programme? Take any church, family or university . . . there is always a tension between what is being said or produced in public and the actual machinery of how we make the sausage. Of course there is some relationship between these two arms of any community and it may be worth investigating exactly what makes this idea tick or that individual sink, but I think that this misses the boat. To do what you are proposing is either a form of muckraker journalism or a call for interdisciplinary study – I would imagine, the easiest fits in our line of work would be anthropology or sociology, or perhaps more recently critical race theory and feminist studies. I am, of course, all for calling a spade a spade and the turn to non-law specific methodologies over the past few decades is probably one of the most important positive changes to the discipline in the last century. And on that count, I think you are being uncharitable to who enters the discipline and for what reasons. It is exactly this opening up of what international law might be allowed to do and who might be employed in its ranks that seems to rebuff your critique of its anti-democratic character. Sure, Harvard, Stanford and Yale produce a lot of the law academics and they tend to come from a relatively closed set of families and life experiences, but you look at the last 20–30 years in the profession and there is also a lot of movement. It has a new look and a new spectrum of what is legitimate and not legitimate to talk about, at least when you step off the podium. And maybe more to the point, I think that there is a danger here in your critique where one could easily slip into a situation where we stop taking seriously the actually ideational frame we inherit when we become initiated into the discipline. It is not that you simply pick up political economy or sociology to now dissect inequality in or through the discipline; those sets of ideas and techniques will be filtered through the conceptual corpus and body politic of our discipline.

We are back at the original thought, that there is no simply getting to the 'real' or 'out there' without passing through the doors of interpretation. And it is exactly this heady world of interpretation that I think we all too often discount when we begin to think about international law in the world. This was the original impetus of asking people to examine commitments/critiques – to explore the intricate conceptual structures that we tend to be endlessly rehearsing. If there were a way out of this professional common sense, it would be through better understanding the ideas and vocabularies that ensnare our best efforts to address the world and each other.

Thomson: Take the expression 'tipping point' . . .

Thompson: I think that is the right type of gesture. Before we even begin to say what we are feeling or what should be done or what and why something or other is happening, I think we would have to get a better handle on this terminology and how it is graphed within our existing mental maps. I do not think you or I have by any means exhausted that inquiry, nor do we really have the space here to experiment chasing that dragon. But I do think we would do well to begin any inquiry into the world with how we speak about it and to appreciate that our descriptions and feelings operate against a background interpretative script which is anything but objective in relation to the 'real' world. I guess the first thing that comes to mind when I think of 'tipping points' is that on the one hand, it seems a relatively new term in international law circles, but on the other hand, it is not a new term within the popular consciousness. Around the same time that we were getting into our project around the concept, I suddenly noticed it was also getting picked up by other colleagues. At the 2019 ILA conference, for instance, 'tipping points' ended up in the title and breakout sessions of the programme, largely to signal the need for renewing the commitment and ensuring the relevance of the rule of law in a world beset by unrestrained politics. To invoke tipping point was to inaugurate a rehabilitation of international law. One might leave such an event wondering if the concept was doing anything that different from what we might imagine at work with a host of other metaphors: revolutionary moment, crisis, metamorphosis, watershed, breaking point, rupture, fall, turn, paradigm shift . . . Depending on your game and the specific audience, any of these words might come in handy to perform very similar functions.

Thomson: So what unites all these words is that they work within a familiar pattern of disciplinary technique: you make a critique, gauged to cognitively persuade the audience of the need to be listened to, and then you offer up a normative suggestion, which is either explicitly or could be more or less easily associated with some recognised-as-legitimate commitment. In this scenario, what you do not want is that your proposal is perceived to fall outside the realm of possible commitment or that your critique is felt to miss its mark, and it is usually on those two grounds that colleagues may try and take you to task. This gets back to that performative aspect of our discipline. Whether or not a claim wins the day is probably only partly due to the merit of the argument, to the logic of the conceptual game. Maybe this is just projection and too cynical, but among the power brokers and protégés within our discipline, any of our cherished professional commitments are always privately felt with a degree of ambivalence, at least when time comes for the rubber to meet the road. The human dignity of all people, sure, but what happens when two very different conceptions of dignity within or between societies come up against each other – how to decide? Is there really a higher norm we could consult to resolve this tension? Can we really turn to the best judgment of our institutions, the discretion or sensibility of the guild, the customary intuition of the profession to act as oracle? If anything, I think the language of commitments and our normative gestures tend to obfuscate what is politically at stake or what might otherwise be possible. And this takes me back again to something we discussed a little while ago, that it is exactly unpacking the specific stakes in any performance – both what it means for the speaker and their audience in those organisational settings and to what extent its content has legs outside that immediate forum, and towards what concrete outcomes. International legal academics as a community, I think, are pretty good at often confusing their work with 'doing politics', at least in the way their professed commitments would otherwise suggest. This is not a new insight. I think David Kennedy has been saying a lot of what we've been talking about so far to anyone that would listen for a long time now. And I see glimpses of this message in the work of a few colleagues from our generation even if they might have different priorities.[4] But for whatever reasons, the message seems hard to operationalise for the discipline. In fact, it seems to me that the discipline has developed a rich set of techniques for discounting anything of this sort.

Thompson: I am sympathetic to what you are raising, though I don't think there is necessarily any virtue in being perceived as the voice of perpetual heterodoxy. For one thing, I think it tempts one to accept the role of the loyal

4 If any of this text looks familiar, that is because it is influenced by a small cadre of intellectuals working in international law academia. I find myself regularly returning to work by David Kennedy and Pierre Schlag (especially from the 1990s), and among my own generational contemporaries, among others, Akbar Rasulov. See, for example, David Kennedy, *When Renewal Repeats: Thinking against the Box* (2000) 32 New York. Journal of International Law and Politics 335; Akbar Rasulov, 'What is Critique? Notes towards a Sociology of Disciplinary Heterodoxy in Contemporary International Law', in Jean d'Aspremont et al. (eds.), *International Law as a Profession* 189 (Cambridge University Press 2017); Pierre Schlag, Normativity and the Politics of Form (1991) 139 *University of Pennsylvania Law Review* 801.

opposition, which actually takes one's emotional and social context as somehow just part of the human condition. Perversely, the very attempt to unsettle things, to denaturalise patterns of thought, to constantly do all those 're' verbs – re-imagine, re-investigate, re-think – just ends up refreshing and ultimately naturalising the existing equilibrium. It tells us there is something here worth finding, worth re-working, just come back again to the fray. Now, I am not against staying inside the game of being an international law scholar and promoting the organisations of international law. I think you can do a lot of good here, and it actually takes quite a bit of technical acumen and professional investment in really knowing how to navigate the corpus of cases, debates, doctrines and organisational procedures to get things done. That might sound like I'm contradicting some of what I said earlier, but well, I'm a lawyer. It is this and it is that. That is what we do, and if you aren't into this sort of game, then maybe you're in the wrong room. Technical immersion blinds you to many doors in the mansion, but it also can be a valuable process of good mental hygiene. All too often, I think we see colleagues identifying as international lawyers, usually with a critical bent, that are teaching and writing without really even knowing, or at least demonstrating that they know, the basic ABCs of what it would mean to practice international law. What is particularly striking to me is that I don't think it is necessarily the case for other fields within the legal academy, at least not so much. But this was not always the case for international legal scholarship. There was a tipping point somewhere in the last decade or two when the new generation just stopped thinking a grounding in the traditional nuts-and-bolts of professional practice was important to being able to teach and write in international law.

Thomson: The manner you just used tipping point is interesting to me. We can see it is referring to an internal situation within the discipline, and maybe not even the discipline at large but what I imagine is particular to certain geographic locations. It raises the question whether this is just a blip in the history of the discipline or something that is here to stay – and so, if it really counts as a tipping point per se – which in turn would mean understanding better exactly how and why it arose and against what contexts it currently interacts. These various contexts would be internal and external to teaching and writing scholarship in international law, and would require a lot of extra-disciplinary skills to unpack. In a lot of ways, the current scholarly tendencies within more critical literature in international law reminds me a lot more of what was being produced in the mid-to-late nineteenth century than it does most of the work from about 1920–1990, at least within the Anglo-American scenes. Maybe that is because the scholars today usually have PhDs and have never practiced or care to practice in the legal field. Maybe it is because we no longer think that law really has very much influence in brokering power, or for that matter, helping us understand how power really is configured nowadays. A lot of this points to much broader trends in our global ecosystem: the erosion of collective deliberative public organisation in favour of private rule under an ideology of spontaneous order, the shift to situating all life within the market, looking to expertise in business management, economics and engineering rather than law, political science, sociology and other humanities and social science orientations. The decentralisation of state power was meant to hand the reigns over to the individual, but if anything, top down power feels simultaneously more ubiquitous and consolidated. This puts patterns of twentieth century establishment international law thinking into a difficult bind. In that worldview, the question was order among formally equal sovereign states. But in our world of unmistakeable and pervasive compulsion, how can we convincingly assert any sovereign is truly autonomous. The consensus answer for about a century was that the modern era is governed by the necessity of interdependence, but that really just restates the problem because it assumes the interdependence of sovereign automatons and it is exactly this autonomous self that seems to be off the table, almost in unison with the shrill insistence on the importance of 'the individual', distrust of all expert rule, faith in the invisible hand of the market, etcetera. But if states are not in the driver seat and we cannot trust in some invisible hand of private ordering, what or who then is at the steering wheel? Traditional international legal doctrines and professional conventions can tell us how to make an argument in court or how to design a formal constitution on paper or structure a complex acquisitions agreement, but they are not really designed to answer or engage directly with this new way of thinking about governance and human existence. In this situation, it could be expected that academics who are in the industry of knowledge production would turn to other disciplines that try and explain things. It is even affecting our more pragmatic, practice oriented colleagues in law departments: we are increasingly told we must rethink how we train the next generation workforce, to produce 'hybrid' lawyers. The fortunes of law, and especially international law, rise and fall on the centrality of public state ordering. If this account has any legitimacy, it suggests that there are a number of tipping points going on across organisations and industries. Now, depending on one's inclination, this could go in different directions. We might say that these various tipping points are all occurring within a broader relatively stable configuration of power, whatever we want to call it. Maybe liberal democracy is teetering, for instance, but capitalism remains strong. Religious passion is back in town, but it is just one of many wares for potential adherents within the secular marketplace. Or maybe these diverse tipping points are traces or instances of a much larger calamity that is already underway. If this is the case, then we get into a whole new range of questions about the extent it is subject to human control or outside our hands at this point, and if so what to do about that. If people are experiencing the world on these terms, then doing traditional international law stuff just feels like a performance in nostalgia, which is only going to be attractive again to a relatively distinct set of folks.

Thompson: I can see how this sends us right back around the bend, from a concentration on the internal vocabulary of the profession to needing extra-disciplinary tools. And then the predictable dilemma that any such tools will be filtered, manipulated, re-assumed into the deep structure of how international law scholars talk to each other. This is itself another way of thinking about tipping points – that moment when we go from one type of position or perspective to another within our disciplinary repertoire. Even if the world beyond our discipline is indeed tipping towards some new equilibrium, we remain constant through this endless recursiveness. I don't know if this a sign of strength or weakness, but it feels a bit narcissistic and depressing. Or maybe that is what it means to actually love – to ignore that much of what one loves is an illusion and be committed nevertheless through better or worse. But of course, I get your point, that this comes with some potentially big opportunity costs. We could maybe be doing something else that would be more meaningful or enjoyable. Then again, maybe safety is our driving emotion – there is nothing wrong with that per se – and if we are naturally such risk attentive people, maybe staying within the law is good for everyone concerned.

Thomson: Right, maybe. What we are finally doing here, though, that I think makes sense is hone in on the various ways we concretely engage this rhetorical devise 'tipping point' as people writing to an international law audience. I want to pick up on a question you asked earlier: what distinguishes tipping point from other metaphors, like paradigm shift? On the one hand, I don't think much of anything, it just all depends on the words you couple before the given metaphor. For example, we are 'undergoing', 'approaching', 'on the cusp' or alternatively, in the past tense, as something having happened and now we have to deal with it. Any of these sort of couplings can then be tacked on to a list of metaphors and have a certain common resonance. We are on the cusp of a revolutionary moment; we are experiencing a fundamental crisis; we have undergone a paradigm shift ... I have a suspicion that this sort of language is more common in social sciences than natural sciences, but maybe I am wrong. Other disciplinary logics probably follow different structural patterns of inquiry and persuasion. Or maybe this sort of terminology acts as a boundary object, soliciting participants across disciplinary orientation and professional context. But I think exactly here we could also get more concrete and think of very discipline-specific ways that the terminology of tipping points is a distinct rhetorical device and reveals a discrete history and conceptual spectrum of what is possible to say and feel.

Thompson: I like this language of feel rather than thought, because what I think we are dealing with is less about a corpus of logic, of schools of thought, of interpretative weights and balances to measure doctrines and direct precedent, and something altogether more experiential. Too often our professional activity ends up trying to clarify technical problems within relatively formalised disciplinary logics when in fact there is so much else actually going on to determine the criteria of validity and where we go on this or that: figurative elements of persuasive communication, aesthetic impulses for coherence, desires to differentiate ourselves from others or to belong, the psycho-bodily dynamics that translate into professional routines. Maybe this makes me all-too-humanist, but I almost think of this in the opposite light: that to really be human, to really empathise, to really listen where it is internalised into a new way of being, all this can only be done if we almost forgo much of what we think is attached to our professional identity and look at the formal levels of communication and production in a non-ideational light. In other words, to think that communication isn't just a process where we receive content and then process it in some internal memory bank that allows us to choose whether to store and implement or reject. It is not simply that we are not fully ready-made rational-wealth maximising, idea-maximising or pleasure-maximising beings, it is that so much of communication and our behaviour is not captured in the substantive lexicons we are trained into, either by birth or career. I think finding a way to speak 'seriously' according to the professional standards while simultaneously being aware and sophisticated in this experiential mode is not only part of what actually makes or breaks one's personal trajectory, but something that should be more incorporated into our professional know-how, or at least what we consider the rules of engagement.

Thomson: I think I hear you, and I am tempted to mirror back what you are saying, just to see if I got it right.[5] That itself would be a good exercise and if it became common practice would be or might lead to a tipping point of some kind. But I also want to get back to this focus on tipping point and how it specifically comes to operate within our law circles. The term has meant

[5] I find actually observing listening in action, by some of the masters of communication, a rewarding exercise. I continue to learn from Carl Rodgers, and many sessions (and lectures) are recorded and available online. See, for example, www.youtube.com/watch?v=QyJ3mvQousc.

different things in different locations and tracing that out, even briefly, may give us some insight into what sort of mental maps it helps generate today. Tipping point is remembered to first gain popularity among expert governance circles with Thomas Schelling's late 1960s essay where he tries to account for white flight to the suburbs. Schelling won his Noble Prize for work as an economist in game theory and he pushed for understanding governance as assessing and then modifying policy around the spontaneous order that emerges from aggregate individual choice distilled from any mediated organised action or pre-existing structural constraints. He wanted to understand why it was that at a specific moment a white neighbourhood went from accepting some degree of integration to completely picking up and moving elsewhere. What Schelling claimed to have discovered is that the white flight to the suburbs had nothing to do with any collective or individual racist prejudice, but that it was an indirect result of complex interpersonal market interactions. A neighbourhood reaching a tipping point was not a good or bad thing, it just (borrowing from natural sciences) describes a situation where the build-up of certain natural occurrence leads to a new equilibrium.

Thompson: The legal and political context is read out of any formal analysis and the focus is on individuals engaged in interpersonal exchange within some sort of non-coercive setting. And of course that naturalises a given very real political situation that is regimented through legal design. This idea of spontaneous ordering keeps coming back into our conversation. Here it is in the context of science and economics, and I can see how we can trace that lineage through an economic tradition of Smith, of Mandeville, or in scientific trends over the last fifty years or so that sees some synchronicity in nature's complexity and tries to translate this into human social ordering. But I cannot help thinking there are other more intimate traditions that do this – for instance, in theology, in philosophy and also within international legal thought. What is customary international law and *opinio juris* if not the working out of a gentle civilising hand in the fate of nations?

Thomson: It is a prevalent message that predates international law – or, for that matter, the Industrial Revolution. But like any message, of course, the context determines its resonance. This idea of spontaneous order existed before the 1970s, but I think it is only from around that decade onwards that it becomes so central and pervasive throughout the logics of governance. When some scholars talk about this thing called neoliberalism as a new strategic management or configuration of capitalism, a lot of what people are attacking is the entrenchment of this belief system. I guess you could call it the rationale for methodological individualism: it is just too complex to figure out, but don't worry, if you just allow all this dispersion to go about its business, the whole enterprise will work itself out in the best possible way. At the same time, that is not the whole story, because if you can situate yourself as an expert who knows how to spot the trends at work, to ride the wave, you can also potentially influence its direction, nudge it this way and that. There is a type of scientific logic to the chaos – just think about the notion of the business cycle and the proliferation of management literature. In fact, it is right around this time that we can see tipping points making a shift from the economists and sociologists into business management and international relations, slowly spreading out through the public and private sectors of what is beginning to be thought of as a truly global society. Notice that the tenet of methodological individualism can only really take off once people stop trusting in collective deliberate decision making – or what I think of as a state-based democratic order. Across the twentieth century, we were witnessing a struggle for expanding enfranchisement of working people, albeit in a very piecemeal fashion, but democracy was clawing its way into policy making. The world wars had only reinforced this trend. So the question is, how could this trust erode so quickly and people at large be willing to so fully swallow the pill of spontaneous ordering and anti-collaborative deliberation? I think at least two historical things happened, and which directly link to our story of tipping point. First, there is the civil rights movement throughout the United States and there is the struggle for emancipation throughout much of the colonial world – this is a story of a former ruling society, that identified as 'white' people, being afraid of what they saw as non-white people saturating their daily culture and the halls of politics. And second, there is the counterculture movement that is willing – albeit in often juvenile ways – to betray the social compact, no longer buying into the promised life of their parents. So, you have dissent within and outside the gates, no longer believing the promise of a liberal rule of law where people are rewarded on merit and can reach their dreams. This promise was felt to be not simply an illusion, it hid a deeply hierarchical system that diminished our individual humanity and relied on massive suffering. It is beyond the scope of this conversation to dive into these histories, but I think one outcome of this is that the establishment was able to strike back through a comprehensive reinvestment in the importance of norms, of principles, of unshakable rights – no longer said to be grounded in politics, but simply in the dignity of each individual. The perfect climate for a human rights regime to really launch. And since human dignity is not in the public, it must be in the private realm, in the marketplace where individuals can barter and exchange norms to find the best fit for themselves, and – here we see the spontaneous order messaging in full force – which would ultimately reflect the best aspects of our common humanity.

Thompson: The rise of the norm entrepreneur . . .

Thomson: Yes, exactly. The link between the norm entrepreneur and tipping points is explicit by the 1980s, with scholars like Sunstein and Finnemore arguing that change occurs by empathetic, passionate individuals exerting the moral energy of a rags-to-riches small business owner, winning over thought consumers in the marketplace of ideas until the norm is fully socialised into the international community. The tipping point signals that threshold when the norm goes viral and becomes part of the new consensus. And a lot of energy went into trying to model this journey, or cycle, and catalogue those traits and tactics for aspiring norm entrepreneurs, or as we might say in international legal terminology, people with projects. So tipping point was a descriptive practice – seeming to put no necessary weight on the virtue of the contagion – but was in fact wrapped around a particular consolidating moral logic.

Thompson: This is an interesting backstory when placed in relation to how we have come, as a population at large and as a profession, to understand tipping points. There was Gladwell's bestseller in 2000 that loosely made the term pop along the lines you mentioned above. But I think we could trace a slightly more nuanced change in the terminology over the last two decades. Around the turn into the millennium, leading scientists working around climate science in Europe and America had become convinced that the ecosystem was reaching an irreversible tipping point that would spell widespread chaos to the species writ large, if not for much of existing plant and animal life. In one sense, it was not all that different from the doomsday clock charting humanity's march to nuclear Armageddon. But in other ways, it was something very different. Sure, humankind might be able to reverse the tide, but whereas nuclear disarmament came down to rational diplomacy between enemies, here there was only nature itself on the other side of the table. Nature did not do empathy or negotiate, so the stakes were more drastic. In this sense, their notion of a tipping point broke the logic of the market, since a market failure might be disastrous for some, but it also meant wins to equal out the losses, and at the end of the day, the market would eventually bounce back. With the climate scientists, there was no bounce back after the threshold and everyone loses. It was also different from a situation like the nuclear context in that while it might be states that led the necessary reform; the problem was not a specific set of state actors that might allow for resolution through careful diplomacy but rather the entire way we globally produce and consume in a capitalist-driven society. The part about capitalism was often kept quiet, but the point was there: the business model of endless growth was simply not sustainable. Of course, others would counter the market might find solutions or that humans might be able to fast forward their technologies to kick-start space colonisation . . .

Thomson: Elon Musk sort of embodies these hedges to the scientists' message.

Thompson: A company man par excellence to allay the fears of ecological and economic collapse. The technological nerd who makes his billions in the market by helping facilitate market transactions and transforms into a norm entrepreneur building industrial revolution era technology to fly ever faster down the open highway on earth and to the stars. It all sounds very risk taking – or in today's lingo, disruptive – but really, Musk peddles a pretty comforting set of images. The open road is already paved; the stars are carefully plotted. It seems to me a fantasy that the market will solve this crisis. But it is wildly attractive to large swaths of the population. And that is exactly what the climate scientists were also finding to their horror – no one in government or industry was sufficiently listening to their warnings. Technology and human innovation would find a solution. So they tried to speak directly to the public through the media, and began experimenting with how to explain the threat. What they came up with was the concept of 'tipping points' and it caught fire in the media and in the popular consciousness. So the term was originally a marketing ploy, the scientists acting in some respects as a type of norm entrepreneur, though I think that terminology is not really accurate here. And then, over the last decade, we have seen natural scientists begin to actually incorporate the term into their conceptual research-led thinking rather than simply the way they speak to the public. But what I think is really important to pick up on here is that unlike the earlier iterations that you raised, this more recent version of tipping points is distinctly negative and largely resists the still dominant market-oriented tendency to think of risk as an opportunity. There is no upside to a new equilibrium. And it shifts the gravitation from scarcity between winners and losers to our collective vulnerability.

. . . .

I like this idea of collective vulnerability and orienting ourselves to the possibility of something other than our current world. I was going to say 'capitalism' rather than 'our current world', but I caught myself. In part, because I think the word would probably need to be unpacked and I think we are coming to the end of our discussion; but also because the word comes with so much different baggage and fantasy for different people and can often turn into a form of virtue signalling. I would like to stop for a moment and take the liberty to actually assign more explicit responsibility in the text for what is being said. *Pour le moment, je suis* John.

One thing I have really enjoyed in this journey together with my co-editor, Jean, is learning how to be a better collaborator, and really in this, I think I mean not only being more competent, but being a better listener. I think this takes trust, and that trust building requires a certain degree of empathy and sincerity. Not taking things too seriously, but saying what you mean and feeling out the context in which you are speaking. I think this is altogether different from being confessional, which is somehow too messy and personal, and often just sublimated narcissism. I thought I might share how I actually am experiencing 'tipping points' and what that might mean, in simple terms, in relation to my professional commitments and critiques. Not as confession, but to take up the same challenge posed to the contributors and as an experiment in how we might talk with one another – if for no other reason, to break out of what often feels like tired patterns.

It might be that what I feel is not an immanent global tragedy of human suffering but only the decline of a way of life designed to be comfortable to your typical Anglo-American bourgeois male. Or maybe I am prone to personal theatrics. But I cannot shake the feeling that we are witnessing the collapse of an entire way of life and everything in it, where there is no second chance for something else. It is just over for most people. I think we are already living through this process unfolding, beginning to sense that the accidents and mishaps are somehow connected and compounding to some ominous future tense. To the extent we might shake this future, I don't know if there is too much momentum pushing the other way against the established hierarchy of social ordering. I also don't know what international law academics can really do about any of this.

Then again, society is not a monolith and the higher education industry is one of its cells.[6] And you can work from there, maybe. And even if not, I think James Baldwin had it right when he said that by the very fact of being alive, one must be an optimist – which I take to mean, don't stop trying.[7] In the last couple years, I have found a lot of inspiration from scholars working around the theme of neo-chartalism and from those communities struggling for popular democratic sovereignty over how we create and use money.[8] If

6 Duncan Kennedy's 1985 lecture at University of British Columbia, available at www.youtube.com/watch?v=1RRVIEvO2l4.

7 For a short recorded clip of Baldwin speaking about how the affirmation "I am alive" means one "cannot be a pessimist," see www.youtube.com/watch?v=nAmL3F5uylo.

8 For example, see Mehrsa Baradaran, *The Color of Money: Black Banks and the Racial Wealth Gap* (Harvard University Press 2017); Christine Desan, *Making Money: Coin, Currency, and the Coming of Capitalism* (Oxford University Press 2015); David Graeber, *Debt: The First 5000 Years* (Melville House 2011); Stephanie Kelton, *The Deficit Myth: Modern Monetary Theory and the Birth of the People's Economy* (Public Affairs 2020).

asked today, I sense that any meaningful future for international law will be re-centred on immediate and tangible wins for working people and will judge institutional arrangements not on the basis of is-ought but the proximity between their current functioning and the possibilities inherent in their design. Let us be known by our politics in the here and now.[9]

Right now it feels like the odds are stacked against change in this direction. But then again, sometimes your bad luck turns out to be your lucky break.

[9] David F. Noble, *Beyond the Promised Land: The Movement and the Myth* (Between the Lines Press 2005).

2

The Literary Performances of the Tipping Point

Jean d'Aspremont

Using the notion of tipping point (hereafter 'the tipping point') to reflect on the dialectics at work between commitment and critique[1] in international legal thought and practice comes with a fundamental ambivalence. On the one hand, there can only be excitement for the resort to such a new symbolic universe out of which innovative arrangements – and possibly thoughts[2] – can emerge.[3] For sure, the tipping point can prove a terribly enabling tool for international lawyers, even more so since the editors of this book and authors of the following chapters are not bound by the meanings, uses and semantics which the tipping point had been filled with in other disciplines.[4] On the other hand, the use of the tipping point as a central conceptual tool limits what can possibly be thought and said about the dialectics between commitment and critique in international legal thought and practice. After all, the words that compose our language always allocate us a position[5] and constrain our imagination, experience and thinking.[6] And yet, the editors of this volume feel

1 For some general observations on how commitment and critique work together, see Edward Said, *Reflections on Exile and Other Literary and Cultural Essays* (Granta, 2001), at 167 and 171.

2 See Martin Heidegger, *What is Called Thinking* (J. Glenn Gray tr, Harper Perennial 1976). For Heidegger, opining, representing, reasoning, or conceiving, while important, do not constitute thinking but rather are accustomed ways of grasping thinking which have their own truth. He adds that science, for him, does not think. For him, thinking is questioning ourselves and the inherited opinions and doctrines we take for granted. It is about going beyond systems and concepts, that is the meta. For him we must think non-conceptually and non-systematically.

3 Barthes expressed a similar feeling about the pleasure of systematicity in semiotics. See Roland Barthes, *L'aventure sémiologique* (Seuil, 1985), at 12.

4 See the account provided by John Haskell in his introduction to this volume.

5 See Jean-Jacques Lercercle, *De l'interpellation. Sujet, langue, idéologie* (Editions Amsterdam, 2019), at 12–13.

6 On how disciplines are constituted around enabling constraints, see gen. Hayden White, *Tropics of Discourses. Essays in Cultural Criticism* (The Johns Hopkins University Press,

that such ambivalence should not deter them from exploiting the enormous literary and critical potential[7] of the tipping point for the sake of their inquiry into the extent to which commitment and critique form a totality.[8]

In the following, I would like to sketch out some of the traits of the formidable literary universe which lies behind the tipping point and which, in a way or another, permeates all the chapters that populate this volume. What follows is meant to neither articulate a normative claim nor provide any kind of overarching framework for this volume but only to shed light on some of the key literary performances of the tipping point when one mobilises it in relation to international law. To do so, the following paragraphs approach the tipping point as a self-sufficient signifier capable of absolute readability, that is irrespective of any of its actual use and context.[9]

2.1 TIPPING POINT AS AN EXTRAORDINARY MOMENT IN THE PRESENT

I understand the invocation of the tipping point as yet another *postulation of an extraordinary moment in the present.* In that regard, I believe the tipping point constitutes a discursive construction similar to that of revolution, crisis, metamorphosis, watershed moment, breaking point, rupture, fall, etc. that so often populate international legal discourses.[10] All those notions postulate an extraordinary moment in the present. It goes without saying that all these

1986), at 126. See also Jean-Jacques Lecercle, *De l'interpellation. Sujet, langue idéologie* (Editions Amsterdam), 75–102.

7 On how literary studies and critique work together, see Paul de Man, *The Resistance to Theory* (University of Minnesota Press, 1986), at 9.

8 On the notion of totality, see gen Jean-François Lyotard, *La Condition Postmoderne* (Editions de Minuit, 1979), p. 25. Theodor Adorno made a similar claim about the voracity of any concept that he sees as creating a totality which draws everything into it, tolerates nothing outside its domain, and translates everything in its own terms, even contradictions to it. On the totalization of thought as a modern phenomenon, see Theodor Adorno and Max Horkheimer, *Dialectic of Enlightenment* (London, Verso, 1997), at 24. See more generally T. W. Adorno, *Negative Dialectics*, trans. E. B. Ashton (Routledge, 1973). See contra Raymond Williams, *Politics and Letters: Interviews with New Left Review* (New Left Books, 1979), at 252.

9 To qualify such an approach Jonathan Culler speaks of the text being orphaned (see Jonathan Culler, *Structuralist Poetics* (Ithaca, 1975), at 133). Roland Barthes speaks of the death of the author. See Roland Barthes, "La mort de l'auteur" in *Le Bruissement de la langue* (Seuil, 1984) 61. See also Stanley Fish, "With the Compliments of the Author: Reflections on Austin and Derrida", 8 *Critical Inquiry* (1982) 693–721. For a criticism of this approach, see Jürgen Habermas, *The Philosophical Discourse of Modernity. Twelve Lectures* (translated by Frederik Lawrence) (Polity Press, 1987), at 166.

10 On the Hegelian dimensions of revolution, crisis, metamorphosis, watershed moment, breaking point, rupture, fall, etc. see Jürgen Habermas, *The Philosophical Discourse of Modernity. Twelve Lectures* (translated by Frederik Lawrence) (Polity Press, 1987), at 7.

postulations of a present being an extraordinary moment would not be possible without the historical consciousness inherited from the Enlightenment.[11] In that sense, the invocation of the tipping point in international legal studies is yet the manifestation of a long-thought tradition. It is a tradition whereby the extraordinariness of the present is constantly staged to justify a specific performance in the present and its continuation in the future.[12] In that regard, it is no coincidence that lawyers, and especially international lawyers, repeatedly mobilise constructions like tipping point, revolution, crisis, metamorphosis, watershed moment, breaking point, rupture, fall, etc. in their discourses.[13]

Whilst I am not surprised that the postulation of an extraordinary moment in the present constitutes a recurring discursive move in international law, I am struck by the lightness and nonchalance with which international lawyers mobilise such postulations of an extraordinary moment in the present, be it through the idea of tipping point, revolution, crisis, metamorphosis, watershed moment, breaking point, rupture, fall, etc. I believe that the act of postulating an extraordinary moment in the present is no simple discursive constructive. The possibility of postulating an extraordinary moment in the present is the result of a wide series of very sophisticated moves and postulations. Indeed, postulating an extraordinary moment in the present entails the designation of an ordinary that is declared to be defunct. The designation of a defunct ordinary, in turn, is a multi-dimensional construction that requires transcending the time of the present from the time of the past as well as transcending the content of the present from the content of the past. The designation of a defunct time ordinary also requires a twofold universalisation, namely the universalisation of a phenomenon, behaviour, standard, state of affairs, perception, etc., which is erected in a type of normality and the localisation of this

[11] Hayden White, *Metahistory. The Historical Imagination in the Nineteenth-Century Europe* (Johns Hopkins University Press, 2014), 51; Michel Foucault, *L'archéologie du savoir* (Gallimard, 1969), p. 23; Michel Foucault, *Les mots et les choses* (Gallimard, 1966), 14 and 381; Michel de Certeau, *L'écriture de l'histoire*, (Gallimard, 1975), at 21; Michel Foucault, *Le gouvernement de soi et des autres. Cours au Collège de France* (1982–1983) (Gallimard Le Seuil, 2008), 16; Peter Sloterdijk, *Après Nous le Déluge*, Editions Payot & Rivages, 2016, at 16; Hans-Georg Gadamer, Truth and Method, Bloomsbury, 2013, at xxiii; Jürgen Habermas, *The Philosophical Discourse of Modernity. Twelve Lectures* (translated by Frederik Lawrence) (Polity Press, 1987), 5–6.

[12] A. McIntyre, *Whose Justice? Which Rationality?* (Duckworth, 1988), at 363.

[13] Ph. Allott, Language, Method and the Nature of International Law, 45 *BY-BIL* 79 (1971), 122; Anne Orford, '*The Destiny of International Law*', 17 *LJIL* (2004) 441–476; Hilary Charlesworth, International Law: A Discipline of Crisis 65 *The Modern Law Review* (2002), pp. 377–392; David Kennedy, '*When Renewal Repeats: Thinking against the Box*', 32 *N. Y. U. J. Int'l L. & Pol.* 335 (1999–2000).

normality in a past held as universal. It is thus no minor thing to postulate an extraordinary moment in the present. It entails a series of moves and assumptions which are all very loaded.

The lightness and casualty with which international lawyers postulate an extraordinary moment in the present is even more surprising, for what the metaphor of the tipping point does is never innocent.[14] Obviously, through the extraordinary present it postulates, the tipping point serves the self-empowerment, self-entitlement, self-promotion, self-vindication, self-congratulation, etc. of whoever invokes it. More importantly, in universalising both a certain normality and certain past, the tipping point silences, orders and governs. Indeed, the tipping point manufactures the real, creates knowledge and writes history; it declares that certain phenomena, behaviours, standards, states of affairs, perceptions, etc., are abnormal or monstrous while empowering certain actors and ostracising others, etc. In that sense, there is a lot of power going into the postulation of an extraordinary moment in the present. I think international lawyers should be much more careful when they resort to discursive constructions like tipping points, revolution, crisis, metamorphosis, watershed moment, breaking point, rupture, fall, etc.

2.2 TIPPING POINT AS SUSPENSION OF TIME

Although the tipping point may belong to this family of postulation of an extraordinary moment in the present, one may still wonder whether there is something that is better said (or argued) with the tipping point rather than with the other postulations of an extraordinary moment in the present like revolution, crisis, metamorphosis, watershed moment, breaking point, rupture, fall, etc. In that regard, I believe that, whilst the tipping point shares similar modes of historicisation, universalisation, silencing, and governance as narrative constructions like revolution, crisis, metamorphosis, watershed moment, breaking point, rupture, fall, etc., the tipping point distinguishes itself from the other postulations of an extraordinary moment in the present by virtue of the very slow and linear temporality it puts in place. It is true that, at first glance, the tipping point projects the image of an non-linear and sudden temporality. After all, we are speaking of a 'point', that is a precise moment in time. Yet, at the same time, the tipping point seems to reverse the temporality. Indeed, in the tipping point, the point is located on a trans-temporal line, this point being neither an end nor

[14] On what the metaphors of legal discourses do, see Steven L. Winter. *A Clearing in the Forest. Law, Life and Mind* (The University of Chicago Press, 2001), at 66. See also Hayden White, *Tropics of Discourses*, at 122–123.

a beginning. In the tipping point, the point that is tipping is stretched between the past and the present, neither ready to leave the past behind nor ready to embrace the present in front of it. In that sense, the temporality informing the tipping point is dialectic. The moment is caught between a past that is never ending and a present that is not yet beginning. I do not think that other postulations of an extraordinary moment in the present like those found in revolution, crisis, metamorphosis, watershed moment, breaking point, rupture, fall, etc. offer such a linear and dialectic temporality.

Such a linear and dialectic temporality can be very convenient for international lawyers. By contrast with revolution, crisis, metamorphosis, watershed moment, breaking point, rupture, fall, etc., the tipping point offers an unmatched flexibility in terms of temporal self-situating. This means, more concretely, that the tipping point allows international lawyers to postulate an extraordinary moment in the present but without being too specific as to where they locate themselves and their action. The tipping point being neither after the past nor before the present, international lawyers can remain very elusive as to where they situate themselves and their actions. In the same vein, the tipping point allows them to constantly move along the trans-temporal line on which the point is located and be somewhat temporally un-situated. As one never knows where that point is, one never knows where and when international lawyers take action. The tipping point facilitates temporal instability as well as what I would call here some kind of 'self-unsituatedness'.[15]

Thanks to its linear and dialectic temporality and its facilitating of temporal instability, one could see an enormous critical potential in the tipping point. In making the temporality more instable, the tipping point, by contrast with revolution, crisis, metamorphosis, watershed moment, breaking point, rupture, fall, etc. can disrupt the traditional temporality that informs international legal discourses. The temporal instability of the tipping point also generates the feeling that the *tipping* of the tipping point is eternal. In fact, in the tipping point, the tipping itself is never tipped but always tipping. As the tipping of the tipping point goes on, time is suspended, thereby allowing deconstruction to do its job.[16]

15 On the idea that dialectics cannot account for the intelligibility of conflict see the remarks of Michel Foucault in Noam Chomsky and Michel Foucault, *The Chomsky-Foucault Debate on Human Nature* (The New Press, 2006), at 147.

16 See gen. Terry Eagleton, The Function of Criticism (Verso, 2005), at 105. See also Jacques Derrida, Force de Loi: Le 'Fondement Mystique de l'Autorité', 11 *Cardozo Law Review* (1990) 920–1046, at 954–956.

2.3 TIPPING POINT AS HESITATION

Besides the temporal instability which tipping point can bring about in international legal discourses, there is another critical aspect of the tipping point which I would like to mention. As the tipping point refers to a *tipping* that is never tipped as well as a *point* that is neither in the past nor in the present, the tipping point denotes a hesitation. It manifests a change unsure of itself, a self-restrained change, a change that does not want to change anything, a change that is having second thoughts. I believe that the hesitation that accompanies the tipping point necessarily infuses with self-reflectivity the claim, the narrative, the story, the argument, etc. which the tipping point serves. As hesitation, the tipping point prompts self-reflection.

There is more to this idea of hesitation that accompanies the tipping point. I believe that this hesitation not only manifests a torn temporality, but there is also probably something even more fundamental than that. I think that the hesitation at work in the tipping of tipping point is, more generally, the expression of the unachievable dimension of modernity. Indeed, modernity has always sought to resist absolutism. By resisting absolutism and assuming the relativity of any discourse, system of truth, representation, perception and experience, modernity has never been able to even vindicate itself, for it has always been predicated on its own historicity, contingency and self-disloyalty.[17] The result is that modern discourses and modern regimes of truth[18] have had only themselves to build their own foundations and entertain claims for truth.[19]

The hesitation at work in tipping point seems to echo this ambivalence of any modern discourse or regime of truth. Caught in a self-confident momentum, the quest for truth is interrupted by the reminder of the historicity and contingency of any claim for truth, thereby provoking a state of tipping. In that sense, the tipping point manifests the crisis with which modernity was born. Any claim, even more so a claim under international law, is left tipping between a past and a present, between the ordinary and the extraordinary, etc. It could even be argued that the tipping point is the normal state of any modern discourse, and thus of any claim made under such a discourse. In that

[17] Paul Ricoeur, *La mémoire, l'histoire, l'oubli* (Seuil, 2000), 386–387; Jean-François Lyotard, *La Condition Postmoderne* (Editions de Minuit, 1979), at 65; Peter Sloterdijk, *Critique of Cynical Reason* (University of Minnesota Press, 1987), 6 and 76 (the expression of self-disloyalty is from Sloterdijk).

[18] On the idea of regime of truth, see Michel Foucault, *Naissance de la biopolitique. Cours au Collège de France* (1978–1979) (Gallimard Seuil, 2004), at 20–22.

[19] Jürgen Habermas, *The Philosophical Discourse of Modernity. Twelve Lectures* (translated by Frederik Lawrence) (Polity Press, 1987), at 7.

sense, the chapters offered in this volume offers wholehearted modern acknowledgments by their authors of the historicity and contingency of the international legal discourse and of any claim entertained thereunder. In that sense, there is a lot of candid modesty in the chapters that follow.

2.4 TIPPING POINT AS A SLIP OF THE LANGUAGE

I would like to return to the temporality that is postulated by the tipping point. The tipping point's temporality remains an indivisible temporality with only two entry points, that is, the past and the present. One can hardly think of a more orthodox temporality. More fundamentally, the tipping point, like all other postulations of an extraordinary moment in the present, always has a rehabilitative dimension as far as the content of the past is concerned. Indeed, the tipping point postulates a past from which the present can never emancipate itself. In other words, the ordinary past is always vindicated by the extraordinary present.[20] The tipping point is thus a very rehabilitative notion.

There is another reason why I think the tipping point is very rehabilitative of a pre-existing ordinary. Whilst the *point* of the tipping point may be neither in the past nor the present but torn between the two, the *tipping* dimension of the tipping point irremediably remains in the present. Let me explain this. The tipping point carries a possibility that cannot but be in the present. There is no possibility that precedes its realisation.[21] Any possibility always follows its realisation. The same holds for the tipping point. By making the turn from the ordinary to the extraordinary a possibility, the tipping point places itself in the present of its saying, not in the past of its occurrence. And this is why the tipping can only be an *ex post* cobbling of a pre-existing ordinary.

This charge against the critical potential of the tipping point could even be pushed further. I wonder whether international lawyers, when invoking the tipping point, commit a slip of language. Indeed, the present can only be extraordinary as long as the past ordinary from which the extraordinary present departs tolerated no exception.[22] If the extraordinary of the present that is postulated by the tipping point falls within the exceptions accepted by the ordinary, the postulated extraordinary cannot be extraordinary but is just the

[20] H. Arendt, *On Violence* (Houghton Mifflin Harcourt, 1970) 237–38; J. Butler, 'Critically Queer' 1 *GLQ: A Journal of Lesbian and Gay Studies* (1993) 17, 24; Noam Chomsky and Michel Foucault, *The Chomsky-Foucault Debate on Human Nature* (The New Press, 2006), at 58–59.

[21] Henri Bergson, *Le possible et le réél* (Quadrige, 2011), 11–17.

[22] Jacques Derrida, *The Beast and the Sovereign*, Volume 2 (University of Chicago Press, 2011), at 140. Comp. with A. McIntyre, *Whose Justice? Which Rationality?* (Duckworth, 1988) 364.

ordinary. In other words, for there to be a tipping point, there must be something unforeseen, unproviding, or unorganised by the ordinary past. Short of being alien to the ordinary past, the tipping point is nothing more than the ordinary which it perpetuates and reinforces. Unalienated from the ordinary past, the tipping point is the ordinary made extraordinary. Yet, I believe that most international lawyers invoke the tipping point for an extraordinary already organised by the ordinary.

Even if international lawyers refer to the tipping point and, by a slip of language, mean the opposite of revolution, crisis, metamorphosis, watershed moment, breaking point, rupture, fall, etc., there still is much to learn from the way in which international lawyers mobilise the tipping point. If the tipping point is just the ordinary made extraordinary in the present and a perpetuation of that ordinary, the tipping point tells us what the ordinary is, could be or should be! It reveals faces of the ordinary which we would not have thought of or could possibly perceive. In that sense, the tipping point can prove a formidable yardstick to gauge what international lawyers hold as an actual or desired ordinary and all what hides therein. Somewhat paradoxically, it is in this loyalty to the ordinary that the tipping point's critical virtue lies. By revealing what international lawyers elevate to the ordinary, the tipping point also unearths the many disciplinary, moral, structural biases, desires, utopias, affects, etc. that inform international legal discourses.

It is by virtue of this loyalty to the ordinary that we can use tipping point as a bellwether of international lawyers' commitments. Whilst expressing a torn temporality and a fundamental hesitation, the tipping point comes to function as an indicator of the commitments of international lawyers and all their disciplinary, moral, structural biases, desires, utopias, affects, etc.

2.5 TIPPING POINT AND NON-COMMITMENTS

The foregoing has tried to show that the tipping point, in telling what the ordinary is, tells us what international lawyers are committed to. This is why the tipping point can be used as a discursive tool that provides a glimpse into international lawyers' commitments. This leads me to formulate a few final remarks on the very idea of commitment that is revealed through the tipping point as well as on whether one should confess one's commitments or simply let them be revealed by discursive tools like the tipping point.

Although, for a long time, a great number of international legal scholars saw their role as being above practice, discourse, current developments, etc. (that is the dream of the meta-standpoint), most of us have come to terms with the fact that anything we do with international law is saturated with commitments.

Commitments are everywhere in what we see, what we hear, what shocks us, what we say, what we react to, etc. Even venturing into saying something about (or in relation to) international law reflects a primitive commitment to give truth-claiming value to such saying. In a way, it seems that international lawyers have finally read their classics.

What I find interesting with respect to the idea of commitment is that a great deal of these commitments are not commitments we have made ourselves. *These are our commitments but not made by us*. I think that the international legal discourse has made these commitments for us, on our behalf. Jacques Derrida said that our native language is not our language because we do not possess it but are possessed by it.[23] Giving it a different twist, Althusser told us that ideology 'interpellates' individuals as subjects.[24] I think the same goes for international law irrespective of whether one sees it as functioning as a language, discourse or as an ideology. International law makes the international lawyers committed to all kind of things: a specific geography, a specific space, a specific temporality, a specific past, a specific real, a specific subject, etc.

If this is the case that international law has committed us to all kind of things, one does not necessarily need to *confess* one's commitments. They are all there, in front of us. Of course, we all have distinct sensibilities as to what we think international law should do. Some of us want justice, others want equality, other wants to protect their parish or their village, other wants a super community, others want money (whatever each and every of these ideals mean to the person pursuing them), etc. Yet, I think our commitments, whatever they are, are already embedded in the pre-discursive categories that populate international law. This is why I think these commitments – which have been made for us and on our behalf – ought not to be confessed. International law having committed us to all kinds of things, it is international law that ought to confess.

That international law already commits international lawyers to all kinds of things should certainly not entail a de-responsibilisation of international lawyers for all what goes wrong with international law. After all, once one engages with a discourse one comes to share responsibility for what that discourse does. And this is the very reason why one should always strive to prevent the discourse from doing what one deems intolerable or indecent. In

[23] Jacques Derrida, *Le Monolinguisme de l'Autre* (Gallilée, 1996).

[24] Louis Althusser, 'Ideology and ideological state apparatuses (Notes towards an investigation)'. In Lenin and Philosophy and Other Essays, pp. 142–7, 166–76. Translated by Ben Brewster. New York and London: Monthly Review Press, 1971.

that sense, more important than our commitments – which after all are made by us and on our behalf by international law – what I find most important is to confess our *non-commitments*, that is what one does not want international law to do. Needless to say that I cannot speak on behalf of the authors of this volume, let alone summarise the non-commitments that their respective chapters bespeak. I can only speak for myself. As far as my own non-commitments are concerned, I have become, in the last years, more sensitive to protecting international law's discursive practice from being recuperated for some sort of post-truth delinquency. In particular, I am wary of having anything I say about international law being used as ammunition by post-truth vandals for their current post-truth rampage. Modern truth was bound to fail simply because it was never going to live up to its own self-imposed standard.[25] We all knew it. Even Kant said it elegantly and repeatedly more than two centuries ago. Nowadays, these post-truth vandals act as if they have just learnt that truth cannot be true. Maybe these post-truth vandals should have spent more time reading their classics than tweeting. Be that as it may, the long-predicted failure of truth – and of the truth regimes – does not mean that anything can be said and done by, through and in the name of international law. No, not everything goes. In this context, the need for international lawyers to come up and say what they are not committed to is even more pressing. So rather than confessing their commitments, I believe that international lawyers should confess their non-commitments.

It must be acknowledged that international legal 'textualists' – who, like me, like to look into how international law, as a discourse, does what it does – certainly have their share in the currently post-truth delinquency. For too long, textualists have indulged in what they perceived as the beauty of structure and have said nothing about what international law should not be doing. They have, in other words, failed to express their non-commitments, thereby facilitating the recuperation of their work by post-truth vandals.[26] It is time that international lawyers indicate clearly what they do not want international law to do, and in so doing, indicate which commitments international law should not be doing for them and on their behalf.

[25] See gen. Peter Sloterdijk, *Critique of Cynical Reason* (University of Minnesota Press, 1987). See also Bruno Latour, *Nous n'avons jamais été modernes. Essai d'anthropologie symétrique* (La Découverte, 1997); Bruno Latour, *An Inquiry into Modes of Existence. An Anthropology of the Moderns* (Translated by Catherine Porter) (Harvard University Press, 2013), at 152–178. Jean-François Lyotard, *La Condition Postmoderne* (Editions de Minuit, 1979), 65

[26] See gen. Bruno Latour, 'Why has Critique Run out of Steam? From Matters of Fact to Matters of Concern', 30 *Critical Inquiry* (2004) 225–248. See also Fuad Zarbiyev, 'International Law in an Age of Post-Shame', *ESIL Reflections*, 2020.

The tipping point, in that it projects a hesitation, provides a great opportunity to claim what cannot be subject to hesitation, namely our non-commitments. Said differently, the tipping point, by postulating an extraordinary moment in the present, can clearly indicate what cannot belong to the realm of the (extra-) ordinary-ness, that is what can be neither ordinary nor extraordinary, and thus what is simply indecent and unacceptable. I hope that elucidating and debating what we do not want international law to ever do, as this book tries to do, will be the greatest takeaway of the following chapters.

3

Authoritarianism

Frank Pasquale

International law presumes some common bonds of belief and empathy among all persons. At the level of individual states, which do more for (and to) their citizens than the present international order, even more is required to maintain social harmony and cohesion. A common understanding of a thicker set of constitutional and social commitments is necessary. But what happens when that common understanding breaks down? For example, what if leaders of one party (and their followers) start to consider other parties illegitimate – inherently disqualified from power? Are there certain "tipping points," or points of no return, when a pluralistic order passes an event horizon toward a black hole of authoritarianism – an unrecoverable decline and collapse of democracy?

Many polities faced these tipping points in the aftermath of World War I. Extreme conditions of deprivation and insecurity left nations ready to try strongman rule, and these strongmen suppressed the opposition ruthlessly. Fascist rulers rallied supporters around blood and soil visions of national greatness. In the 2010s and 2020s, a similar ethnonationalism (fueled by racism, xenophobia, and economic anxiety) has been effectively manipulated by a new generation of right-wing authoritarian and quasi-authoritarian rulers. They tend to target immigrants, blaming them for economic insecurities caused far more directly by their own commitments to neoliberalism and what Susan Strange deemed "casino capitalism."[1]

In some of these jurisdictions, democracy is well and truly gone, short of revolution. For example, Viktor Orbán and Vladimir Putin have orchestrated *Gleichschaltungen* so deep and entrenched that effective opposition has been rendered impossible. In others, such as Wisconsin, glimmers of hope remain.

[1] Susan Strange, Casino Capitalism (London: Blackwell, 1983). Some of the discussion of Balkin & Levinson's *Democracy and Dysfunction* in this chapter was originally published in a blog symposium on their book at the Balkinization blog, at this URL: https://balkin.blogspot.com/2019/05/crisis-or-rot-dueling-metaphors-of.html.

While the Republican Party of the state has both deeply gerrymandered the legislature and taken away many powers from the state's governor, the state's elected Supreme Court might declare the gerrymander violative of the state's constitution. The U.S. as a whole narrowly escaped a second term of Trumpism in 2020, with courts and local election officials by and large resisting enormous pressure from the President and many of his Republican followers to subvert the election results. Had a few hundred thousand votes shifted in key states, the U.S. may well have passed a tipping point toward the type of authoritarian governance now evident in Hungary and Russia.

Asked to contemplate the theme of "tipping points" for this volume, I wish to examine both the theory and practice of metaphorically analyzing politics. I start that process by reflecting on the debate between Jack Balkin and Sanford Levinson concerning the proper metaphor for organizing thought about recent decades of democratic dysfunction in the United States (Section 3.1). The metaphor of constitutional crisis, with its attendant biological and medical resonances, generatively suggests further families of metaphors, including the category of "tipping points." These metaphors disclose the urgency of the present conjuncture, and Section 3.2 expands upon them. The metaphors also suggest that, in times of crisis, the duty of the analyst is not only to describe harsh realities, but also to propose ways of ameliorating them. Section 3.3 suggests some ways to do so.

3.1 CRISIS OR ROT?

The Balkin–Levinson dialogue on American constitutionalism is a model of academic conversation: two learned scholars reasoning together on some of the deepest problems the topic poses.[2] But it is also a debate intended to shape ongoing public clashes with the highest stakes – a debate that pivots on dueling metaphors for contemporary crises of legitimacy. Levinson, self-describedly "semi-apocalyptic" at one point, suggests the United States is in or near a constitutional crisis. Balkin instead diagnoses "constitutional rot."

Some definitional clarity is in order. In an earlier article, both Balkin and Levinson defined crisis as:

> [A] potentially decisive turning point in the direction of the constitutional order, a moment at which the order threatens to break down, just as the body does in a medical crisis. It may lead back to a slightly altered status quo, that is, a crisis averted. The fever provoking

[2] Sanford Levinson & Jack M. Balkin, Democracy and Dysfunction (Chicago: University of Chicago Press, 2019).

> a medical crisis breaks, and the patient returns to her prior condition little the worse for wear. On the other hand, the conclusion of a crisis may indeed be an important transformation in the forms and practices of power or, in the most extreme cases, the dissolution of the existing constitutional order and the creation of a new order in its place. The ultimate medical crisis, after all, is death, as demonstrated most spectacularly in our lifetime by the demise of the Union of Soviet Socialist Republics or the dissolution of Yugoslavia.[3]

The mention of the demise of the U.S.S.R. was uncomfortably resonant for the United States by late 2020. As President Trump's baseless allegations of election fraud continued unabated after dozens of court losses, the chairman of the Texas Republican Party floated the possibility of red states' secession. Many residents of blue states welcomed the chance to bid them adieu.

Levinson and Balkin go on to distinguish emergencies ("perceptions of urgency caused by facts on the ground or by the way that people perceive those facts") from constitutional crises ("conflicts about the legitimate uses of power by persons or institutions"). Their diagnoses of crisis and rot are reminiscent of other notable metaphors in social theory.[4] Inspired by Wittgenstein's classic observation that the "meaning of a word is its use in the language," we can ask: what is the work that "rot" is doing here? Could other metaphors do similar work, while also disclosing additional dimensions of the problem?

The rhetorical power of a particular metaphor in part relies on the strength (and weakness) of rival metaphors, as scholars articulate narratives and comparisons designed to inspire new forms of recognition and action.[5] What is particularly rewarding, in working with the metaphors of scholars like Balkin and Levinson, is to connect their "crisis/rot" debate to the larger skein of meanings and resonances that have structured their work over decades.

An earlier Balkin project, *Constitutional Redemption*, deployed metaphors of religious faith and storytelling to explain (and encourage) American constitutionalism.[6] According to Balkin, "The legitimacy of our Constitution depends … on our faith in the constitutional project and its

[3] Sanford Levinson & Jack M. Balkin, *Constitutional Crises*, 157 U. Pa. L. Rev. 707 (2009).

[4] Richard H. Brown, *Social Theory as Metaphor: On the Logic of Discovery for the Sciences of Conduct*, 3 Theory & Soc'y 169 (1976).

[5] Frank Pasquale, *The Substance of Poetic Procedure: Law & Humanity in the Work of Lawrence Joseph*, 32 Law & Literature 1 (2020).

[6] Jack M. Balkin, Constitutional Redemption: Political Faith in an Unjust World (Cambridge: Havard University Press, 2011).

future trajectory."[7] His rot metaphor evokes the many parables of building, home, and shelter found in religious texts, participating in political theology.[8] Recalling the preacher who warns a sinning congregation that it is not too late to repent, it is both admonitory and optimistic: some warning sign may shock us into action. Perhaps some roof beams will collapse in from termites and alert neglectful homeowners to hire carpenters. Balkin posits an objective correlative to this "repent and polarise no more" metaphor: perhaps some partisan gerrymanders will be so egregious, he suggests, they will provoke the Supreme Court to intervene. That hope has now been dashed – not only has the Supreme Court refused to fix partisan gerrymanders, but it has also repeatedly intervened to quash lower courts' efforts to make elections marginally fairer. But there is always another fix—say, court expansion, which could lead to a better balanced court reconsidering the new rotten boroughs now created by grotesque gerrymanders.

The greatest danger of rot is that, at some point, deterioration may go past a point of no return. Thus, Levinson masterfully marshals the medical metaphor to counter Balkin's building metaphor. As US President Trump ignored basic pandemic advice, threatened not to respect the results of the 2020 election, and otherwise ignored the most basic norms of liberal democracy, Levinson's post from mid-November 2016 appears all the more prophetic:

> Imagine two soldiers in Iraq (or anywhere else). One is killed, then other incurs traumatic brain injury. We would say of the second that he/she "survived" the war in a way the first did not, but we would also go on to say that "he/she will never be the same again. It is as if we're dealing with a very different person; I feel so sorry for the spouse . . . . " We would go on to speak of the living envying the dead. So in that sense the U.S. will survive, but anyone who believes we are the same country today as two weeks ago is deluded. Indeed, we are only beginning to get a glimpse of how truly terrible it may

[7] *Ibid.* at 2. *Compare* Mary Anne Franks, The Cult of The Constitution (Stanford: Stanford University Press, 2019).

[8] See, e.g., the parable of the wise and foolish builder: "Therefore everyone who hears these words of mine and puts them into practice is like a wise man who built his house on the rock. The rain came down, the streams rose, and the winds blew and beat against that house; yet it did not fall, because it had its foundation on the rock. But everyone who hears these words of mine and does not put them into practice is like a foolish man who built his house on sand. The rain came down, the streams rose, and the winds blew and beat against that house, and it fell with a great crash." Matthew 7:24–27. On the importance of theological structures of thought to political concepts, see Carl Schmitt, Political Theology: Four Chapters on the Concept of Sovereignty, trans. George Schwab (Cambridge: MIT Press, 1986).

> turn out to be .... The United States is, I believe, in the most precarious position since 1860.[9]

Levinson's metaphor of the traumatically brain injured soldier may have seemed melodramatic in 2016, but the grueling Trump era has proven it prophetic. Tactics that seemed unimaginable in the U.S. before Trump—subversion of postal voting, baseless allegations of millions of illegal votes being cast in 2016, 2018, and 2020, reckless circulation of conspiracy theories by the President and his allies, winks and nods to vigilante justice and armed private militias, and general approval for all this and more from a political party with tens of millions of adherents—have damaged U.S. democracy, perhaps irreparably. Nor are strongman tactics unique to the U.S. They are becoming increasingly popular among authoritarians eager to rig elections and courts to keep themselves in power, and to expand their powers once ensconced in office.

Both Balkinson's and Levinson's metaphors incline the reader toward their overall diagnosis and approach to constitutional order. As anyone who has walked down the streets of Florence or Rome can attest, buildings (the source of Balkin's metaphor) may exist in perpetuity if they are maintained (and avoid the sudden destructive power of, say, a bomb). They can also be replicated and end up as good or better than new. Levinson's state-as-body metaphor implies inevitable loss. Yes, bodies often heal, especially the young and strong. But a 245-year-old country should have some sense of its own mortality. Empires have risen and fallen in shorter periods.

3.2 THREE METAPHORS OF SELF-REINFORCING CHANGE

Metaphors help us comprehend these troubled times, by enabling nonconceptual strategies for evoking our predicament. As Martin Jay (explicating the work of Hans Blumenberg) explains, "Metaphors lessen anxiety by guiding us through the unfamiliar and distant via a healthy detour through the familiar and proximate."[10] While it is difficult to condense decades of political history into a compelling narrative, there are metaphors we live by, conceptual maps

9 Sandy Levinson, *Will America Survive the 2016 Election? A Union on the Brink of Civil War*, BALKINIZATION (November 19, 2016), https://balkin.blogspot.com/2016/11/will-america-survive-2016-election.html.

10 MARTIN JAY, SPLINTERS IN YOUR EYE: FRANKFURT SCHOOL PROVOCATIONS (New York: Verso, 2020). As Blumenberg himself put it, "Demythicization is in large measure nothing more than remetaphorization." Hans Blumenberg, "Prospect for a Theory of Nonconceptuality," in HANS BLUMBENBERG, SHIPWRECK WITH SPECTATOR, 83 (trans. Steven Rendall, 1996).

for orientation and lights for illumination. The figurative can also be affirming, disquieting, or both. Metaphors like "rot" and "crisis" crystallize our justified sense of unease at the present conjuncture, but they are not the final story. We can plumb their resonance and limits by comparing them to other metaphors.

One such tool of thinking is the "tipping point," or point of no return. Levinson's sense of urgency and crisis becomes much more compelling if we think we are about to pass a tipping point: when small changes aggregate to the point where they create a much larger, more important, and irreversible change. For example, any particular intervention in the post-2010 Project REDMAP may have been insignificant in political time, but a critical mass of them (combined with their sequelae) may have ensured that Democrats can never take power again in certain states.[11] What is the point at which that happens at the federal level? It is well within the realm of possibility that, by 2040, "half the country will have 16 senators, and half will have 84."[12] Every incremental step the United States takes toward such an imbalance makes it harder to cure the imbalance, given predictably homophilic mechanisms of social sorting.[13] At some point, twenty-six of the smallest states may durably unite to oppose policies preferred by 60 percent, 75 percent, or more of the United States. Or they may follow Dennis Hastert's policy of "majority of a majority rules," whereby the thirteen smallest states could block whatever the thirty-seven largest states want. In that case, it is quite conceivable that representatives of 20 million persons could block the will of representatives of 300 million. Such a situation cannot be called a democracy. It would be a moldering relic of a past *modus vivendi* that effectively let accidents of geography and population sorting culminate in permanent potential for tyranny of the minority.

In addition to the tipping point, a second metaphor of ineluctable progress toward extremity is the slippery slope. We often hear that if Democrats were to push back too hard against gerrymanders and voting restrictions, and to act as aggressively in constitutional ways (to expand the Supreme Court, say, or add states to the Union) to build their own power, that would put us on a slippery

[11] Elizabeth Drew, *American Democracy Betrayed*, N.Y. REV. BOOKS (August 18, 2016), www.nybooks.com/articles/2016/08/18/american-democracy-betrayed/ (reviewing DAVID DALEY, RATFUCKED: THE TRUE STORY BEHIND THE SECRET PLAN TO STEAL AMERICA'S DEMOCRACY (New York: Liveright Press, 2016).

[12] Ezra Levin (@ezralevin), TWITTER (May 5, 2019, 9:57 AM), https://twitter.com/ezralevin/status/1125051905368047617.

[13] Aaron Retica, *Homophily*, N. Y. TIMES MAG. (December 10, 2006), www.nytimes.com/2006/12/10/magazine/10Section2a.t-4.html.

slope to constitutional crisis. But it seems like the United States is already on that slippery slope thanks to past asymmetrical polarization, since "decisions to change the voting rules (such as rules related to voter eligibility, ease of registration, apportionment, or supermajority requirements) may lead to more changes in the future."[14] That accumulation of power has tilted the playing field in very close elections in North Carolina and Florida, leading to further entrenchment of GOP power. It has now almost entirely unraveled Florida voters' resounding decision to give the franchise back to over a million persons.[15] The slippery slope is here, and we need a metaphor for how to avoid slipping further down it.

The lack of urgency among Democrats in the U.S. (and small-d democrats in some other polities with fragile democracy) as they face these crises suggests a third metaphor for the present dilemma: the boiling frog – an evocative (if apocryphal) model of how a blasé amphibian may end up cooked if it gradually accommodates increasingly uncomfortable surroundings.[16] The U.S. house speaker's stark warning to Democrats in 2019 – to stay in the center lest the president contest a close election – exemplifies boiled frog dynamics.[17] Think of how much it accommodated: an erratic leader who has already claimed that there were millions of illegal votes in an election he won;[18] partisan courts capable of reprising *Bush* v. *Gore*; and mass appeals to violence and vigilantism on internet platforms more than eager to profit from demagoguery.[19] As constitutional law expert Steven Vladeck has observed, "We've all been desensitized over

14 Eugene Volokh, *The Mechanisms of the Slippery Slope*, 116 HARV. L. REV. 1026, 1118 (2003).

15 Gary Fineout, *Florida GOP Moves to Rein in Felon Voting Rights*, POLITICO (May 2, 2019), www.politico.com/states/florida/story/2019/05/02/florida-gop-moves-to-rein-in-felon-voting-rights-1005333.

16 On the utility of models in legal theory, *see* Jeffrey M. Lipshaw, *Models and Games: The Difference Between Explanation and Understanding for Lawyers and Ethicists*, 56 CLEV. ST. L. REV. 613 (2008).

17 Ben Mathis-Lilley, *Four Things that Don't Make Sense about Nancy Pelosi Saying 2020 Could Be a Huge Democratic Disaster that Triggers a Coup*, SLATE (May 6, 2019), https://slate.com/news-and-politics/2019/05/nancy-pelosi-times-interview-moderate-coup.html.

18 Mark Joseph Stern, *Trump Crony Proves Widespread Voter Fraud Doesn't Exist*, SLATE (May 30, 2018), https://slate.com/news-and-politics/2018/05/new-hampshire-investigation-by-bill-gardner-shows-widespread-voter-fraud-doesnt-exist.html; Gary Fineout, *Supreme Court Allows Limits on Felon Voting in Florida*, POLITICO (July 16, 2020), www.politico.com/states/florida/story/2020/07/16/us-supreme-court-keeps-florida-felon-voting-law-in-place-1301508.

19 Sheldon Whitehouse, *A Right-Wing Rout: What the "Roberts Five" Decisions Tell Us about the Integrity of Today's Supreme Court*, ACS ISSUE BRIEF (April 24, 2019), www.acslaw.org/issue_brief/briefs-landing/a-right-wing-rout-what-the-roberts-five-decisions-tell-us-about-the-integrity-of-todays-supreme-court/. On the irresponsibility of the automated public sphere of which Twitter is a part, see FRANK PASQUALE , NEW LAWS OF ROBOTICS: DEFENDING HUMAN EXPERTISE IN THE AGE OF AI (2020), chapter 4.

the past four years, but the President of the United States even discussing the possibility of 'deploying the military' in some amorphous response to an election he lost is equal parts chilling and insane." If one side is disproportionately willing to risk a slippery slope, and the other does nothing, the noble liberal statesmen of moderation and civility are all too likely to end up as boiled frogs.

These temporal metaphors of decline can intensify into the master metaphor motivating this chapter: "cascading tipping points." Both the boiled frog and the slippery slope scenarios can occur fractally at higher and lower levels of resolution. As they do so, empowering those ruthless enough to press their current advantages into ever more advantages, they form their own feedback loops. A gerrymandered legislature may only approve the appointment of judges who will endorse and entrench ever more biased gerrymanders. Russian authoritarians promote the Trump regime in the United States, which in turn supports a Bolsonaro or Boris Johnson, who in turn orient their own foreign policies to promote tin-pot dictators like Viktor Orbán. The dynamic calls to mind the concrete origin of the cascading tipping point metaphor: recent scientific research on anthropogenic climate change that shows how easily feedback loops of warming and its consequences can occur. Excess carbon can warm the air, which in turn heats Siberian permafrost, which then releases methane, another greenhouse gas that again heats the air and restarts the cycle. There are numerous examples of such feedback loops in nature. They are a powerful metaphor for the ways in which one ruthless or authoritarian party's success can spread in space or ramify through time, creating an environment where ruthlessness and authoritarianism further thrive.

Some critics dismiss metaphors as inexact or speculative. But when it comes to thinking about social change as abstract and complex as democratic politics, metaphors can be quite useful – and influential.[20] They can be performative, activating the very attitudes and dynamics they claim merely to model.[21] The science-fiction writer Liu Cixin's metaphor of the "dark forest" in his "Remembrance of Earth's Past" trilogy could, for example, fuel a turn toward a more realist and aggressive foreign policy.[22] His wildly popular *The Dark Forest* universalized a reversal of the golden rule (destroy or be destroyed) as

[20] Alessandro Morelli & Oreste Pollicino, *Metaphors, Judicial Frames and Fundamental Rights in Cyberspace*, AMERICAN JOURNAL OF COMPARATIVE LAW (2020), https://papers.ssrn.com/sol3/papers.cfm?abstract_id=3422946.

[21] They can also be counterperformative, undoing the very factors their accuracy relies on. Donald McKenzie & Alice Bamford, *Counterperformativity*, NEW LEFT REVIEW (2018), https://newleftreview.org/issues/II113/articles/donald-mackenzie-alice-bamford-counterperformativity.

[22] Gerry Canavan, *Quiet, Too Quiet*, L.A. REV. BOOKS (February 12, 2016), https://lareviewofbooks.org/article/quiet-too-quiet/ (reviewing CIXIN LIU, THE DARK FOREST (2015)). The trilogy makes the metaphorical dark forest quite literal at many points in the story, including

a resolution of Fermi's Paradox (which highlights the strangeness of humans never discovering or being discovered by advanced alien civilizations, despite the immensity of the universe and ample opportunities over eons for such beings to develop). For one of Liu's key protagonists, the answer to Fermi's Paradox is obvious, if depressing: Evolution would favor the success of any civilization that simply destroyed any rival before that rival could overwhelm it. In the last novel of the trilogy, one "civilization" is portrayed as doing just that, incinerating worlds as nonchalantly as a human being might flick on an electric mosquito zapper. In a dark forest, the safest response to hearing a noise is simply to shoot in the noise's direction, killing whatever animal or person may be pursuing oneself. The parallel to Schmittian political theory is obvious: enemies must be neutralized, left utterly unable to vie for power, lest they do the same to oneself. Indeed, in Liu's fantastic though hard-science-fictional imagination, much of the universe is destroyed thanks to the development of a "two-dimensional attack"—a strange advance in physics that initiates a chain reaction toward flatness. It is hard to think of a better metaphor for the grave risks imposed by U.S.'s current Schmittian impasse, where any matter of public concern, no matter how urgent or trivial, is liable to be flattened into a battle of red versus blue, Republican versus Democrat. The loss of dimensionality is palpable.

Sadly, metaphors of conflict are more entertaining (and thus more viral) than metaphors of cooperation. If a renewed political public sphere is possible, it may depend on a common capacity to imagine new and decentralized forms of cooperation and respect.[23] The next section explains such grounds of cooperation. Schmitt's "friend/enemy" distinction is scarcely definitive or exhaustive as a theory of politics. As Theodore Heuss explained in 1951:

> Carl Schmitt squeezed the "essence of the political" into the tenuous formalism of the "friend-enemy" relationship. This throttled the infinite variety of interrelations and interactions in political life because the dynamic tension, which can also belong to this infinite variety, was isolated and overemphasised. This infinite variety, which does not just look at the friend-enemy relationship, but goes beyond the limits of formal logic to the place

a portrayal of a ruthless US space ship succeeding by acting upon the "dark forest" metaphor more quickly than its European and Chinese rivals.

[23] In this way, key utopian works in the science fiction of Kim Stanley Robinson may stand as a counterpoint to the dystopian realism of the "dark forest" metaphor. See, e.g., Kim Stanley Robinson , New York 2140 (2019); Carol Franko, *Working the "In-Between": Kim Stanley Robinson's Utopian Fiction*, 21 Science Fiction Studies 191 (1994).

> where the substance of public life can be seen – a substance that carries values and is carried by values that are, by nature, transcendent.[24]

An insistence on these transcendent values, all too often obscured in the pulling and hauling of Robert Dahl-style liberal pluralism, can stay the slide toward authoritarianism. However, it must be combined with a clear-eyed understanding of the highest stakes of politics.

3.3 TWO THEORIES OF POLITICS: ZERO-SUM VERSUS SELF-REINFORCING CHANGE

Journalist Edward Luce recently judged that "America's intellectual energy is now on the left."[25] With light comes heat, and there are vigorous debates among progressives on fundamental questions in technology, health, employment, energy, and finance policy. I am less concerned about the infighting than about the outdated theories of political change it sometimes presumes. A broad popular front united against Trumpist patrimonialism may fragment if too many within it are committed to too narrow an approach to policy.[26] This danger should motivate a theory of political change to justify policy bricolage.[27] Creative ideas should be welcomed, and the hermeneutics of suspicion instead directed toward those eager to thwart ambitious policy agendas.

Consider, for instance, the recent pile-on by economists jostling to discredit Modern Monetary Theory (MMT). The core idea behind MMT is that government spending faces a flexible inflation constraint, not a hard-and-fast debt constraint.[28] Sometimes government spending can spark demand-pull inflation: too much money chasing too few resources and goods. However, wise macroeconomic investment can reduce prices as well, or produce a mixture of raised and lowered prices. Think of the extraordinary decline in the price of software,

[24] Heuss is quoted in Pádraig Murphy, *The White Raven*, Dublin Review of Books (January 7, 2020), at www.drb.ie/essays/the-white-raven.

[25] Edward Luce, *The Clinton-Obama Era Ends as US Democrats Seek a Radical New Voice*, Financial Times (January 13, 2019), www.ft.com/content/12ab216c-1587-11e9-a581-4ff78404524e.

[26] Dylan Riley, *What Is Trump?*, New Left Rev., November/December 2018, https://newleftreview.org/issues/II114/articles/dylan-riley-what-is-trump.

[27] J. M. Balkin, Cultural Software: A Theory of Ideology 23 (New Haven: Yale University Press, 1998).

[28] Frank Pasquale, *Realities and Relationships in Public Finance*, Provocations (February 5, 2010), www.provocationsbooks.com/2019/02/05/realities-and-relationships-in-public-finance/; Ben Walsh, *Stephanie Kelton Wants You to Rethink the Deficit*, Barron's (September 13, 2018), www.barrons.com/articles/stephanie-kelton-wantsyou-to-rethink-the-deficit-1536853788.

computing capacity, and data storage over the past two decades. Investment paid dividends there – and can do so on a much larger scale. Moreover, as Cornell law professor Robert Hockett has argued, there are many ways to identify inflation early, and nip it in the bud, if government spending causes certain scarcities.[29]

Some aspects of MMT are established features of macroeconomic thought. For example, its emphasis on government's central role in the economy recalls Keynes's *General Theory of Employment, Interest, and Money*. Keynesianism took root amidst a global depression, when unemployment sparked enormous personal suffering and political upheaval. Its revival now is unsurprising, given the problem of youth unemployment in much of the industrial world, and the decades-long worsening of work conditions for those suffering the indignities of "fissured workplaces" in the developed world.

Liberals like Paul Krugman and leftists like Doug Henwood have passionately attacked MMT.[30] I have neither the time nor the space here to adjudicate all the merits of their critiques, and the many forceful responses developed by economists like Stephanie Kelton[31] and Pavlina Tcherneva.[32] But I think a common problem for the critics is that they fail to contextualize the conditions out of which MMT arose, as Brian Beutler does here:

> For decades now, Republican administrations have created enormous deficits with regressive, inequality-widening tax cuts, then turned around and cited those very deficits as a pretext to demand that their Democratic successors adopt austerity budgets without raising taxes at all.... It was against that backdrop that MMT began making headway on the left. Only later, in response to stagnant wages, the Republican assault on the Affordable Care Act (ACA), ecological crisis, and Donald Trump, did the progressive agenda shift leftward.
>
> Everyone on the left who supports the emerging Democratic presidential primary policy consensus should stop and remind themselves that any effort Democrats put into making sure their priorities are "paid for" in the orthodox sense will be wasted the moment Republicans take back over and pass their next tax cut. ... The left is either going to beat conservatives at the game of

29 Robert Hockett, *The Green New Deal: How We Will Pay for It Isn't a "Thing" – and Inflation Isn't Either*, Forbes (January 16, 2019), www.forbes.com/sites/rhockett/2019/01/16/the-green-new-deal-how-we-will-pay-for-it-isnt-a-thing-and-inflation-isnt-either/#5ad2884d4d7f.

30 Lars Syll, *Kelton and Krugman – MMT vs IS-LM*, Real World Econ. Blog (March 3, 2019), https://rwer.wordpress.com/2019/03/03/kelton-and-krugman-mmt-vs-is-lm/; Doug Henwood, *Modern Monetary Theory Isn't Helping*, Jacobin Mag. (February 21, 2019), www.jacobinmag.com/2019/02/modern-monetary-theory-isnt-helping.

31 Stephanie Kelton, Bloomberg, www.bloomberg.com/opinion/authors/ASym14c8hEQ/stephanie-kelton.

32 Pavlina Tcherneva, *MMT Is Already Helping*, Jacobin Mag. (February 27, 2019), https://jacobinmag.com/2019/02/mmt-modern-monetary-theory-doug-henwood-overton-window.

chicken they have forced us into, or it is not. In either case, squabbling over the merits of MMT is just more whistling past the graveyard.[33]

Indeed, the dynamic of "deficit spend for the right's priorities, cut deficits by sacrificing the left's priorities" is exactly the type of self-reinforcing political change evoked by the tipping point and slippery slope metaphor. They are more urgent than "crisis" or "rot" because they indicate that the situation is not stationary: the longer it drifts unchanged, the harder it is to solve.

Of course, there are difficult questions for MMT advocates to answer. Few can now say whether ambitious social spending needs to be 60, 70, or 90% "paid for" by taxes or reallocation of extant government spending, and how much could be funded by monetary operations or currency creation.[34] But neither do MMT critics, who look increasingly out-of-touch as central banks create more money to float COVID-19-ravaged economies.[35] The key question now is how the keep unfounded demands for austerity from stifling real reform.[36] MMT helps by emphasizing the government's power to create credit on good terms for everyone, not just the well-connected, or those traditionally supported by central banks.

Thus Steve Randy Waldman is right to argue that "If you think MMT is good politics but bad economics, it may be worth asking whether there isn't some tweak or reform that would render the economics acceptable and retain the good politics."[37] The alarm about MMT seems to be built on an idea that political economy is not a Lindblom-ian muddling through, but rather some kind of exacting science, where we have one chance to "get things right" and must elaborate in advance a perfected calculus of government action.[38] This

[33] Brian Beutler, *What's Missing from the Most Important Debate on the Left*, CROOKED (February 28, 2019), https://crooked.com/articles/whats-missing-from-the-most-important-debate-on-the-left/.

[34] Jack M. Balkin, *3 Ways Obama Could Bypass Congress*, CNN (July 28, 2011), www.cnn.com/2011/OPINION/07/28/balkin.obama.options/index.html.

[35] Jeff Spross, *Medicare-for-All Has a Modeling Problem*, THE WEEK (March 4, 2019), https://theweek.com/articles/826609/medicareforall-modeling-problem ("If the U.S. actually succeeded in passing a Medicare-for-all program with dollar-for-dollar matching taxes, it would be overkill. The country would offset the spending too much, remove too much demand [via, for instance, mass unemployment of workers now ensconced in a bloated private insurance system], and leave the economy below full employment.").

[36] Frank Pasquale, *Fair Value Accounting Debunked Again – Will the Congressional Budget Office End its FVA Crusade?*, BALKINIZATION (March 15, 2016), https://balkin.blogspot.com/2016/03/fair-value-accounting-debunked-again.html; Frank Pasquale, *The CBO Needs to Answer Some Questions for the Public*, MEDIUM (July 27, 2017), https://medium.com/@FrankPasquale/the-cbo-needs-to-answer-some-questions-for-the-public-c861cd957d47.

[37] Steve Randy Waldman, *Three Levels of Controversy over MMT*, INTERFLUIDITY (March 3, 2019), www.interfluidity.com/v2/7097.html.

[38] Charles E. Lindblom, *The Science of "Muddling Through,"* 19 PUB. ADMIN. REV. 79 (1959).

precisionist view in turn feeds on a zero-sum vision of political change, where any energy put into, say, a health reform program that is too ambitious, is energy that could have been better spent on, say, boosting technocratic alternatives.

The right has a very different theory of political change – where initiatives large and small, foundational or incremental, are welcomed as ways of weakening the opposition and building resources for political fights in the future.[39] Rather than zero-sum, the right's vision of politics is one of self-reinforcing change, where a fight builds power, which is then used to set the terms of the next fight more in their favor, which makes it easier to build even more power later. That dynamic is most obvious in serial redistrictings that will tilt US politics rightward for decades on end.[40]

Self-reinforcing change is also clear in capital's siege of labor over the past eighty years. In the U.S., the Taft-Hartley Act of 1947 sapped unions' strength, rendering them too weak to fight back against other hostile legislation. In the EU, neoliberal labor reforms and budget constraints have performed a similar (if weaker) role, as Stephanie Mudge's work has shown. Weakened unions were not able to stop more generally anti-worker legislation. Once union density in the private sector was reduced, increasingly precarious private sector workers rallied to right-wing political appeals to pull public sector workers down to their level of wages and benefits. The final frontier of capital's political war on labor is a blunderbuss attack on occupational licensing, coupled with the cynical deployment of antitrust law to hamstring independent workers who want to collectively bargain with tech giants like Uber.[41] Meanwhile, the use of contracts to eviscerate workers' privacy protections (and other rights) helps bosses police the restive workers that remain.[42]

39 For illuminating analyses of the results of this asymmetry between the right and a liberal/left popular front, see Chantal Mouffe, The Return of the Political (New York: Verso, 2019); Nancy Fraser, The Old Is Dying and the New Cannot Be Born (New York: Verso, 2020).

40 David Faris , It's Time to Fight Dirty: How Democrats Can Build a Lasting Majority in American Politics (2018). For a practical proposal for addressing this asymmetry, see Note, *Pack the Union: A Proposal to Admit New States for the Purpose of Amending the Constitution to Ensure Equal Representation*, 133 Harv. L. Rev. 1049 (2020).

41 Marshall Steinbaum, *Antitrust Implications of Labor Platforms*, CPI Antitrust Chron. (May 2018), www.competitionpolicyinternational.com/wp-content/uploads/2018/05/CPI-Steinbaum.pdf; Sandeep Vaheesan and Frank Pasquale , *The Politics of Professionalism: Reappraising Occupational Licensure and Competition Policy*, 14 Annual Review of Law and Social Science 309 (2018).

42 Victoria Graham, *DOJ Seeks "Rule of Reason" in Fast-Food No-Poach Antitrust Policies*, Bloomberg (March 7, 2019), www.bloomberglaw.com/document/XFQGLUDG000000?bna_news_filter=mergers-and-antitrust&jcsearch=BNA%252000000016959dcdb02a57f5fde48210002#Sjcite.

I have seen little evidence that those on the right, seeking to reduce the power of labor relative to capital, were overly worried about whether there were some conceptual or even practical tensions between these many facets of anti-labor policy. Rather, they realized that there was a relatively clear-cut divide, and they would take the side of capital (sometimes rationalized as consumer interests) in order to reduce wages and benefits of workers. By bringing many liberals on board, they also helped create an impression among some marginalized workers that the state was simply unwilling or unable to help them.[43] That learned helplessness was another self-reinforcing dimension of political change, enabled by its instigators' clear-eyed view of the fundamental tension between capital and labor shares of national income.

By contrast, MMT is a powerful set of ideas for building confidence in the state's ability to fund and promote a more efficient, robust, and equitable economy.[44] And in an era of climate emergency and threats to employment from automation and trade, the real question is not "can we afford a Green New Deal," but how we can afford to go without one.[45] Experimentalism is necessary. [46]

The same type of big tent thinking needs to be popularized on the left as well. For example, those in the U.S. who endorse Medicare for All should not try to tear down proposals to increase the medical loss ratio for insurers, or reduce the age of eligibility for Medicare. Yes, it is necessary to have a broader vision of the ultimate goal of reform: better care for all. But given many regions' Democratic primary voters' lingering allegiance to centrists or long-serving office-holders, something like Pramila Jayapal's model of single-payer may be very hard to pass.[47] Chipping away first at the power of the big insurers and pharma, and then at monopolistic hospital chains and parasitic intermediaries, will be crucial. And each effort to weaken them, taking away funds they'd otherwise use to gain more political power, will in turn make it easier to

[43] Jennifer M. Silva , Coming Up Short: Working-Class Adulthood in an Age of Uncertainty (2013).

[44] Rutger Bregman (@rcbgreman), Twitter (March 10, 2019, 12:47 PM), https://twitter.com/rcbregman/status/1104800955210567680.

[45] David Wallace-Wells , The Uninhabitable Earth: Life After Warming (2019).

[46] Conor Sen, *History's Lesson for Democrats: Don't Be Afraid of Economic Experiments*, Bloomberg News (March 7, 2019), www.bloomberg.com/opinion/articles/2019-03-07/modern-monetary-theory-democrats-should-try-new-economic-ideas.

[47] Sarah Kliff, *Medicare-for-all: Rep. Pramila Jayapal's New Bill, Explained*, Vox (February 26, 2019), www.vox.com/policy-and-politics/2019/2/26/18239630/medicare-for-all-pramila-jayapal-bill.

support further efforts to promote the interests of patients (and workers) in the health care system.[48]

As David Kaib puts it, "winning begets winning."[49] Whatever your critique of Affordable Care Act (ACA), it performed a crucial function in changing the conversation away from a "consumer-directed health care" approach.[50] The ACA's Rube Goldberg neoliberalism is not sustainable,[51] but it was at least a step in the right direction when the leading rival options were health saving accounts and stripped down employer-sponsored insurance.[52]

In short: both bold visions and incremental improvements have a place in popular front politics. Those who would unite to address climate crisis, a broken health care system, excess financialization, and tech platform power may not agree on everything, and may even disagree on ultimate ends. The situation is now so dire that "all of the above" makes far more sense than deductive elimination of options. The tipping point toward authoritarianism has not yet been reached in the U.S. But awareness of it (and other metaphors of decline, ranging from "rot" to "crisis" to "slippery slope" and beyond) should fuel a renewed appreciation of the stakes of a united defense of democratic processes and their social bases, both in the U.S. and in democracies around the world.

[48] Rick Ungar, *Busted! Health Insurers Secretly Spent Huge to Defeat Health Care Reform While Pretending to Support Obamacare*, FORBES (June 15, 2012), www.forbes.com/sites/rickungar/2012/06/25/busted-health-insurers-secretly-spent-huge-to-defeat-health-care-reform-while-pretending-to-support-obamacare/#SSS3c12e2b44248; Frank Pasquale, *The Hidden Costs of Health Care Cost-Cutting: Toward a Postneoliberal Health-Reform Agenda*, LAW & CONTEMP. PROBS., Fall 2014, at 171.

[49] David Kaib, *Every Inch Won Should Lead Us to Demand More*, NOTES ON A THEORY (May 23, 2014), https://notesonatheory.wordpress.com/2014/05/23/every-inch-won/.

[50] TIMOTHY JOST , HEALTH CARE AT RISK: A CRITIQUE OF THE CONSUMER-DRIVEN MOVEMENT (2007).

[51] Frank Pasquale, *Rebuilding Health Care Policy from the Ground Up*, BALKINIZATION (November 12, 2016), https://balkin.blogspot.com/2016/11/rebuilding-health-care-policy-from.html.

[52] Steve Forbes, *Bush, Congress Could Have Avoided Obamacare*, NORTHJERSEY.COM (July 11, 2017), www.northjersey.com/story/opinion/contributors/2017/07/11/bush-congress-could-have-avoided-obamacare/467607001/.

4

China

Larry Catá Backer

The first several decades of the twenty-first century have constituted themselves as a time of great dread. It is an age that appeared to mark both the beginning of a century and the end of an age; an end augured by assaults on the physical and financial manifestations of the power of a worldview that had been dominant since 1945. The physical assault on the Twin Towers in New York marked a challenge to the power of the established order to maintain it. The intangible assault followed the near collapse of the power of the established order to protect and project its wealth.

Dread, however, is a complicated matter. Certainly, dread suggests the sort of fear and apprehension, the common meanings of dread,[1] that have produced the strong reaction that has been the history of the first two decades of this century, marked in turn by the great trajectories of national and domestic legal orders. But that sort of dread also connotes a fear or apprehension of a higher (usually but not always divine) authority—a four year old dreads the discovery by one's parent of the consumption of the contents of the family cookie jar not because of the consumption but out of an apprehension of a higher power (and to a four year old, nearly divine authority); so, too, a political or economic community in the face of an apparently irresistible power.[2] Dread also suggests awe or to be held in awe; that is, the holding of a thing in awe. That sense of a thing of awe, an awful apprehension, also marks this age. It follows then, that this is an age that is marked by a frightful apprehension of that which is held in awe. That which causes fright, that

[1] From the etymology of dread, see www.etymonline.com/word/dread.

[2] "And he took a yoke of oxen, and hewed them in pieces, and sent them throughout all the coasts of Israel by the hands of messengers, saying, Whosoever cometh not forth after Saul and after Samuel, so shall it be done unto his oxen. And the fear of the Lord fell on the people, and they came out with one consent." 1 Samuel 11:7 (King James Version). This fear of the Lord drives international law and religions as well.

which awes; is in turn a thing, a cause, or a future. Dread comes from the anticipation of a dreadful thing. It signals consciousness of the accumulations of fears that themselves can now be incarnated, or can incarnate time, into an epoch – one that is going (and thus the fear and apprehension), and one that is coming (and thus the awe).

All of these senses of dread are very much on display in the context of the (re)construction of international law and the core principles through which the worldview is necessary to its animation as custom, practice, rule, and popular expectation. Within that self-reflexive world there has arisen a dread (among some in the West) of the steady approach to a tipping point. In the West, and especially in its sciences, one has come to understand a tipping point as a threshold which, when exceeded, opens the possibility of significant changes from an old status quo. In Marxist Leninist political systems, the concept of tipping points is sometimes naturalized through the application of concepts of historical materialism, "a mass of productive forces, capital funds and conditions, which, on the one hand, is indeed modified by the new generation, but also on the other prescribes for it its conditions of life and gives it a definite development, a special character."[3]

And it is in dread and awe – in the dreadful anticipation of the future from out of the past, in the awful realization that the unimagined is now at the gates – that serves as the foundation of the emerging reality that troubles, and the passing of the commitment increasingly understood only in the past tense. And so the dread of this age is one that comes to those who having been inattentive, having been arrogant in their sense of the entitlement, the naturalness of their commitments, of the principles that may have instilled dread and awe in others, but provided comfort for themselves, now on the cusp of being swept away serves only, perhaps too late, to instill the dread that arises from finally sensing (to the extent that such sensation is still possible) of something wrong, something troubling, something that will soon go missing. The current generation of those entrusted with the commitment to liberal democracy and the international order founded on its core principles, having stood on the shoulders of giants, now gaze out on a field in which other giants roamed the space once unquestionably theirs. The dread that arises at the start of the twenty-first century, then, is one that that grows out of the awe with which a realization that the commitments of the prior age are now threatened to be swept away by another set of commitments, one that has always been troubled by what had been taken for granted by those committed to

3 Karl Marx, A *Critique of the German Ideology*, www.marxists.org/archive/marx/works/download/Marx_The_German_Ideology.pdf.

a specific worldview from out of which they constructed the reality of international relations between 1945 and 2016.

This contribution examines a very small aspect of this age of dread, and of the tipping point to which it appears to lead. Appearing as a distant speck on the horizon of power in 2001, fresh from its accession to the World Trade Organization, by 2020 China could more clearly be seen as the dreadnought (without dread; drede ich nawiht)[4] now threatening the battlements of the great fortifications of what had once appeared to be the universal (and universally disciplined) structures of global governance through international institutions as well as the authority of its leading power within the system.[5] Its focus is on one key manifestation of this approaching dread – the emergence of an increasingly sophisticated and well-structured challenge by China to the current framework for international human rights law and norms, both in conception and application. Section 3.2 briefly describes the evolution of the contemporary Chinese engagement with international law and norms and its consequences for economic persons and institutions caught in the middle. Section 3.3 analyzes a core instance of that application of that emerging sensibility, the successful effort of China to embed the conception of "Mutually Beneficial Cooperation" within the human rights discourse of the UN. From these, the basic structural elements of the accumulation of dread sufficient to tip what had been settled conceptions of international human rights law and norms become visible. But in what direction? What clearly emerges is that the state of certainty about the shape and meaning of human rights and the human rights mission of the international community will be reshaped to some extent, as will be the power structures from which it proceeds. And for both to yield is dreadful, but to resist ought also to fill each with dread.

4.1 THE EMERGING SOCIALIST AND CHINESE FRAMEWORK FOR HUMAN RIGHTS

China has been developing its own Socialist Human Rights, one deeply embedded within the political and economic ideology of the Chinese

4 For the etymology of dreadnought, see www.etymonline.com/word/dreadnought.

5 Gabe Lipton, 'The Elusive 'Better deal' With China', The Atlantic (August 14, 2018), www.theatlantic.com/international/archive/2018/08/china-trump-trade-united-states/567526/; Gabe Lipton, 'The Elusive 'Better deal' With China', The Atlantic (August 14, 2018), www.theatlantic.com/international/archive/2018/08/china-trump-trade-united-states/567526/; Jordan Weissmann, 'Waking the Sleeping Dragon,' Slate, 28 September 2016, https://slate.com/business/2016/09/when-china-joined-the-wto-it-kick-starte d-the-chinese-economy-and-roused-a-giant.html.

state.[6] These have begun to take distinctive form after the 19th Chinese Communist Party (CPC) Congress and the official recognition of the new era of Chinese development.[7] "It makes clear that major country diplomacy with Chinese characteristics aims to foster a new type of international relations and build a community with a shared future for mankind."[8]

Socialist Human Rights is closely tied to national context – one that rejects the possibility of universal standards beyond general principles.

> There is no universal road for the development of human rights in the world. As an important element in the economic and social development of each country, the cause of human rights must be promoted on the basis of the national conditions and the needs of the people of that country, and cannot be defined on the basis of a single authority.[9]

But more importantly, it is a rights-based system that is tied to development and collective well-being.[10] That has been the theme expressed since 2017 in the Beijing Declaration of the first South–South Human Rights Forum: "According to the Beijing Declaration issued at the forum, participants agreed that the right to subsistence and the right to development are the primary basic human rights. The main body of the right to development is the people."[11]

6 "China proposes to build a new type of international relationship featuring mutual respect, fairness, justice and win-win cooperation, to build a community with a shared future for mankind, and to provide a Chinese proposal for promoting the healthy development of the international cause of human rights." 'People's Republic of China National Report', Human Rights Council Working Group on the Universal Periodic Review, 31st Session, Geneva, 5–16 November 2018, https://undocs.org/en/A/HRC/ WG.6/31/CHN/1 (hereafter, China National Report 2018).

7 "Since our 18th National Congress, changes both in and outside China . . . have presented us with a profound question—the question of an era. Our answer must be a systematic combination of theory and practice and must address what kind of socialism with Chinese characteristics the new era requires us to uphold and develop, and how we should go about doing it." Xi Jinping, 'Secure a Decisive Victory in Building a Moderately Prosperous Society in All Respects and Strive for the Great Success of Socialism with Chinese Characteristics for a New Era,' 19th National congress of the Communist Party of China, 18 October 2017, http://www.xinhuanet.com/english/download/Xi_Jinping's_report_at_19th_CPC_National_Congress.pdf.

8 *Id.*

9 China National Report 2018, *supra.*

10 "China gives due regard to both the universality and the particularity of human rights, combines promotion of democracy and people's livelihood, coordinates the pursuit of peace and development, and promotes and protects human rights in the process of development." *Id.*

11 Jie Meng, 'South-South Human Rights Forum calls for protection of people's right to development', Xinhua, 8 December 2017, www.xinhuanet.com/english/2017-12/08/c_136811509.htm.

The emerging approach was prominently articulated in the second South–South Human Rights Forum, organized by the Chinese State Council Information Office and the Ministry of Foreign Affairs, held in Beijing, China December 10–11, 2019. The thrust of the South–South Human Rights Forum points to an interesting emergence of a counter-narrative to the human rights discourse even as the structures of post-1945 international human rights principles, especially relating to human rights in economic activity, have also become far more important. The almost-simultaneous convening of the influential UN Forums on Business and Human Rights - the eighth Forum, which was held in late November 2019 and the second South–South Forum - suggest both tangible and intangible divisions that produce dread in the sense of fear as well as awe. The character of the approaching dreadnought that is Socialist and national human rights internationalism has already taken on an identifiable form, most clearly visible in the shadow of conventional human rights principles.

First, this emerging international human rights discourse effectively abandons the post-1945 Western model that was grounded in the centrality of the individual and the premise of human dignity as the unalterable foundation of all human rights structures. From the time of the Universal Declaration of Human Rights, the global project of human rights was grounded in the fundamental principles of "the inherent dignity and … the equal and inalienable rights of all members of the human family," and of "the dignity and worth of the human person and in the equal rights of men and women." It also found its way into the constitutions of states (e.g., German Basic Law, 1949, Art. 1), and of the great regional human rights instruments (e.g., European Convention, 1953). It became, as Jurgen Habermas suggested, the "moral 'source' from which all of the basic rights derive their sustenance."[12]

Second, the emerging approach substitutes collective development for individual human dignity. "'The most fundamental human right is the right to a safe life, and only by ensuring people's safety can human rights be protected,' the official Xinhua news agency."[13] This can be understood in an interesting advance of the development – from the time of the great human rights debates of the 1970s that saw the UDHR fracture between

[12] Jürgen Habermas, 'The concept of human dignity and the realistic utopia of human rights' in Amos Nascimento and Matthias Lutz Bachmann (eds), *Human Dignity: Perspectives from a Critical Theory of Human Rights* (Taylor & Francis, 2018).

[13] 'China Ramps Up Campaign', Bangkok Post, 13 December 2019, www.bangkokpost.com/world/181533p/china-ramps-up-campaign-to-redefine-human-rights.

civil and political rights, on the one hand, and economic, social, and political rights on the other.[14] In place of the centrality of the individual to human rights, what is offered is an elaboration of the notion derived from the UN Declaration of the Right to Development (1986) in which the human being becomes the central subject of development (Art. 2.1), development becomes the central element of human rights (Art. 1.1), and both must be expressed with reference to national conditions and culture. "The people of each country," the Chinese vice foreign minister Ma Zhaoxu told delegates, "all have the right to decide for themselves their human rights development path."[15]

Third, centering collective rights produces a substantial possibility of temporal flexibility in the construction and realization of rights. This makes possible a view of human rights measured in the long term (that is one that is based on aggregate long-term improvement even at the cost of short-term deficiencies deliberately tolerated for the greater good in the future). It follows that under this approach to human rights, a political community might have to sacrifice individual human rights now (assuming agreement on the nature and extent of that sacrifice) so long as it is done for the likelihood of a brighter collective future – measured in terms of economic, social, cultural, and environmental progress. This is a very different vision from that cultivated in Geneva.

Fourth, this model is already being offered as a substitute for the individual rights standard of post-1945 consensus standards. On the eve of the 2019 eighth UN Forum for Business and Human Rights, for example, China's UN Mission in Geneva declared: "Countries need to bear in mind the practical circumstances, consider both universality and specialty, and strive to find a tailored and effective model of promoting and protecting human rights."[16] (Countries must follow path of human rights development suited to national conditions: Chinese envoy, 2019). This aligns with the language in China's national report on human rights presented to the UN Human Rights Council in 2018.

[14] Hurst Hannum, 'The Status of the Universal Declaration of Human Rights in National and International Law' (1995–1996) 25 *Georgia Journal of International and Comparative Law* 287; Susan Waltz, 'Reclaiming and rebuilding the history of the Universal Declaration of Human Rights' (2002) 23 *Third World Quarterly* 437.

[15] China Ramps Up Campaign, *supra*.

[16] 'Countries must follow path of human rights development suited to national conditions', South-South Human Rights Forum Portal, 27 November 2019, http://p.china.org.cn/2019-11/27/content_75452706.htm.

Fifth, the template for this approach to human rights is China's own political model. The model uses the template of Socialist Modernization, a project in which the productive forces of the nation were to be developed to produce greater wealth and opportunity for the people as a whole. Human rights are effectively conflated with the core responsibilities of a Leninist vanguard with national characteristics.

> The 70 years of New China are the 70 years that the Chinese nation has ushered in from standing up, becoming rich, and becoming stronger. It is also the 70 years when the fundamental rights of the Chinese people have been continuously respected and guaranteed. It is also China 's continuous contribution to the development of the world 's human rights cause. 70 years ... The Communist Party of China has always taken the pursuit of happiness for the people as its original intention, and the socialist system with Chinese characteristics has always been based on safeguarding the interests of all people.

The China model of human rights, then, combines the theory of Reform and Opening Up with the fundamental premises of Socialist Modernization (the focus on the development of productive forces). Once that is undertaken (over the course of a generation or so), then the state and its apparatus will be ready to more precisely inculcate appropriate values – to engage in the political work that then refocuses from productivity and development of the economic resources of the nation to the development of the cultural and social position of the community within that productive culture. That is the baseline against which Socialist Human Rights will be developed. And that is precisely what is being offered as the South–South win-win variation on human rights.[17]

Sixth, the divergence in approaches, then, can be understood in the context of the political and constitutional theories under which these two systems have developed.[18] On the one hand, Western liberal democracy developed its liberties-based baseline of individual human rights against the backdrop of producing a democratic governmental order designed to preserve the social and cultural expectations of its populations (that is to preserve and perfect the customs and traditions of the people). There was no other specific goal. And indeed, until the 20th century there was a singular unwillingness to engage in

[17] Larry Catá Backer, 'Voices From the 2019 South–South Human Rights Forum Organized by the Chinese State Council Information Office and the Ministry of Foreign Affairs–Human Rights as Development? Law at the End of the Day', lcbackerblog, 15 December 2019, http://lcbackerblog .blogspot.com/2019/12/human-rights-as-development-human.html.

[18] Larry Catá Backer, 'Party, People, Government, and State: On Constitutional Values and the Legitimacy of the Chinese State-Party Rule of Law System' (2012) 30 *Boston University International Law Journal* 331.

social engineering (as opposed to class-based animal husbandry as social policy), though that unwillingness did not produce opposition to more "organic" cultural evolution.[19] At its worst, this is the society that perpetuates discrimination; it is a society as comfortable with slavery as it is with a pluralistic and multicultural society. And it is one that tends to revolve around an abstraction, human dignity, with precious few baselines that do not move across space and time.[20]

On the other hand, Marxist–Leninist states start from a transformative basic premise for legitimacy – the core obligation to establish a communist society within the nation. It is against this that all of the work of vanguard parties is judged. That baseline, then, does not look to perfection of the present as to an inevitable transformation for a more perfect future. At its worst and most corrupt, of course, it becomes a facade behind which all sorts of atrocities may be perpetuated – a *Darkness at Noon* society. But it need not always be at its worst. That is the point that China has sought to make over the last generation with its focus on the construction of Socialist Rule of Law.[21] And in the process, it offers itself as a model for preventing the sort of Soviet decadence (and the less spoken Cultural Revolution error) that can tumble this approach.

Seventh, this model is not offered merely for China; the Chinese model is offered as transposable (and indeed more transposable given the positions of developing states) than the liberal democratic model that has not appeared to have had much traction outside of its states of origin. This is in part a new form of Communist internationalism; but it is also more than that. It is also a model that might be harmonized with or contribute to the development of the global human rights project which, to date, has not embedded many of these sensibilities of the Marxist Leninist or developing world within its conceptual universe or in its sensibilities.[22] Chinese policy is crafted around the idea that there is room for further development of a human rights discourse which had to date focused primarily on the detritus of the Second World War from the Anglo-European perspective. "China no longer passively accepts the rules as the rules, but has rather begun to make them, turning itself into a positive contributor and decision-maker."[23]

[19] Larry Catá Backer, 'Culturally Significant Speech: Law, Courts, Society, and Racial Equity' (1999) 21 *University of Arkansas Little Rock Law Review* 845.

[20] Larry Catá Backer, 'Reifying Law – Government, Law and the Rule of Law in Governance Systems' (2008) 26 *Penn State International Law Review* 521.

[21] John Garrick and Yan Chang Bennett (eds), *China's Socialist Rule of Law Reforms Under Xi Jinping* (Routledge, 2016).

[22] Ted Piccone, *China's Long Game on Human Rights at The United Nations* (Brookings, 2018).

[23] Xinmin Zhou, Xi Jinping's *Governance and the Future of China* (Skyhorse, 2017) 105.

China's approach has not gone unchallenged, criticized within the institutional framework in which international human rights norms and standards are developed. That criticism, in turn, has generated harsh responses from the Chinese state organs that emphasize the conceptual divide between these perspectives.[24] The international community continues to apply its developing standards to Chinese action, even as the Chinese develop their own metrics to measure compliance with international norms. The result is that key actors tend to ignore the role of the Chinese state in the constitution and enforcement of human rights norms even within China, focusing instead on foreign actors in the global production chains with some connection to China. An example is the 2019 report on labor conditions in Chinese toy factories.[25]

4.2 MUTUALLY BENEFICIAL COOPERATION AND THE RECENTERING OF INTERNATIONAL HUMAN RIGHTS LAW AND NORMS

What happens when the trajectories of the development of a Chinese and Socialist Human Rights framework collide with the emerging global consensus on business and human rights responsibilities in global production chains? That is a question that used to be academic and conceptual but no longer.[26] A recent situation illustrates the consequence in the investment decisions of non-Chinese firms within China.

The context is the highly controversial (outside of China) policy of the Chinese authorities in the Xinjiang Autonomous Region. Chinese human rights self-assessment focused on a development centered assessment. It emphasized progress in income and housing, along with education program benefits.[27] Measured by the standards of Chinese human rights principles, there is nothing in its policies or practices that suggests any need for human

[24] Lily Kuo, 'China says UN criticism of human rights record is politically driven', Guardian, 6 November 6, 2018, www.theguardian.com/world/2018/nov/06/china-un-criticism-human-rights-record.

[25] The Report Concluded: "Year after year, we have called on brand companies to address the ongoing rights violations at their factories and to ensure that the workers in their supply chain are fairly treated. Brand companies and factories are well aware of the labor laws in China and also international labor standards... Therefore, it is the responsibility of brand companies to take serious measures in fundamentally reforming the working conditions in their supply chain." 'The Dark Side of the Glittering World: A Report on Exploitation in Toy Factories in China', China Labor Watch, 20 November 2019, www.chinalaborwatch.org/upfile/2019_11_14/1120.pdf.

[26] Larry Catá Backer, 'Human Rights without Chinese Characteristics and Global Production Chains Within China', lcbackerblog, 24 January 2019, https://lcbackerblog.blogspot.com/2019/01/human-rights-without-chinese.html#more.

[27] China National Report 2018, *supra*.

rights due diligence assessments with respect to business activities generally in China or more specifically in the Xinjiang Autonomous Region. This aligns with Chinese approaches to the implementation of international human rights norms through national measures.

Measured by interpretation of international human rights standards by states and other actors outside of China, however, the metrics point in a different direction. The United States has its own interpretation of international human rights principles to assert violations of the rights of individuals on the basis of religion and ethnic differences, and their ill treatment by the state. Elements of the US government have suggested that these practices ought to be invested as crimes against humanity. That view finds echoes in other places outside of China as well. Germany called on China to "end all unlawful detentions in Xinjiang," while Iceland and Japan expressed concern about the rights of minorities in Xinjiang. Several states urged China to allow UN observers into Xinjiang. The US called on China to abolish all internment camps in the far western territory and release the "possibly millions" detained there. The United Kingdom has also become a vocal critic of Chinese state practices in the Xinjiang Autonomous Region. "British diplomats who visited Xinjiang have confirmed that reports of mass internment camps for Uighur Muslims were "broadly true", [then] UK foreign secretary, Jeremy Hunt, … told parliament."[28] Chinese delegates said internment centers were not reeducation camps but vocational centers that offered free training in the law, language, and workplace skills.

This puts Western businesses operating in China in an awkward position. Such enterprises are worried about both legal compliances throughout their operations and the societal expectations of its stakeholders outside of China that could affect their worldwide operations, including their access to financial markets. Legal and business risks are augmented for an enterprise that by complying with Chinese legal and business expectations is then deemed complicit in Chinese actions deemed to be in breach of international norms outside of China. In late 2019, a US sportswear manufacturer announced that it would no longer use a Chinese supplier because it was concerned that continuing to do so would increase the risk of using forced labor from camps in Xinjiang. "Out of an abundance of caution and to eliminate any concerns about our supply chain given the controversy around doing business in northwestern China, we will no longer source any product from Hetian Taida or

[28] Lily Kuo, 'UK confirms reports of Chinese mass internment camps for Uighur Muslims', Guardian, 31 October 2018, www.theguardian.com/world/2018/oct/31/uk-believes-china-has-interned-about-1-million-uighur-muslims.

this region of China."[29] Xinjiang has now become a conflict point between the emergence of Chinese perspectives on the application of global human rights norms against the consensus practices and sensibilities developed around China respecting supply chain human rights responsibilities.

The issue is not merely one of legal violation (legal or public risk) but risk management and compliance (societal or market risk).[30] In the case of Badger Sportswear there appeared to be no question of legal compliance in their sourcing from Xinjiang facilities either under Chinese or US law. The issue centered around their own internal governance systems – their domestic legal order for their production chain.[31] Badger worried that the relationship violated its own internal Global Sourcing Policy (Founder Sport Group, ND). That determination would have required careful balancing following the processes of human rights' due diligence had Badger thought to undertake its responsibilities fully in compliance with international standards (something that it was not required to do as a matter of law but which might have been treated as important under their compliance-risk management parameters).

Badger's Global Sourcing Policy consists of a compilation of a number of key principles including the following: "FORCED LABOR: Founder Sport Group prohibits business partners from engaging in forced labor, including prison, bonded, indentured, and other forms of forced labor." The issue arose, as these things tend to do, when a highly visible and influential news outlet reported on the possibility that Badger's local supplier was using labor from camps that Chinese authorities had established to implement their policy objectives in Xinjiang.[32] Badger also effectively undertook a form of UNGP human rights due diligence in response to receipt of reports that the Xinjiang facility was being operated contrary to its Global Sourcing Policy. Rather than undertake the investigation themselves, Badger chose to outsource its internal compliance. The reasons were risk reducing – a third party with a good reputation would reduce the possibility that an internal investigation would have been discredited as self-serving.

[29] 'US clothing company drops Chinese supplier over Xinjiang forced labour concerns', Guardian, 10 January 2019, http://www.theguardian.com/world/2019/jan/11/us-clothing-company-drops-chinese-supplier-over-xinjiang-forced-labour-concerns (hereafter, US Clothing).

[30] Parveen P. Gupta and Tim Leech, *The Next Frontier for Boards: Oversight of Risk Culture* (The Conference Board, 2015).

[31] Gunther Teubner, *Constitutional Fragments: Societal Constitutionalism and Globalization* (Oxford University Press, 2012).

[32] US Clothing, *supra*.

To conduct the review, Badger chose Worldwide Responsible Accredited Production (WRAP), "an independent, objective, non-profit team of global social compliance experts dedicated to promoting safe, lawful, humane, and ethical manufacturing around the world through certification and education". The review revealed no violation of policy ("we found those operations to be consistent with our Global Sourcing Policy"). One might have thought that would have concluded the matter. But their due diligence revealed more: "historical documentation provided … was insufficient to conclude with certainty that it had met Badger's Global Sourcing Policy." It is not clear what that means in plain English – one would imagine that it took several lawyers and business officials some time to craft such obtuse language. But the point was clear enough: it was too risky to do business there. That risk took two forms. The first was a risk that the information provided by local suppliers was unreliable and that (reading between the lines) there was no guarantee that political conditions would improve that situation. More important from a risk perspective, however, was the implied assessment that no matter what the evidence showed, popular sentiment among key consumer and investor stakeholders about Badger activity in Xinjiang might adversely affect their operations.

This, then, is the global context in which the consequences of Chinese policy may play out. The calculation is economic rather than political, but it points in the direction of markets and finance rather than on production costs to manufacturers. That calculus makes sense; one can (at sometimes great cost) move production, but customers and financial relationships are much harder to substitute. For China, in this context of dissonance among different views of human rights compatible behaviors, political choices will have economic effect. For China, the solution may well be found in its Belt and Road Initiative whereby building its own global production chains serve as a hedge against these sorts of actions. The other solution is to project its own approaches onto the global approaches to human rights. It is to this effort that the essay now turns.

The rights-based approach developed for the Chinese context have also been proffered to the rest of the world as an alternative basis for the ordering of international relations, including human rights.[33] These efforts have been bearing fruit in the reconstruction of the normative basis for human rights within the architecture of the UN's Geneva based Human Rights Council. The UN Human Rights Council Resolution, "On promoting mutually beneficial cooperation in the field of human rights", sponsored by and reflecting an

[33] China National Report 2018, *supra*.

important new perspective of the People's Republic of China, is worth considering in some detail.[34] That resolution has been embraced and condemned by leading states and the press.[35] Yet those reactions have uniformity missed the central important element of that resolution: Chinese internationalism is now fully engaged. Yet to understand the nature of that internationalism (and the new fourth Communist International) requires a better understanding of the development and focus of Chinese Communist "New Era" Thought, which adds substantial meaning to the new operative language of an internationalized "Socialist Human Rights": "mutually beneficial cooperation."

The resolutions of the UN Human Rights Council rarely get much coverage. Sometimes they serve to articulate positions of various multilateral factions (always shifting) in the constant struggle for influence and the management of the international system in "mutually beneficial" ways (understood in the sense that such mutual benefit for all is evidenced by the work of the vanguard able to cobble together sufficient votes to make that point). Beyond the space where states play, civil society and the masses who must bear the consequences of the games, these resolutions often serve as evidence of some already formed belief about the HRC and its predilections, or about the character and motives of those states that drive these resolutions.

Resolution A/HRC/37/L.36 appears at first blush fairly innocuous, even by the low standards of HRC practice. It starts with the usual reaffirmation of core international declarations and then recalls "all relevant human rights treaties." It also concedes the universality, indivisibility, interrelatedness, and interdependence of human rights, all of which "must be treated in a fair and equal manner" (again, as we will be a judgment special in the context in which it might be made) and all of which derive from the dignity and worth of the individual human person who remains at the central subject of the human rights project. This archetypal human person is acknowledged to have, as among their rights, that of "participating actively in the realization of those rights and freedoms" accorded to them by those who have taken the power to establish them.

It then starts taking an interesting turn. It recalls prior resolutions "on international cooperation in the field of human rights" and then reaffirms (although that is a bit of a stretch here even by the usual principles of looseness

34 'On promoting mutually beneficial cooperation in the field of human rights', UN Human Rights Council, Resolution A/HRC/37/L.36, 19 March 2018, https://undocs.org/A/HRC/37/L.36 (hereafter UN Resolution).

35 Stephanie Nebehay, 'US and China clash at UN rights forum on Beijing text', Reuters, 23 March 2018, https://mobile.reuters.com/article/ amp/idUSKBN1GZ1D0?__twitter_impression=true.

in these sorts of writings) that the principles of universality, impartiality, objectivity, and non-selectivity in the work of the HRC will be guided by "constructive international dialogue and cooperation." To that end, the key part of the resolution acknowledges "the important role that mutually beneficial cooperation plays among all relevant stakeholders in promoting and protecting all human rights in an increasingly interrelated world."

From there the Resolution turns to the consequences of embracing the principle of "mutually beneficial cooperation" in the development of the architecture of human rights in the HRC. The first is to tie the principle of mutually beneficial cooperation to the objective of "capacity building and technical cooperation" as an expression of human rights in law and norm. It is thus recognized in a very specific and fractionalized way "the importance of technical assistance and capacity-building provided in consultation with, and with the consent of, the States concerned in promoting mutually beneficial cooperation in the field of human rights." The second is to tie human rights to strengthening the "capacity of States to comply with their human rights obligations for the benefit of all human beings." The concept suggests not just individual but collective measures of application. The third is to transpose the managerial techniques of big data management to the business of human rights with national characteristics "establishing a cooperative mechanism based on objective and reliable information and on interactive dialogue." The fourth, to the end of "mutually beneficial cooperation", the initial objective is dialog and the fostering of international relations. Dialog in the field of human rights is to be held among "religions, cultures and civilizations," an odd aggroupment in a document heavily tilted toward states and the individual holder of human rights. Intentional relations take up that lacuna by aiming for the "building a community of shared future for human beings, in which human rights are enjoyed by all."

It is on this critical ideological foundation that the Resolution then quite briefly gets to the substance of its business in five short bursts of instructions for implementation. States are called upon to "promote mutually beneficial cooperation in the field of human rights, and encourages other stakeholders, including international and regional organizations and non-governmental organizations, to contribute actively to this endeavor".[36] It references the application of the mutually beneficial cooperation principle in the context of technical assistance and capacity building. Resolution A/HRC/37/L.36 constrains the scope and context of periodic human rights reviews of one "based on cooperation and constructive dialogue." It then centers the concept

[36] UN Resolution, *supra*.

of mutually beneficial cooperation in the work of relevant United Nations human rights mechanisms and procedures. Lastly, it directs the Human Rights Council Advisory Committee to "conduct a study on the role of technical assistance and capacity-building in fostering mutually beneficial cooperation in promoting and protecting human rights."[37]

The essence of the resolution appears to move the discourse of human rights both backward and forward. It moves back by resurrecting the ideological and discursive tropes of the old New International Economic Order.[38] Reading the instruments produced a welling of nostalgia, a *recherche du temps perdus*. Yet it also points forward by reframing the old Soviet–Third World discourse into one that merges individual human rights into the collective imperative of development, reconstitutes development as the foundational right of humans, and then aligns that fundamental right into a state-based expression. These, then, are the refinements then built into the 19th CPC Congress Report delivered in October 2017, the approach focusing on human progress understood in terms of well-being, on peaceful development within a context of mutually beneficial cooperation, and on the construction of a community with a shared future – but all of this grounded in the respect for all states to choose their own "development path" under the guidance of their vanguards. In the process, as the Japanese delegation noted, it effectively decenters the principle that "[t]he individual was the central subject for human rights."

To understand the meaning of the concept of "mutually beneficial cooperation" from the perspective of China, it is necessary to consider in some detail the development of the concept in the pronouncements of Xi Jinping and their translation into core elements of Chinese foreign policy (tied of course intimately with crucial objectives of national public policy). Those, in turn, represent an effort, over the course of the last several years, to expand and refine the well-known "Five Principles of Peaceful Co-Existence," of equality, mutual benefit and mutual respect for territorial integrity and sovereignty. Both expansion and refinement were expressed in a recent speech of Xi Jinping: "The Five Principles of Peaceful Coexistence give concrete expression to the purposes and principles of the UN Charter and facilitate their implementation. The key elements of the Five Principles, namely, 'mutual' and 'coexistence', demonstrate the new expectations the Asian countries have for international relations and the principle of international rule of law that

37 *Id.*

38 Sakiko Fukuyda-Parr, 'The Right to Development: Reframing a New Discourse for the Twenty-First Century' (2012) 70:4 *An International Quarterly* 839.

give countries rights, obligations and responsibilities."[39] Those principles, now further expanded and refined, now make their way into the core of approaches to the project of human rights in Resolution A/HRC/37/L.36.

Xi Jinping first appeared to unveil the concept of "mutually beneficial cooperation" in a keynote speech delivered at the fifth BRICS Leaders Meeting, Durban South Africa on March 27, 2013.[40] "No matter how international situations may unfold, we should stay committed to pursuing peaceful development and mutually beneficial cooperation … While pursuing our own interests, we should also accommodate the legitimate concerns of other countries … We should respect the right of all countries to independently choose their social systems and development paths and the diversity of civilizations."[41]

The two elements of mutually beneficial cooperation were that (1) "the internal affairs of a country should be handled by its own people," and (2) "international affairs should be managed by all countries through consultation."[42] Moreover, mutually beneficial cooperation was strongly tied to the principles of socialist modernization styled economic development and the advancement of the objectives of creating a moderately prosperous socialist state, as well as the link between the principle of mutually beneficial cooperation and capacity building and technical assistance and between development and cooperation. "We BRICS countries should not seek our own development, but also work for the common development of all countries."[43] "Our development endeavour is a cooperative one, as we will work for common development, carry out economic and technological cooperation with all other countries on the basis of equality and mutual benefit, and promote our own development and the common development of all countries through cooperation."[44]

The theme of cooperation was again raised by Xi Jinping in a speech delivered at the Boao Forum for Asia Annual Conference, April 7, 2013.[45] Cooperation was grounded on sustainability as an animating concept, but with Chinese characteristics. It was expressed in four key points: common development, upholding peace to secure common development, boosting

[39] Xi Jinping. '*Work Hand in Hand for Common Development*', in Xi Jinping, The Governance of China (Foreign Languages Press, 2014) 355.

[40] *Id.* at 355–359.

[41] *Id.* at 356.

[42] *Id.*

[43] *Id.*

[44] *Id.* at 358.

[45] *Id.* at 360.

cooperation as an effective vehicle for enhancing common development, and remaining "open and inclusive to broaden the scope for enhancing common development."[46] Mutuality of self-interest rather than a universal vision are at the base of this perspective. "China cannot develop itself in isolation from the rest of Asia and the world. On their part, the rest of Asia and the world cannot enjoy prosperity without China."

These notions were not to be understood within the narratives of human rights and liberal globalization, but rather through the ideological lens of the Chinese 18th Congress of its Communist Party. "As a Chinese proverb goes, 'Neighbors wish each other well, just as loved ones do to each other.' China will continue to promote friendship and partnership with its neighbors, strengthen friendly ties, intensify mutually beneficial cooperation and ensure that its development will bring even greater gains to its neighbors."[47] Here, then, is the core of the concept of mutually beneficial cooperation, now applied to frame the narrative of human rights: a Leninist and internationalist view of the centrality of mutual development toward the development of productive forces at the center of the human rights project.

These ideas were further refined at the G20 Leaders' Summit, September 5, 2013, where Xi Jinping articulated an "opening up strategy."[48] Building on the "single flower" proverb, Xi Jinping noted: "China will continue to adhere to the opening up strategy of mutual benefit, . . . and resolve trade disputes with relevant countries through consultations."[49] These comments were further refined in his Speech at the 13th meeting of the Council of Heads of Member States of the Shanghai Cooperation Organization in Bishkek, 13 September 2013.[50] The core of the remarks sought to develop the concepts of the "Shanghai Spirit". The "essence of the 'Shanghai Spirit', he explained, is "mutual trust, mutual benefit, equality, cooperation, respect for diverse civilizations, and seeking common development."[51] For Xi Jinping, the essence of the Shanghai Spirit was centered on the objectives to "build up trust and conduct mutually beneficial cooperation based on equality, consultation, mutual understanding and mutual accommodation."[52] To that end,

46 Xi again reaches for literary metaphor: "The ocean is vast because it is fed by hundreds of rivers. We should respect the right of a country to independently choose its social system and development path, ease distrust and misgivings, and turn the diversity of our world and differences among countries into dynamism and momentum." *Id.* at 364.

47 *Id.* at 365.

48 *Id.* at 368–372.

49 *Id.* at 372.

50 *Id.* at 373–377.

51 *Id.* at 377.

52 *Id.* at 374.

practical cooperation was emphasized. For Shanghai Cooperation Organization members that revolved around what eventually would become the One Belt One Road Initiative.[53]

And again, on October 7, 2013, in his speech at the APEC CEO Summit, Bali, Indonesia, the concepts of mutually beneficial cooperation, of the development of productive forces, and of the vanguard approach to national characteristics based internationalism was further refined.[54] The challenge for the world, including the human rights of its people, was grounded in economic instability. But more than that, the entire economic order now found itself "in the middle of profound readjustment" which required "new drivers for growth." Those new drivers can be found, Xi Jinping asserted, with the economies (the political economies) of the Asia Pacific region. "To push for recovery in the sluggish world economy, economies in the Asia Pacific region should have the courage to do what has never been done before and build an open growth mode featuring innovation, interactive growth and converging interests."[55] Here is nicely laid out the direct connection between mutual benefit, capacity building, and technical cooperation built on the foundations of economic growth, which then indirectly augments the economic, social, and cultural (human) rights of individuals. And again, for Xi Jinping, profundity lies in the Chinese classics: "A Chinese poem runs, 'When one doubts whether there is a way out from the endless mountains and rivers, one suddenly finds a village shaded in soft willows and bright flowers.'"[56] That village is China and its vanguard the ideology and the CPC Basic Line, now serving as a platform for multilateral internationalism under the leadership of the CPC line – the beginnings of Xi Jinping's construction of a Markets Marxism based on the 4th Communist International.[57]

> China is drawing up a master plan for the continuation of reform in all respects. Our general approach is to press ahead with reform in the economic, political, cultural, social and ecological fields in a balanced manner. … We will attract foreign investment and encourage companies to 'go global' at the same time, and enhance international economic cooperation. … We will make overall planning for bilateral, multilateral, regional and sub-regional opening up and cooperation, and accelerate the

53 *Id.* at 375.
54 *Id.* at 377–388.
55 *Id.*
56 *Id.*
57 *Id.* at 379–381.

implementation of the FTA strategy and promote communication and exchanges with our neighboring countries.[58]

Mr. Xi appears quite conscious of the challenge to the traditional organization of power and the world order. "We are aware that the reform is a profound revolution that involves the adjustment of major interests and improvement of systems and institutions in various fields."[59] And it is from these internal revolutionary refinements of Chinese Leninism and the implementation of CPC leadership for the purpose of moving forward the project of the establishment of a Communist society that the leadership of international efforts consonant with those profoundly important objectives is developed. This leadership is grounded in notions of solidarity and cooperation toward shared national goals under the leadership of a vanguard with legitimately valid constitution. "China will firmly uphold regional peace and stability and help cement the foundations for a mutually beneficial situation in the Asia Pacific region."[60] Harmony, peace and common prosperity are to serve as the basis of the mutual benefit of such cooperation.

That mutually beneficial cooperation in the Asia Pacific region is to be built around the leadership of China. "China will commit itself to building a cross-Pacific regional cooperation framework that benefits all parties."[61] And indeed, that template also serves the One Belt One Road Initiative as well. Mutual benefit cooperation grounded in development of productive forces producing better quality of life for the masses becomes itself the marker of solicitude for the economic, social, and cultural rights of individuals from out of which the legitimacy of the structures of civil and political life that produced those benefits is legitimated. It is a brilliant refinement of Leninist principles embedded within contemporary international architectures. It is to that end, Xi Jinping announced his proposal for what became the Asia Infrastructure and Investment Bank and signalled the intention to leverage those structures into the international arena "to undertake more international responsibilities."[62]

In 2014, Xi Jinping added one final dynamic to this human rights approach. "As a Chinese saying goes, 'A wise man changes his way as circumstances change; a knowledgeable person alters his means as times evolve.'"[63] Here mutually

58 *Id.* at 382–383.
59 *Id.* at 383.
60 *Id.* at 384.
61 *Id.* at 385.
62 *Id.* at 387.
63 *Id.* at 390.

beneficial cooperation migrates from the economic to the security field. A "community of common destiny" emerges from this discourse (compare the narrative of "community of shared future for human beings" in Resolution A/HRC/37/L.36). "Asia is a region of great diversity. . . . However, we are all part of the same Asian family. With our interests and security so closely intertwined, we will sink or swim together, and we are increasingly becoming a community of common destiny."[64] How might this "community of common destiny" be bound? It is bound up by principles. "Security must be equal . . . Security must be inclusive . . . Comprehensive security means upholding security in both traditional and non-traditional fields . . . .[to adopt] a multi-pronged and holistic approach."[65] This is to be accomplished through the application of a quite specific principle of cooperation (one that echoes as well through Resolution A/HRC/37/L.36). "Cooperative security means promoting the security of both individual countries and the region as a whole through dialogue and cooperation. . . . We should expand the scope and means of cooperation and promote peace and security through cooperation."[66]

Built into the concept of cooperation and communication is also that of sustainability. Sustainability, in turn, reinforces the Marxist notion of.leading through economic development rather than through the construction of discursive spaces for the masses without the guide of vanguard leadership.[67] Thus, the inextricable interlinking of development, cooperation, security and human rights is to be measured by the improvement of people's lives, the measurement of which must, as in all matters, be contextually derived. And the foundational source of the insight is again revealed: "As a Chinese saying goes, 'For a tree to grow tall, a strong and solid root is essential; for a river to reach far, an unimpeded source is necessary.'"[68] Of course, that insight can be the subject of some engagement; it is as powerful to consider the inverse of the Chinese saying quoted by Mr. Xi. How would one approach the issues if in fact one drew from the inverted saying in this way: for the roots to continue to build a strong network, a vigorous mechanism for acquiring nutrients from the sun and rain is necessary; for an unimpeded source to remain in harmony with its surroundings, a fat river is necessary. The clash of those two sayings may well mirror the clash of approaches to international engagement and especially to the narrative structures of approaches to human rights. That, in metaphorical terms will be the basis of the conflict of narrative between the new approach

64 *Id.* at 390–391.
65 *Id.* at 391.
66 *Id.* at 392.
67 *Id.* at 393.
68 *Id.*

built into Resolution A/HRC/37/L.36 and the historical approaches of the human rights built into the contemporary Western narrative.

And thus, with Resolution A/HRC/37/L.36, one can trace the concept of "mutually beneficial cooperation" from a genesis in the economic and security fields into international human rights. For a vision that grounds the attainment of human happiness in the progress toward economic, social, and cultural harmony, it makes perfect sense to focus on the mechanisms of leadership driven cooperation of mutual benefit that leads from the economic and cultural to the political and civil – but in ways that are contextually driven. Eventually, Leninist theory understands all roads lead to the same ends: a historical determinism built into the bones of both Marxism and Leninism. In that sense, the great principles matter. But principle does not require discipline and orthodoxy among states, just contextually driven commitment. And that appears to be the essence of Resolution A/HRC/37/L.36 as it quite correctly, from a Leninist international perspective, draws together the modalities of leadership in the economic, social, security, and cultural fields within the umbrella of human rights narratives.

4.3 CONCLUSION – 'BY DRED THINGS I AM COMPELLED'

> "Like one, that on a lonesome road
> Doth walk in fear and dread,
> And having once turned round walks on,
> And turns no more his head;
> Because he knows, a frightful fiend
> Doth close behind him tread."
>
> (Samuel Coleridge, 1798, The Rime of the Ancient Mariner)

The global order has been walking along a steady path toward a coherent internationally driven framework for human rights since the adoption of the Universal Declaration of Human Rights.[69] That road has been both lonesome and frightening – the project has been one undertaken in dread of the past that gave rise to the expression of the project after 1945. Yet dread of the past, for those on that path, is giving way to a dread of another that is walking with increasing confidence along the same road. Both are destined to walk along the same path – perhaps together, perhaps apart. One embraces the centrality of the individual and the relevance of the present in a society that can be advanced only through the development of the individual. The other

69 Sophocles, Electra before 406 B.C.

embraces the centrality of a collective and the relevance of the future whose welfare may be attained through development of society.

Both have proven to be conceptually elegant and fundamentally incompatible. They have become instruments in the battle for control of the narrative around which compelling world views can be enforced. Both arise from a dread of and as expiation for a past too brutal to repeat and a fear of any deviation that may invite the past forward to the future.

As instruments, they have sought to tip the balance of dread in favor of their respective narratives and in the process have transformed high concept into politics. That hides, in turn the true character of the dread with which each ought to regard the other. Most states abstaining from (or in the case of the United States voting against)[70] the incorporation of regimes of mutually beneficial cooperation within international human rights may not have grasped the extent to which the effort represented a substantial transformation (potentially) of the narrative (and thus the course) of the human rights project. Yet from the perspective of China, it was intended as a step toward that objective. Most enterprises are now caught between the construction of human rights conceptual world orders in which compliance with one standard risks liability for complicity with the other in the realms of societal, legal, and normative orders. Such has been the context in which the evolution of contemporary Chinese engagement with international law and norms has emerged.

70 The "Action on Resolution" also noted the strong opposing position of the United States: "United States, in a general comment, said it was clear that China was attempting through this resolution to weaken the United Nations human rights system and the norms underpinning it. The 'feel good' language about 'mutually beneficial cooperation' was intended to benefit autocratic States at the expense of people whose human rights and fundamental freedoms all were obligated, as States, to respect. For these reasons, the United States was calling for a vote and would vote against this resolution, and encouraged all other countries not to support this resolution."

5

Democracy

Lua Kamál Yuille

For all of its contemporary challenges, the European Union (EU) continues to be framed as a path breaking, novel actor in the field of international law and global governance.[1] By its adherents, the EU is heralded as a model, even if imperfect, of the potential for multi-level/post-national/post-modern government and governance.[2] Other regional international organizations struggle to recreate its successes, and regional integration efforts across the globe – the *Mercado Común del Sur* (Mercosur), the *Comunidad Andina* (CAN), the Association of Southeast Asian Nations (ASEAN), the Common Market for Eastern and Southern Africa (COMESA), and even the North American Free Trade Agreement (NAFTA) – have drawn inspiration from and are influenced by the EU.

[1] The work of numerous others has expertly explained and summarized the basic history and functioning of the EU, so a recreation of it here is unnecessary. For the purposes of the proceeding discussion, it suffices to mention that the EU is merely the current incarnation of the project of European regional integration that began at the end of World War II. For an introduction to the European Union and its development see, for example, THE EVOLUTION OF EU LAW 2d ed. (Paul Craig & Gráinne de Burca, eds. 2011); J. H. H. Weiler, *Transformation of Europe, The Transformation of Europe*, 100 YALE L. J. 2403 (1991) (theorizing the development of the European Communities during its first forty years as three distinct phases, and predicting the challenges the community would face moving forward).

[2] Conspicuously positioned in the cadre of pro-Europe voices are outspoken politicians like former-German Foreign Minister Joschka Fischer, *see* Joschka Fischer, *From Confederacy to Federation: Thoughts on the Finality of European Integration, Speech at the Humbolt University, May 12, 2000* (concluding that the "simple answer" to Europe's problems is "the transition from a union of states to full parliamentarisation as a European Federation"), and powerhouse of political theory Jurgen Habermas, *see, e.g.*, Jurgen Habermas, *The European Nation-State and the Pressures of Globalization*, 235 NEW LEFT REV. (1999); Jurgen Habermas, *Remarks on Dieter Grimm's 'Does Europe Need a Constitution?'* 1 EUR. L. J. 303, 304 (1995). *See also*, Koen Laenarts, *Constitutionalism and the Many Faces of Federalism*, 38 AM. J. COMP. L. 205 (1990); Giandomenico Majone, *Delegation of Regulatory Powers in a Mixed Polity*, 8 EUR. L. J. 319–339 (2002); Gary Marks, Leisbeth Hooge , & Kermit Blank, *European Integration from the 1980s: State-Centric v. Multi-level Governance*, 34 J. COMM. MKT. STUD. 341 (1996).

Its detractors, most prominent among them – the so-called Euroskeptics, deconstruct its strictures and structures to illustrate the impossibility of "good" supranational government and governance.[3] The supranational technocracy created by the EU's constitutive treaties is opaque, disconnected from the needs and wants of those governed and thereby condemned as micro-managed, unwieldy, and substantively unsatisfactory. Such problems were only exacerbated by the sustained "widening" of the EU,[4] which grew from six to a zenith twenty-eight Member States since the births of the EU's direct predecessors.

From these divergent visions of the EU,[5] the Commission of the European Union, the engine of European integration, was led to conclude that "political leaders throughout Europe are facing a real paradox."[6] The Commission styled this paradox as a problem of expectation, distrust, and disinterest. Simply put: Europeans want political actors to fix their problems, but they do not trust those same actors with the task.[7]

3 For an emblematic, though not exhaustive, summary of such critiques see Joseph H. H. Weiler, Ulrich R. Haltern, & Franz C . Mayer, *European Democracy and its Critique: Five Uneasy Pieces in* THE CRISIS OF REPRESENTATION IN EUROPE (Jack Hayward, ed. 1995). *See als o* Robert Oulds & Lee Rotherham, *Eurosceptics Tell Brussels How It Is: Top Down is the Wrong Way Up!* The Bruges Group (2002) (urging that EU policy aimed at uniformity is "out-dated and out-moded" and should be replaced by flexible, intergovernmental cooperation); Dieter Grimm, *Does Europe Need a Constitution?* 1 EUR. L. J. 282 (1995) (arguing the essential impossibility of supranational democracy because of the lack of a *demos* upon which to base it).

4 The term "widening" of European integration connotes the process by which the EU embraces more countries. The original six partners to European integration were France, Germany, Italy, and the Benelux countries (Belgium, the Netherlands, and Luxembourg). Through events in 1973 (the first enlargement), 1981–86 (the second enlargement), and 1995 (the third enlargement), the United Kingdom, Denmark, Ireland, Greece, Spain, Portugal, Austria, Finland, and Sweden joined the EU. In May 2004 in the largest enlargement in history, ten countries—Slovenia, the Czech Republic, Estonia, Hungary, Poland, Cyprus, Latvia, Lithuania, Slovakia, and Malta—joined the Union. On January 1, 2007, Bulgaria and Romania acceded to the EU. And Croatia became the most recent state admitted to the EU in July 2013. On January 31, 2020, the UK withdrew from the EU as the culmination of the controversial "Brexit" movement.

5 A comprehensive review of the multitude of perspectives on the EU is far beyond the scope of this chapter. Between the poles of the federalists and the Euroskeptics – each itself a broad category that masks the variety of viewpoint encompassed thereby – one could position numerous other categorizations that fail to reflect the diversity embedded therein. For a very accessible tour of the approaches to the EU see Paul Craig, *The Nature of the Community: Integration, Democracy, and Legitimacy in* Craig & de Búrca at 1–50. *See also* Simon Hix, *The Study of the European Union II: The 'New Governance' Agenda and its Rival*, 5 J. EUR. PUB. POL'Y 38, 39 (1998).

6 Commission of the European Communities, *European Governance: A White Paper*, COM (2001) 428 final (25.7.2001) 3 ("On the one hand Europeans want them to find solution to the major problems confronting our societies. On the other hand, people increasingly distrust institutions and politics or are simply not interested in them.").

7 *Id.*

By others, this paradox has been called a crisis of legitimacy. Indeed, the European Union's protracted mid-life crisis may be one for the history books. More than a decade before the project of European integration that evolved into the EU neared its fiftieth anniversary – which was officially celebrated throughout 2007 – critics and supporters (both Euroskeptics and Europhiles, politicians, and academics, alike) began arguing about, lamenting over, and strategizing to fix Europe's "democratic deficit," the principal feature of its crisis of legitimacy.[8] These calls manifest themselves today across the European space in the politics of nostalgia, the rise of right and left wing populism, in the mass strikes for economic sovereignty in France and the Brexit vote in the UK. In part complementing and responding to calls to cure the deficit, the EU itself has engaged in a sustained project of governance reform. This effort is reflected not only in the "semi-permanent"[9] treaty revision process, which regularly constitutionalizes or Europeanizes changes in the EU, but also in the general implementation of EU policy and the institutional positions of the primary actors on the EU level.

This chapter examines two such reform mechanisms: the creation of a Committee of the Regions (CoR) and the widespread adoption of the Open Method of Coordination (OMC). Part 1 provides a brief introduction

[8] For an early explicit academic discussion of the democratic deficit and crisis of legitimacy in the context of European integration, see J. H. H. Weiler, *The Transformation of Europe, supra* note __ at 2466–74. *See also* J. H. H. Weiler & Joel P. Trachtman, *European Constitutionalism and Its Discontents*, 17 Nw. J. Int'l L. & Bus. 354 (1996–97); J. H. H. Weiler, *Does Europe Need a Constitution? Demos, Telos, and the German Maastrict Decision*, 1 Eur. L. J. 217 (1995). Although there is an extensive corpus of literature problematizing and analyzing the EU's crisis of legitimacy and democratic deficit – far too vast to list here – Weiler's works are considered foundational expositions of the central critiques of the EU. *See also* Koen Lenaerts and Marlies Desomer, *New Models of Constitution-Making in Europe: The Quest for Legitimacy*, 39 Common Mkt. L. Rev. 1217, 1228 (2002); Andrew Moravcsik, *In Defense of "Democratic Deficit": Reassessing Legitimacy in the European Union*, 40 J. Common Mkt. Stud. 603 (2002) (arguing that there is no deficit); G. Federico Mancini, *Europe: The Case for Statehood*, 4 Eur. L. J. 29 (1998) (proposing the move to a federal European state); Giandomenico Majone, *Europe's "Democracy Deficit": The Question of Standards*, 4 Eur. L. J. 5 (1998) (arguing that traditional notions of majoritarian democracy are inappropriate in the EU); Gráinne de Burca, *The Quest for Legitimacy in the European Union*, 59 Mod. L. R. 349 (1996); Karlheinz Neunreither, *The Democratic Deficit of the European Union: Towards Closer Cooperation between the European Parliament and the National Parliaments*, 29 Gov. & Opp. 13 (1994) (proposing the superimposition of domestic-style democracy on the EU: "Do we not dramatically need European political parties, European trade unions, a far-reaching European organizational structure … if we want to move forward substantially … ?").

[9] Neil Walker, *The White Paper in Constitutional Context* in Symposium: Mountain or Molehill? A Critical Appraisal of the Commission White Paper on Governance, Jean Monnet Working Paper No. 6/01 22 (Christian Joerges, Yves Mény & J. H. H. Weiler, eds. 2001). After the first major of treaty reform, the Single European Act (1986), the European Community has not passed a decade without revising its constitutive treaties, and since the 1992 birth of the EU, major treaty reform has occurred every three or four years.

to the new governance as a partial response to the EU legitimacy crisis and sketches a picture of its European poster child, the OMC. It focuses on the primary actors in selected policy areas in which the "new mode of governance"[10] is implemented. Part 2 provides a snapshot of the CoR and its role in the EU. It argues, in line with the general consensus, that the CoR plays only a very minor direct role in EU policy and law making and exercises limited influence over the primary actors in EU governance.

Finally, Part 3 explores the implications of what is described herein as a disconnect between the legitimizing legal mechanisms being explored through the OMC and the potentially most "legitimate" political actor in Europe – the regional and local representatives. In so exploring, Part IV preliminarily suggests that these disconnects might not be missteps but represent an effective strategy for muting the voices of dissidence echoing throughout the EU. As democracy increasingly seems to hang in the balance around the world, a dive into the operations of widely perceived exemplars of democratic systems allow us to examine some of the limits and possibilities of the current democratic imagination in global governance – and how we might rebuild our commitment to a more robust model of shared power.

5.1 THE OPEN METHOD OF COORDINATION AS A PATH TO LEGITIMACY

For several decades, the capability, efficiency, suitability, and propriety of government institutions as principal actors in "the activity or process of governing," as the center of "a condition of ordered rule," as the "people charged with the duty of governing," and as the sculptors of "the manner, method or system by which … society is governed" has been seriously questioned.[11] In place of the classical government-centered modalities, the search for and experimentation with alternatives has been explored in earnest.

In the EU, the realities of *sui generis* supranational law making,[12] as well as the concomitant crisis of legitimacy were catalysts of efforts to find alternatives to traditional governance strategies (represented by the classic "Community

[10] Joanne Scott & David M. Trubek, *Mind the Gap: Law and New Approaches to Governance in the European Union*, 8 EUR. L. J. 1 (2002).

[11] These textbook "definitions" of government can be found in R. A. W. Rhodes, UNDERSTANDING GOVERNANCE: POLICY NETWORKS, GOVERNANCE, AND ACCOUNTABILITY 46 (1997) (quoting S. E. FINER, COMPARATIVE GOVERNMENT 3–4 (1970)).

[12] *See, e.g.*, Markus Jachtenfuchs, *The Governance Approach to European Integration*, 39 J. COMMON MKT. STUD. 245, 252–55 (2001); Markus Jachtenfuchs, *Conceptualizing European Governance in* REFLECTIVE APPROACHES TO EUROPEAN GOVERNANCE (Knud Erik Jørgensen, ed. 1997); Iain Begg, *Introduction: Regulation in the European Union*, 3

Method").[13] As commentators long recognized, patterns and sources of democratic accountability and legitimacy within the EU are difficult to pinpoint.[14] This elusiveness gives power to claims that EU policy formation is distant from the people, is hyper-controlled and micromanaged by barely accountable institutions (i.e., Commission and the Council),[15] by-passes democracy by delegating authority to unaccountable technocrats, and takes place behind an iron curtain, which prevents transparency and fosters *über*-complex legislation.[16]

The convergence of these factors led to the March 2000 introduction of the Lisbon Strategy and the so-called Open Method of Coordination. This new governance mechanism was suggested as a response to then (and still) raging critiques of the EU. In eschewing concentration, (traditional) hierarchy, and autonomy, new governance mechanisms embrace the participation of decentralized political actors like subnational representatives and civil society. Such actors, characterized by smaller constituencies, geographic proximity to those constituencies, and greater opportunities for direct involvement by individuals, bridge the expanse between the governors and the governed. Moreover, at the root of the "distance" argument is the inability of the EU to respond to the heterogeneous characteristics of problem arenas with one-size-fits-all legislation. The flexibility envisioned by the new governance permits such diversity to animate rather than hinder policymaking.

New governance, with its emphasis on outputs (e.g., results and outcomes) rather than inputs (e.g., procedures), also addresses the performance element of the legitimacy crisis faced by the EU. Intimately tied to the performance consideration, new governance constitutes a more palatable mode of addressing policy areas in which successful EU-level action promotes confidence in the EU – say, employment – but are not (or are less) amenable to the Community Method because of the politically sensitive nature, or the sheer complexity, of the problems facing governments . When used in this way, as it

J. EUR. PUB. POL'Y. 527 (1996); Beate Kohler-Koch, *Catching Up with Change: The Transformation of Governance in the European Union*, 3 J. EUR. PUB. POL'Y. 359 (1996).

13 Trubek and Trubek describe it as "differ[ing] radically" from approaches used so far. David M. Trubek & Louise G. Trubek, *Hard and Soft Law in the Construction of Social Europe: The Role of the Open Method of Co-ordination*, 11 EUR. L. J. 343, 347 (2005).

14 *See* Neil MacCormick, *Democracy, Subsidiarity, and Citizenship in the European Commonwealth*, 16 L. & PHIL. 331 (1997); Kevin Featherstone, *Jean Monnet and the Democratic Deficit in the European Union*, 32 J. COMMON MKT. STUD. 149 (1994).

15 The European Council, which brings together the heads of state or government of the member States and is charged with providing the "necessary impetus" for the development of the EU, TEU Art. 4, is often cited as part of the legitimacy problem, as well.

16 *See* Weiler, *supra* note 8.

often is, new governance can be described as a legitimizing discourse – a way to mobilize support.[17]

As many have recognized, at is core, the EU's legitimacy crisis debate is beset by competing notions of what democracy and legitimacy mean (or should mean) in the EU.[18] Necessarily, which responses are satisfactory depends on which vision of democracy or legitimacy the observer takes. Describing the Open Method of Coordination, Bowman has claimed new governance "best captures the capacity of freedom as non-domination to deal with the prevailing forms of multiculturalism that are problematic for traditional forms of republicanism."[19] For example, for a proponent of classical representative democracy, commingling illegitimate and legitimate actors does not necessarily erase illegitimacy.[20] Nevertheless, the new governance constitutes a way to engage in the dialogue necessary to find broadly satisfactory answers.

Touting change as "the way forward," the European Council called for a reform of governance to facilitate the achievement of its strategic goal, namely, "a new open method of coordination" to be used in a wide range of policy areas.[21] Most important, the European Council explained,

> [a] fully decentralised approach will be applied in line with the principle of subsidiarity in which the Union, the Member States, the regional and local levels, as well as the social partners and civil society, will be actively involved, using variable forms of partnership.[22]

17 *See Claudio M. Radelli,* The Open Method of Coordination: A New Governance Architecture for the European Union? *The Open Method of Coordination: A New Governance Architecture of the European Union?* Swedish Institute for European Policy Studies (SIEPS) Report 1/2003 7 (describing the OMC as a legitimizing discourse within the EU).

18 Craig, *supra* note 5at 32–42 (describing a selected set of competing visions); see Walker, *The White Paper in Constitutional Context supra* note 9at 4–12 (discussing a threefold typology of legitimacy: performance, regime, and polity).

19 Jonathan Bowman, *The European Union Democratic Deficit: Federalists, Skeptics, and Revisionists,* 5 EUR. J. POL. THEORY 191, 194, 196–201 (2006) (outlining three approaches to legitimacy).

20 Fritz W. Scharpf, *European Governance: Common Concerns vs. the Challenge of Diversity in* Joerges et al. *supra* note 9; *see also* Iain Begg, *Policy Responses to Marginalization: The Changing Role of the EU in* RESISTING MARGINALIZATION: UNEMPLOYMENT EXPERIENCE AND SOCIAL POLICY IN THE EUROPEAN UNION 255–56 (Duncan Gallie, ed. 2004) (describing legitimacy concerns connected with new governance in the EU).

Similarly, it can be argued that this increases the accountability problems already inherent in the EU by adding another layer of such problems attendant to new governance. On one level, the institutions are not accountable because they are not directly responsible to a constituency; on another, they are not accountable because, having involved a wide range of actors they are able to disclaim responsibility for policy choices.

21 *Id.* at ¶37.

22 *Id.* at ¶38.

With the OMC, the EU proclaimed it was convinced that new governance could reconcile the tension between EU-level action and subsidiarity,[23] which mapped onto the tension between efficiency and legitimacy.[24] (Theoretically) operationalizing that principle, the OMC – though in each policy area functioning distinctly – is characterized by four essential characteristics:

(1) *Setting European-level guidelines or objectives.* This process involves identifying issues or problems and advancing a common vision about desired outcomes.
(2) *Establishing indicators, targets, or benchmarks.* This process, as it is generally understood, consists of defining standards or best practices with respect to the objectives of the relevant policy.[25]
(3) *Independent translation into national contexts.* This process, permitting wide margins of variation, envisions individual states, regions, or localities implementing policies designed to achieve the Europe-wide goals but tailored to relevant national, regional, or local conditions.
(4) *Periodic monitoring, evaluation, and peer review.*[26] This process proposes creating fora for sharing and judging the policy experimentation fostered by the OMC. The result of this regular process is revision of the guidelines, benchmarks, and national policies developed through the OMC.

These four iterative processes – with their preference for generality, nonbinding norms, reliability, flexibility, and outcomes (versus inputs) – have made the OMC the paradigmatic instance of new governance within the EU.[27] Today, it is a primary, complementary, or clandestine policy mechanism in more than thirteen arenas.[28]

[23] "Subsidiarity" is used here to denote a generic version of the term of art: decision making and policy implementation at the most appropriate level of organization (local, provincial, national, regional, supranational).

[24] Armin Schäfer, *Beyond the Community Method: Why the Open Method of Coordination Was Introduced to EU Policymaking*, 8 EIoP 11 (2004) *available at* http://eiop.or.at/eiop/texts/2004-013a.htm.

[25] *See* Janine Goetschy, *The European Employment Strategy, Multi-level Governance and Policy Coordination: Past, Present and Future in* GOVERNING WORK AND WELFARE IN A NEW ECONOMY: EUROPEAN AND AMERICAN EXPERIMENTS (Jonathan Zeitlin & David Trubek, eds. 2003).

[26] *Id.*

[27] *See* Scott & Trubek, *Mind the Gap*, supra note 10(arguing that the OMC is but one new governance mechanism within the EU).

[28] Erika Szyszczak, *Experimental Governance: The Open Method of Coordination*, EUR. L. J. 486 (2006) (creating a four tier typology of the OMC: developed areas (e.g. employment),

The OMC was only a part of the larger new governance trend slowing unfolding in the EU. The high water mark of which was Commission's publication of the White Paper *European Governance*.[29] The reform proposals made by the Commission in that document were extremely far reaching, setting out five principles underlying good governance: openness,[30] participation,[31] accountability,[32] effectiveness,[33] and coherence.[34]

The Commission paired its principles of good governance with specific actions to be undertaken to put the principles into practice. Important among those for the present discussion, the Commission committed itself to improving the involvement of local and regional actors in EU policymaking.[35] Explaining that "[d]emocracy depends on people being able to take part in public debate,"[36] the Commission aimed at creating a "more systematic" dialogue with subnational actors.[37] It also called on the Committee of the Regions to become more proactive, organize a best practice exchange, and think about how EU law could become more flexible.[38]

The links between the EU's legitimacy concerns and the White paper on governance are clear, and they have been discussed at depth elsewhere.[39] Also clear are the links between the Commission's proposals and the new governance. For example, the commitment to more involvement of local and regional actors is reminiscent of the polycentric and centerlessness (versus

adjunct areas (e.g. pensions), nascent areas (e.g. research and development), and unacknowledged areas (e.g. tax or enlargement)).

29 Commission of the European Communities, *supra* note 6.

30 *Id.* at 10 (requiring institutions to "actively communicate about what the EU does and the decisions it takes,").

31 *Id.* (explained as "wide participation throughout the policy chain – from conception to implementation").

32 *Id.* (claiming that "each of the EU institutions must explain and take responsibility for what it does in Europe").

33 *Id.* (describing effectiveness as "delivering what is needed on the basis of clear objectives, an evaluation of future impact and . . . past experience").

34 *Id.* (explaining, "action must be coherent and easily understood").

35 *Id* at 14.

36 *Id.* at 13.

37 *Id.* at 15.

38 *Id.*

39 *See, e.g.*, Marlene Wind, *The Commission White Paper: Bridging the Gap between the Governed and the Governing? in* Joerges et al. *supra* note 20(arguing that the White Paper is a step toward creating "habitual trust" in the EU, which nations have built up over the centuries and is at the root of the legitimacy debate); Walker, *supra* note 9(situating the White Paper's themes within a theoretical epistemology of legitimacy); Scharpf, *supra* note 20 (contending that the White Paper's authors "seem to be happily unaware of any legitimacy constraints on European institutions").

hierarchical) characteristic of new governance.[40] The aims of creating a more systematic dialogue with regional and local government at an early stage of policy shaping,[41] and of increasing policy examination by a variety of actors[42] also evokes new governance's rejection of rigid hierarchy. The promise to "[d] evelop . . . a more systematic and pro-active approach to working with key networks to enable them to contribute to decision shaping and policy execution"[43] echoes the principle that "[new g]overnance is by definition about collective problem-solving, not dominance."[44]

Given the origins of the OMC and the Commission's concurrent pledge in the White Paper on governance to embracing increased participation of subnational actors,[45] it would be reasonable to imagine that the OMC formalized an important direct role for regions and cities within the EU policy machine. However, despite its auspicious veneer, the OMC has failed to deliver all it has promised, and the polycentricity it augured remains unseen.[46] Independent of substantive outcomes, the OMC processes themselves have been criticized, as well. Specifically, the promise that the EU would embrace a range of actors has failed to materialize: "So far the OMC has not been very 'open.'"[47]

While, practically, the EU project of governance reform has amounted to little more than lip service, theoretically, it is a very important development. Optimistically cast, it is an acknowledgment that traditional government may not hold the answers to the "paradox" being faced by local, national, supranational, and intergovernmental policy makers. More optimistically still, armed with the rhetoric of new governance, citizens and civil society have the tools they need to transform pretense into effective action.

40 *See e.g.*, RHODES, *supra* note 11at 51.
41 Commission of the European Communities, *supra* note 6at 16.
42 *Id.*
43 *Id.* at 18.
44 *Id.*
45 The Commission's White Paper has been criticized on many fronts. Among the main arguments is that it represents more an attempt to consolidate the Commission's power than an attempt to embrace new governance.
46 Indeed, in the wake of disappointing performance described by the European Council as "mixed" results, the Lisbon Strategy was revised and relaunched in 2005. *See, e.g.*, Robert Kaiser & Heiko Prange, *Missing the Lisbon Target? Multi-Level Innovation and EU Policy Coordination*, 25 J. PUB. POL'Y 241 (2005); Radelli, *supra* note 17at 27–38, 43–48; Stijn Smismans, *EU Employment Policy: Decentralization or Centralization through the Open Method of Coordination?* EUI Working Paper LAW No. 2004/1 (2004); *see also* Carlo Chiatelli, *The Reform of the Lisbon Strategy's Governance Framework—the "New Governance" the Way Forward?*, 2 JCER 4, 6 (2006).
47 *Id.* at ¶¶4–41.

What optimism fails to explain, however, is *why* subnational actors have not been welcomed into OMC policy processes. At first blush, it is easy to point to the difficulty of coordinating cross-border, trans-scalar, multi-actor cooperation, especially in the absence of binding, enforceable norms. Yet, that answer is unsatisfactory because the OMC has not excluded only those actors that it is more difficult to coordinate. The EU-level institutionalized voice of subnational actors too has been marginalized in the OMC. It serves, now, to turn to the role of that institutionalized voice, the Committee of the Regions.

5.2 THE COMMITTEE OF THE REGIONS AS A PATH TO LEGITIMACY

If the Economic and Social Committee – on which it was modelled – is the EU's "perennial bridesmaid,"[48] the Committee of the Regions (CoR) is its neglected foster child who hopes to receive an invitation to the wedding. Not an institution of the EU, it is virtually ignored by the major institutional actors. A consensus has persisted that recognizes the weak position of the CoR within the EU; so minor is the CoR, that it seems wholly disconnected from the debates about EU policymaking mechanisms as tools for building legitimacy. The discussion that follows opens that conversation.

Although histories of subnational participation in the European Union and its predecessors have been written, the story is less familiar than the evolution of other EU institutions. Accordingly, it serves to outline briefly the major events in the birth and development of this facet of European development.

By 1988, the European Community (the EU had not yet been born) faced three important and interrelated circumstances.[49] First, the initial breaths of the illegitimacy charges that would plague it throughout the 1990s and the new

48 Charlie Jeffrey, *Wither the Committee of the Regions? Reflections on the Committee's "Opinion on the Revision of the Treaty in European Union"*, 5 REG. & FED. STUD. 247 (1995).

49 The factors leading to the creation of the CoR have been cataloged and characterized in various ways. *Compare* John Loughlin, *Representing Regions in Europe: The Committee of the Regions*, 6 REGIONAL & FED. STUD. 147, 147 (1996)(describing three sets of factors: (1) developments within the European Community, (2) the "evolving political systems of the member states," and (3) "growing inter-regional mobilization") *with* Roht-Arriaza, *The Pinochet Effect: Transnational Justice in the Age of Human Rights* 418–20 (2005)(outlining four major consideration: (1) domestic decentralization (2) "intractable" problems of nationalism, socialism, ethnic conflict, and threat of succession (3) theories of government stressing the importance of local and regional control over resources, and (4) perceived democratic deficits); *see also* Dennis Kennedy, *The Committee of the Regions: An Assessment*, 7 REG. & FED. STUD. 1, 1 (1997) (outlining additional factors).

millennium were expelled.[50] Second, two waves of enlargement had introduced more acute cultural and economic cleavages among the Member States.[51] Third, the expanding sphere of competences simultaneously usurped evermore decision-making authority from, and vested implementation responsibility with, subnational actors, which may be described as the "ascendant" and "descendant" aspects of European integration.[52]

In a response that was as proactive as it was reactive,[53] the Commission created the Consultative Council of Regional and Local Authorities to serve as a "sounding board"[54] for the increasing number of EU policy initiatives that were seen to have particular relevance or impact at the subnational level.[55] Prominent among such EU regional policies was (and continues to be) the "economic and social cohesion" policy and the European Regional Development Fund that preceded it.[56] Although the English terminology is

[50] These early breaths emanated powerfully from the nationalist and separatist voices seeking political autonomy within domestic systems. *See* Roht-Arriaza, *supra* note 49at 418–19 (describing the claims of Catalonians in Spain); Michael Keating, *Europeanism and Regionalism in* THE EUROPEAN UNION AND THE REGIONS 4–6 (Barry Jones & Michael Keating, eds. 1995) (describing mobilization of the Basque country, which lies in France and Spain). Equally powerful were the German *Länder* and the *Bundesrat*, whose constitutionally vested rights were circumvented by the European Community. *See* Roht-Arriaza, *supra* note 49at 423–24. Though possibly less powerful than the *Länder* given Spain's European infancy (it acceded to the European Community only in 1986), the *Comunidades Autónomas*—most prominently, Catalonia and the Basque Country, as well as Galicia and Andalusia—also sought to maintain the territorial balance of power enshrined in the Spanish constitution.

[51] *See* Keating, *supra* note 50at 7–8 (describing increased economic disparity among the regions occasioned by enlargement).

[52] Roht-Arriaza, *supra* note 49at 415.

[53] The year 1988 also saw a drastic overhaul of the community's cohesion policy; the formal inclusion of subnational actors responsible for implementing much of that policy on the ground is a natural (though not necessary) outgrowth of that development. *See* Bruce Millan, *The Committee of the Regions: In at the Birth*, 7 REG. & FED. STUD. 5, 5 (1997) (describing the decision by the Commission to create the Consultative Council).

[54] Roht-Arriaza, *supra* note 49at 446.

[55] Commission Decision 88/487/EEC 1988 O.J. (L247) 23. This immediate predecessor to the CoR itself was preceded by a number of efforts are mobilizing the regions of Europe that were independent of any international organization. Prominent among these, one finds the Assembly of European Regions (ARE), established in 1985. Earlier still, the Council of Europe (CoE), of ECHR fame, created space for subnational voices with its Standing Conference of Local and Regional Authorities of Europe (SCLRAE). These developments, no doubt, influenced later developments in the European Community by modeling forms of subnational mobilization and responses thereto. *See* Roht-Arriaza, *supra* note 49at 430–32.

[56] For a brief but comprehensive early history of the development of regional policy in the European Community see Harvey W. Armstrong, *The Role and Evolution of European Community Regional Policy in* Jones & Keating, eds., *supra* note 50at 34–50.

fuzzy,[57] the aim of cohesion policy is to reduce regional and social "disparities" and "backwardness" in the community[58] – that is to promote economic equality (and development) across both the diverse territorial units that comprise the EU (the regional element) and the socio-economic groups (the social element).[59] It seemed that redoubling efforts within this policy area and drawing on the subnational authorities who were to implement measures and distribute structural funds stemming from the cohesion policy was an answer to each of the three major issues facing the European Community.

Despite the creation of the Consultative Council of Regional and Local Authorities, regional voices were not satisfied. Without a treaty basis for the operation, the Commission was the sole dictator of the direct involvement of subnational actors in European Community-level policymaking. And, in its short history, the Consultative Council was a "practically invisible" body.[60] Invisibility was insufficient. The call was for a "Europe of the Regions." In its most ambitious form, the phrase envisioned the obsolescence of the state in a federated Europe constituted of regions.[61] In its tempered, more popular version, the notion advocated either a third level of European institutionalization (i.e. the addition of the regional level to the supranational and national) or the introduction of a second house of the European Parliament to represent subnational interests.[62]

Accordingly, when the EU began a new round of treaty reform with the Intergovernmental Conference (IGC) on Political Union, the Commission

57 Most versions of the treaty use an equally opaque term: *coesione* (in Italian), *cohésion* (in French), *cohesión* (in Spanish), and *Zusammenhalt* (in German, roughly translated as "cooperation"). The clearer Dutch term *samenhang*, though, might be translated as "consistency," which appears to better reflect the concept. *See* EC Treaty Art. 158.

58 EC Treaty Art. 158.

59 Thus, under the banner of cohesion policy the major activities, financed through structural funds, provide financing for infrastructure, local development projects and aid for small firms (the European Regional Development Fund (ERDF)) but also promotes the return of the unemployed and disadvantaged groups to the workforce, mainly by financing training measures and systems of recruitment assistance (the European Social Fund). Other structural funds focus more specifically on agricultural and fisheries development, areas in which research has shown European integration exacerbates economic disparity. For a comprehensive analysis of social and economic cohesion through the mid-1990s *see* COHESION POLICY AND EUROPEAN INTEGRATION: BUILDING MULTI-LEVEL GOVERNANCE (Liesbet Hooghe, ed.1996).

60 Kennedy, *supra* note 49at 1 (noting that "it is difficult to find any mention of its activities in Commission documentation").

61 *See, e.g.*, John Loughlin, *Representing Regions in Europe: The Committee of the Regions*, 6 REGIONAL & FED. STUD. 147, 147 (1996); John Loughlin, *"Europe of the Regions" and the Federalization of Europe*, 26 PUBLIUS 141 (1996).

62 *See, e.g.*, Thomas Christiansen, *The Committee of the Regions at the 1996 ICG Conference: Institutional Reform*, 7 REG. & FED. STUD. 50 (1997).

urged the heads of state to consider creating a formal advisory body within the community to represent regional and local concerns.[63] Though ultimately included in the Maastricht Treaty, the new body barely was discussed during the treaty negotiations, especially during the crucial final exchanges.[64] Nevertheless, with the entrance into force of the Maastricht Treaty (and the creation of the EU) in 1992, the CoR was born, a political afterthought: "A Committee consisting of representatives of regional and local bodies hereinafter referred as 'the Committee of the Regions', is hereby established with advisory status."[65] The Council and Commission were required to consult the advisory body during the legislative process in five major policy areas (education, vocational training and youth; culture; public health; trans-European networks for transportation; and economic and social cohesion).[66]

Early reflecting the body's marginal status, the actual establishment of the CoR and appointment of its members took nearly two years. Further, the body that emerged in 1994 was "truncated".[67] Despite the mandatory consultation process, which was broader than which the Consultative Council had enjoyed, nothing in the treaties required that the Council and Commission seriously consider the CoR's opinions. In any event, the body had no legal recourse should it be ignored because it was not granted standing before the Court of Justice. Furthermore, the Council and the Member States controlled the appointment of the body's members.

In light of these realities, a stream of pessimistic critiques followed.[68] By this time, the legitimacy debate had gained momentum and was at the forefront of EU discourse. For the small cadre of observers watching its development, the CoR appeared to be a valuable source of legitimacy for the polity in crisis. As discussed above, one of the "five uneasy pieces" of the legitimacy critique is distance from the people: "'foreigners' should not be telling 'us' how to run our lives;" "'government' should not be telling 'us' [the individual or local

[63] Kennedy, *supra* note 49at 1–2.

[64] Millan, *supra* note 53at 7; Loughlin, *Representing the Regions in Europe*, *supra* note 61at 157.

[65] Art. 198a

[66] *See* TEU (amending EC Treaty Arts. 126 [now 149(4)], 128 [now 151(5)], 129 [now 152(4)], 129d [now 156], and 130a-e [159–162]).

[67] Loughlin, *Representing the Regions in Europe*, *supra* note 61at 157.

[68] *See, e.g.*, Thomas Christiansen, *Second Thoughts on Europe's Third Level: The Committee of the Regions*, 26 PUBLIUS 96 (1996); Charlie Jeffrey, *Whither the Committee of the Regions?* 5 REGIONAL & FED. STUD. 253 (1995); Peter van der Knaap, *The Committee of the Regions: The Outset of the Europe of the Regions?* 4 REG. POL. & POL'Y 86 (1994). *But see, e.g.*, Elizabeth Meehan, *The Citizen and the Region*, 7 REG. & FED. STUD. 70, 75–76 (1997) (projecting that over time the CoR would develop into a meaningful institution).

community] how to run our lives."[69] Layered as the distance argument may be, its salient feature is the physical distance of the EU machine – situated in Brussels and dominated by remote national actors – from its constituents. In this sense, subnational actors necessarily are closer to the people. Resting on the assumption that regional and local actors are more democratically accountable[70] and better able to gauge the needs and desires of the governed from whom they are less removed, the CoR was also seen as a way to insert the call for greater respect of subsidiarity within EU decision-making. This great potential, observers lamented – and continue to lament – was thwarted by the shadow of an institution that the Maastricht Treaty produced.[71]

Just one year after the CoR held its first meeting, the EU was on the road back to the drawing board with another round of treaty reform. In the run up to the negotiations, the CoR's 1995 Pujol Report[72] called for a significant reinforcement of the body's role. However, the outcomes from the IGC were negligible. The Treaty of Amsterdam resulted in a greater number of areas of mandatory consultation,[73] but the CoR still ranked only as an advisory body and had no way to enforce its role in the European Courts.

When the EU embarked on further treaty reform in 1999, the CoR, again, called for a stronger role in the EU.[74] The Nice Treaty ultimately revised the Article establishing the CoR to require that its members be either elected officials or directly responsible to an elected body.[75] This success, though

69 Weiler et al., *supra* note 9at 7.

70 This assumption draws on Paul Hirst's argument that the burgeoning size of modern democracy dilutes the vote – and voice – of the individual. *See* PAUL HIRST , REPRESENTATIVE DEMOCRACY AND ITS LIMITS (1990). It is reminiscent of Neunreither's call for a more active role of national parliaments in the EU, which also draws on the idea that national parliaments are closer to the constituents than the European institutions. See Neunreither, *supra* note 8.

71 Jeffrey, *Whither the Committee of the Regions? supra* note 48.

72 *See* Committee of the Regions, Opinion of the Committee of the Regions on the Revision of the Treaty on European Union and of the Treaty Establishing the European Community, 136/1995 (Rapporteur Jordi Pujol i Soley).

73 With the additions transport, employment, the European Social Fund, and industry and cross-border cooperation expanded the scope of the CoR's advisory responsibility. It also prohibited the dual mandate for members of the CoR, ensuring that they could not also serve on the European Parliament, fostered greater internal independence for the body by eliminating the Council's control over its rules of procedure, and permitted the European Parliament to consult with it as well.

74 *See* Committee of the Regions, Resolution of the Committee of the Regions of 3 June 1999 on the Next Intergovernmental Conference, 54/99 (urging the recognition of the CoR as an institution of the EU, the right to initiate proceedings in the European Court of Justice, and the requirement that members of the CoR be democratically accountable within the domestic system).

75 Treaty of Nice Art. 2(42) February 26, 2001, O.J. C 80/01 (amending EC Treaty Art. 263).

limited, was seen as an important advance in the role of the CoR as a legitimizing body. Nevertheless, the CoR itself declared that

> the Treaty of Nice falls well short of what the Committee has deemed necessary ... if the Union's ability to enlarge is to be strengthened, its democratic legitimacy, transparency and 'closeness to the people' is to be enhanced and lasting improvements are to be made to the effectiveness of its decision-making.[76]

The Convention on the Future of Europe, the distinctive round of treaty reform that produced the Treaty Establishing a Constitution for Europe, proved the biggest success for the CoR. Though failing to gain any legislative prerogatives or status as an institution of the EU, the CoR was given a limited right to bring actions before the European Court of Justice.[77] Though the ratification of the Constitution was indefinitely abandoned, the subsequently ratified Lisbon Treaty incorporated these enhanced roles.

Despite its formally strengthened position and through twenty-five years of rapid and substantial change in the EU, the CoR stagnated in the embryonic stage that observers – optimistically or fatalistically – heralded as merely a first stepping-stone on the path to a more influential body.[78]

Observers have concluded that the CoR has little impact on EU policy. While the Commission solicits its opinion with relative regularity, it has boxed the CoR out of those areas where it might have the most significant impact. And, though some claim that CoR opinions are taken seriously,[79] it is widely agreed that the CoR's role is negligible.[80]

Various explanations have been offered for the weakness of the CoR. In the wake of a 2003 censure by the European anti-fraud authority for "systematic and flagrant incompetence,"[81] the body itself was blamed for failing to make an impact. More consistently, Member State resistance is charged with responsibility, as has EU institutional tension – especially from Parliament.

76 Committee of the Regions, Resolution of the Committee of the Regions on the Outcome of the 2000 Intergovernmental Conference and the Discussion on the Future of the European Union, 430/2000.

77 *See* Treaty Establishing a Constitution for Europe Art. III-270(3); Protocol on the Application of the Principles of Subsidiarity and Proportionality Art. 7.

78 *See, e.g.*, Christiansen, *supra* note 68at 50.

79 Roht-Arriaza, *supra* note 49at 456–57 (noting report of former-CoR president that 40 of 74 CoR opinions resulted in some changes to the Commission's proposal).

80 Peter John, *Europeanization of Sub-National Government*, 37 URB. STUD. 877, 889 (2000); *but see* Christiansen & Lintner, *supra* note 68at 7 (stating that the CoR is a "fixture" in Europe that has made its mark).

81 Financial Times, October 19, 2003, *Cursed, spat at, ignored. The ordeal of an EU whistleblower*).

The waning interest of CoR members from more powerful subnational divisions, like the German *Länder* and the Spanish *comunidades autonomas*, is also cited as the cause of the CoR's power stagnation. However, the most common argument contends that structural factors explain the CoR's weakness. Simply, if the CoR is never given any power, how is it expected to exercise influence? These explanations, though critical to a holistic understanding of the CoR, are somewhat unsatisfactory when positioned within the framework of governance reform addressing the legitimacy crises that have emerged here.

5.3 IMPLICATIONS: MULTILEVEL GOVERNANCE OR MULTILEVEL COOPTATION?

Juxtaposed, the preceding sketches of the governance schemata of the OMC, the CoR, and its current role in the EU reveal a fundamental disconnect within the EU's pursuit of legitimacy. This disconnect recasts the foundational question with which CoR scholarship has grappled: why is an institution created (at least in part) to respond to the EU's crisis of legitimacy – a crisis that is emblematized by distance from the citizens and virtually excluded from the governance mechanisms (the OMC), but which should be the most fertile ground for cooperation?

Unfortunately, it is not possible to conclude by tying together the strands of this story with that neat, yellow ribbon called an "answer". As is so often the case, the broader picture is too messy for frilly bows. The time has come to mention some possibilities, facts, and observations conveniently (though neither disingenuously nor maliciously) obscured by the broad strokes painted above.

First, the CoR is not the only place where there is an opportunity for formal, direct subnational participation in EU-level policymaking. EU law permits regional level actors to represent the Member States in the Council.[82] Second, there are additional sites of subnational influence within the EU. Receiving the most attention are two phenomena: the proliferation of lobbying offices and domestic decentralization. The first reflects the recognition by several actors that the main role for subnational interests in the EU today is through negotiation and lobbying. Thus, both cities and regions have opened offices in Brussels to be closer to those opportunities. The second, motivated in many cases by European integration, describes the process through which subnational actors gain power within the domestic system. That power, in turn,

[82] This limited right is afforded only to those Member States meeting certain qualifications.

filters to the shaping of national positions at the EU level. As yet unexplored in the subnational literature, are those ways in which subnational actors may participate in legal dialogue in ways that engage European Community law directly but go unrecognized as law making. One such example might be the activities of meta-subnational representative bodies unconnected with the EU.[83]

Despite these levels of complexity, the basic questions asked by this chapter remain relevant. What (institutionalized) role are subnational actors playing in the EU? What is the proper place for such involvement? Why have they been formally boxed into ostensibly low-stakes forms of participation and excluded even from the most inclusive governance mechanism employed within the EU? And, why are so few voices raised in opposition? The answers to these questions might well lurk within the nuances identified here. The answers might lie in nuance assuredly overlooked.

The following discussion explores one possible answer: The CoR is a wonderful success; it does exactly what it was meant to do. It mutes potentially powerful dissident voices by pigeonholing them within the cacophony of intra-EU inter-institutional power struggles.

5.3.1 *Coopting the Subnational through the CoR*

There is a view of the law as instrumental. Such views treat the law as an end in itself that achieves (or aims to achieve) specified results. Thus, anti-discrimination laws are passed to induce individuals not to engage in employment practices that disadvantage women. Murder is prohibited to encourage individuals to refrain from taking the lives of others. Or, from the perspective of the EU, the European Community Treaty prohibits "quantitative restrictions" on the importation of goods in order to force the Member States to treat all goods originating within the EU as they treat domestic goods.[84] It is within the contours of this perspective on law that the lawyers are trained. Most doctrinal legal scholarship seeks to evaluate how well a particular law is achieving its literal or instrumental objectives.

83 For example, the Assembly of European Region (often in collaboration with other such bodies) frequently issues declarations calling for action or decrying actions taken within the EU. For a recent example, see Assembly of European Regions & European Regions for European Federation of Regional Energy and Environment Agencies (FEDARENE), Joint Declaration: European Regions for Energy efficiency and Renewable Energy Sources *available at* www.a-e-r.org/fileadmin/user_upload/Commissions/RegionalPolicies/EventsAndMeetings/2006/Strasbourg/WorkingDocuments/Declaration-en.pdf.

84 EC Treaty art. 28

Yet, law need not be seen (solely) as such. There is also a symbolic aspect to every law. As Edelman convincingly set forth, "every political institution and act evokes and reinforces a particular response in its audiences."[85] The anticipated responses are as important to the adoption of laws and the creation of political institutions as any instrumental aim of the law. Arguably, "[t]he rational and dialectical phases of politics are subsidiary to the process of redefining an emotional consensus."[86] From a strictly legal standpoint, the instrumental objectives of the law may take a back seat to the statement that is being made by that law. Thus, anti-discrimination laws might be passed to convince women that they are being treated fairly. Murder might be prohibited to induce the sensation of physical security. And, from the perspective of the EU, the prohibition on "quantitative restrictions" might be intended to produce the feeling that there is robust competition among goods.

At a practical level, the expected responses of the audience – the citizens of the Member States – drives the EU to engage in governance reform aimed at increasing its legitimacy. After all, at the heart of the crises of legitimacy is the emotional response to the particular set of institutional settlements represented by the EU. EU scholarship has recognized the importance of such symbols within the law. Indeed, others have suggested that one of the largest contributions of the CoR is as a symbol of the importance of subnational voices in the EU.

What has not been explored, however, is the potential that the CoR project has been wholly that of creating a symbol, the instrumental aspects of law playing little or no role at all. Stated bluntly, the CoR does nothing (or little) because it was created to do nothing (or little). This design may not have been carefully intentioned, but it is the almost unconscious driver of its anatomy – its power – and even its most adamant advocates do not necessarily realize their own complicity.

The value of such a symbol at the creation of the CoR – and its continuing value – is readily apparent. As discussed above, numerous factors precipitated the birth of the CoR: the early recognition of the legitimacy crises; concerns of autonomous and domestically influential subnational actors about loss of authority to the EU; and broad ranging but diverse socio-economic concerns sharpening with the continued widening of the polity. Each of those factors,

85 Murray Edelman, The Symbolic Uses of Politics 12 (1964).

86 *Id.* at 29 (quoting Harold D. Lasswell, Psychopathology and Politics (1930)); *see also* Charles D. Elder & Roger W. Cobb , The Political Uses of Symbols (1983); Harold D. Lasswell et al., The Comparative Study of Symbols (1952). For an exposition of the legal implications, see J. M. Balkin, *Ideological Drift and the Struggle Over Meaning*, 25 Conn. L. Rev. 869 (1993).

persisting and sometimes heightened today, called for greater subnational participation in the EU. And, the institutionalized form taken by CoR imbued the participation with a sense of permanency. That sensation, in turn, induced a feeling of well-being: the resolution of the tensions that prompted the creation of the CoR.[87]

The continued activity of the CoR reproduces and perpetuates this cycle. Its activities "can most confidently be expected to convey a sense of well-being to the onlooker because they suggest vigorous activity while in fact signifying inactivity."[88] This misdirection is reflected clearly in the functioning of the CoR as outlined above. Though issuing hundreds of opinions and launching ambitious monitoring initiatives, the CoR's efforts amount to little. The assertion that the symbolic work done by the CoR is the body's ultimate purpose, also explains why the CoR plays so little a role in the OMC.

This brief exposition of the symbolic role of the CoR, however, does not lead inevitably to the conclusion that dissident voices have been coopted. Such an argument requires a different thread to be drawn through the pictures of the OMC and the CoR presented here.

Radelli has posited that the OMC serves to "mute" political controversies.[89] The CoR has operated in a similar fashion to mute a particular controversy. Before the existence of the CoR, subnational actors had an unassailable claim that the EU's institutional structure was deficient. Since its creation, efforts have turned toward carving out a place for itself within the institutional structure of the EU. Accordingly, the CoR's efforts are focused self-consciously on creating a higher profile for the institution as a resource for subnational actors and as a valuable player in the legislative process. As Wolfgang Clement presaged, before the CoR can be upgraded to the level of an equal partner in European integration, "the states, regions and autonomous communities should prove that they are able to use their knowledge, expertise and political resources constructively and in the interest of the Union as a whole."[90] Participation in the OMC process, which results in soft European law, does not fulfill this aim.

Most important, through the CoR, subnational actors who might otherwise be inclined toward criticism of the EU are given a stake in its future. Before the

87 Edelman, *supra* note 85at 38 (explaining that "it is one of the demonstrable functions of symbolization that it induces a feeling of well-being: the resolution of the tension").

88 *Id.*

89 Radelli, *supra* note 46.

90 Wolfgang Clement, *The Committee of the Regions: More than an Alibi?* in REGIONS IN EUROPE: THE INSTITUTIONALISATION OF THE COMMITTEE OF THE REGIONS (Joachim Jens Hesse, ed. 1995).

creation of the CoR, subnational actors were increasingly framing their claims in European terms. This trend has only increased with the dedication of a subnational space within the polity. Moreover, what little attention is paid to the CoR is focused on its development as an institution within the EU structure, larger concerns that may emanate from subnational actors somehow not making their way to the political forefront. And, in its perpetual state of weakness, the CoR is unable to realize the potential already available to it within the EU structure.

Combined, these effects produced a type of cooptation. They do not buy off opposition, but incorporate it within the political discourse in a way that maintains the balance between the dominant forces within the EU's institutional system. The function of the CoR is to co-opt the subnational voices: silencing opposition is the purpose of the body, not an undesirable side effect.[91]

What of new governance commitments? The CoR's exclusion as the muting of dissidence also reframes the OMC critique. Rather than an "open method of centralization," as the OMC it is the same type of multilevel governance already observed in EU, which envisions the appropriate players as national and supranational.

5.3.2 *The Dangers of Cooptation*

So, why should anyone care whether the CoR is involved in the EU? Why should the cooptation of regional voices be a cause for concern?

Unarguably, there is no empirically sound basis for concluding that one should. Whether or not EU policy – especially in OMC arenas – would be "better" if it were founded on genuine multi-level deliberation is a profoundly theoretical matter whose resolution depends on the philosophical stance adopted by the observer. Thus, from the pluralist democratic view of Cohen and Sabel's directly deliberative polyarchy, the cooptation of the CoR stifles the potential for learning and leads to substantive inferior legislation. In contrast, the vision of a Schumpeterian competitive elite model of democracy would find no problem *per se* with the exclusion of the CoR because the participation of ordinary people – which the CoR is supposed to facilitate – is not an important element of democracy and, indeed, could have negative consequences. Accordingly, remaining philosophically neutral, this essay

91 This exposition draws liberally from Susan Rose-Ackerman's short discussion of the co-optive effective of cooperative federalism in the United States. *See* Susan Rose-Ackerman, *Cooperative Federalism and Co-Optation*, 92 YALE L. J. 1344, 1344–45 (1983).

need not urge that there is any *a priori* reason to be concerned with the position of the CoR.[92]

There is, however, a side effect of this situation that deserves attention independent of how one frames democracy or legitimacy. In coopting the subnational and muting subnational-specific dissidence, the EU squelched an interesting niche in the on-going debate regarding the European polity and its legitimacy. That is, underlying the debate is the notion that the spaces over which the EU, its Member States, and their constituent parts exercise jurisdiction are uncontested, settled, and independently meaningful. The unique status of many of the powerful regional actors at work around the birth of the CoR – notably the Basque separatists, Catalonian nationalists, and the German *Länder* navigating a reunited Germany – created room for such notions to be interrogated. The creation of the CoR, by reanointing the accepted subnational boundaries as valid and inevitable, ended this debate.

Yet, legal spaces (e.g., territorial jurisdictions) are artificially conceived inventions.[93] The territorial borders of the Member States are the products of the wars European integration was implemented to prevent.[94] Within domestic legal systems, partitioning is also the consequence of at least somewhat conscious decision-making. A clear example of the manufactured jurisdiction can be seen in the federalization of Belgium through four state reforms, which transformed it from a unitary state to a fully federal state divided territorially into three regions and substantively into three language communities.[95] The widening boundaries of the EU are set and defined by accession treaties and Commissioners pronouncing who is and is not in Europe. Despite its half century long candidacy, which predates the first enlargement of the European Community in 1973, transcontinental Turkey

92 Elsewhere the value of subnational actors and local/regional autonomy has been praised.

93 *See* Richard T. Ford, *Law's Territory (A History of Jurisdiction)*, 97 Mich. L. Rev. 843, 929 (1999). Beyond the scope of this paper (and further beyond the ken of the author) is any sustained engagement of geographic tools of evaluation – terms, like place, space, and scale, that are highly contested and resist definition – on which a growing number of legal scholars are drawing.

94 As has been much discussed elsewhere, the earliest justification for European integration, formulated by Jean Monnet and articulated by Robert Schuman, was the end to the warring that plagued the continent of Europe for centuries. *See* Robert Schuman, The Schuman Declaration, (May 9, 1950), *reprinted in* 2 The European Union: Readings on the Theory and Practice of European Integration 13, 13 (Brent F. Nelsen & Alexand er C-G. Stubb eds. 1998) (proclaiming that the aim of the European Coal and Steel Community was to make ware "not merely unthinkable, but materially impossible").

95 *See, e.g.*, Frank Hendriks, *Belgium: Federalism and Subnational Democracy in a Divided Country in* Loughlin supra note 61289–90 (summarizing the impetus for the federalization of Belgium)

remains outside the EU without serious prospects of joining in the near future.[96] The rejection of Morocco was far less protracted; that country is simply "not in Europe."[97]

So too, the borders between various actors within the EU are envisioned as inherently static. There is government and there is civil society. There are the various institutions of the EU upon which specific functions must be mapped. Indeed, a major critique of the EU is the treaties inadequate division of powers among the distinct actors. To respond to this critique, Giandomenico Majone constructs a different set of boundaries for European actors, which he calls "estates."[98] Rejecting Montesquieu's *séparation des pouvoirs* model as inappropriate within the EU, Majone posits a separation of interests in which "estates" represent national (the Council), supranational (the Commission), and popular interests (the Parliament).[99]

As Ford has described with respect to other countries, these divisions are treated as inevitable facts – "[t]he jurisdiction is either an arm of the state, of no particular interest except as a matter of narrow administrative technique … or it is an organic political community, a self-validating form of self-rule."[100] Yet, as Charlie Jeffery has analyzed, the very idea of a committee of regions begs the question of what is a region.

Deeper still is this question: what should be a region? The CoR was created, at least in part, to calm the EU's crisis of legitimacy by bringing Europe closer to its citizens. Revising the treaty to ensure that its members are democratically accountable at the subnational level is seen as an infusion of more democracy within the polity. The CoR's own rhetoric positions the body as a protector and pursuer of these ideals. Yet, busying the body with ineffectual tasks and putting it into the EU structure mutes the debate on what interests are supposed to be reflected within the CoR, whether the scope of those interests are meaningful or legitimate, and whether potentially flawed domestic institutional settlements need be replicated within the EU. Creating an impotent body like the CoR reinforces the idea about the proper framework in which to actualize

[96] Turkey straddles (or bridges) unevenly the line where cartographers have separated Europe from Asia.

[97] Morocco submitted an application to become a member of the European Community in 1987. That same year, the Council rejected the application because that country was not deemed geographically, culturally or politically European.

[98] Giandomenico Majone, *Delegation of Regulatory Powers in a Mixed Polity*, 8 Eur. L.J., 3, 319–339 (September 2002).

[99] *Id.* at 320, 326. The factual accuracy of Majone's epistemology have been challenged Elizabeth Bomberg & Alexander Stubb, eds. The European Union: How Does It Work? 136–53 (2003).

[100] Ford, *supra* note 93at 851–52.

representation, serves as a symbol that those interests are being paid attention to, and quiets the debate about the framework itself.

5.4 CONCLUDING REFLECTIONS

This chapter has attempted to draw closer together three often-segregated streams of European literature. In so doing, it has highlighted a layer of inquiry ignored by the legal and political science literature. Traveling hand in hand with the questions about the level(s) at which democracy operates and governance (and government) should occur – the questions with which the OMC, the legitimacy debate, and the CoR are preoccupied – should be the territorial question about the nature of the jurisdictions that make up those levels.

These (usually technocratic) debates often assume a democratic character and progress narrative to institutional reform. When things do not work, failures are attributed to the pragmatic limitations inherent to pluralistic governance, rather than the failure of policy design to meaningfully embrace substantive democratic commitments. If Europe is the model par excellence for the world of democracy, it is all too often a story of unacknowledged exclusions and unnecessarily constrained governance choices. For democracy to thrive and Europe to reclaim its democratic possibility, technical questions need to be comprehensively reoriented to a more substantive vision of popular sovereignty, to what it means to say power to the people.

6

Development

Jamee K. Moudud

The decades of the 1970s and 1980s together constituted a tumultuous period with inflation and unemployment ravaging the global economy. Many countries in the Global South also accumulated massive amounts of foreign debt. High interest rates prevailing at the time exacerbated the debts of a number of poorer countries; and falling export revenues, as global demand for their exports fell during the crisis, made this debt unsustainable. The 1980s were also significant because they constituted a watershed moment with regard to the nature of economic and social policies and their legal underpinnings in conventional thinking. After the Second World War through the 1970s many countries pursued a policy which, among other things, involved high tariff protection of imports with the goal of promoting domestic industry, linked at times to export promotion, via interventionist public policies such as direct subsidies[1] The legal underpinning of this state-led development strategy has been called the First Moment in Law and Development (L & D). In contrast, the Second Moment in L & D, originating in the crisis alluded to above promoted deregulation, free markets, and free trade (i.e., neoliberalism).

In the Second Moment free trade came to be seen as a *sine qua non* to jump start countries mired in crises. At the heart of the new market-oriented framework that gained hegemonic status was the view that social, labor, and taxation policies need to be subsumed under a fundamental business investment-driven model of development. Central to this variant of the neoliberal framework was the use of "shock therapy" which involved draconian austerity measures involving cuts in the social safety net, downsizing of public sector jobs, and removal of trade barriers. However, by the 1990s a new L & D discourse, intellectually rooted in New Institutional Economics (NIE)

[1] James M. Cypher and James L. Dietz, *The Process of Economic Development*, vol. 3 (London and New York: Routledge, 2009).

and the contributions of Douglass North, had begun to gain popularity in international development institutions such as the World Bank. This has come to be known as the Third Moment in L & D.[2]

In addition to generally maintaining the commitment to free trade, balanced budgets, and "sound money," two theoretical themes appear prominently in the Third Moment framework, one of which is consistent with Friedrich Hayek's framework and the other one is not. One the one hand, as in Hayek in the NIE framework, the "free market" cannot arise spontaneously via a minimal state but requires a strong political and legal framework to enclose markets and insulate them from political interference by the state.[3] Thus the "rule of law" to enforce free markets and property rights is a central plank of the Third Moment view. On the other hand, as David Kennedy discusses, the Third Moment approach also stresses the importance of "market failures" to explain economic problems.[4] Hayek, however, was intellectually opposed to the putative existence of perfect competition[5] and perfect markets more generally.[6]

In addition to market failure, neoclassical economics also tends to focus on "government failure" where the latter pertains to corrupt governments that engage in predatory, including rent-seeking, behavior thereby not securing property rights.[7] "Government failure" is said to constitute a major cause of economic underdevelopment in both the Hayekian and Third Moment approaches.[8] Corruption and rent-seeking by public elites in collusion with powerful private ones with negative consequences for trade and growth have been central concerns of New Political Economy (NPE) which, as Douglass North observed, is closely related to NIE.[9] Fused into the broad Third Moment framework of the World Bank[10] the NIE/NPE integration

[2] David M. Trubek and Alvaro Santos, *The New Law and Economic Development: A Critical Appraisal*, ed. David M. Trubek and Alvaro Santos (New York, NY: Cambridge University Press, 2006).

[3] Quinn Slobodian, *Globalists: The End of Empire and the Birth of Neoliberalism* (Cambridge MA and London, England: Harvard University Press, 2018), 7.

[4] David Kennedy, "The 'Rule of Law', Political Choices, and Development Common Sense," in *The New Law and Economic Development: A Critical Appraisal*, ed. David M. Trubek and Alvaro Santos (New York, NY: Cambridge University Press, 2006), 151.

[5] Friedrich Hayek, "The Meaning of Competition," in *Individualism and Economic Order* (London and Chicago: The University of Chicago Press, 1948), 92–106.

[6] Slobodian, *Globalists: The End of Empire and the Birth of Neoliberalism*, 271.

[7] Cypher and Dietz, *The Process of Economic Development*, vol. 3, Chapter 7.

[8] Slobodian, *Globalists: The End of Empire and the Birth of Neoliberalism*, 251.

[9] Camille Landais, Thomas Piketty , and Emmanuel Saez , Pour Une Revolution Fiscale (Editions de Seuil et La Republique des Idees, 2011), 979.

[10] Chantal Thomas, "Law and Neoclassical Economic Development in Theory and Practice: Toward an Institutionalist Critique of Institutionalism," *Cornell Law Faculty Publications*, 2011, 994.

emphasizes the need for robust political institutions to create free markets, with historical contexts and path dependencies shaping how "efficient" the rule of law is to promote property rights and market development. Simply put, institutional development may or may not improve trade performance and economic development. Finally, as a big tent, development goals also include poverty reduction and social inclusion although these are linked to market-driven objectives that would be ensured via human capital development (entailing the promotion of education) and small-business promotion. Such goals are in line with the World Bank's *Doing Business* project, with the aim to "drive inclusive, sustainable economic growth; and bring us one step closer to ending poverty on the face of the earth."[11] The key underlying assumption is that markets are inherently private (i.e., they arise from private exchange) and the rule of law should make them more efficient and equitable. In short, property rights are fundamentally in the Lockean tradition.[12]

Drawing on the broad Critical Legal Studies (CLS) tradition's approach to property and money, this paper will challenge the Third Moment framework by rejecting the twin notions of "market failure" and "government failure". The see-sawing of the conventional perspective along these dichotomies has foreclosed the consideration of alternative policies beyond those proposed by neoclassical economics whose "vision" on how the economy should be structured has remained dominant since Reagan/Thatcher. The problem is that this "vision" has also culminated in the multiple crises we confront now from massive wealth concentration to labor precarity and a burgeoning ecological catastrophe. Clearly a new direction is necessary and it is argued that the CLS framework does just that.

Neoclassical economics fundamentally assumes that the economy is barter-based with money entering the economy at the discretion of the central bank. By drawing on the broad constitutional theory of money approach,[13] which has discussed the public foundations of money, this paper shows that politics and the law cannot be separate from markets since they construct the latter in various contextual ways with crucial implications for foreign trade and social

[11] The World Bank, "Doing Business 2019: Training for Reform" (Washington DC, 2019), v, www.doingbusiness.org/content/dam/doingBusiness/media/Annual-Reports/English/DB2019-report_web-version.pdf.

[12] Jeremy Waldron, *The Rule of Law and the Measure of Property* (Cambridge, UK: Cambridge University Press, 2012).

[13] Christine Desan, *Making Money: Coin, Currency, and Coming of Capitalism* (Oxford: Oxford University Press, 2014), Robert C. Hockett and Saule T. Omarova, "The Finance Franchise," *Cornell Law Review* 102 (2018): 1143–1218, Jamee K. Moudud, "Analyzing the Constitutional Theory of Money: Governance, Power, and Instability," *Leiden Journal of International Law* 31, no. 2 (2018): 289–313, Morgan Ricks, "Money as Infrastructure," *Vanderbilt Law Research Paper* 17–63 (2018): 1–79.

policy. Section 6.1 provides the theoretical foundation to the paper by discussing the CLS view of property and money. Section 6.2 discusses the neoclassical theory of international trade and shows why the classic debates between Jagdish Bhagwati and Paul Krugman regarding trade policy was an internal controversy within the neoclassical tradition, implicitly based on the Lockean theory of property. Finally, the paper suggests that the burying of false dichotomies such as "free trade versus protectionism" and "free markets versus state intervention," which are the heart of neoclassical theory, opens up new political possibilities to bring about economic transformation. This is elaborated in section 6.3. Section 6.4 is the conclusion.

6.1 PROPERTY, MONEY, AND THE GOING CONCERN: RECONCEPTUALIZING THE PROFIT MOTIVE

In the neoclassical view, markets are fundamentally pre-political whereby property and contractual relations between buyers and sellers occur in the private sphere. In order for Pareto-efficient and perfectly competitive markets to flourish, the legal institutional framework should protect them. Thus the law is essentially conceptualized as an apolitical technology[14] that should operate to protect free markets, a legal formalist view that traces its ancestry to nineteenth century jurisprudence.[15] The figure of Robinson Crusoe looms large in this neoclassical framework where each property owner (or state) is considered to be an island-unto-herself and trades the goods they have with other similarly isolated Crusoes. In such an anarchistic world of interstate competition and international trade, the mantra of regulation becomes the ethical maxim, *sic utere tuo ut alienum non laedas*: property owners should only use their property in a way that others are not harmed.[16] Not only is the state kept out of market activity (except as umpire) but it relies on an apolitical view of market and property institutions in which at a benchmark level there are no social consequences (zero externalities) of private actions. The property owners are assumed to be capable of acting individually and as an aggregate in ways that do not entail nonconsensual coercion.[17]

14 Curtis J. Milhaupt and Katharina Pistor, *Law and Capitalism* (Chicago and London: University of Chicago Press, 2008), 21.

15 Morton J Horwitz, *The Transformation of American Law 1780–1860* (Cambridge MA and London, England: Harvard University Press, 1977).

16 Joseph William Singer , "The Legal Rights Debate in Analytical Jurisprudence from Bentham to Hohfeld," *Wisconsin Law Review*, 1982, 975–1059; Horwitz, *The Transformation of American Law 1780–1860*.

17 As the late Stephen Hymer discussed in his classic article, it is this Crusoe-like model that is the basis of all neoclassical textbook discussions of international trade. See Stephen Hymer, "Robinson Crusoe and the Secret of Primitive Accumulation," in *Growth, Profits, and*

This apolitical vision of global markets and property transactions is reflected in the mainstream explanations of market failure.[18] Market failure is said to occur when the invisible hand does not allocate resources optimally (in the Pareto sense). Two instantiations of market failure are noteworthy of mention here. The first is a deviation from perfect competition and the second one is the presence of externalities. The benchmark "free market" from which all deviations are measured is assumed to be perfectly competitive where the latter market structure is populated by a large number of identical tiny firms that are passive takers, produce identical products, have identical costs, and access to perfect information flows. Neoclassical theory conceptualizes the perfectly competitive firm as "profit-maximizing" and yet, as follows from critiques of this model by a number of authors such as Friedrich Hayek, Joseph Schumpeter, and P. W. S Andrews,[19] it has neither the ability nor the inclination to damage any other firm by taking the latter's market share away – for example, by price and cost-cutting, product differentiation, and advertising.

The remarkably rich theoretical work of P. W. S. Andrews and others of the Oxford Economists' Research Group (OERG), based on extensive interviews of businessmen and field work, provided a powerful critique of the neoclassical framework revealing that real-world firms behaved nothing like the models discussed in neoclassical textbooks.[20] For example, in both perfect and monopolistic competition models, firms do not engage in strategic behavior and have neither the ability nor the inclination to cut prices and costs in order to expand market shares.[21] And yet, while the principle of *sic*

Property: Essays in the Revival of Political Economy, ed. Edward J. Nell (New York, NY: Cambridge University, 1980), 29–40.

18 See for example Robert E. Hall and Marc Lieberman, *Microeconomics: Principles & Applications*, vol. 6 (Mason, Ohio: South-Western, Cengage Learning, n.d.).

19 Hayek, "The Meaning of Competition"; Joseph Schumpeter, *Capitalism, Socialism and Democracy*, vol. First Harp (New York, NY: Harper Perennial Modern Thought, 2008); P. W. S. Andrews, "Competition in the Modern Economy," in *The Economics of Competitive Enterprise: Selected Essays of P. W. S. Andrews*, ed. Frederic S. Lee and Peter E. Earl (Aldershot, UK and Brookfield, VT: Edward Elgar, 1993), 323–62; J. K. Moudud, *The Hidden History of Competition and Its Implications, Alternative Theories of Competition: Challenges to the Orthodoxy*, 2012.

20 Fred S. Lee and J. Irving-Lessmann, "The Fate of an Errant Hypothesis: The Doctrine of Normal-Cost Prices," *History of Political Economy* 24, no. 2 (1992): 273–356; Frederic S. Lee and Peter E. Earl, *The Economics of Competitive Enterprise: Selected Essays of P. W. S. Andrews* (Aldershot, UK and Brookfield, VT: Edward Elgar Press, 1993).

21 In neoclassical economics a defining feature of oligopolistic competition is strategic behavior, with certain models allowing for price- and cost-cutting behavior (Giocoli 2014). However, neoclassical theory considers oligopolistic along with monopolistic competition as forms of imperfect competition.

utere' implicitly appears as the foundation to contemporary international *laissez faire* policies such as free trade, over the course of the nineteenth century it became relatively obsolete with domestic courts and legal scholars as it could not be reconciled with the need to promote industrialization and urbanization, both of which invariably resulted in adverse social consequences from private actions. Technological change increasingly came to be seen as creatively destructive since industrialization involved rivalrous competition between firms armed with the adoption of newer and/or cheaper technologies.[22] In short, "the essential attribute of property ownership was the power to develop one's property regardless of the injurious consequences to others".[23] Increasingly, therefore, the principle of *damnum absque injuria*[24] came to dominate the jurisprudence of capital accumulation.[25]

Of course, and this is an important point, it was not that the law was adapting to the "needs" of the economy but that the courts were actively involved in shaping property rights. This is consistent with the broader point made by John R. Commons, that property is fundamentally determined by the legal structures in place as they change through history.[26] In short, the law does not passively reflect the "needs" of economic development as mainstream international trade and law and development scholarship would suggest.[27] Rather the law constitutes the "genetic" code of capital.[28]

When economic crises occur, for instance like the recent one of 2008, a conventional view is to claim that government over-regulation was the cause with the normative conclusion that markets should be de-regulated and made more "competitive". However, this familiar argument rests on two fallacious foundations. First, it assumes that markets can fundamentally be made to be free of state involvement. However, this was the view that was challenged by Karl Polanyi, the Legal Realists, and the "old" institutionalists such as Commons. If markets are fundamentally the products of politics acting through the law, then the notion of "over-regulation" makes no sense. One

22 Horwitz, *The Transformation of American Law 1780–1860*, 133.

23 Horwitz, 99.

24 That is, economic injury to others from the use of one's property was not a legal injury requiring compensation.

25 Horwitz, *The Transformation of American Law 1780–1860*; Singer, "The Legal Rights Debate in Analytical Jurisprudence from Bentham to Hohfeld."

26 John R. Commons, *Legal Foundations of Capitalism* (New York: The Macmillan Company, 1924).

27 Robert W. Gordon , "Critical Legal Histories," *Faculty Scholarship Series, Paper 1368*, 1984, 57–125.

28 Katharina Pistor, *The Code of Capital: How the Law Creates Wealth and Inequality* (Princeton and Oxford: Princeton University Press, 2019).

could certainly argue that the underlying regulatory framework was poorly constructed thereby producing the sub-prime mortgage collapse.[29] Second, with regard to the claim that markets should be made more "competitive", neoclassical economists imply that they should be brought closer to perfect competition. However, this is completely unrealistic as Friedrich Hayek and Joseph Schumpeter argued. And of course as discussed above, the remarkably rich theoretical work of P. W. S. Andrews and others of the Oxford Economists' Research Group (OERG), based on extensive interviews of businessmen and field work, is particularly significant in providing a critique of neoclassical theories of the firm.

Some important theoretical consequences follow from the above discussion for international law scholars. First, as profit-making institutions, firms from early capitalism have attempted to grow by minimizing internal costs, and thus by externalizing them on to society at both domestic and international terrains.[30] This necessarily involved transformations in the background laws.[31] Beginning with some of earliest corporations in capitalism's history, such as The Virginia Company – a joint-stock company established in Jamestown in 1607 in the British Colony of Virginia – there have always been close interconnections between globalized corporations and domestic legislatures, with the latter providing a wide range of legal and other financial subsidies to promote investment.[32] In fact, in tracing corporations' efforts to increase their "civil rights" from the early nineteenth century to *Citizens United*, Adam Winkler underscores the profoundly political and socially embedded nature of corporations, linked directly to their profit motive. In short, policy (political) choices are always encoded in the background rules between diverse interests, which shape and express struggle – Robinson Crusoe is quite simply, fiction.

Second, it must be recalled that Wesley Hohfeld's legal taxonomy[33] necessarily implies the bipolar nature of individual property rights. Not surprisingly,

29 Jennifer Taub, *Other People's Houses: How Decades of Bailouts, Captive Regulators, and Toxic Bankers Made Home Mortgages a Thrilling Business* (New Haven & London: Yale University Press, 2014).

30 Robert A. G. Monks and Nell Minow, *Corporate Governance*, 5th ed. (Chichester, UK: John Wiley & Sons, Ltd., 2011), 4.

31 Duncan Kennedy, "The Stakes of Law, or Hale and Foucault!" *Legal Studies Forum* XV, no. 4 (1991): 327–66.

32 Erik Dean et al., *Principles of Microeconomics: Scarcity and Social Provisioning* (OpenStax Economics, Principles of Economics. OpenStax CNX. May 18, 2016, 2016), Chapter 14, https://doi.org/http://cnx.org/contents/69619d2b-68f0-44b0-b074-a9b2bf90b2c6@11.330.

33 Wesley N. Hohfeld, "Some Fundamental Legal Conceptions as Applied in Legal Reasoning," *Yale Law Journal* 23 (1913): 16–59.

Warren Samuels argued that in Robert Lee Hale's framework, externalities are ubiquitous since "every exercise of volitional freedom tends to restrict or change the volitional freedom of others, through the coercive impact on the alternatives open to others."[34] However, if externalities are ubiquitous then so are "market failures." This raises a logical problem for neoclassical theory: there cannot be a deviation from any idealized market, given this ubiquity. A key theoretical underpinning of the Third Moment framework thus falls apart.

Third, the principle of *damnum absque injuria* as the legal foundation of business competition necessarily implies attempts by each firm to invest as it grows and to exploit economies of scale at the expense of others. This requires that profit-making by firms be understood in two related ways, one of which pertains to *what* they do and the other to *how* they attempt to do so. In regards to the former, an important strand of heterodox economics, drawing on classical political economy and the path-breaking contributions of P. W. S. Andrews and the Oxford Economists' Research Group[35] rejects the perfect versus imperfect competition dichotomy *in toto*. Authors in this literature argue that all firms, big and small, are profit-making *institutions* in which the objective is to set prices in order to grow and undercut rivals via cost-cutting and product differentiation. Investment is undertaken with the expectation of monetary profits or *pecuniary value* as Veblen and others have argued.[36] In contrast to neoclassical

34 Warren J. Samuels, "The Economy as a System of Power and Its Legal Bases: The Legal Economics of Robert Lee Hale," *University Miami Law Review* 27 (1973): 286.

35 James A Clifton, "Administered Prices in the Context of Capitalist Development," *Contributions to Political Economy* 2, no. 1 (1983): 23–38; Fred S. Lee and J. Irving-Lessmann, "The Fate of an Errant Hypothesis: The Doctrine of Normal-Cost Prices," *History of Political Economy* 24, no. 2 (1992): 273–356; Jamee K. Moudud, *Strategic Competition, Dynamics, and the Role of the State: A New Perspective* (Brookfield, VT: Edward Elgar Press, 2010); Jamee K. Moudud, Cyrus Bina, and Patrick L. Mason, *Alternative Theories of Competition: Challenges to the Orthodoxy* (New York, NY: Routledge (Advances in Heterodox Economics), 2012); Anwar Shaikh, *Capitalism: Competition, Conflict, Crises* (New York, NY: Oxford University Press, 2016).

36 Thorstein Veblen, *The Theory of Business Enterprise* (New Brunswick, NJ: Transaction, Inc., 1978); Jonathan Levy, "Capital as Process and the History of Capitalism," *Business History Review* 91, no. 3 (2017): 483–510; John Maynard Keynes, *The General Theory of Employment, Interest, and Money* (San Diego and New York: Harcourt Brace Jovanovich Publishers, 1953); Say's law is central to neoclassical economics but this assumes implicitly a passive view of business investment in which, given an increase in household savings, firms automatically increase investment proportionately. It is not obvious why these additional savings would increase production capacity, R&D, and other long-term goals. They could be channeled into short-term speculative financial activities (Krippner 2011) and/or stock buybacks. On the latter see www.nytimes.com/2018/02/26/business/tax-cuts-share-buybacks-corporate.html. In short, the notion of a "savings glut" with secular stagnation is very much a possibility as prominent neoclassical economists such as Lawrence Summers and former Fed chair Ben Bernanke observed over a decade ago. See https://slate.com/business/2016/09/saving-glut-and-the-failure

models,[37] this requires that they set prices over cost to attain some target rate of return.[38] In short, every firm attempts to be a *going concern* (i.e., be financially viable).[39]

On the other hand, economic analysis on its own cannot explain how firms have the ability to behave as above. Too often international lawyers abdicate questions of markets to the economists when in fact, markets can only be understood within a legal context. For instance, security of expectations in the face of pervasive uncertainty – the typical context of business decisions – requires a foundational legal structure for a business enterprise to function coherently.[40] As a type of property it cannot possibly be the benchmark perfect competition model[41] as it has to operate in a political and social context where the "law takes center stage in enhancing the reliability of others' expected behaviour."[42] Sales, as Commons put it,[43] do not involve merely the exchange of commodities but a transfer of titles so that behind every bilateral transaction there has to be a third party that adjudicates disputes – in other words, whether on the domestic or international level, a state-enforced legal system is necessary.[44] The *ex ante* nature of any decision making necessarily requires promises which constitute the basis of all transactions and need to be legally

-of-capital-in-the-21st-century.html and www.nytimes.com/2018/02/26/business/tax-cuts-share-buybacks-corporate.html. On the other hand, if investment is determined by expected profit rates which, given production costs, are determined by sales there is no reason why an increase in savings will automatically increase investment.

37 David Romer, *Advanced Macroeconomics*, 4th ed.(New York: McGraw-Hill Irwin, 2012).

38 William G. Nickels, James M. McHugh, and Susan M. McHugh, *Understanding Business*, 11th ed. (New York: McGraw-Hill Education, 2016), 407–8; Dean et al., *Principles of Microeconomics: Scarcity and Social Provisioning*; Alfred Eichner, "Prices and Pricing," *Journal of Economic Issues* 21, no. 4 (1987): 1555–84.

39 As Atkinson put it: "A going concern is a social unit that organizes and controls individuals and directs them toward a common purpose. They limit individual discretion but provide a security of expectations because they shape customary and expected behavior. In addition to limiting individuals, going concerns expand the ability of the individual to act. These concerns are governed by working rules, which change in the face of new circumstances." See Glen Atkinson, "Going Concerns, Futurity and Reasonable Value," *Journal of Economic Issues* 43, no. 2 (2009): 434. Commons, *Legal Foundations of Capitalism*.

40 As Jonathan Levy, following Veblen and Commons, concludes "[C]apital is legal property assigned a pecuniary value in expectation of a likely future pecuniary income. Capital valuation is prospective, always occurring under conditions of uncertainty". See Jonathan Levy, "Capital as Process and the History of Capitalism," *Business History Review* 91, no. 3 (2017): 487.

41 In this model each firm faces a horizontal demand curve and thus has no ability to change its price. Thus the question of bargaining with customers or competing with other firms is not possible.

42 Pistor, *The Code of Capital: How the Law Creates Wealth and Inequality*, 12.

43 Commons, *Legal Foundations of Capitalism*, 245.

44 Commons, 242.

enforced if there is going to be market stability.[45] Market participants will only enter into voluntary contracts to promise to buy and sell property if there is a stable set of background laws in place to enforce promises[46] since no one will enter into market transactions with strangers on the basis of empty promises. As Commons argued, it is the law which creates the foundation of negotiable bills of exchange and thus the basis of future revenue flows from these, promoting in the process the expansion of credit and thus the expansion of business investment.[47] In short, if the multinational firm is a going concern, global markets cannot be pre-political and the "state versus markets" debate, at the heart of neoclassical policy debates, makes no sense.[48]

Fourth, contrary to neoclassical economics, if markets and property are deeply legal and political – so is money. The supply and demand of commodities involves the exchange of titles, which of course requires the prior existence of a unit of account in which the titles are denominated – money. The creation and stability of the unit of account is central to how property is measured and current as well as future market transactions are made reliable.[49] It should be noted here that neoclassical theory conceptualizes both the domestic economy and foreign trade[50] purely in barter terms, with money entering the economy at the discretion of the central bank. However, such an approach is inconsistent with the business enterprise which, as discussed above, is a monetary institution. It will always attempt to be financially solvent to pay its bills. For example, it will try to have adequate cash on hand given the time lag between future revenues from current output and current debt obligations.

Fifth, introducing the centrality of money opens up the proverbial can of worms. It is one thing to say, as do heterodox economists, that money is endogenous

45 Commons, chap. VII.

46 Firms are legally required to pay dividends if they earn adequate profits. For example, as demonstrated in the landmark case *Dodge v. Ford Motor Co.* (1919), the Michigan Supreme Court required Ford to pay dividends to its shareholders as a legal duty to them rather than use the firm's massive retained earnings for other purposes by paying no dividends (Monks and Minow 2011, 56–57). In the same way, while a labor contract between a worker and their employer is not transferable to third parties, debt contracts are.

47 Commons, *Legal Foundations of Capitalism*, 253.

48 John Martinussen, *Society, State and Market: A Guide to Competing Theories of Development* (London & New York: Zed Books, 1997).

49 For example, a businessperson whose input costs are in US dollars needs to be assured that all their domestic sales are in the same unit of account and not some foreign currency one whose random fluctuations against the domestic currency could generate uncertainty in the calculation of profits.

50 William Milberg, "Say's Law in the Open Economy: Keynes's Rejection of the Theory of Comparative Advantage," in *Keynes, Uncertainty and the Global Economy: Beyond Keynes*, ed. Sheila C. Dow and John Hillard, vol. 2 (Cheltenham, UK and Northhampton, MA: Edward Elgar Press, 2002), 239–53.

because of the nature of credit.[51] However, heterodox economists generally do not ask how money is created; in other words, that it is a legal institution that derives out of a political process. Contextually driven politics create the laws that provide the context over which "market forces" operate, thereby generating distributional struggles and business production costs. In other words, politics acting through the law creates and circulates money and thus produces markets with different institutional foundations. As Christine Desan put it:[52]

> In fact, a community determines which goods and services can be alienated and thus what counts as a 'commodity' when it decides what items or services money can buy . . . transactions involving money would not be enforced if they were improperly made or inappropriately targeted a resource that could not be considered a 'commodity.' Later societies would return, notoriously, to allow the sale of Africans. Debate over the sale of free labor continues, with disputes about what constitutes real choice . . . Those debates are joined by myriad others, contests over what else is 'for sale,' from honors to votes, sex to kidneys.

Simply put, if politics and the law are central to money and money defines investment, then of course all private investment necessarily has a public foundation.[53] Further, in such an approach to money and markets, perfect competition is not possible. Consider agriculture with many small-sized farms located in different jurisdictions across the world. Neoclassical economists, for instance, routinely evoke grain markets as approaching the perfectly competitive ideal. And yet, with different bundles of rights (i.e., wage differences) in various jurisdictions, it is impossible for the firms to have close to identical monetary costs. There simply cannot be any baseline "normal" market structure since politics acting through different legal arrangements create different types of markets.[54]

6.2 FREE TRADE VERSUS PROTECTIONISM: THE NEOCLASSICAL FALSE DICHOTOMY

Today, we commonly hear among private international lawyers and policy-makers that a key problem in world affairs is increasing economic protectionism

51 Wynne Godley and Marc Lavoie, *Monetary Economics: An Integrated Approach to Credit, Money, Income, Production and Wealth* (Basingstoke: Palgrave Macmillan, 2007).

52 Christine Desan, "Money as a Legal Institution," in *Money in the Western Legal Tradition: Middle Ages to Bretton Woods*, ed. David Fox and Wolfgang Ernst (Oxford: Oxford University Press, 2016), 21–22.

53 See the extensive literature on state-led industrialization, e.g., Amsden (1989, 2001), Chang (2002), and Wade (1990).

54 See Daniel K. Tarullo, "Beyond Normalcy in the Regulation of International Trade," *Harvard Law Review* 100, no. 3 (January) (1987): 546–628.

and the breakdown of cosmopolitan free trade. Often, the claims are dismissed by non-economists or non-specialists because of the seeming technical nature of the analysis – but it is important for us to begin to understand the terms of debate and the logic at play. At the heart of the free trade debate is the Heckscher-Ohlin -Samuelson (HOS) model with its core claim that a country's trade performance is determined by its relatively abundant factors of production (land, labor, and capital). Consider trade between two countries (US and China) involving two types of goods, computers and cloth, and two factors of production (labor and capital), such that computers involve a capital-intensive production method while cloth involves a labor-intensive one. The US is assumed to be capital-abundant and China labor-abundant, where labor and capital get the wage rate (w) and the profit rate (r) as remunerations, respectively. The central argument of HOS is that capital-abundant countries should export capital-intensive goods and labor-abundant ones should do likewise for labor-intensive goods with free trade producing balanced trade.

The following assumptions are central to this theory that trade produces win-win economic gains for all countries, whatever their levels of economic development.[55] First, perfect competition prevails. Second, trading countries have access to identical production technologies thereby leading to the absence of product differentiation. And third, markets and trade operate as if existing in a pure barter system that allows full employment of all factors of production.

The first assumption implies fully flexible prices in all countries since perfectly competitive firms cannot set prices. If the general price level in the US is p and China is p* and e is the nominal exchange rate, then it follows that the relative prices in common currency, ep/p*, or the real exchange rate will automatically vary to clear any trade imbalances. If this suddenly is looking too 'economic', we will speak in non-economic terms in the next paragraph, but it is worth pausing a moment to digest this seemingly technical language. Ultimately, once you get a handle on the grammar, the actual arguments look increasingly familiar. Now, under fixed exchange rates, the Quantity Theory of Money holds that when a country experiences a trade surplus (China), the inflow of money will raise prices thereby lowering its surplus. Under flexible exchange rates the global excess demand for the surplus country's output will appreciate its nominal exchange rate, thereby making its exports more expensive internationally and lowering its trade surplus. In

55 Steve Suranovic, *International Trade: Theory and Policy* (The Saylor Foundation, 2010), Chapter 5, https://doi.org/http://www.saylor.org/site/textbooks/International%20Trade%20-%20Theory%20and%20Policy.pdf.

other words, firms in the trade surplus country will passively see their global market shares shrink and will do nothing about it. The opposite will happen for the trade deficit country (US) whose prices will fall under fixed exchange rates because the monetary outflows and nominal exchange rate will depreciate under flexible exchange rates. To summarize, in either exchange rate regime, as long as trade imbalances exist, variations in the real exchange rate will eliminate such disequilibria.[56]

From the early proponents of free trade such as David Hume, David Ricardo, and John Stuart Mill, foreign trade is essentially conceptualized as one nation exchanging its goods for another nation's goods. Foreign trade is considered equivalent to barter with money acting purely to make exchange more convenient.[57] In this regard, free trade is an extension to the open economy of the general equilibrium model in which money is assumed to be *neutral* so that changes in the money supply only affect prices and not output.

Now the key problem with the HOS model's prediction (and its mainstream adoption among global governance experts) is that trade balances tend to show persistent disequilibria over long periods of time. This can be easily verified by looking at trade balance data from the World Bank's *World Development Indicators* database.

In fact, the assumption of automatic balanced trade falls apart once one unpacks some of the key assumptions. First, suppose that for the deficit country its international price level declines by 1 percent (say because its currency depreciates). Then for the monetary value of exports to rise, the quantity of exported goods has to increase by more than 1 percent. But this depends on the price elasticity of demand for the goods which in turn depends on the qualitative characteristics of home goods versus foreign ones. It is entirely possible that the foreign demand for domestic goods rises by less than 1 percent, which would engender a decline in the dollar value of exports, thereby exacerbating the trade deficit.[58]

Second, international money flows will not affect prices but the quantity of bank reserves and, by extension, interest rates. Thus, a trade surplus country will experience an increase in bank reserves and a fall in interest rates; trade

[56] That is, for a deficit country there has to be a decline in its international price level compared to its foreign rivals thereby generating an increase in the quantity of exports. Similarly, for a surplus country a relative increase in its international price level has to decrease its quantity of exports.

[57] Milberg, "Say's Law in the Open Economy: Keynes's Rejection of the Theory of Comparative Advantage."

[58] Anwar M. Shaikh, "The Economic Mythology of Neoliberalism," *in Neoliberalism: A Critical Reader*, ed. Alfredo Saad-Filho and Deborah Johnston (London, England and Ann Arbor, MI: Pluto Press, 2005), 41–49.

deficit countries will experience the opposite, with falling bank reserves and rising interest rates. Of course, if the impact of trade flows is on interest rates rather than prices it follows that the latter will not adjust to bring about balanced trade.

Third, outside the perfect competition framework, real-world business enterprises set prices to be going concerns as discussed above. These prices are set to cover their costs and yield their target rates of return. It would be highly unlikely, and indeed coincidental, if these relative international prices emanating from firms in different countries would also adjust to bring about balanced trade.[59]

Fourth, following American legal theorists such as Hale and Hohfeld, if one conceptualizes markets as fundamentally political constructions, then an economy's legal foundation will also constitute the context for distributional struggles. Firms in different countries will thus be internationally competitive to different extents and one would expect trade imbalances to be persistent.[60] *Trade imbalances do not arise from "market distortions" caused by state interventionist policies quite simply because there is no benchmark perfectly competitive market that is free of state regulation.* All markets, and the flows of money that define them, are the outcomes of different combinations of laws that are politically enforced.[61] In short, the free trade versus protectionist-cum-industrial policies, at the heart of neoclassical debates on foreign,[62] rests on a false dichotomy.

6.3 BEYOND AUSTERITY AND "SOUND MONEY": TOWARD A PROGRESSIVE ECONOMIC FRAME WORK

The pursuit of balanced budgets and central bank independence (CBI) has been a central feature of both the Second and Third Moments in Law and Development. CBI involves legal and institutional restraints on the part of the legislature or the executive to influence the money supply. The claim is that "experts" at central banks should control inflation by stabilizing the growth of the money supply so that the economy remains at the NAIRU (non-accelerating inflation rate of unemployment) level. This is said to stabilize

59 Id.

60 Id.

61 Gordon, "Critical Legal Histories"; Tarullo, "Beyond Normalcy in the Regulation of International Trade".

62 Jagdish Bhagwati, "Free Trade: Why AFL-CIO, the Sierra Club, and Congressman Gephardt Should Like It," *The American Economist* 43, no. 2 (1999): 3–12; Paul Krugman, "Is Free Trade Passé?," *Journal of Economic Perspectives* 1, no. 2 (1987): 131–44; Paul R. Krugman, "Making Sense of the Competitiveness Debate," *Oxford Review of Economic Policy* 12, no. 3 (1996): 17–25.

property rights and thus investor expectations,[63] and long-run growth will be driven by productivity and thrift. In fact, the pursuit of balanced budgets and "sound money" to promote exports and growth are central features of all L&D policy programs.

Monetary neutrality, exogeneity, and the NAIRU are rejected by heterodox economists.[64] As for the role of thrift, a central feature of Keynes's contribution to macroeconomic theory was his rejection of Say's law[65] and his emphasis on the role of effective demand in promoting output and employment.[66] Investment plays a central role in Keynes's framework and is determined by the expectation of profits and not savings as discussed earlier. So the real question becomes: can an alternative export-oriented development paradigm be conceptualized that convincingly eschews austerity?

There is a considerable literature that has argued there is indeed a "high-road" to globalization involving both export promotion and social democratic policies – and not just in the wealthy countries but also some of the poorer ones too.[67] But even here, there are perspectives that continue to rely on neoclassical approaches and other approaches that might offer something truly different. The rejection of the "one-size-fits-all" approach to global integration, for instance, has been the hallmark of the *varieties of capitalism* (VoC) school, pioneered by Peter Hall and David Soskice.[68] With its firm-centered approach, at the heart of the VoC framework is the distinction between what it calls *liberal market economies* (LME), with the US being an archetype, and coordinated market economies (CME) such as Germany.

These two broad categories of economies have different institutional environments within which firms are embedded. LMEs are said to have more "competitive" environments while CMEs involve strategic behavior involving firms and other institutions such as the state or unions.[69] This polarity implicitly

63 Sylvia Maxfield, *Gatekeepers of Growth: The International Political Economy of Central Banking in Developing Countries* (Princeton, NJ: Princeton University Press, 1997).

64 L. Randall Wray, "The Dismal State of Macroeconomics and the Opportunity for a New Beginning," *Levy Economics Institute of Bard College Working Paper Series*, no. 652 (2011): 1–22.

65 Say's law states that supply creates its own demand. For example, in this perspective an increase in business savings (say from a corporate tax cut) will automatically be ploughed back into higher investment.

66 Keynes, *The General Theory of Employment, Interest, and Money*.

67 See for example Milberg and Houston (2005) and Sandbrook et al. (2007).

68 Bob Hancke, *Debating Varieties of Capitalism: A Reader* (Oxford and New York: Oxford University Press, 2009).

69 Peter A. Hall and David Soskice, "An Introduction to Varieties of Capitalism," in *Debating Varieties of Capitalism: A Reader*, ed. Bob Hancké (New York: Oxford University Press, 2009), 27–28.

accepts the neoclassical distinction between perfect and oligopolistic competition since only the latter market structure involves strategic interactions between firms. In fact, as Colin Crouch argues,[70] the VoC literature dichotomizes neoliberalism and social democracy, and thus assumes the free-market framework of neoclassical economics as the baseline and then deviations from it.[71]

In reality, the US government has historically played a central role in promoting innovation policies via the allocation of finance to target sectors, acting in fact like a developmental state.[72] At a theoretical level, the LME vs. CME distinction replicates the familiar "regulation vs. deregulation" dichotomy. In the Legal Realist tradition, all economies are regulated in different ways. The relative stinginess of social protection mechanisms in the US compared to Germany reflects a particular political allocation of power relations that favors employers more in the former than the latter.[73]

Beyond the VoC framework, institutional variations of capitalist economies need to be explained. The CLS tradition's focus on *legal indeterminacy*[74] constitutes a central theoretical foundation to not only understand how varieties of capitalism arise but also how one can conceptualize alternatives to neoliberalism. This requires the denaturalization of capitalist markets in order to reveal their fundamental legal and political foundations. Economic policy has either advocated the promotion of small business solutions or using the power of the state to 'prime the pump' and regulate big business for socially desirable outcomes. Both strands of progressive reform ironically take the basic market system as given, including its power relations, and implicitly accept the perfect vs. imperfect competition dichotomy.

Instead, the goal of progressive reform should be to reconstitute or re-regulate markets by, among other things, restructuring the role of finance. Banks and other financial institutions would need to be restrained from speculative activities and their investments would have to be subsumed to the needs of long-term industrial finance. At the core of the financial system is

70 Colin Crouch, "Typologies of Capitalism," in *Debating Varieties of Capitalism: A Reader*, ed. Bob Hancké (New York: Oxford University Press, 2009), 75–94.

71 Crouch, 77.

72 Fred L. Block and Matthew R. Keller, *State of Innovation: The US Government's Role in Technology Development* (Boulder, CO and London, UK: Paradigm Publishers, 2011); Mariana Mazzucato, *The Entrepreneurial State: Debunking Public vs. Private Sector Myths* (Philadelphia, PA: Public Affairs, 2015).

73 This after all, was the critique of Lochner vs. New York by Hale and others, that is, the absence of labor protection was not a deregulated state of the economy but a particular allocation of state-enforced coercive power. See Barbara H. Fried, *The Progressive Assault on Laissez Faire* (Cambridge MA and London, England: Harvard University Press, 1998).

74 Gordon, "Critical Legal Histories".

of course central banks, which could be used to promote different institutional design of the markets. This is not a mere "pie in the sky" proposal, but is consistent with the industrialization experiences of a large number of countries.[75]

In other words, since all money and credit creation ultimately has a public basis (Desan 2016; Hockett and Omarova 2018; Ricks 2016) and money is constitutive of markets, restructuring the monetary system to make the economy more socially inclusive while promoting investment and exports tantamount to redistributing power relations. One is reminded of Sabeel Rahman's insightful book which, drawing on the insights of Louis Brandeis and John Dewey, forcefully argues against what he calls managerialist approaches to market reform whose goal is to channel "market forces" in a progressive direction.[76] Instead, Rahman proposes the need for a restructuring of markets to reduce inequalities of wealth and power. To many authors, especially those in the Marxist tradition, this appears unrealistic given capitalist power. The problem with these reservations is that the history of property has always involved contested struggles over what it is and does, and sometimes such property destabilization has gone against capitalists' interests.[77] One can consider the Factory Acts in the UK or the New Deal and environmental and consumer regulations in the US in the 1970s, all of which were opposed by industry.[78] Finally, there is an extensive business history literature that deals with the question of institutional variation.[79]

Clearly the context matters in how money and markets are shaped. But does legal indeterminacy imply lack of theoretical rigor in which intellectual work collapses into descriptive empiricism? Does an inductive approach to the study of economics, as pioneered by Institutional Economists in the interwar period, imply a lack of theoretical analysis as critics of this tradition claimed?[80]

75 Gerald Epstein, "Post-War Experiences with Developmental Central Banks: The Good, the Bad and the Hopeful," *G-24 Discussion Paper No. 54, Geneva: UNCTAD*, no. 54 (2009): iv–25, www.g24.org/wp-content/uploads/2016/01/54.pdf.

76 K. Sabeel Rahman, *Democracy against Domination* (New York, NY: Oxford University Press, 2017).

77 Ezra Rosser, "Destablizing Property," *Connecticut Law Review*, 2015.

78 Kim Phillips-Fein, *Invisible Hands: The Businessmen's Crusade against the New Deal* (New York, NY: W. W. Norton, 2009); Katherine A Moos, "The Political Economy of State Regulation: The Case of the English Factory Acts," *UMass Economics Working Papers* 233 (2017): 1–31, https://scholarworks.umass.edu/cgi/viewcontent.cgi?article=1234&context=econ_workingpaper.

79 See the symposium on business history and varieties of capitalism in the *Business History Review* (2010) 84 (4).

80 On this issue see Yuval P. Yonay, *The Struggle for the Soul of Economics: Institutionalist and Neoclassical Economists in America between the Wars* (Princeton: Princeton University Press, 1998).

One can respond to both these questions in the negative by arguing that the very nature of property as a socially and politically embedded institution automatically produces the need for context-based analysis. This central insight on property necessarily relates its contextual nature to both constitutional and nonconstitutional law and how these are interpreted and fought over in constructing a particular property rights regime or obstructing the creation of a new one.[81] And of course since money can also be treated in property (and contract) terms, the CLS view of money property creates a particular theoretical and methodological framework which is quite distinct from neoclassical economics. All this implies that a progressive policy framework has to go beyond the demand-side versus supply-side dichotomy which is a core one in economics, since the political and legal foundations of a market economy of a given type simultaneously determine both the nature of demand (via the distribution of income) and supply (costs and sales of firms).

6.4 CONCLUSION

"Free trade versus protectionism," "free markets versus state intervention", "efficient markets versus market failure," and "distribution versus redistribution" are some of the most prevalent dichotomies that make up public discourse over international development and trade This essay has shown that such dichotomies are false as they implicitly rest on a Blackstonian notion of absolute property rights and a view of the firm that is inconsistent with real-world business competition. In a world where our legal and political institutions feel increasingly fragile in the face of economic constraints and financial precarity, international lawyers and experts in global governance need to bury the myths that have helped us dig our current ditch.

A monetary production economy necessarily implies that real-world firms behave as going concerns in which their chief objective is to be financially viable. In such a world, as monetary institutions there is no such thing as a perfectly competitive market or any deviation from it. Thus real-world business competition inherently involves damaging other firms as legal jurists argued a long time ago with the principle of *damnum absque injuria*.[82] The profit-making firm as a going enterprise is necessarily embedded in a particular legal and political context which determines its bundles of

[81] Gregory Alexander, *The Global Debate Over Constitutional Property: Lessons for American Takings Jurisprudence* (Chicago and London: University of Chicago Press, 2006); A. J. van der Walt, *Property in the Margins* (Portland, Oregon: Hart Publishing, 2009).

[82] Singer, "The Legal Rights Debate in Analytical Jurisprudence from Bentham to Hohfeld".

entitlements and prohibitions and thus its financial viability. Since flows of money across the economy are logically linked together via balance sheets, each going concern is by definition a social creature.[83] Politics are at the heart of the firm, determining the accounting rules,[84] the ways in which capital assets are coded,[85] and in the final instance the unit of account itself.[86]

All this implies that one would hardly expect to see balanced trade. The pursuit of a socially equitable trade strategy cannot be accommodated within the neoclassical economic framework, however much the group *Economics for Inclusive Property* claims otherwise.[87] A new international law and development framework needs to jettison the tyranny of false dichotomies and begin with the CLS view of property rights and money.

83 Godley and Lavoie, *Monetary Economics: An Integrated Approach to Credit, Money, Income, Production, and Wealth.*

84 Steven K. Vogel, *Marketcraft: How Governments Make Markets Work* (Oxford University Press, 2018).

85 Pistor, *The Code of Capital: How the Law Creates Wealth and Inequality.*

86 Desan, *Making Money: Coin, Currency, and Coming of Capitalism.*

87 See https://econfip.org/.

7

Digital

Rohan Grey

Contemporary international law is driven by advances in financial and information technology. These twin systems together function as a common linguistic and physical infrastructural layer for the entire planet, transcending national boundaries and cultural divisions. Financial and informational considerations dictate the budgetary and administrative practices of international legal institutions and practitioners, as well as the domestic legal systems upon which they rely. More broadly, the capacities and constraints of "Big Finance" and "Big Tech" shape the contours of legal and policy debates in fields ranging from war and global health, to ecological sustainability and intellectual property. While these debates and the underlying material forces that condition them have always been in flux, there is good reason to believe that we are approaching – or indeed, are in the middle of – an epochal inflection point on the scale of the transition from oral to literate society, or the invention of the printing press.

The digitization of society, a process which first began centuries ago, has accelerated rapidly in recent decades as a result of the maturation of electronic communication technologies, most notably the internet, as well as the expansion of the logic of capitalist accumulation into every facet and sphere of daily life. For arguably the first time in history, the "digital" has become the explicit locus of our social imaginary and shared political experience, rather than a superimposition on top of it.[1] This new mode of collective ordering, like those that came before it, is precipitating the emergence of a new global legal regime, fashioned out of a combination of old and new jurisprudential tools

Rohan Grey is an Assistant Professor of Law at Willamette University, the President of the Modern Money Network, and the Research Director of the Digital Fiat Currency Institute.

[1] *See, e.g.*, Melinda Sebastian & Wesley Shumar, *The Digital Age and the Social Imaginary*, *in* Remembering and Forgetting in the Digital Age 188 (Florent Thouvenin et al. eds., 2018); Christopher Kelty, Geeks, Social Imaginaries and Recursive Publics, 20(2) *Cultural Anthropology* 185.

and principles. While this regime will necessarily address and incorporate a wide range of issues and considerations – many of which are discussed elsewhere in this book – one area of particular importance to international lawyers is the design and regulation of digital money.

Money lies at the core of all financial systems, and innovations in monetary media and their accompanying institutional structures have played a defining role in many periods of major social transformation.[2] At the same time, key innovations in information technology, including the invention of writing itself, first began as monetary innovations, before taking on wider social and cultural significance later. Today, digital money functions as a microcosm of and vanguard for a paradigmatic shift in global governance in the wake of the maturation of information capitalism, highlighting key areas of legal tension and revealing a general agenda of legislative and regulatory priorities. Political debates over the appropriate balance between social welfare and profit-seeking, privacy and surveillance, and local and global sovereignty in the context of digital money represent the tip of the spear of a broader geopolitical realignment, whose societal consequences will be far-reaching and comprehensive.

Legal scholars and practitioners committed to the project of international law have important contributions to offer these debates, as part of a larger movement to construct a just, equitable, and functional global governance regime. These include articulating and prioritizing an agenda of political and legal reforms in light of practical considerations, and coordinating and harmonizing the efforts of various stakeholders and experts by serving as "boundary-spanning intermediaries" and systemic change agents.[3] In order to do so effectively, however, international lawyers must take the transformative social implications of digital money seriously. This, in turn, requires going beyond the traditional theoretical silos of international law, and instead, conceptualizing digital money as a small-c constitutional project that spans both public and private governance at the global level.[4]The remainder of this chapter proceeds as follows: Part I revisits early legal debates over the social significance of the internet, particularly in relation to older digitally networked technologies that shaped the modern international financial system. Part II explores the historical and legal

2 *See, e.g.*, William N. Goetzmann, *Money Changes Everything: How Finance Made Civilization Possible* (2017).

3 *See, e.g.*, Susan Sturm, Activating Systemic Change Toward Full Participation: The Pivotal Role of Boundary-Spanning Institutional Intermediaries, 54 *St. Louis Uni. L. J.* 1117 (2010).

4 *See, e.g.*, Christine Desan, *The Constitutional Approach to Money: Monetary Design and the Production of the Modern World, in* Money Talks: Essays in Honor of Viviana Zelizer 109 (Nina Bandelj, Frederick Wherry, & Viviana Zelizer eds., 2017).

foundations of money, and the ways in which monetary systems and informational processes have evolved in the wake of the transition from industrial capitalism to information capitalism. Part III evaluates contemporary debates over the design and regulation of digital money, and considers their legal and political implications for the future of the global economy.

7.1 THE FINANCIAL FOUNDATIONS OF THE NETWORK SOCIETY

Electronics has been a handmaiden to commerce ever since the telegraph . . . Given this long history, new problems in cyberlaw may be very old issues in banking law.

- Joseph Sommer[5]

Digital historians trace the origins of the modern internet to networked computer systems developed by the US military in the 1960s.[6] It was not until the 1990s, however, that personal and commercial use began to take off. This development, in turn, inspired techno-utopians and hackers, who until then had been relegated to the fringes of popular culture, to confidently declare the dawning of a new era of mankind, encapsulated most vividly in John Perry Barlow's infamous "Declaration of the Independence of Cyberspace" in 1996:

> Governments of the Industrial World, you weary giants of flesh and steel, I come from Cyberspace, the new home of Mind. On behalf of the future, I ask you of the past to leave us alone. You are not welcome among us. You have no sovereignty where we gather.[7]

Around the same time, a spirited debate broke out among legal theorists over whether "cyberlaw" constituted a new, distinct legal subfield, worthy of its own independent study, or merely the latest iteration in a longstanding dialectical relationship between law and technological innovation.[8] The most prominent advocate of the "skeptical" view was US Court of Appeals Judge Frank Easterbrook, who in 1996 accused cyber law-enthusiasts of "multidisciplinary dilettantism" and the "cross-sterilization of ideas."[9] According to

[5] Joseph Sommer, Against Cyberlaw, 15 *Berkeley Tech. L.J.* 1145, 1201 (2000).

[6] See, e.g ., Yasha Levine, *Surveillance Valley: The Secret Military History of the Internet* (2018).

[7] John Perry Barlow, A *Declaration of the Independence of Cyberspace*, Electronic Frontier Foundation (February 8, 1996), www.eff.org/cyberspace-independence.

[8] For an overview, *see* Paul Schiff Berman, *Introduction, in* Law and Society Approaches to Cyberspace, xi, xiii (Paul Schiff Berman, ed., 2007).

[9] Frank H. Easterbrook, Cyberspace and the Law of the Horse, 1996 *U. Chi. L. Forum* 207, 207 (1996). *See also* Lawrence Lessig, The Law of the Horse: What Cyberlaw Might Teach, 113 *Harv. L. Rev.* 501.

Easterbrook, cyber law was no more a distinct field than the "Law of the Horse" had been in the nineteenth century, and any attempt to understand it solely on its own terms was "doomed to be shallow and to miss unifying principles."[10] Instead, Easterbrook argued, "[o]nly by putting the law of the horse in the context of broader rules about commercial endeavors could one really understand the *law* about horses."[11]

In 1999, legal historian Eben Moglen argued that it was a mistake to try to understand the legal significance of the internet solely in terms of its impact on the laws governing the underlying technology.[12] According to Moglen:

> We often discuss "the Internet" as though it were either a thing or a place, but we do better at grasping the legal and political issues the net presents if we think of "the Internet" as the name of a social condition: the fact that everyone living in the networked portions of the world can now communicate with anyone else directly, without intermediaries, reaching very large numbers of people at almost no cost. A society in which everyone is connected to everyone else behaves differently from any society that has ever existed before; past "principles" of social and economic law, things that seemed always true everywhere, aren't anymore.[13]

In practice, Moglen's vision of a "networked society"[14] defined by universally disintermediated social interconnection has since been – at least thus far – belied by the persistent centralizing influence of telecommunications operators, internet service providers, and more recently, online platforms such as Google, Amazon, and Facebook. On the other hand, his insistence that the historical significance of the internet be understood primarily in sociological rather than technological terms serves to both reframe and clarify the stakes of the underlying legal debate.

In 2000, Federal Reserve attorney Joseph Sommer offered an alternative cyber-skeptic take, arguing that many of the legal issues raised by the internet were prefigured by the laws governing earlier digital financial networks, which in turn were derived from much older jurisprudential principles.[15] According

10 Easterbrook, *supra*.

11 Easterbrook, *supra* at 208.

12 Eben Moglen, Anarchism Triumphant: Free Software and the Death of Copyright, 4(8) *First Monday* (1999), https://journals.uic.edu/ojs/index.php/fm/article/view/684/594.

13 Eben Moglen, Free Software Matters: When Code Isn't Law, *Linux User* (April 23, 2000), http://moglen.law.columbia.edu/publications/lu-01.html. *See also* Eben Moglen & Pamela S. Karlan, The Soul of a New Political Machine, The Online, The Color Line, and Electronic Democracy, 34 *Loy. L. A. L. Rev.* 1089, 1105 (2001).

14 This term was first coined in 1991 by Manuel Castells. *See* Manuel Castells & Gustavo Cardoso (Eds.), *The Knowledge Society: From Knowledge to Policy* (2005).

15 Sommer, *supra. See also* James Rogers, The New Old Law of Electronic Money, 58 *S. M. U. L. Rev.* 1253 (2005);

to Sommer, "The law of electronic commerce has . . . been around since at least the 1860s and has been the topic of legal analysis since at least the 1920s."[16] Additionally, questions of political sovereignty, such as "how does the law of a state deal with communities not defined by that state?" and "How do such communities govern themselves?" were "old [problems] with many manifestations."[17] In particular, Sommer noted that banking was a "quintessentially networked activity," and the "international banking community . . . is a good example of a . . . 'virtual community' . . . [and] shows us that the problem of autonomous or transnational communities is an old one, often resolved satisfactorily."[18]

Notwithstanding the clear difference in tone and emphasis, there is less daylight between Moglen and Sommer than initially appears. In particular, Sommer agrees that new information technologies often "wreak major social change," and acknowledges that "[i]f [movable type and the television] were not socially transformative, nothing is."[19] In his view, however, social transformation often results in novel deployment of existing law, rather than the development of new law *per se*. For example, the basic informational flow of digitally networked systems is governed by the laws of records and messages, which have "been around since the telegraph . . . [T]he Internet is merely bringing them to our attention."[20] Moreover, to the extent technology spurs legal innovation, there tends to be a significant lag, "in part because [new technologies] are unlikely to generate new [social] practices immediately."[21] For example, Sommer notes that "the first 'cyber-statute' may have been Article 4A of the Uniform Commercial Code, promulgated in 1989, codifying the practice of bank wire transfers . . . [Yet] [w]ire transfers have existed since at least the days of the transatlantic cable, so Article 4A codified well over a century of practice."[22]

By comparison, Moglen views the internet as the perfection of a networked communication system whose origins lie millennia ago with the introduction of the postal service by the Roman Emperor Augustus.[23] To that end, he readily acknowledges that the radical implications of transitioning to a "network society" may not be fully realized for at least one or two more

16 Sommer, *supra* at 1188.
17 *Ibid.* at 1190.
18 *Ibid.* at 1192–93.
19 *Ibid.* at 1148–49.
20 *Ibid.* at 1229.
21 *Ibid.* at 1148.
22 *Ibid.*
23 Eben Moglen, *Snowden and the Future, Part I: Westward the Course of Empire*, Lecture at Columbia Law School (October 9, 2013), www.snowdenandthefuture.info/PartI.html.

generations, and will be at least partly contingent on political and technological decisions that have yet to be made.[24] Furthermore, Moglen recognizes the underlying technical similarities between the internet and earlier forms of digital technology. In his view, however, the ability to capture and share an extremely diverse range of symbolic information via identical bitstreams across a globally integrated network represents a qualitative leap in communicative capacity, which in turn generates novel forms of radical legal instability.[25]

Both Moglen and Sommer, therefore, situate the emergence of the internet within a larger narrative of evolving communications technologies, in which media initially designed for narrow purposes take on new functions and social significance as they mature. In addition, both recognize that the internet's disruptive potential lies primarily in its capacity to transform broader social dynamics, rather than the narrow legal principles that govern the underlying technology. Notably, both authors first articulated their views over twenty years ago, and while they remain highly relevant, there have been significant technological advances in the intervening years, particularly in the realm of digital finance. Given these developments (discussed further in Part III), it is entirely possible that Sommer's claim that "new problems in cyberlaw may be very old problems in banking law," and Moglen's claim that in the network society, "past 'principles' of ... economic law ... that seemed always true everywhere, aren't anymore," may ultimately both prove correct.

7.2 MONETARY INFORMATION AND MONETIZED INFORMATION

Cash, Rules, Everything, Around, Me
C.R.E.A.M.
Get the money
Dollar, dollar bill y'all

- Wu-Tang Clan[26]

Money is commonly understood to have emerged as a technologically superior alternative to barter, solving the problem of the "double coincidence of wants" by functioning as a "ur-commodity" that individuals could use to buy and sell other goods and services.[27] This narrative, while superficially plausible, lacks any basis in the historical or anthropological record. In fact, money

[24] Eben Moglen, *Why Freedom of Thought Requires Free Media and Why Free Media Requires Free Software*, Address at Re:Publica, Berlin (May 2, 2012), www.softwarefreedom.org/events/2012/Moglen-rePublica-Berlin/transcript.html.

[25] Moglen, *supra* note 11.

[26] Wu-Tang Clan, *C. R. E. A. M.*, *on* Enter the Wu-Tang (36 Chambers) (Loud Records 1993).

[27] L. Randall Wray, Alternative Approaches to Money, 11(1) *Theor. Inq. Law* 29, 30 (2010).

first emerged as a form of standardized record-keeping to facilitate the governance of social units too large to manage solely via face-to-face relationships.[28] Political leaders and their bureaucratic agents imposed non-reciprocal obligations, including taxes, fees, fines, and recognized tithes, and determined what tokens or commodities were acceptable in payment.[29] These legally recognized 'tax-credits' then circulated as money among private actors, who used them to establish subsidiary systems of credit and mutual exchange.[30] Over time, public and private actors developed increasingly sophisticated administrative institutions and accounting methods to keep track of complex webs of financial obligations and flows of real resources.

According to archaeologist Denise Schmandt-Besserat, the origins of modern writing itself can be traced back to early monetary practices.[31] Public authorities first issued (and subsequently collected) tax receipts in the form of three-dimensional clay tokens, which were later sealed in tubes with markings on the outside to denominate the tokens included therein for safekeeping. Eventually, these tubes were replaced with flat, two-dimensional tablets, and the markings expanded from basic numerical quantities to include other kinds of legally relevant information. Finally, these grammatical and scribal technologies were adapted for non-administrative purposes, such as writing poetry and fiction.

While accounts of money often focus on the evolution of record-keeping practices and financial instruments (i.e. "money-things"),[32] the underlying unit in which such money-things are denominated is arguably more fundamental.[33] As anthropologist David Graeber notes, "the big question in

[28] *See, e.g.*, David Graeber, *Debt: The First 5,000 Years* (2011); Michael Hudson, *The Role of Accounting in Civilization's Economic Takeoff, in* Creating Economic Order: Record-Keeping, Standardization, and the Development of Accounting in the Ancient Near-East, 1 (Michael Hudson & Cornelia Wunsch, eds., 2004).

[29] *See, e.g.*, Christine Desan, *Money as a Legal Institution, in* Money in the Western Legal Tradition: Middle Ages to Bretton Woods, 18 (David Fox & Wolfgang Ernst, eds., 2015); Wray, *supra* at 39; Pavlina Tcherneva, *Chartalism and the Tax-Driven Approach to Money, in* A Handbook of Alternative Monetary Economics, 69 (Philip Arestis & Malcolm Sawyre, eds., 2007).

[30] Desan, *supra* at 25. *See also* Robert Hockett & Saule Omarova, The Finance Franchise, 102 *Cornell L. Rev.* 1143 (2017); Stephanie Bell, The Role of the State and the Hierarchy of Money, 25(2) *Cambridge J. of Econ.* 149 (2001).

[31] Denise Schmandt-Besserat, *The Evolution of Writing* (2014), https://sites.utexas.edu/dsb/files/2014/01/evolution_writing.pdf.

[32] *See, e.g.*, Benjamin Geva, *'Bank Money': The Rise, Fall, and Metamorphosis of the 'Transferable Deposit'*, in Money in the Western Legal Tradition: Middle Ages to Bretton Woods, 359 (David Fox & Wolfgang Ernst, eds., 2015).

[33] *See, e.g.*, Alla Semanova, Would You Barter with God? Why Holy Debts and Not Profane Markets Created Money, 70(2) *Am. J. of Econ. & Socio.* 376 (2011).

the origins of money is how a sense of obligation – an 'I owe you one' – turns into something that can be precisely quantified."[34] According to Graeber, the transformation of previously qualitative, socially mediated relationships into formalized "exact equivalents" occurs when there is a "potential for violence:"

> If you give someone a pig and they give you a few chickens back you might think they're a cheapskate, and mock them, but you're unlikely to come up with a mathematical formula for exactly how cheap you think they are. If someone pokes out your eye in a fight, or kills your brother, that's when you start saying, "traditional compensation is exactly twenty-seven heifers of the finest quality and if they're not of the finest quality, this means war!"[35]

Throughout history, money has functioned as a common unit of account for a wide range of legislative and judicial value calculations, from the common law of obligations and criminal law through to regulatory cost-benefit analysis and human rights.[36] Contrary to orthodox economic theory, however, money is not merely a neutral veil for underlying real economic activity. Rather, monetary values are determined in large part by the legal structure of the monetary system itself,[37] as well as the processes by which monetary values are aggregated across different contexts to establish a general system of prices.[38] Consequently, as German monetary theorist Georg Friedrich Knapp argued, "[m]oney is a creature of law. A theory of money must therefore deal with legal history."[39]

According to legal historian Christine Desan, the transition from feudalism to industrial capitalism was precipitated by the emergence of a new mode of

34 Philip Pilkington, What is Debt? An Interview With Economic Anthropology David Graeber, *Naked Capitalism* (August 26, 2011), www.nakedcapitalism.com/2011/08/what-is-debt-%E2%80%93-an-interview-with-economic-anthropologist-david-graeber.html.

35 *Ibid.*

36 *See, e.g.*, Desan, *supra* note 27; Lua Yuille & Rohan Grey, Money and Property, *Law and Political Economy* (May 16, 2019), https://lpeblog.org/2019/05/16/money-and-property; Raúl Carrillo, Keeping It Real: Law, Coercion, and the Frontiers of Public Finance, *New Economic Perspectives* (June 25, 2014), https://neweconomicperspectives.org/2014/06/keeping-real-law-coercion-frontiers-public-finance.html.

37 *See, e.g.*, Yair Listokin, *Law and Macroeconomics: Legal Remedies to Recessions* (2019); Simon Deakin et al., Legal Institutionalism: Capitalism and the Constitutive Role of Law, 45(1) *J. of Comp. Econ.* 188 (2015); Katharina Pistor, A Legal Theory of Finance, 41(2) *J. of Comp. Econ.* 315 (2013); Roy Kreitner, The Jurisprudence of Global Money, 11 *Theor. Inq. Law* 177 (2010).

38 *See, e.g.*, Blair Fix, The Aggregation Problem: Implications for Ecological and Biophysical Economics, 4(1) *Biophysical Econ. and Resource Quality* 1 (2019); David Grewal, The Laws of Capitalism, 128 *Harv. L. Rev.* 626 (2014).

39 George Friedrich Knapp, *The State Theory of Money* (1924). *See also* Roy Kreitner, Legal History of Money, 8 *Ann. Rev. of L. & Soc. Sci.* 415 (2012).

monetary production, in which the power to create public money – previously the exclusive prerogative of the sovereign – was for the first time shared with a class of profit-seeking investors and banking intermediaries.[40] By aligning the self-interest of private capital with the physical and legal systems by which money itself was created, Britain unleashed a wave of financial innovation that permanently transformed the productive dynamics of the entire global economy. Presently, a similar transition is underway. However, in this case the interests of private capital are aligned with the physical and legal systems that create, store, and process *monetizable information*, rather than money *per se*. As Julie Cohen argues:

> In referring to the shift from industrialism to informationalism … [I] mean to indicate two kinds of fundamental transformations. First is a movement away from an economy oriented principally toward manufacturing and related activities toward one oriented principally around the production, accumulation, and processing of information … Second is a transformation in the conduct of even traditional industrial activity … information technology assumes an increasingly prominent role in the control of industrial production and in the management of all kinds of enterprises.[41]

As with the earliest forms of written record-keeping, the aim of these new technologies and systems of information production is to improve the ability of governing entities to monitor and condition social behavior in large social units. In contrast to earlier economic regimes, however, the dominant governing entities in question are not sovereign states, motivated by concerns of political legitimacy, but rather transnational corporations motivated by the pursuit of profit. Thus, as Shoshana Zuboff argues:

> 'Big data' is above all the foundational component in a deeply intentional and highly consequential new logic of accumulation … This new form of information capitalism aims to predict and modify human behavior as a means to produce revenue and market control … While 'big data' may be set to other uses, those do not erase its origins in an extractive project founded on formal indifference to the populations that comprise both its data sources and ultimate targets.[42]

[40] Christine Desan, *Making Money: Coin, Currency, and the Coming of Capitalism* (2014). *See also* Andrew David Edwards, The American Revolution and Christine Desan's New History of Money, 42(1) *L. & Soc. Inq*. 252.

[41] Julie Cohen, The Regulatory State in the Information Age, 17 *Theor. Inq. Law* 369, 371 (2016).

[42] Shoshana Zuboff, Big Other: Surveillance Capitalism and the Prospects of an Information Civilization, 30 *J. of Inf. Tech*. 75, 75–76 (2015).

More broadly, monetary systems not only translate existing social and economic information into monetizable information, but also generate new forms of information from within. Indeed, as both Karl Marx and John Maynard Keynes observed, modern capitalist economies are driven by a self-referential cycle of monetary accumulation, rather than external considerations of social well-being or material prosperity.[43] Furthermore, as sociologist Viviana Zelizer has documented, although "modern money seems starkly homogeneous ... [in reality] [w]e assig[n] different meanings and separate uses for particular kinds of monies ... Not all dollars are equal."[44] Recording and processing new forms of internally generated monetary information necessitates the creation of new administrative and governance technologies, which in turn become sites for the production of yet more monetary information.[45] In this sense, money functions simultaneously as a specific type of information, a mode of ordering other types of information, a means of producing new information, and a self-contained information ecosystem.[46]

7.3 DIGITAL MONEY: FROM FRONTIER TO ENCLOSURE

[When] the empire of the Romans filled the world ... the world became a safe and dreary prison for [its] enemies ... On every side [they were] encompassed with a vast extent of sea and land, which [they] could never hope to traverse without being discovered, seized, and restored to [their] irritated master ... "Wherever you are," said Cicero to the exiled Marcellus, "remember that you are equally within the power of the conqueror."

- Edward Gibbon[47]

Digital money has been a central concern of internet theorists for decades. As Sommer noted in 1998, "[m]ost of what occurs in the Internet is commercial. Most commercial transactions require payment in money ... Therefore, the

43 John Maynard Keynes, Drafts of the General Theory, in *Collected Writings Vol. XXIX*, 81 (1979); Karl Marx, *Capital, Vol. I*, Chapter 4 (1867 [1977], trans. Ben Fowkes).

44 Viviana Zelizer, The Social Meaning of Money: "Special Monies," 95(2) *Am. J.* of Socio. 342, 342–343. *See also* Viviana Zelizer, *The Social Meaning of Money* (2017).

45 *See, e.g.*, Shoshana Zuboff, *The Age of Surveillance Capitalism: The Fight for a Human Future at the New Frontier of Power* (2019); Frank Pasquale, *The Black Box Society: The Secret Algorithms That Control Money and Information* (2016); Martha Poon, Corporate Capitalism and the Growing Power of Big Data, 41(6) *Sci. Tech. & Human Values* 1088.

46 *See* Annalise Riles, *Collateral Knowledge: Legal Reasoning in the Global Financial Markets* (2011).

47 Edward Gibbon, *The Decline and Fall of the Roman Empire, Vol. I*, 95 (1776).

commercial part of the internet – most of the Internet – is regulable through the money."[48] For early internet freedom activists, this concern manifested in a commitment to developing technologies that allowed for anonymous, decentralized, and non-censorable digital transactions in a manner similar to physical currency.[49] For example, in 1993, Eric Hughes penned "A Cypherpunk's Manifesto," which declared that:

> Privacy is necessary for an open society in the electronic age . . . [and] requires anonymous transaction systems . . . We cannot expect . . . large, faceless organizations to grant us privacy out of their beneficence . . . We must defend our own privacy if we expect to have any . . . We the Cypherpunks are dedicated to building anonymous systems . . . We are defending our privacy with . . . electronic money.[50]

For most cypherpunks, an instinctual (left- or right-leaning) skepticism of the state led them to downplay the importance of public monetary reform, in favor of cryptographic technologies that they believed would facilitate competing – and superior – forms of privately issued money. Ironically, however, the most successful of these early efforts, such as David Chaum's Digicash, were ultimately licensed or acquired by commercial banks and credit card companies, whose payments systems were in turn built upon a foundation of public money.[51]

In the mid- to late-2000s, the previously nascent digital consumer finance industry began to expand exponentially, driven by new developments in hardware and software infrastructure, as well as widespread skepticism toward traditional banking institutions in the aftermath of the global financial crisis.[52] In particular, the rapid proliferation of mobile phones capable of processing transactions and storing value locally allowed consumers to eschew traditional point-of-sale payments devices in favor of "digital wallets" that they could carry in their pockets, wherever they went. This, in turn, provided a new entry point

48 Sommer, *supra* at 1190–91.

49 *See, e.g.*, David Chaum, *Blind Signatures for Untraceable Payments, in* Advances in Cryptology Proceedings of Crypto 82, 199 (David Chaum, Ronald Rivest, & Alan Sherman eds., 1982).

50 Eric Hughes, A *Cypherpunk's Manifesto* (March 9, 1993), www.activism.net/cypherpunk/manifesto.html.

51 DigiCash, *DigiCash's Ecash to be Issued by Deutsche Bank* (May 7, 1996), www.chaum.com/ecash/articles/1996/05–07-96%20-%20DigiCash_s%20Ecash%E2%84%A2%20to%20be%20Issued%20by%20Deutsche%20Bank.pdf. Indeed, many of the most prominent early cypherpunks came from professional backgrounds in the corporate sector. Jamie Bartlett, Cypherpunks Write Code, 104(2) *Am. Scientist* 120 (2016).

52 *See, e.g.*, Douglas Arner, Janos Nathan Barberis, & Ross Buckley, The Evolution of Fintech: A New Post-Crisis Paradigm? 47 *Geo. J. Int'l L.* 1271 (2015–2016).

into the financial services sector for telecommunications and technology companies, particularly in communities with limited access to more traditional banking services.[53]

Around the same time, advances in cryptographic and consensus-driven data management software, combined with the growth of social media-driven 'meme' culture, set the stage for the emergence of Bitcoin and similar 'crypto-currency' and 'blockchain' initiatives. Many of the early and most vocal proponents of these initiatives presented them as natural successors to the earlier cypherpunks dream of a truly decentralized, privacy-respecting internet.[54] In doing so, however, they often disavowed the social nature of money itself, encapsulated most succinctly in the claim by early Facebook investors, the Winklevoss twins, that by investing in Bitcoin, they had "elected to put [their] money and faith in a mathematical framework that is free of politics and human error."[55]

In reality, however, this "second wave" of digital currency pioneers, like their predecessors in the 1990s, were from the outset deeply entangled in existing legal and regulatory structures.[56] Moreover, they proved highly vulnerable to capture or absorption by established financial and technological interests. Indeed, many of the promising early "cryptocurrency" projects have since either devolved into yet another layer of the formal banking system, or been superseded by "stablecoin" projects that combine private payments technology with a stable underlying value based upon existing public money. Or, in some cases, both.

53 *See, e.g.*, Rohan Grey, Mobile Money in Developing Countries: Macroeconomic Implications and Potential, *Global Institute for Sustainable Prosperity Working Paper No. 116* (June 2017), www.global-isp.org/wp-content/uploads/WP-116.pdf.

54 *See, e.g.*, Sarah Jeong, *The Bitcoin Protocol as Law and the Politics of a Stateless Currency* (May 8, 2013), https://papers.ssrn.com/sol3/papers.cfm?abstract_id=2294124.

55 Nathaniel Popper & Peter Lattman, Never Mind Facebook; Winklevoss Twins Rule in Digital Money, *New York Times* (April 11, 2013), https://dealbook.nytimes.com/2013/04/11/as-big-investors-emerge-bitcoin-gets-ready-for-its-close-up.<int_i> See also Yanis Varoufakis, *Bitcoin and the Dangerous Fantasy of Apolitical Money* (April 22, 2013), www.yanisvaroufakis.eu/2013/04/22/bitcoin-and-the-dangerous-fantasy-of-apolitical-money.

56 *See, e.g.*, The Law Library of Congress, *Regulation of Cryptocurrency Around the World* (June 2018), www.loc.gov/law/help/cryptocurrency/cryptocurrency-world-survey.pdf; Richard Levin, Aaron Obiren, & Stephanie Osterman, Dread Pirate Roberts, Byzantine Generals, and Federal Regulation of Bitcoin, 27(4) *J. of Tax. & Reg. of Fin. Inst.* 5; Securities and Exchange Commission, *Release No. 81207 – Report of Investigation Pursuant to Section 21(a) of the Securities Exchange Act of 1934: The DAO* (July 25, 2017), www.sec.gov/litigation/investreport/34-81207.pdf; Yuki Furukawa, Former Mt. Gox CEO Mark Karpeles Gets Suspended Jail Term, *Bloomberg* (March 15, 2019), www.bloomberg.com/news/articles/2019-03-15/former-bitcoin-baron-mark-karpeles-gets-suspended-jail-term.

In 2019, Facebook announced plans to launch its own global digital currency, called "Libra," that it claimed would be provided as a "public good," despite being governed by a Facebook-led conglomerate that included commercial banks, tech giants, and credit card companies.[57] In the wake of considerable public backlash and regulatory skepticism, Libra has since pivoted toward a "stablecoin" approach that fuses a new transnational payments ecosystem on top of existing domestic public monetary infrastructure.[58] Ostensibly, Libra's goal is to facilitate global peer-to-peer and consumer-to-business payments through existing web-based platforms. In practice, however, it provides yet another opportunity for Facebook (and its corporate partners) to generate and collect data on a 2+ billion consumer base, and to further perfect their already considerably detailed social graphs of the entire human race.[59]

Notwithstanding its amorphous business model,[60] the sheer scale and scope of Libra's ambition – that is, to become the "internet of money"[61] – has ignited a sense of urgency among policymakers as to the need for digital public monetary reform. In 2019, for example, Benoit Couere, head of the Bank of International Settlements' "Innovation Hub" and former governor of the European Central Bank, described Libra as a "wake-up call," and argued that "whatever fate awaits private digital money, they will likely change the international monetary and financial system in one way or another, either directly or by driving global central banks to innovate."[62] That same year, during a Congressional hearing with Libra founder, David Marcus, US

57 Libra, White Paper (June 2019, rev. April 2020), https://libra.org/en-US/white-paper. *See also* Josh Constine, Facebook Announces Libra Cryptocurrency: All You Need to Know, *TechCrunch* (June 18, 2019), https://techcrunch.com/2019/06/18/facebook-libra.

58 Libra, *supra*.

59 *See, e.g.* Americans for Financial Reform & Demand Progress, *Banking on Surveillance: The Libra 'Black' Paper* (June 2020), https://ourfinancialsecurity.org/wp-content/uploads/2020/06/Libra-Black-Paper-FINAL-2.pdf.

60 *See, e.g.*, Dirk Zetzsche, Ross Buckley, & Douglas Arner, Regulating Libra: The Transformative Potential of Facebook's Cryptocurrency and Possible Regulatory Responses, *European Banking Institute Working Paper Series 2019/44* (July 2019), https://papers.ssrn.com/sol3/Papers.cfm?abstract_id=3414401; Raúl Carrillo, Don't Buy What Zuckerburg's Selling on Libra, *American Banker* (October 22, 2019), www.americanbanker.com/opinion/dont-buy-what-zuckerbergs-selling-on-libra; Raúl Carrillo Following Mark Zuckerburg's Hearing, Facebook's Libra Project Hangs in the Balance, *The American Prospect* (November 5, 2019), https://prospect.org/power/mark-zuckerberg-congressional-hearing-facebook-libra-project.

61 Libra, *supra*.

62 Benoît Cœuré, *Digital Challenges to the International Monetary and Financial System*, Panel Remarks at the Banque Centrale du Luxembourg-Toulouse School of Economics Conference on "The Future of the International Monetary System" (September 17, 2019), www.ecb.europa.eu/press/key/date/2019/html/ecb.sp190917~9b63e0ea23.en.html.

Representative Ayanna Pressley (D.-Mass.) noted that "the reason that [Facebook] even has this opportunity to pursue [a digital currency] is because the Federal Reserve has failed . . . to offer Americans an equitable, reliable, efficient, safe and secure system to access and move their monies."[63]

Presently, over eighty percent of central banks around the world are evaluating or experimenting with their own central bank digital currency ("CBDC") systems.[64] Many countries, from China to the Bahamas, are already at the stage of mass rollout, even as many of the underlying practical and legal issues remain unresolved.[65] Many of these issues, including the appropriate balance between social welfare and profit-seeking, privacy and surveillance, and local and global sovereignty, have echoes in earlier debates over the internet, and before that, the international payments system. While it is tempting to reduce such debates to a dichotomous struggle over the merits of state versus market ordering, in reality they cut deeper, implicating the very nature of public governance itself. Consequently, as Moglen has argued, even "when the private parties have reduced their grip we will still have a great deal to accomplish by way of making political freedom."[66]

In 1999, legal theorist Yochai Benkler noted that society was "in the midst of an enclosure movement in our information environment . . . that [would] subject more of the ways in which each of us uses information to someone else's exclusive control."[67] At the time, his focus – like that of many internet theorists – was on the increasingly proprietarian flavor of copyright law as applied to digital networks, and the implications it posed for the future of freedom of speech. While such issues are undoubtedly important, arguably even more fundamental to expressive freedom is the ability to engage in economic activity via money itself. As attorney and journalist Sarah Jeong noted in 2014:

63 C-SPAN, *Facebook Digital Currency* (July 17, 2019), www.c-span.org/video/?462708–4/facebook-digital-currency. *See also* Rohan Grey, Facebook Wants Its Own Currency. That Should Scare Us All, *The Nation* (July 22, 2019), www.thenation.com/article/archive/facebook-libra-currency-digital.

64 Codruta Boar, Henry Holden, & Amber Wadsworth, Impending Arrival – A Sequel to the Survey on Central Bank Digital Currency, Bank of International Settlements Papers No. 107, 3 (January 2020), www.bis.org/publ/bppdf/bispap107.pdf.

65 Jonathan Cheng, China Rolls Out Pilot Test of Digital Currency, *Wall Street Journal* (April 20, 2020), www.wsj.com/articles/china-rolls-out-pilot-test-of-digital-currency-11587385339; Farah Johnson, Complete Bahamian Digital Dollar Roll-Out By Year End, *The Tribune* (February 13, 2020), www.tribune242.com/news/2020/feb/13/complete-bahamian-digital-dollar-roll-out-by-year.

66 Eben Moglen, *Free Software and Free Media*, Speech at the Internet Society of New York (May 3, 2006), https://en.wikisource.org/wiki/Free_Software_and_Free_Media.

67 Yochai Benkler, Free as the Air to Common Use: First Amendment Constraints on Enclosure of the Public Domain, 74(2) *N. Y. U. L. Rev.* 354, 354–55 (1999).

> Money is speech . . . as immensely unpopular as [Citizens United v. Federal Election Commission] is, the court had a point—money is essential to political participation, and restrictions on the use of money in political activities can silence the cause of both the plutocrat and the dissident. But if money is speech, and free speech can require a certain degree of privacy, even anonymity, particularly so when the speaker supports an unpopular political cause—then why don't we have a right to anonymous payments?[68]

Today, the clearest manifestation of this political struggle is the so-called War on Cash; a concerted international campaign by governments and businesses to drive consumers away from physical currency and toward forms of digital money that can be more easily monitored, data-mined, and censored.[69] This "war" is justified on the basis of reducing crime and promoting "efficiency," "inclusion," and, in the aftermath of COVID-19, "public health."[70] In practice, however, it is waged through both soft propaganda and the violent suppression of non-digital payments practices, embodied most starkly in Indian Prime Minister Narendra Modi's 2016 shock-move to demonetize a significant fraction of all high-denomination currency notes in private circulation.[71] While there have been some scattered attempts to resist the tide, such as the recent enactment of a law in the city of Philadelphia prohibiting "cashless" businesses,[72] they have thus far met with only limited success.

If central bank digital currency is the contemporary financial vanguard of the network society's drive to establish a "pervasive global nervous system across [the] planet,"[73] then the War on Cash is its rearguard. What the invention of the telegraph in the nineteenth century began, the eradication of physical currency in the twenty-first century will complete. As Brett Scott

68 Sarah Jeong, Is Bitcoin Free Speech? *Slate* (February 7, 2014), https://slate.com/technology/2014/02/bitcoin-as-free-speech-regulating-cryptocurrency-has-ramifications-for-democracy.html.

69 *See, e.g.*, Brett Scott, The War on Cash, *The Long+Short* (August 19, 2016), https://thelongandshort.org/society/war-on-cash; Daniela Gabor & Sally Brooks, The Digital Revolution in Financial Inclusion: International Development in the Fintech Era, 22(4) *New Pol. Econ.* 1356.

70 *See, e.g.*, Stephen O'Neal, Coronavirus Crisis Accelerates CBDC Race, Cash No Longer Untouchable, *CoinTelegraph* (April 10, 2020), https://cointelegraph.com/news/coronavirus-crisis-accelerates-cbdc-race-cash-no-longer-untouchable.

71 *See, e.g.*, Indrajit Basu, Life After Demonetization: How India's Poor are Paying the Price, *Al Jazeera* (June 14, 2019), www.aljazeera.com/ajimpact/life-demonetisation-india-poor-paying-price-190614135641262.html.

72 *See, e.g.*, Karen Zraick, Philadelphia Bans 'Cashless' Stores Amid Growing Backlash, *New York Times* (March 7, 2019), www.nytimes.com/2019/03/07/business/cashless-stores-philadelphia.html.

73 Leonard Kleinrock, The Invisible Internet, *Internet Society* (October 29, 2019), www.internetsociety.org/blog/2019/10/the-invisible-internet.

observed in 2016, "the Death of Cash means the Rise of Something Else. [The war against the 'War on Cash' is thus a] battle to maintain alternatives to the growing digital panopticon that is emerging all around us."[74] In this sense, perhaps the greatest threat to human freedom in the twenty-first century lies not in the legal enclosure of the digital, but rather the digital enclosure of the analog, and with it, the homogenization and standardization of previously diverse modes of social and economic interaction.

7.4 CONCLUSION

Money, information technologies, and global governance regimes are deeply interconnected. Monetary systems are – at least in part – information systems, capable of both producing new social dynamics, and refracting existing social dynamics through the logic of monetary accumulation. In turn, monetary and informational practices shape, and are shaped by, prevailing legal governance structures.

Over the past nearly two centuries, the increasing digitization of society has transformed both money and information technologies. As the networked society begins to enter its mature phase, decisions we make today regarding the design and regulation of public and private money, the balance between digital and analog modes of monetary activity, and the uses and limits of monetarily significant data, will reverberate for generations to come.

Contemporary debates over the future of digital money thus implicate questions of state sovereignty and global governance that cut to the heart of contemporary international law. Addressing these questions will require international legal scholars and practitioners to embrace new forms of interdisciplinary and practical expertise relating to both money and digital technology, and take responsibility for articulating a just and equitable vision for the future of digital money.

74 Scott, *supra*. *See also* John Haskell & Nathan Tankus, Virtual Currency (in the Shadows of the Money Market), *Just Money* (April 9, 2010), https://justmoney.org/j -haskell-n-tankus-virtual-currency-in-the-shadows-of-the-money-markets.

8

Environment

Usha Natarajan and Kishan Khoday

We live in a time of ecological change. Climate change is occurring alongside other interrelated environmental transformations. We are amid the biggest disruption to Earth's nitrogen cycle in two and a half billion years,[1] and a mass extinction of species for the first time in sixty-six million years.[2] When it comes to climate, the last time there was this much carbon dioxide in the atmosphere was three and a half million years ago.[3] Change on a scale unprecedented in human history combined with our inability to stem these trends thus far contributes to a sense of being at a tipping point – that unless these challenges are addressed effectively and soon, human life will become irrevocably unpredictable and volatile.

Our planetary history evidences cyclical recurrence of such events, but in the past nature played the dominant causal role, whereas this time colossal human injustice is at the heart of the matter. The lifestyles of today's wealthy few are sustained not only by increasing economic inequality but the systemic collapse of ecosystems.[4] The richest twenty percent consumes eighty percent of the world's natural resources and generates over ninety percent of its

Parts of this chapter are abridged with permission from U. Natarajan & J. Dehm, "Where is the Environment? Locating Nature in International Law" (2019) 3 *TWAILR Reflections*; and U. Natarajan, "Climate Justice" in M. Valverde et al. (eds), *The Routledge Handbook of Law & Society* (Routledge, Abingdon, 2021). The views expressed here are those of the authors and do not reflect the views of the United Nations, UNDP or member states.

1 W. Steffen , et al. "Planetary Boundaries: Guiding Human Development on a Changing Planet" (2015) 347(6223) *Science* 1259855.

2 T. Pievani , "The Sixth Mass Extinction: Anthropocene and the Human Impact on Biodiversity" (2014) 25(1) *Rendiconti Lincei* 85–93.

3 M. Willeit , et al., "Mid-Pleistocene Transition in Glacial Cycles Explained by Declining $CO_2$and Regolith Removal" (2019) 5(4) *Science Advances* eaav7337.

4 M. Lawson , et al. *Public Good or Private Wealth* (Oxfam, Oxford, 2019); IPBES, *Global Assessment Report on Biodiversity and Ecosystem Services* (2019) https://ipbes.net/.

pollution and waste.[5] For most people, the poorer eighty percent, their grossly unequal access to natural resources is compounded by also bearing the brunt of the pollution generated by the rich.[6]

Climate change is but one example of such inequities. Anthropogenic climate change (climate change caused by human influences as opposed to natural processes) is caused by increased greenhouse gases in the atmosphere from activities such as burning fossil fuels and changing land use patterns. The United Kingdom, with a population of 60 million, emitted more greenhouse gases than Egypt, Nigeria, Pakistan, and Vietnam combined with a total population of 472 million. One state in the United States, Texas, with a population of 23 million, had a deeper carbon footprint than the whole of sub-Saharan Africa with a total population of 720 million. And the 19 million people in New York state emitted more than the 766 million people living in the 50 least developed countries.[7]

Disparities on such scale are not happenstance, they are systemic. Globalized capitalism ensures the profligately wealthy not only stay rich but get richer.[8] As the impact of climate change is borne by others, there is no immediate incentive for the rich to change their behavior. The poor contribute very little to climate change but are on the frontlines of environmental harm because of their vulnerable geographic locations; lack of resources and regulatory capacity to protect themselves; ongoing extraction of their natural resources and labor to fuel an unequal global economy; and a systemic transfer of pollution from the rich to the poor.[9] Today over 2 billion people are poor or near-poor, and estimates indicate that by 2030 over 100 million more people could fall back into poverty due to climate change.[10] For these reasons, people concerned about climate change frequently turn to the language of justice and look to law, especially international law, for redress.

Unfortunately, international laws have been unsuccessful in stemming climate change. This chapter examines why and points to avenues for fruitful

5 UNDP, *Human Development Report 2019*; *Human Development Report 2007–8*; *Human Development Report 1998* (Oxford University Press, New York).

6 U. Natarajan, Environmental Justice and the Global South in S. Atapattu et al (eds), *The Cambridge Handbook of Environmental Justice and Sustainable Development* (Cambridge University Press, Cambridge, 2021).

7 UNDP, *Human Development Report 2007–8* (Oxford University Press, New York, 2008).

8 D. Hardoon, *An Economy for the 99%* (Oxfam, Oxford, 2017).

9 Natarajan n 6; K. Khoday, *Environmental Justice: Comparative Lessons in Legal Empowerment* (UNDP, New York, 2014).

10 Global Commission on Adaptation & World Resource Institute, *Adapt Now: A Global Call for Leadership on Climate Resilience* (GCA, Rotterdam, 2019).

disciplinary progress. Part 2 considers the turn to international environmental law and provides three reasons why this project has failed. Section 2.1 examines the divide between the rich and poor that has prevented international cooperation on climate change. On the international level, environmentalism and the laws that it fashions are shaped predominantly by those who caused environmental problems, enabling them to indefinitely evade the consequences of their actions. Section 2.2 describes the predetermination of economic and ecological priorities by disciplinary structures, making ecological destruction inevitable. Section 2.3 explains that even if the rich–poor divide is overcome and environmental protection becomes a disciplinary priority, international laws cannot stem climate change because the discipline has an inaccurate and unhealthy understanding of what and where exactly the environment is. Without reconfiguring basic assumptions about nature to more accurately reflect scientific and social realities, international law cannot provide solutions to climate change and other environmental challenges. Part 3 outlines avenues for disciplinary rejuvenation through reconceptualizing foundational disciplinary concepts by incorporating sustainable world views and becoming a genuinely international discipline. International law plays an important part in causing climate change and thus disciplinary transformation is a necessary part of any solution.

8.1 LEGAL FAILURE IN A WARMING WORLD

The climate is in perpetual interaction globally with species extinction, desertification, deforestation, ozone layer damage, increasing pollution, and toxicity of air, water and land. In addition to being interrelated, environmental issues transcend state borders. International law provides a forum to address such issues coherently and cooperatively. Unfortunately, so far international lawyers have been unable to stem environmental harm. For fifty years we brought to bear our treaties, principles, institutions, research, and teaching to create an increasingly specialized and technocratic expertise in international environmental law. Yet each of the above-mentioned crises continues to steadily deteriorate. For instance, the United Nations Framework Conventions on Climate Change and Biodiversity were signed in 1992 at the Rio Earth Summit.[11] Yet more greenhouse gases have been emitted in the last thirty

[11] *UN Framework Convention on Climate Change* (1992) 31 ILM 849; *UN Convention on Biological Diversity* (1992) 31 ILM 818.

years than in all human history,[12] one million species are now at risk of extinction,[13] and other environmental issues such as desertification, deforestation, and pollution have also significantly worsened.[14] Repairing the ozone layer was accomplished through international cooperation, but sadly in a manner highly detrimental to the climate, thus necessitating urgent remedial action now.[15]

Why have international environmental laws failed? The two most frequented critiques are that the rich and poor cannot agree on how to protect the climate (usually called the North–South divide) and a lack of political will (people have other priorities). Such critique allows international lawyers to dodge responsibility for the failures of international environmental law. We point instead to politicians and the private sector for either preventing us from making good laws or, when such laws are made, failing to abide by them. Do unequal economies and fickle electoral politics mean lawyers are not to blame? Letting ourselves off-the-hook allows our disciplinary expertise to proliferate despite extant failures. For example, our inability to regulate climate change on the global level has only spurred a flourishing of climate law-related job opportunities, research funding, degree programs, textbooks, and so on. Indeed, since the advent of international environmental law in the 1970s, we may have struggled to achieve sustainable development but have enjoyed unmitigated success in sustaining the relevance of our expertise. It may be the case that past failures stimulate the search for better legal solutions but, after five decades, we need to consider whether international lawyers are contributing to the problems we claim to solve.

Sections 2.1 and 2.2 posit that international lawyers share the responsibility for environmental harm because we help maintain the North–South divide and shape global priorities. Section 2.3 argues that underlying these two oft-observed critiques is a deeper problem: Our discipline has constructed "the environment" in a manner that endlessly reproduces environmental harm and ensures the impossibility of remedy. That is to say, redistribution of wealth and reordering of political priorities are indispensable to stemming environmental harm, and international lawyers have agency and responsibility to bring about such a transformation. But even such radical change is insufficient unless

12 A. Vaughan, "Global carbon emissions from energy hit a record high," *New Scientist* (26 March 2019) www.newscientist.com/article/2197643-global-carbon-emissions-from-energy-hit-a-record-high-in-2018/#ixzz62sPsy9Xo.

13 IPBES, *Global Assessment Report on Biodiversity and Ecosystem Services* (2019) https://ipbes.net/.

14 Ibid.

15 Ibid.

accompanied by a more accurate understanding of what exactly it is that we are attempting to regulate.

8.2 EMPIRE AS APOCALYPSE

International law has a particular understanding of the environment stemming from western environmentalism in the 1960s and 1970s. Stirrings of environmental consciousness in these decades are attributable to two factors. First, the middle classes of Western Europe and North America began feeling the impact of industrialization: higher levels of air and water pollution, more oil spills, fears of nuclear fallout, and so on. Second, advances in western science increased public awareness about the complexity, uniqueness, and fragility of our planet. The first pictures of Earth from space were symbolic of this knowledge for western environmental movements at the time.[16] In the United States, these decades witnessed the 1963 *Clean Air Act*, 1972 *Clean Water Act*, and establishment of the Environmental Protection Agency in 1970.

From these domestic developments stemmed international law's engagement with environmentalism at the 1972 *Stockholm Conference on the Human Environment*, usually identified as the genesis of international environmental law. In the wake of Stockholm came other summits (notably the 1992 *Rio Earth Summit*, the 2002 *Johannesburg Summit*, and 2012 *Rio +20*), treaties (including Framework Conventions on Climate Change and Biodiversity, as well as treaties on hazardous wastes, endangered species, and protecting the ozone layer, among others),[17] and legal principles (such as the principle of common but differentiated responsibilities, the precautionary principle, and so on), through which the specialization evolves and constitutes itself.

This origin story provides the textbook introduction to international environmental law.[18] According to this narrative, the "environment" first appears within international law in the 1970s as the object of our stewardship, as this was when international lawyers assumed such protection to be both desirable and possible. Standard texts observe that humanity's understanding of nature changed in the 1960s. In the past, states and peoples were exhorted to control nature through science, industry, and modernity. But, with the advent of

16 S. Jasanoff, "Heaven and Earth: The Politics of Environmental Images" in S. Jasanoff and M. Martello (eds), *Earthly Politics: Local and Global in Environmental Governance* (MIT, Cambridge, 2004),

17 *International Environmental Agreement Database Project* hosts a catalog of laws: https://iea.uoregon.edu/.

18 See eg., P. Sands and J. Peel, *Principles of International Environmental Law* (2012); P. Birnie, et al. *International Law and the Environment* (2009).

environmentalism, humanity turned away from mere mastery and toward protecting and cherishing nature. Thus, the environment was created as an object of international regulation.

While conventionally narrated as a global paradigm shift, this type of environmentalism is the product of a particular western history and culture. Such a conceptualization of the "environment" is not necessarily self-evident to, or shared by, most of the world for whom the story started much earlier. Through centuries of colonialism, genocide, slavery, apartheid, and racial discrimination, western states systemically looted the natural resources of the third world to fuel the accumulation of western wealth.[19] Western industrialization, fuelled by an ever-expanding reliance on fossil fuels, was predicated on accessing the natural resources and labor of their colonies.[20]

A core tenet of the colonial enterprise was to more efficiently exploit nature.[21] European Enlightenment philosophy understood the control of nature as "a primordial act, transforming chaos into order, imbuing the environment with human form – a divine-like act to craft a new world."[22] From the seventeenth century onward, this philosophy increasingly informed the so-called civilizing mission. Not only was nature a "standing reserve of resources for man to serve his development,"[23] but the "[m]astery of nature came to be regarded as an expression of cultural superiority and the key mark of civilization."[24] Natives were incentivized to internalize these hierarchies through brute force, access to material privileges through collusion with imperial masters, and promises of dignity and salvation through mirroring western culture.[25]

Western understandings of progress were more systematically universalized through the decolonization process by conditioning third world independence upon a commitment to industrial development.[26] While postcolonial states adopted varied stances on the spectrum between capitalism and communism, including non-alignment, societies that dared disavow industrial

19 For our usage of the term "third world," see U. Natarajan, "TWAIL and the Environment" in A. Philippopoulos-Mihalopolous & V. Brooks (eds), *Research Methods in Environmental Law* (Elgar, Cheltenham, 2017).

20 C. Ross, *Ecology and Power in the Age of Empire* (Oxford University Press, Oxford, 2017); J. Beattie et al. eds), *Eco-Cultural Networks and the British Empire* (Bloomsbury, London, 2015).

21 I. Porras, "Appropriating Nature" (2014) 27(3) *Leiden Journal of International Law* 641.

22 P. Fitzpatrick, *Mythology of Modern Law* (Routledge, London, 1992) 10–11.

23 Ibid 2.

24 Ibid.

25 U. Natarajan, "TWAIL and the Environment: The State of Nature, the Nature of the State, and the Arab Spring" (2013) 14 *Oregon Review of International Law* 177.

26 Ibid.

development altogether were denied sovereignty, as evidenced most clearly by the ongoing self-determination struggles of many tribal and Indigenous peoples.[27] Hence, colonization forever transformed the landscape of the global south, with devastating consequences for ecosystems and societies.[28] Not only does much of the greenhouse gas infusing our atmosphere today originate from the colonial period,[29] but also, emissions that arise in the postcolonial era are the legacy of a philosophy of violence against nature and non-western peoples.

The formative role of international law in universalizing and normalizing these values and hierarchies is well-canvassed by the Third World Approaches to International Law (TWAIL) movement, so we will not revisit it here except to reiterate Anghie's canonical observation that the discipline of international law emerged through the colonial encounter.[30] International law originated in Europe, in the context of enterprises setting out to access riches in the non-European world, through lawyers justifying such exploitation in universal terms.[31] Our disciplinary evolution is intimately shaped by colonization, decolonization, and imperialism.[32] The environmental consequences of such a history were that, for the third world, international environmental law was not seen as a new era of environmental stewardship but symptomatic of the longstanding use of international law to universalize western values.[33]

Western states' desire to globally regulate the harmful consequences of industrial development in the 1970s came too close upon the heels of the south finally achieving a degree of economic independence, raising fears of "environmental colonialism".[34] The third world's responses to environmental change included unsuccessful attempts to articulate different visions of

27 U. Natarajan, "Decolonization in Third and Fourth Worlds" in A. Alvez et al (eds), *Decolonizing Law* (Elgar, Cheltenham, 2020).

28 K. Mickelson & U. Natarajan, "Reflections on Rhetoric and Rage: Bandung and Environmental Injustice" in L. Eslava et al. (eds), *Bandung, Global History and International Law* (Cambridge University Press, Cambridge, 2017).

29 H. Ritchie, "Who has Contributed Most to Global CO_2 Emissions?," *Our World in Data* (1 October 2019) https://ourworldindata.org/contributed-most-global-co2.

30 A. Anghie, *Imperialism, Sovereignty and the Making of International Law* (Cambridge University Press, Cambridge, 2007)

31 Ibid; Porras n 21.

32 J. T. Gathii, "'TWAIL': A Brief History of its Origins, its Decentralized Network and Tentative Bibliography" (2011) 3 *Trade, Law & Development* 26 provides a helpful entry into the large body of TWAIL scholarship that elaborates on this point.

33 E. DeLoughrey & G. Handley, *Postcolonial Ecologies* (Oxford University Press, Oxford, 2011) 5–6.

34 A. Agarwal & S. Narain, *Global Warming in an Unequal World* (Center for Science & Environment, New Delhi, 1990).

development that promoted a more just international economic order,[35] including forms of self-reliance that accounted for both the "inner limit" of satisfying human needs as well as the "outer limit" of planetary boundaries.[36] When international climate laws were negotiated in 1992, third world stances aligned with their position on previous international environmental issues: an insistence on legal recognition that the rich caused climate change and should shoulder most of the responsibility for fixing it. Indeed, international law principles such as sustainable development and common but differentiated responsibilities articulate precisely this.[37] But international law has been unable to turn these principles into action by getting the rich to change their behavior.

Under the umbrella of the 1992 *United Nations Framework Convention on Climate Change (UNFCCC)*, climate law initially allocated strict and clear emission reduction targets to rich states through the 1997 *Kyoto Protocol*.[38] However, the United States – the world's biggest emitter then – refused to participate and this demotivated other rich states from meeting their targets. Instead, the US led a movement to replace *Kyoto* with the 2016 *Paris Agreement*, which allows all states rich and poor to volunteer their own aspirational non-binding targets.[39] The result is a regime that still exonerates the poor from responsibility for climate change but has not modified the harmful practices of the rich. Lucrative extractive industries today are responsible for 50 percent of greenhouse gas emissions (as well as 80 percent of biodiversity loss),[40] while the poor remain on the frontlines of climate catastrophes. Thus, in three decades of international climate law, not only has more greenhouse gas been emitted than ever before, but the US has led a concerted effort to erode legal acknowledgment that climate justice matters.

Although international climate law has been unsuccessful in stemming greenhouse gases, it remains an important terrain where climate justice struggles are articulated and contested. For instance, in the lead up to the *UNFCCC*, the 1987 Brundtland Commission introduced the concept of sustainable development.[41] At the time it had a straightforward meaning:

35 *Coçoyoc Declaration*, UN Doc AC2/292, Mexico (8–12 October 1974).
36 J Galtung et al (eds), *Self-Reliance: A Strategy for Development* (1980).
37 S. Alam et al (eds), *International Environmental Law and the Global South* (Cambridge University Press, Cambridge, 2015).
38 *Kyoto Protocol to the United Nations Framework Convention on Climate Change* (1998) 37 ILM 22.
39 M. Jernnas & B. Linner, "A Discursive Cartography of Nationally Determined Contributions to the Paris Climate Agreement" (2019) 55 *Global Environment Change* 73.
40 International Resource Panel, *Global Resources Outlook* (UNEP, Nairobi, 2019).
41 Brundtland Commission, *Our Common Future* (Oxford University Press, Oxford, 1987).

development that meets the needs of the present without compromising the ability of future generations to meet their own needs. Sustainable development kept economic development within the absorptive capacity of ecosystems, acknowledging systemic limits. In line with this, in the years that followed, climate scientists estimated the maximum change in global temperature that could sustain human life and calculated the remaining emissions quota to remain within this safe zone. Their calculations indicated that between 1990 and 2050 the world should reduce its overall emissions by 50 per cent. As per the principle of common but differentiated responsibilities, the United Nations advised that rich states reduce their emissions by 80 per cent by 2050.[42] Not only were these obligations ignored by many rich states, but in the decades that followed, the concept of sustainable development also lost all trace of its original meaning. Today, it is used in such a broad variety of contexts that it is routinely exploited for the purposes of obfuscation and double-speak.[43]

Both the regulatory and symbolic aspects of climate law continue to matter a great deal to states and peoples. Third world states were cognizant that the shift from *Kyoto* to *Paris* not only meant a shift from mandatory to voluntary standards but a sharp turn away from the principle of common but differentiated responsibilities. The US argued that "emerging" economies such as China and India could no longer be considered poor, hence differentiation between responsibilities of rich and poor states should be done away with, and instead all states should choose voluntary targets. But it is possible to address rising third world emissions without shifting to voluntary targets or distracting from the dominance of western emissions. Almost half the greenhouse gas in the atmosphere today was produced by western states before 2000, and their emissions have been increasing too.[44]

Leading up to *Paris*, "emerging" states proposed multiple ways to curb their increasing emissions in equitable ways. India proposed a recalculation based on per capita emissions in the past, present, and future. China suggested targets based on carbon intensity per gross domestic product. Mexico and Indonesia added that recalculations could also include projected increases of gross domestic product. Brazil recommended that rich country commitments be based on proportionality between historical responsibilities, current greenhouse gas concentration levels, and related temperature increases. Bolivia united aspects of all these approaches, dividing available emissions based on

42 UNDP (2007–8) n 5, 111.

43 G. Rist, *The History of Development* (Zed, London, 2014).

44 Ritchie n 29.

a set of indexes that considered historical responsibility, per capita ecological footprints, technological and economic capability, and development levels. Calculation on these bases were in line with *Kyoto* estimates, allocating more than two-thirds of the remaining carbon budget to the global south, with the global north needing to radically reduce because it used up most of its budget.[45] Ultimately, the US defeated each of these proposals as a precondition for its participation in *Paris*, rendering a regulatory and symbolic setback for climate justice.

In the wake of spectacularly unsuccessful attempts to reduce emissions, international climate lawyers today increasingly focus on trying to get rich states to help poor states adapt to climate change through transferring technological and financial aid. Rich states routinely block attempts to develop legal mechanisms for redress. For instance, reparation claims potentially arise under state responsibility for transboundary harm and the resulting loss and damage. But rich states prefer the language of aid and largesse to that of causation and responsibility. By channeling their contributions through global funds, rich states control the distribution of finance and technical know-how for climate adaptation. To make matters worse, regular assurances of scaled-up funding for climate adaptation and resilience are echoed in international meetings, yet rich states are yet to deliver on the bulk of it.[46]

8.3 PREDETERMINED CHOICES

Climate injustice is reproduced not only through the legacies of imperialism but the related phenomenon of disciplinary fragmentation. Climate struggles usually transpire in the context of international environmental law, which aims to protect the natural environment. However, the fossil fuels that cause climate change are regulated under a different legal regime. International law characterizes fossil fuels as natural resources, which are governed by the principle of maximizing efficient exploitation, through a mixture of private international law (international business transactions) and public international law (international economic, trade, and investment law). International environmental law focuses on mitigating the harmful environmental consequences of development through managing pollution and waste. At the same time, international economic laws encourage a type of development fueled by the increasing consumption of natural resources.

45 Jernnas & Linner n 39.
46 GCA n 10.

When competing governance objectives are directed at an identical object, the result is regulatory dysfunction. When the two legal regimes collide, economic law inevitably prevails as it has a much deeper disciplinary history. Our disciplinary origins lie in doctrines that allowed European private actors to exploit natural resources elsewhere, whether Vitoria's arguments for free commerce in the Americas or Grotius' defense of the Dutch East India Company's untrammelled pursuit of colonial labor and resources.[47] The drive to economically develop in this exploitative vein has remained a propelling force of our disciplinary evolution ever since.[48]

Indeed, the power of private law over the public imagination overshadows the climate regime itself, which in both *Kyoto* and *Paris* turns to economic incentives for climate solutions.[49] The "green economy" and "green growth" are our supposed salvation, with blind faith that capitalism will simultaneously solve the problems it creates. This contradiction is epitomized in ostensibly virtuous calls for more efficient use of fossil fuels, instead of directly tackling the problem of overconsumption. Such approaches ultimately exacerbate climate change through by making more fossil fuels available for unlimited (albeit more efficient) use. Indeed, many so-called green solutions, from biofuels to electric vehicles, from carbon offsets to carbon trading, are creative ways to fuel economic growth but do not stabilize the climate. Whether we like it or not, economy and ecology are inextricable, as are the chains that link consumption and waste, as are natural resources and the environment. International lawyers' ability to compartmentalize them produces convenient regulatory schizophrenia that allows environmentalism itself to be captured by pro-market forces in the untrammelled pursuit of economic growth.

Notwithstanding western narratives of stewardship that gave rise to international environmental law and Enlightenment myths of limitless progress that drive international economic law,[50] the environment is more than the object of our protection; it is more than a resource for economic activity. It encompasses all life, all human endeavor. The segregation of environmental concerns from other aspects of public and private international law predetermines disciplinary priorities and prevents humane and orderly climate response. To take the example that provokes perhaps the greatest fear within rich states, it is estimated that hundreds of millions of people are being displaced from the third world as a result of climate change.[51] International

[47] Porras n 21, Anghie n 30.

[48] S. Pahuja, *Decolonising International Law* (Cambridge University Press, Cambridge, 2011).

[49] J. Hickel & G. Kallis, "Is Green Growth Possible?," *New Political Economy* (2019).

[50] Rist n 43.

[51] GCA n 10.

law currently addresses population movement in such limited ways that it cannot conceive of a shift in our planet's habitable zones. Refugee law provides international protection only for a narrow category of people who face specific extreme forms of discrimination (0.34% of the global population has refugee status).[52] Everyone else crossing an international border is dependent on the discretion of host states for permission. Such a legal framework obfuscates the mass protracted displacement habitually produced by dominant development patterns so systemically destructive that they foment conflict, insecurity, inequality, drought, famine, desertification, environmental toxicity, and of course climate change.[53] Yet attempts to provide redress through the *Paris Agreement* for those displaced by climate change, including extreme cases where entire sovereign territories are submerging, were deferred by rich states.[54]

8.4 WHERE IS THE 'ENVIRONMENT'?

North–south inequities and regulatory dysfunction are symptomatic of a more fundamental problem: conceptualizing the environment as the object of international regulation risks, scientific inaccuracy, and hubris. The foundational role of the environment in shaping economy and human migration illustrates the broader point that the environment underlies every area of international law as it provides the basis for life. International lawyers cannot physically separate ourselves from the environment. Yet we occupy a conceptual position outside it from which we putatively observe and govern. Such a standpoint can only be understood by tracing its cultural evolution within western modern thought. Argyrou in *The Logic of Environmentalism* characterizes western modernity as having a tendency toward "metaphysical totalizations" stemming from "the need to make a decision about what exists in its entirety."[55] The western modern subject is compelled to venture beyond the world because "it is only from such an external position that the boundaries of the world can be drawn and knowledge of what exists guaranteed."[56]

52 UNHCR, *Global Trends* (UNHCR, Geneva, 2019).

53 I. Awad & U. Natarajan, "Migration Myths and the Global South," *Cairo Review of Global Affairs* (Summer 2018).

54 O. Karasapan, "Refugees: Displaced from the Paris Agreement?," *Brookings Institute* (7 December 2015) www.brookings.edu/blog/future-development/2015/12/07/refugees-displaced-from-the-paris-climate-change-agreement/.

55 V. Argyrou, *The Logic of Environmentalism* (Berghahn, Oxford, 2005) 102.

56 Ibid.

As with other modern disciplines, international law continually adopts such external postures. Fitzpatrick and Anghie,[57] among others, observe how international law is justified and dynamited by the continuous assertion of universal values from a professed position of external objectivity. This is followed by the identification of those places and people that remain unaware of such values despite their ostensive universality, necessitating the creation of laws to enlighten them. In the context of a discipline that continually makes such governance moves, international environmental law can be better understood. It is the necessary culmination of the western legal enterprise, enabling the ultimate modern move of casting international law around everything: "the environment". Aptly symbolized by the first photographs of Earth from space, environmentalism as it arose in the United States in the 1960s assumed a conceptual posture external to Earth, allowing it sufficient distance to look back and see a single globe. Argyrou observes that this position of externality "is to say, in effect, that it is we who surround the environment, not the other way around."[58]

The environment cannot be accurately understood as an object of governance because exiting it is as much a conceptual impossibility as a scientific one. As scientific knowledge about the complex web of interactions that create and sustain life accumulates, we realisatomisede how far we are from fully understanding nature and ourselves as part of it. Instead of producing regulatory solutions, the law's ability to conceptually isolate itself from the natural world has helped create and foment environmental catastrophes. Law plays a crucial role in transforming a unified planet into discrete sovereign territories, in converting nature into exchangeable property, in turning interconnected ecosystems into realms of infinite commodification and exchange, and in extracting and conceptually isolating an atomized human individual from the intertwined ecosystems that create life.[59] Law not only enables environmental destruction but understands the natural environment in a manner that ensures the impossibility of remedy. To remedy this conceptual dislocation of nature requires an exit from the confines of western modernity.

8.5 LOCATING NATURE

Environmentalism as it exists today within international law reconfirms the position of the west as the source of all acceptable meaning. But the extant

[57] Fitzpatrick n 22; Anghie n 30.

[58] Argyrou n 55, 95.

[59] U. Natarajan & K. Khoday, "Locating Nature: Making and Unmaking International Law" (2014) 27 *Leiden Journal of International Law* 573.

failures of international environmental law demand alternatives. A genuinely international solution to environmental problems requires an openness to diverse philosophical and theoretical understandings of the relationship between nature and law. Disciplinary willingness to embrace those understandings of nature that gauge more accurately the parameters of our ability to govern it offers us a pathway to address environmental crises and toward more sustainable ways of life. Environmental change on the scale we are witnessing now seriously challenges knowledge production within social sciences because many of these disciplines assumed the stability of natural systems.[60] When nature is destabilized, the foundations of economics, politics, and law need to change; and an openness to elementary transformation increases the likelihood of disciplinary responses being useful and relevant to a time of environmental change.

The environment cannot be the subject of a discrete disciplinary specialization. Understandings about the natural world underpin and organize the entire international legal order, and these assumptions need to be identified, unpacked, and radically reworked if we are to think our way out of destructive development patterns and ecological crises. This is the premise of the *Locating Nature Project*, an ongoing effort to unite international lawyers from all continents together with scholars from cognate disciplines to unpack the central constructs of international law and remake them in a more inclusive and sustainable vein. What role have international law concepts such as sovereignty, jurisdiction, territory, development, human rights, and so on, played in destroying the natural environment? How can we reconfigure these concepts to promote sustainable living? What are the lessons we can draw from local, domestic, and transnational developments usually ignored or silenced?[61]

An ecological basis for international law unmakes disciplinary commitments to Eurocentrism and anthropocentrism. Human agency does not by itself shape the world and nature is not a mechanistic automaton at our service. Rather, humanity is in constant interaction within natural systems including the climate.[62] More than an academic exercise, these insights already contest dominant legal frameworks and transform them. Examples

60 B. Latour, *Down to Earth* (Polity, Cambridge, 2018) 43; *Facing Gaia* (Polity, Cambridge, 2017) 8.

61 K. Khoday, et al, "Introduction to the Locating Nature Symposium" (2014) 27(3) *Leiden Journal of International Law* 571; U. Natarajan & J. Dehm (eds), *Locating Nature: Making and Unmaking International Law* (Cambridge University Press, Cambridge, forthcoming 2022).

62 J Bennett, *Vibrant Matter* (2010) ix.

include peasant movements in Ecuador that demand the right to preserve their way of life; class actions on behalf of future generations in the Philippines; transnational tribal mobilization against extractive industries across South Asia; law reform recognizing the rights of Mother Earth in Bolivia; recognizing the legal personality of non-human entities in India and New Zealand; the rights of Indigenous and Tribal peoples to hunt protected species in the Arctic; climate justice demands of sinking small island states; massive environmental protests across China; international rights of nature tribunals; and Mother Earth summits held alongside international environmental law summits.[63] Targeting entrenched transnational and global structures of violence that reproduced inequality and ecological destruction for centuries, the high stakes are evidenced most starkly in the increasing murder of environmental defenders worldwide.[64]

Despite these risks, movements continue to grow, necessitated by environmental change looming large and inescapable. Global climate protests are also increasing and show no signs of abatement. Such movements increasingly prioritize a "process of transversalism" as opposed to universalism, where diverse groups generate "cross-identity solidarities and inter-ideological hybridizations."[65] In the same way, international law can engage the diversity of legal traditions in the world so that "the global and local come together, not by way of synecdoche ... but in a way that each interrupts and distorts the

[63] La Via Campesina, https://viacampesina.org/en/; *Minors Oposa v Factoran*, Philippines Supreme Court GR No 101083 (30 July 1993); Samina Luthfa, "Transnational Ties and Reciprocal Tenacity: Resisting Mining in Bangladesh with Transnational Coalition" (2017) 51(1) *Sociology*; *Ley de Derechos de la Madre Tierra*, Bolivia, Ley 071 (21 December 2010); *Lalit Miglani v State of Uttarakhand & others*, WPPIL 140/2015 (High Court of Uttarakhand) 2017 [64]; *Mohd Salim v State of Uttarakhand & others*, WPPIL 126/2014 (High Court of Uttarakhand) 2017 [19]; *Te Awa Tupua (Whanganui River Claims Settlement) Act*, New Zealand, Public Act 2017 no 7 (20 March 2017); *EU Regulation 2015/1775 on Trade in Seal Products* (6 October 2015); L van Scheik et al, "Fighting an Existential Threat: Small Island States Bringing Climate Change to the UN Security Council," *Planetary Security Initiative Policy Brief* (March 2018); Klaus Mühlhahn, "Can Environmental Activism Succeed in China?," *Literary Hub* (28 January 2019) https://lithub.com/can-environmental-activism-succeed-in-china/; *Rights of Nature Tribunals*, http://therightsofnature.org/rights-of-nature-tribunal/; *Peoples' World Conference on Climate*, "Bolivia calls for urgent high-level talks on cutting climate pollution" (17 June 2011) https://pwccc.wordpress.com/; *Peoples' Summit on Climate Change COP20*, 'For Climate Justice and a World fit to Be Lived In' (8–11 December 2014) http://rio20.net/en/iniciativas/peoples%E2%80%99-summit-on-climate-change-cop20/.

[64] Global Witness, *Enemies of the State* (30 July 2019) www.globalwitness.org/en-gb/campaigns/environmental-activists/enemies-state/.

[65] A. Salleh, et al, "From Sociological Imagination to Ecological Imagination" in J. Marshall & L. Connor (eds), *Environmental Change and the World's Futures* (Routledge, London, 2016).

other . . . the local and often unassimilable aspects of culture and history . . . uphold a sense of alterity while still engaging a global imaginary."[66]

8.6 CONCLUSION

Climate change confronts international lawyers with the systemic injustice we help create and maintain. It brings to the fore a sense of crisis, of standing on a precipice where, if greenhouse gas emissions are not abated soon, we will be precipitated into a future of irreversible harm and chaos. But climate change is not an emergency we can react to with specialized legal regimes, extreme measures, and extra-budgetary resources. It has been a long time in the making and the inevitable consequence of a legal system that protects the rich and powerful from the harmful consequences of their actions. International law helps structure a system of climate apartheid,[67] where the privileged few treat everything and everyone else as superfluous.

For those interested in mitigating climate change, there are several reasons why international law deserves our attention. The discipline provides the global framework for facilitating and normalizing efficient fossil fuel extractivism. Hence dismantling this legal structure is an inescapable part of stemming climate change. Without such harmful structures, international law could potentially play a useful role in addressing environmental problems. The complexity and globality of environmental problems such as climate change would benefit from a degree of international cooperation and coordination. Furthermore, seeking alternatives to dominant development patterns that have proven damaging to the environment requires an openness to more sustainable world views and a genuinely international forum would allow for such voices to emerge and be nurtured in a helpful way. For international lawyers, a sense of justice demands that we take responsibility for the suffering we inflict. More fundamentally, climate change points to basic disciplinary misconceptions, and reminds us that it is neither desirable nor possible to indefinitely separate ourselves from our environment.

66 S. O'Brien, "Articulating a World of Difference: Ecocriticism, Postcolonialism and Globalization" (Winter 2001) 170/171 *Canadian Literature* 140; K. Khoday & U. Natarajan, "Fairness and International Environmental Law from Below" (2012) 25 *Leiden Journal of International Law* 415.

67 P. Alston, *Climate Change and Poverty: Report of the Special Rapporteur on Extreme Poverty and Human Rights*, UN Doc A/HRC/41/39 (25 June 2019); Ban Ki-moon & Patrick Verkooijen, "Time is Running Out to Stop the Forces Driving a New Climate Apartheid," *Devex Opinion* 18 October 2019) www.devex.com/news/opinion-time-is-running-out-to-stop-the-forces-driving-a-new-climate-apartheid-95841.

Environmental change on the scale we are witnessing today demands an acceptance that we were mistaken in thinking we could construct and then govern the environment. It necessitates that we transcend the confines of western modernity and embrace instead other narratives about our relationship with the natural world that more accurately estimate human ability to regulate it. Beyond protection and remedy, causation and responsibility, loss and damage, liability and insurance, we need to make disciplinary space for the different, uncomfortable, unknown, and unknowable. Through relinquishing our conviction that western philosophy is the epitome of human thought, and more importantly that humans are the epitome of the natural world, we could break our illusion of separateness from each other and from the natural environment and notice that it is in fact nature that governs us.

9

Health

Sara De Vido

2020 will be remembered by posterity as the year of COVID-19 crisis, which has spread around the entire world starting from China. In such a complex moment of world history, it seems difficult as an international lawyer to conceive possible alternatives to the current legal approach used to tackle issues of health, which, in my understanding, must incorporate considerations on both global health and the individual human right to health, along with the environment. Aggregated data on death rate, scientific information on how contagious the coronavirus is, and the discovery of vaccines are surrounded by an aura of incertitude, and have been the object of a wave of misinformation that this globalized world has fueled, increasing the (understandable) chaos.[1] Yet, the advent of the 2020 pandemic has not come out of the blue. It has been years, at least since the spread of SARS, that scientists have warned against a possible pandemic that could reach the magnitude of the Spanish influenza of 1918.[2] What went wrong? Why were states not prepared for the pandemic? Why has the response been so far predominantly "national"? The ongoing emergency has also disoriented lawyers, who have reacted to the health crisis through an endless amount of first glance posts, connecting the pandemic to any possible sector, and has produced a feeling of inadequacy of the present state of the art of the law, and not only of international law. The approach might be twofold: either we abandon international law altogether or we take

[1] See Laurie Garrett, "The Art of Medicine. Covid-19: The Medium is the Message," *The Lancet* 395 (March 2020): 942–943, and on misinformation during the pandemic, Marko Milanovic, "Viral Misinformation and the Freedom of Expression: Part I, II, III," *EJIL: Talk!* (April 2020).

[2] See, for example, the warning launched by 32 scientists, "Scientists' Warning to Humanity: Microorganisms and Climate Change," *Nature Reviews* 17 (2019): 569–586, and www.environmentandsociety.org/mml/pandemics-context for a series of articles and databases on the history of the pandemics with shocking lessons never learned from the past.

the challenge to propose alternatives to the traditional mindset of international lawyers, even taking the risk of being, to a certain extent, idealistic.

The pandemic urges a reconsideration of existing rules on global health and the human right to health, which was needed well before its outbreak and seems non-deferrable now. In the first part of this chapter (Part 1), my main argument is that the weaknesses underlying the system depend on the fact that international law, in its current state of the art, is anthropocentric and patriarchal. This argument echoes feminist concerns,[3] which I thoroughly endorse, pointing out that it is not only the male structure of international law that has to worry, but also the human-centered (adjective that should be linked to a part of humanity, as I will further explain) structure of international law, which misses the point of embracing eco-centric considerations, according to which human beings are an essential part of nature. In the critical appraisal, I will evaluate the way in which international legal scholarship has tackled the issue of health, missing the connections between the individual right to health and global health and failing to locate the debate within a broader context, which inevitably includes the environment. The lack of an autonomous field of "global" or "international" health law does not explain the silence of the law concerning environmental matters *as intersecting* health issues. I will illustrate the piecemeal approach to health, considered in all its facets. I will then briefly reflect on the relation between the human right to health and global health, arguing that they are not in antithesis, and, as it was contended, that global health policy is more than just securing human rights – it also entails duties.[4]

In Part 2, I will show how my evaluation of the current state of international legal thought and practice is informed by my belief in possible alternatives to emerge. I will show that my argument builds on an utopia that is eco-centric, which changes the perspective from humans to the environment,[5] and appreciates the intersections between the individual human right to health, global health, and the environment, the latter eventually embracing the previous ones. This change of perspective has the potential to expand to all fields of international law. I will examine the complexity of a similar commitment for international legal scholarship and discuss possible scenarios in dealing with communicable diseases and also contextualize two concepts in international law in the field of health, unravelling their under-explored potential, namely common concern of humankind (CCHK) and common but differentiated

[3] Christine Chinkin and Hilary Charlesworth, *The Boundaries of International Law* (Manchester, 2000).

[4] John Tasioulas and Effy Vayena, "The Place of Human Rights and the Common Good in Global Health Policy," *Theor. Med. Bioeth* 37 (2016): 365–82.

[5] This recalls the "post-human" in Rosi Braidotti. *The Posthuman* (Cambridge, 2013).

responsibilities (CBDR). In the final part (Part 3), I will offer some thoughts on the possibility to conceive a "cosmological" health law which recalls Plato's "cosmological medicine" and responds to the challenge launched by some scientists who started to talk about "planetary health."[6]

9.1 THE CRITICAL APPRAISAL

The critical appraisal starts from the acknowledgment of the fragmented way in which international law currently approaches global health. It then grasps the connections between global health and the individual human right to health and draws out the underlying cause of the existing anxiety determined by the absence of practical and effective responses to health emergencies, namely the anthropocentric nature of international law, where the environment is the object of a specific branch of international law, but stays at the margin of other sectors, including health, and is considered as a "component" of other – always human and not non-human – rights.

9.1.1 *The Fragmented International Legal Panorama on Global Health*

Global health has its roots in the ancient science of "public health," aimed at "preventing diseases, prolonging life and promoting health through the organised efforts and informed choices of society, organizations, public and private, communities and individuals."[7] Tobin argued that the *history of public health* reveals how "societies have long accepted the necessity – whether for humanitarian, economic, and/or political reasons – of taking measures to protect the health of individuals."[8] There is not such a thing as international health law as an autonomous branch of international law, though there have been remarkable attempts to theorize it. Gostin defined global health law as "the study and practice of international law – both hard law [. . .] and soft instruments [. . .] that shapes norms, processes and institutions to attain the highest attainable standard of physical and mental health for the world's population," arguing

[6] See Richard Ostfeld, Cary Institute of Ecosystem Study in Millbrook, NY, www.planetaryhealthalliance.org/planetary-health. It is a field focused on the health impacts of human-caused disruptions of Earth's natural systems.

[7] Charles Edward A. Winslow, "The Untilled Fields of Public Health," *Science* 51 (1920): 23–33. See the history of global health in Mark W. Zacker , and Tania J. Keefe (eds), *The Politics of Global Health Governance. United by Contagion* (New York, 2008). Linking public health and global health, John Coggon, "Global Health, Law, and Ethics," in *Law and Global Health*, eds. Michael Freeman, Sarah Hawkes, and Belinda Bennet (Oxford, 2014), 369–85, 372.

[8] John Tobin, *The Right to Health in International Law* (Oxford, 2012), 15. See the history of health in Adam Gaffney, *To Heal Humankind: The Right to Health in History* (London, 2018).

that the potential of international law in the field had not been appreciated at its best.[9] For this analysis, I will consider global health as the system of actors and legal instruments aimed at the prevention, protection, and response to transboundary health issues, taking into consideration social and economic disparities that exist between and within countries.[10] A more advanced concept should also include the effects of the degradation of the environment and the imbalance of natural ecosystems on global health.[11] Toebes supported the idea that we should talk about international – rather than global[12] – health law, which she admitted has never acquired the status of an entirely autonomous field of research and studies. She considered international health law as including the World Health Organization (WHO) law, composed of the Framework Convention on Tobacco Control and Protocol, the International Health Regulations (IHR), and the International Code on Marketing of Breast-milk Substitutes; international human rights law, including the human right to health; and some overlapping issues, such as international humanitarian law, international environmental law, and international trade law.[13] It is possible to contend that global health has been mainly the law of the WHO, not related to the human right to health, as I will show in the next paragraph. Even though it is crystal clear that achieving global

9 Lawrence O. Gostin, *Global Health Law* (Cambridge, London, 2014), 59–61.

10 This concept was elaborated after reading, among others, David Fidler, *Global Health Governance* (Geneva, 2002); David Fidler, *Global Health and Global Governance* (New York, 2010); John Harrington and Maria Stuttaford (eds)., *Global Health and Human Rights* (London, 2010) Solomon R. Benatar and Ross Upshur, "What is Global Health?," in *Global Health and Global Health Ethics*, eds. Solomon R. Benatar and Gillian Brock (Cambridge, 2011), 13–23, 14; Solomon R. Benatar , "Health: Global," in *Encyclopedia of Global Bioethics* (Cham, 2014), 1–11; Angus Dawson and MarcelVerweji, "The Meaning of 'Public' in Public Health," in *Ethics, Prevention and Public Health*, eds. Angus Dawson and Marcel Verweji (Oxford, 2007), 1–12; Charles Foster and Jonathan Herring, "What is Health?," *in Law and Global Health*, eds. Michael Freeman FBA, Sarah Hawkes , and Belinda Bennett (Oxford, 2014), 23–36; *La tutela della salute nel diritto internazionale ed europeo tra interessi globali e interessi particolari*, ed. Laura Pineschi (Napoli, 2017); Michael Freeman, "Global Health: An Introduction," in *Law and Global Health*, 1–10. Thérèse Murphy, "Hardwired human rights: A health and human rights perspective on global health law," in *Research Handbook on Global Health Law*, eds. Gian Luca Burci and Brigit Toebes (Cheltenham, Northampton, 2018), 82–103, defining global health as a "collection of problems." I will not even attempt here to define what health is in general. See, among others, Foster and Herring, "What is," 23.

11 The rephrasing of the definition of public health elaborated by Charles-Edward A. Winslow in 1920 included global efforts for the maintenance of a safe environment.

12 Brigit Toebes, "International Health Law: An Emerging Field of Public International Law," *Indian Journal of International Law* 55:3(2015): 299–328, 301. See also, however, Toebes, "Global Health Law: Defining the Field," in *Research Handbook on Global Health*, 2–23, explaining the reasons for using the idea of "global health law."

13 Toebes, "International Health Law, 305. On the WHO, see, for a complete analysis, Gian Luca Burci and Claude-Henri Vignes, *The World Health Organization* (The Hague, 2004).

health ultimately realizes the right of the individual to health, a law that is only focused on the prevention and response to diseases fails to appreciate the connections and the conceptualization of duties for state and non-state actors alike that intertwining global health and the human right to health entails.

The fragmentation of international norms pertaining to health is mirrored in the fragmentation of actors and competences. Despite playing the major role, the WHO is not the only entity that works in the field of health. Along with international organizations and UN programs, such as the Food and Agriculture Organization, the International Labor Organization, the UN Development Program, UNICEF, UNESCO, the World Trade Organization, the UN Environment Program, the World Food Program, and the World Organization for Animal Health; there are global funds such as the one for HIV/AIDS, malaria and tuberculosis, NGOs, foundations, pharmaceutical businesses, and public–private partnerships. With the emergence of avian influenza, the role of civil society has more strongly emerged, both in terms of preparedness and disease surveillance.[14] Governments alone cannot deal with the crisis in an effective way, and the recent pandemic has adamantly shown that no national infrastructure, even in the most industrialized countries, has proved to effectively handle the multiple effects of the pandemic, including its (long-standing) social and economic impacts. States' action has failed to appreciate the connections between global health and the human right to health.

9.1.2 *Failing to Grasp the Connections: Global Health and the Human Right to Health*

Contemporary global health and the individual right to health have both developed as normative systems after the Second World War. They should not have evolved in parallel and non-communicable ways, but rather as two intersecting systems of rules, based on the assumption that global health contributes to the realization of the human right to health and that the realization of the right to health contributes to global health. Yet, despite Article 12 of the Covenant on Economic, Social and Cultural Rights (ESCR), interpreted by the ESCR Committee in its General Comment No. 14(2000) as including action of prevention, education and "promotion of social determinants of good health, such as environmental safety,"[15] the global health regime

[14] Kathryn White and Maria Banda , "The Role of Civil Society in Pandemic Preparedness," in *Innovation in Global Health Governance*, eds. Andrew F. Cooper and John J. Kirton (Farnham, 2009), 105–28, 111.

[15] General Comment No. 14 (ESCR Committee, 2000), para. 16.

and human right to health have evolved in different, and even conflicting, ways. In Italy, for example, the decision, leaked and published by several newspapers, to "save" the youngest among the patients affected by COVID-19, due to the insufficient number of ventilators, appalled the public opinion. Who must be saved? Should the individual right to health be limited for the benefit of the entire society to the point of sacrificing an entire generation, one that has witnessed as a child the Second World War? The decision sounds almost unbearable, but I consider that the question is quite misplaced. It should not be whom practitioners are going to save, but rather who bears the responsibility for having to make this choice as a consequence of the failure of states in the adoption of measures of preparedness to possible pandemics (global health), and as a consequence of the inefficient, discriminatory and not affordable access to basic health services and medicines (right to health).[16]

The incommunicability of the global health and human rights regimes (and global health with international law more generally) is as old as the WHO itself; in 1948, the President of the first World Health Assembly, Sir Wilson Johnson, held that "legal technicalities" were beyond the competency of public health experts and should therefore be omitted from the debate.[17] The never-amended definition of health as a "status" in the WHO Constitution undoubtedly supports the "medicalization" of the organization's public health mandate.[18] On the positive side, it must be acknowledged that the WHO law has evolved, as a consequence of the adoption of an innovative normative framework represented by the IHR of 2005, from a state-centric to a post-Westphalian structure, involving more actors than states and activating a naming and shaming campaign against countries for their reluctance in promptly responding to health emergencies.[19] The WHO has published manuals on the preparedness to influenza pandemics,[20] and elaborated a "checklist"[21] for countries to assess their level of readiness to possible outbreaks.[22]

16 Ibid., para. 12 mentions the essential elements of the right to health: availability, accessibility, acceptability and quality.

17 Obijiofor Aginam, "Mission (Im)possible? The WHO as a 'Norm Entrepreneur' in Global Health Governance," in *Law and Global Health*, 563.

18 Ibid., 564.

19 A "revolution" according to Fidler, *The challenges*, 6. See for the evolution and the urgent revision of 2013, Gian Luca Burci, "Health and Infectious Disease," in *The Oxford Handbook on the United Nations*, eds. Thomas G. Weiss and Sam Daws, 2018, 2nd ed., 679–692, 682.

20 www.who.int/influenza/resources/pip_framework/en/

21 www.who.int/influenza/preparedness/pandemic/influenza_risk_management_checklist_2018/en/

22 We will not deal with the issue of chronic diseases in these pages. See, in that respect, Geoffrey B. Cockerham and William C. Cockerham, "International Law and Global Health," in *Law and Global Health*, 492–502.

On the negative side, however, the right to health and the protection of the environment[23] do not find any place in the IHR.[24] The organization has been accused of delays in the announcement of the severity of epidemics[25] and acting *ultra vires* in containing SARS.[26] I am not criticizing the powers of the WHO and I am not trying to establish whether or not it has exercised *ultra vires* powers, in response to SARS and to COVID-19. However, I agree with a scholar saying that the WHO "has consistently fallen short of achieving the culture of prevention."[27]

The evolution of the human right to health has not been devoid of criticism, either.[28] In General Comment No. 14, for example, the UN ESCR Committee considered the individual right to health as an inclusive right, which encompasses not only the access to health care but also the "underlying determinants of health," including, *inter alia*, healthy environmental conditions.[29] This broad definition jeopardizes the justiciability of this right in front of courts. To solve the tension and reflecting on health-related human rights and common goods, Tasioulas and Vayena argued that the human right to health should be defined by reference to obligations regarding healthcare services and public health measures.[30] Their legal reasoning is based on the concepts of justice and interest. What is interesting to note is that they did not consider the relationship between the human right to health and common goods, such as public health, as mutually exclusive. Global health incorporates the human right to health and other rights, as well as "health-related duties to oneself and duties to foster health-related common goods."[31]

23 There is only a provision on the protection of the environment which can be damaged by disinfection (Article 22 IHR).

24 On the reference to human rights but the absence of its practical implementation, see Andraž Zidar , "WHO International Health Regulations and Human Rights: From Allusion to Inclusion," *International Journal of Human Rights* (2015), 505–526.

25 See also the ongoing criticism on when the spread of coronavirus started. Burci, "Health," 683.

26 See, in this sense, David Fidler, *SARS: Governance and the Globalization of Disease* (New York, 2004), 139–45. *Contra*, Adam Kamradt-Scott, "The WHO and SARS: The Challenge of Innovative Responses to Global Health Security," in *Innovation*, eds. Cooper et al., 63–79.

27 Fidler, *The Challenges*, 15.

28 It goes beyond the scope of this chapter to discuss the complexity of the content of the right to health and corresponding states' obligations. See, in that respect, among others, Tobin, *The Right to Health*, and bibliography therein.

29 Gostin, *Global Health*, 257 ff. In the conclusions of his book, Gostin conceived the right to health as a collective right, encouraging a population-based approach.

30 Tasioulas, Vayena, "The place," 371.

31 Ibid., 380.

9.1.3 *Whither the Environment? The Anthropocentric Approach to International Law*

There is a missing point in the current approach to health in international law, beyond the underestimated connections between the global health regime and human rights discourse as explained in the previous paragraph. The environment has been constantly and systematically excluded or considered from the health discourse as a "determinant" of health.[32] In the common understanding of the word, "environment" is a synonym for nature. The "natural environment" can be considered as composed of non-human beings and natural elements such as rivers, mountains, oceans, and forests. Conventions in international environmental law protect one or more of these natural elements, reinforcing the dichotomy culture/nature or human/nature, with the first element dominating the second one. In the critical appraisal, I am considering the environment according to this restrictive, and, as I will contend, anthropocentric and patriarchal, approach. The natural environment is particularly relevant for health. Ecological disasters and pandemics are the tip of the iceberg of a long process of destruction. This process has been called "slow violence,". meaning "a violence that occurs gradually and out of sight, a violence of delayed destruction that is dispersed across time and space, an attritional violence that is typically not viewed as violence at all."[33] What we experience now has been the product of decades of environmental exploitation and domination of human beings – the privileged category composed, as highlighted by feminist legal scholarship, of able-bodied, middle class, heterosexual men[34] of developed countries – on the natural environment. The effects of human activities on the environment are certainly not unknown,[35] and the process of destruction has been emphasized by civil society, acknowledged by international organizations, and endorsed by some governments. Slow violence is difficult to appreciate from a legal perspective, because the traditional approach of state responsibility focuses on the relation cause–consequence and the "neighbourliness" of a dangerous activity.[36]

32 General Comment No. 14.

33 Rob Nixon, *Slow Violence and the Environmentalism of the Poor* (Cambridge, London, 2011) 2.

34 Emily Jones and Dianne Otto, *Thinking through Anthropocentrism in International Law: Queer Theory, Feminist New Materialism and the Postcolonial* (London, 2020), www.lse.ac.uk/women-peace-security/assets/documents/2020/Final-Jones-and-Otto-Anthropocentrism-Posthuman-Feminism-Postcol-and-IL-LSE-WPS-Blog-2019–002.pdf. Braidotti (*The Posthuman*, 88) warned against humanity as a category for all human beings, *all other differences notwithstanding*.

35 See, for example, Intergovernmental Panel on Climate Change, Global Warming of 1.5°, 2019.

36 Daniel Bodansky, Jutta Brunnée, and Ellen Hey, "International Environmental Law: Mapping the Field," *in The Oxford Handbook of International Environmental Law*, eds.

Hence, states might be held responsible for the violation of the procedural law of the WHO, – late notification, for example – but it would be much more difficult to demonstrate the causal relation between the human attacks to biodiversity and ecosystems, on one hand, and the creation of viruses that affect human health worldwide, on the other. Rachel Carson was a pioneer in unraveling the disconnections between human beings and the environment and paved the way for the work of ecofeminism worldwide. Receiving a prize for her book *The Sea around Us*, she made a strong affirmation that one can hardly believe it was pronounced in 1952:

> Mankind has gone very far into an artificial world of his own creation. He has sought to insulate himself, in his cities of steel and concrete, from the realities of earth and water and the growing seed. Intoxicated with a sense of his own power, he seems to be going farther and farther into more experiments for the destruction of himself and his world.[37]

There have been timid attempts to acknowledge the connections between the pandemic and the destruction of the environment, for example, in the work of the UN. In 2016, the UNEP found that 75 per cent of all emerging infectious diseases in humans were zoonotic and that these were interlinked with the health of the ecosystems.[38] Yet, this acknowledgment has not determined a change in the work of the WHO. In my understanding, international law – and not merely international environmental law – has been conceived following an anthropocentric and patriarchal approach, characterized by patterns of oppression and domination. This argument echoes post-human and post-anthropocentric feminism and emphasizes how the human/nature dichotomy has been used to determine patterns of oppression and discrimination *among* and *beyond* humans, including non-human animals and "natural objects."[39] The law, as the Earth Jurisprudence has pointed out,[40] has been theorized in a specific association human/nature, where the former dominates

Daniel Bodansky, Jutta Brunnée, and Ellen Hey (Oxford, 2008), 9. See also Christopher Stone, *Should Trees Have Standing?* 3rd. ed. (Oxford, 2010), 128.

37 Linda Lear, *Lost Woods. The Discovered Writing of Rachel Carson* (Boston, 1998). Carson published in 1962 *Silent Spring*, where she highlighted the toxic connections between pesticides, environmental degradation and inter-species health.

38 *Coronaviruses: Are they here to stay?*, www.unenvironment.org/news-and-stories/story/coronaviruses-are-they-here-stay

39 See Anna Grear , "Deconstructing Anthropos: A Critical Legal Reflection on "Anthropocentric" Law and Anthropocene "Humanity," *Law Critique* 26 (2015): 225–249, 241.

40 Mumta Ito and Massimiliano Montini, "Nature's Rights and Earth Jurisprudence – a New Ecologically Based Paradigm for Environmental Law," in *The Right to Nature. Social Movements, Environmental Justice and Neoliberal Natures*, eds. Elia Apostolopoulou and Jose A. Cortes-Vazquez, (London, 2019), 221–233.

the latter.[41] The concepts we use in international law inevitably incorporate "traces of power and domination."[42] Scholars have already contended that international environmental law has had anthropocentric biases since its inception, because it deals with the protection of the environment "not for its own sake, but because of its value to humans – its importance for human health, economics, recreation, and so forth."[43] The analysis of this chapter goes beyond international environmental law and focuses on health issues to appreciate how the rules on global health and the human right to health, and in general international law in its entirety, center on (some categories of) humans and replicate oppression. Even though the pandemic, because of globalization, has spread everywhere in the world, it has not been equal in its impact and has shown an intersectional impact, exacerbating existing inequalities.[44] So have the measures adopted in response to the pandemic that have further reinforced patterns of discrimination: the exclusion of women and migrants from the political decision making is illustrative.[45] Ecosystems in all continents have been jeopardised as a consequence of a human action characterized by an exploitation guided by economic profits. As it was argued, the "ideology of anthropocentrism [. . .] does not necessarily apply to all humanity, but to discriminating practices and society *en masse*—anthropocentrism is also an ethical failing that ought to be resolved."[46] Against this backdrop, global health and the human right to health have only considered the environment at the margin, as functional to humans. This approach misses the long-term and inter-generational perspective:[47] it is only focused on the here and now.

41 Val Plumwood, *Feminism and the Mastery of Nature* (London and New York, 1993), 69.

42 On the use of concepts in international law, see Sahib Singh and Jean d'Aspremont, "Introduction: The Life of International Law and its Concepts," in *Concepts for International* Law, eds. Jean d'Aspremont and Sahib Singh (Cheltenham, 2019), 1–24, 18.

43 See, as early as the end of the nineties, Alexander Gillespie, *International Environmental Law, Policy and Ethics* (Oxford, 1997) and 2nd ed. (2014); Prue Taylor, *An Ecological Approach to International Law* (London and New York, 1998); more recently, Bodansky et al., "International Environmental," 15.

44 Lisa Forman, "The Evolution of the Right to Health in the Shadow of COVID-19," www.hhrjournal.org/2020/04/the-evolution-of-the-right-to-health-in-the-shadow-of-covid-19/

45 Hilary Charlesworth, "International Law: A Discipline of Crisis," *Modern Law Review* 65 (2002): 377–392, 388. The language of crisis silences structural inequalities and injustices.

46 Helen Kopnina, Haydn Washington, Bron Taylor, and John J. Piccolo, "Anthropocentrism: More than Just a Misunderstood Problem," *J. Agric. Environmental Ethics* 31 (2019): 109–27, 122.

47 On the inter-generational perspective, Edith Brown Weiss, "Our Rights and Obligations to Future Generations for the Environment," in *American Journal of International Law* 85 (1990), 198–207.

But something has started to change. The images of the fires in the Amazon in summer 2019 raised widespread protests worldwide on the need to safeguard ancestral forests where oxygen is produced. The same reaction cannot be said to have occurred in these times of pandemic that raised more economic rather than ecological concerns. In the rules pertaining to global health and the human right to health, the international law regime fails to unveil the complexities, and shows the blindness of governments and international organizations that do not (or do not want to) see the interconnections between the ongoing pandemic and decades of environmental exploitation. David Boyd affirmed that "protecting the environment is impossible if we continue to assert human superiority and universal ownership of all land and wildlife to pursue endless economic growth."[48] As international lawyers, we need a change of perspective.

9.2 THE COMMITMENTS

In the critical appraisal, I have shown the limits of a legal approach to health that does not grasp the connections between global health and the human right to health and is anthropocentric in nature. Against this backdrop, the change of perspective I propose for a realized utopia starts from the consideration of the environment as "us," hence in a way that does not separate the human beings on one hand and non-human animals and natural objects on the other. I will explore ecocentrism as a valuable alternative not only for international environmental law, but for international law more generally, whose characteristics of anthropocentrism and patriarchy have been unveiled in the critical appraisal. I will then connect global health, the human right to health and the environment, and will elaborate the concept of "environmental global health" as a definition that enriches the notion of global health by changing the focus from humans to the environment to which they belong. I will eventually dig into the possibility of using the concepts of CCHK in the elaboration of CBDR for states and non-state actors alike. The analysis will zero in on the prevention of communicable diseases, but the underlying legal theory might be apt to be applied, *mutatis mutandis*, to all health issues.

[48] David Boyd, *The Rights of Nature* (Toronto, 2017), xxxiv. See also UNEP, CBD, WHO, Connecting Global Priorities: Biodiversity and Human Health (Geneva, 2015), www.cbd.int/health/SOK-biodiversity-en.pdf, and the campaign https://natureneedshalf.org/

9.2.1 *The Environment Is "Us:" Ecocentrism and its Legal Relevance for International Law*

In this second part, I endorse a definition of "environment" that includes natural objects and human and non-human beings, where humans are not the dominant factor but rather a part of a holistic whole. The idea of the environment as "us" was introduced by Christopher Stone in his pioneering article and book almost fifty years ago: "because the health and well-being of [human]kind depend upon the health of the environment, these goals will often be so mutually supportive that one can avoid deciding whether our rationale is to advance 'us' or a new 'us' that includes the environment."[49] I am not entering in the discussion of legal rights of forests, oceans, rivers, lakes, and other natural objects, thus central in Stone's argument,[50] but I will explore eco-centric moves in international law, already present in regional and national environmental jurisprudence and international environmental law,[51] but hardly ever extended to all fields of the discipline, and I will provide a rough assessment of what this might entail before exploring its application to health. For this chapter, I consider eco-centrism as the encompassing idea that disrupts the human/nature divide and considers the relationships between organisms and the healthy interaction of all components of ecosystems, including human beings. The adjective "healthy" stresses that ecocentrism does not mean a complete absence of interference with nature or that humanity cannot defend itself from lethal viruses.[52] It considers the inherent value of nature and recognizes the holistic and mutual relationship of humanity with it.[53]

International environmental law, originally conceived as strictly anthropocentric and patriarchal, has already experienced some eco-centric developments since the nineties, and acknowledged that environmental disasters are mainly caused by actors other than states.[54] As it was argued, "environmental

[49] Stone, *Should Trees*, 23. His original article dates back to 1972.

[50] "I am quite seriously proposing that we give legal rights to forests, oceans, rivers, and other so-called natural objects in the environment – indeed, to the natural environment as a whole" Stone, *Should Trees*, 3.

[51] For this article, I will use the concept of international environmental law, though some scholars have used global and/or transnational environmental law.

[52] Taylor, *An Ecological Approach*, 40.

[53] The definition is based on Taylor, *An Ecological Approach*, and Patrick Curry, *Ecological Ethics*, 2nd ed. (Cambridge, 2011).

[54] On different "phases" of international environmental law evolution toward ecocentrism: Susan Emmenegger and Axel Tschentscher, "Taking Nature's Rights Seriously: The Long Way to Biocentrism in Environmental Law," *The Georgetown International Environmental Law Review* 6 (1994): 545–592.

law looks to ecology both as postmodern epistemology and as new ethical framework in order to find [...] a normative, epistemological and ethical reference framework adequate to meet contemporary challenges."[55] Ecocentrism is not a monolith and has shown different facets, from ecofeminism to deep ecology.[56] However, for international legal analysis, what matters is the shift from humans to the environment, and how this shift translates into law.[57] In this way, ecocentrism is not the mere opposite of anthropocentrism, with the risk of proposing a new dichotomy in place of the disrupted one, but rather seeks to reconceive relationships among the different elements of the environment.[58]

In legal terms, eco-centric aspects were first introduced in provisions of international treaties establishing that some elements of nature, such as biodiversity, constitute a CCHK,[59] or that habitats and wildlife have an intrinsic value.[60] The legal reasoning does not seem *prima facie* adequate to disentangle the complex network of the relationships that ecocentrism promotes. The vague provisions in the preambles of treaties are insufficient to reorient the relation of domination human/nature in a relational and mutual supportive way. The 2017 Whanganui Agreement in New Zealand is more advanced in that respect, both because of the actors that negotiated the agreement (the Crown and the Whanganui Land Settlement Negotiation Trust) and because of the consideration of the river as a holistic system, in which the Maori are physically and spiritually embedded.[61] This eco-centric move contributes to disrupting patterns of oppression within human beings and in the relationship of humanity with nature because it grants participation to the indigenous

55 Vito De Lucia, "Beyond Anthropocentrism and Ecocentrism: A Biopolitical Reading of Environmental Law," *Journal of Human Rights and the Environment* 8(2017): 181–202, 185. Bateson extended ecology beyond its biological-anthropological origins to embrace a transdisciplinary approach in all the field of humanities. See Hubert Zapf, "Cultural Ecology, the Environmental Humanities, and the Transdisciplinary Knowledge of Literature," in *Environmental Humanities*, eds. Serpil Oppermann and Serenella Iovino (London, New York, 2017), 61–80, 64.

56 See, for example, Plumwood, *The Mastery*, and Freya Mathews, "Deep Ecology," in *A Companion to Environmental Philosophy*, ed. Dale Jamieson (Malden-Oxford, 2001), 218–232, and ivi, Victoria Davia, "Ecofeminism," 233–248.

57 For a transition from environmental to ecological law, see Massimiliano Montini, "The Double Failure of Environmental Regulation and Deregulation and the Need for Ecological Law," *Italian Yearbook of International Law* 26 (2017): 265–285.

58 De Lucia, "Beyond," proposed biopolitics as alternative.

59 Convention on biodiversity of 1992, preamble.

60 Convention on the conservation of European wildlife and natural habitats of 1979, preamble.

61 Boyd, *The Rights*, 139.

communities and is guided by the rights – and not by the human property interests that lay upon – of this natural object. Resolutions of international organizations have also tried to capture the essence of ecocentrism. Starting from the World Charter on Nature of 1982, the UN General Assembly (UNGA) has adopted a series of non-binding Harmony with Nature resolutions, stressing the coexistence of humankind in harmony with nature.[62] Moving to regional, human rights jurisprudence, the Inter-American Court of Human Rights has begun to incorporate eco-centric legal reasoning in its recent decisions. In a landmark advisory opinion of 2017 and the contentious case decided in February 2020, the Court derived an autonomous right to a healthy environment from Article 26 of the American Convention of Human Rights.[63] In the Court's view, the human right to a healthy environment, which sounds like another anthropocentric example in international law, protects nature, even absent evidence of possible risks for human beings, because of its importance to the rest of the living beings.[64] At national level, eco-centric considerations have determined the advent of a new "environmental constitutionalism," which has led to the inclusion of the rights of nature in constitutions.

This transition to ecocentrism, a "legal and cultural revolution,"[65] should characterize all fields of international law, including, as I will argue in the next paragraph, health issues. Even though it is not the purpose of this chapter to further develop this argument, one can only imagine the potential of embracing an eco-centric approach in transitional justice settings, where the environment becomes one of the pillars of post-conflict actions. We can also imagine how the law regulating the prohibition of the use of force would change when informed by environmental considerations. A revolution in this sense will be guided by non-domination,[66] and would address feminist and post-colonial concerns, because it would question the underlying causes of oppression.[67]

62 See the latest one, A/RES/74/224 (17 January 2020).

63 Inter-American Court of Human Rights, advisory opinion OC-23/17 of November 15, 2017, and *Aboriginal Community of Lhaka Honhat v. Argentina*, judgment of 6 February 2020.

64 Opinion, para. 180.

65 Boyd, *The Rights*, xxxvi.

66 This recalls Philipp Pettit, *Republicanism: A Theory of Freedom and Government* (Oxford, 1997).

67 See for example Greta Gaard in "Where Is Feminism in the Environmental Humanities?" in *Environmental Humanities*, 81–97, expressing her concerns that "the culture/nature, mind/body, white/non- white, man/woman and human/animal binaries [. . .] impede our interdisciplinary collaborations in addressing the eco- social emergencies of climate change."

9.2.2 *Connecting the Dots: Global Health, the Human Right to Health and the Environment*

Having assessed the evolution of ecocentrism in international environmental law and sketched its (yet under-explored) potential in international law more generally, in this paragraph I will apply the eco-centric approach to international law to health issues. As I argued, the environment is always at the margin of legal reasoning in health issues, either not considered (as in the IHR) or diminished to the role of the determinant of the right to health. An eco-centric approach appreciates the connections between global health and the human right to health and the environment, which have been already addressed by science. In 1994, the American science author Laurie Garrett wrote *The Coming Plague*. Reading this book in the middle of a pandemic, it does not sound like science fiction at all. She wrote about deforestation and the disruption of natural balances, viruses whose existence becomes notorious with the outbreak of epidemics, and social disparities in the access to health services. What can international law do? Our commitment as scholars should be to propose feasible, but also courageous alternatives, trying to find a balance between the need for order/pragmatism and creativity/emancipation.[68] The Framework Convention on Global Health (FCGH) constituted an interesting proposal in this sense, though being still basically anthropocentric. It was elaborated by Gostin and other scholars in 2008 and endorsed by the WHO and the UN Secretary General some years later.[69] Grounded on the right to health, it includes commitments of universal coverage, theorizes equal access as immediate obligations, encourages a global fund for health, establishes a compliance mechanism, and creates a network of actors.[70] The project is inspiring and well structured – it was these scholars' realized utopia – though it presents some points of weaknesses, including the nature of the proposal: an international treaty whose negotiation, ratification, and compliance encounter several obstacles. It considers the environment as an essential element for a healthy life but does not put it at the center of the legal reasoning.

The creative thinking in this chapter appreciates that the environment encompasses both global health and the human right to health. More than a human right to a healthy environment,[71] what is needed is the recognition of

68 John Haskell, "Identity," in *Concepts*, 378–392, 381.

69 www.who.int/bulletin/volumes/91/10/12-114447/en/

70 Lawrence O. Gostin and Eric A. Friedman, "Towards a Framework Convention on Global Health: A Transformative Agenda for Global Health Justice," *Yale J. Health Pol'y L. & Ethics* 13 (2013):1–76. In the long paper there is no relevant reference to the environment.

71 See in this sense Alan Boyle, "Climate change, the Paris Agreement and Human Rights," *International Comparative Law Quarterly*, 67 (2018): 759–777, 768.

every human, non-human being and ecosystem's right to be part of a healthy environment, where prevention is fundamental, and where all actions are taken in light of their impact on the environment, considering all possible alternatives and guided by the principles of precaution and proportionality.[72] The shift is courageous and probably premature. It is not far, however, from what the UNGA has achieved with the Harmony with Nature resolutions – which have included an unprecedented eco-centric move.[73] Where global health law can find "a secure place to anchor itself in the right to health,"[74] both aspects can anchor themselves in the environment, because they are part of it. To go back to where I started, "environmental global health" consists in a system of actors, including non-human animals and natural objects, and legal instruments, measures, and policies, aimed at the prevention, protection, and response to transboundary health and environmental issues, taking into consideration social and economic disparities, and going beyond the humans to address imbalances of natural ecosystems.[75] At the moment, this concept is fragmented in a series of legal instruments. It might be combined in a unique resolution of the UNGA, which can appreciate the connections, and endorse an eco-centric approach to (environmental) global health. It might focus on prevention, ensuring campaigns to raise awareness, for example, of how wet markets represent ticking bombs for the environment, but also of how increasing emissions, plastics, disruption of ecosystems, land grabbing, water grabbing, weak public health systems characterized by inequalities and lack of participation, fuel the spread of pandemics and/or the effects of them. These measures have an inevitable cost,[76] but surely less than reacting to a pandemic and its economic and social consequences.[77]

72 Cfr. Makane Moïse Mbengue, Susanna Waltman, "Health and International Environmental Law," in *Research Handbook on Global Health*, 197–238.

73 Though the eco-centric approach was absent from the resolution on global health A/RES/74/20. See the reference to the "fundamental interconnections between humankind and nature" in the most recent resolution A/RES/75/220 of December 2020.

74 John Tobin, "Still Getting to Know You: Global Health Law and the Right to Health," in *Research Handbook on Global Health*, 56–81, 80.

75 As argued by Tom A. Faunce, Anton Wasson, and Kim Crow, "Environmental Sustainability and Global Health Law," in *Law and Global Health*, 465–77, 468: "issues of climate change, poverty, and lack of access to healthy food could then be viewed [. . .] as global environmental pathologies to be remedied in part by commitment to environmental sustainability amongst systems of global health law."

76 Lawrence O. Gostin, "Global Health Security After Ebola: Four Global Commissions," *The Milbank Quarterly* 94 (2016): 34–38, and David H. Peters et al., "Financing Common Goods for Health: Core Government Functions in Health Emergency and Disaster Risk Management," *Health Systems & Reform* 5:4 (2019): 307–321.

77 See, for example, here https://daily.jstor.org/the-true-costs-of-managing-pandemics/.

9.2.3 *The Realized Utopia: The Concepts of Common Concern of Humankind and Common but Differentiated Responsibilities*

In an ideal world, we would have a comprehensive international treaty on environmental global health, modeled on the project by Gostin and others' and rewritten following an eco-centric approach. We would have a UN Security Council (UNSC), in which no country has a veto power, that establishes how pandemics and health emergencies constitute a threat to peace and security, and impose binding measures to be adopted by states, international organizations and other non-state actors alike. The reality is that countries struggle to reach agreements and to comply with them, and that the UNSC is an anthropocentric and patriarchal body *per se*: it has declared Ebola, which mainly affected developing countries, as a threat to peace and security,[78] but it is arguably going to declare COVID-19 as such due to its Chinese origin. The UNGA has been the most prominent actor in encouraging eco-centric moves, but not entirely in the field of global health. In its pre-pandemic resolution on global health, health is merely considered as "precondition for and outcome and indicator of the social, economic and environmental dimension."[79] To chase the utopia which, despite being a bit idealistic, is rooted in law, we should change perspective and angle. Putting the environment at the center, and considering it as "us," my argument is that what I have been calling "environmental global health" should be considered as CCHK.[80] One might object that the idea of CCHK is anthropocentric, because it refers to humanity and which concerns it considers valuable enough to get this label. However, we can look at it as an acknowledgment of the negative impact of human beings – as I said, a part of humanity, owing to structural intra-species hierarchies[81] – on the environment, to which they belong. CCHK is not a new concept. Despite being criticized for its vagueness, it has an under-explored potential, which should not be limited to the environment.[82] It is relatively uncontroversial that environmental global health is an urgent contemporary problem, which cannot be tackled from

78 UN SC Resolution No. 2177(2014). See P. Acconci, "The Reaction to the Ebola Epidemic within the United Nations Framework: What Next for the World Health Organization?" in *Max P. YB. Un. Nat. Law* (2014): 405–424.

79 A/RES/74/20.

80 On the "global public health" as common concern, Matiangai Sirleaf, "Responsibility for Epidemics," *Texas Law Review* 97 (2018): 285–354, 319.

81 Grear, "Deconstructing," 231.

82 Philippe Cullet, "Common but Differentiated Responsibilities," in *Research Handbook on International Environmental Law*, eds. Malgosia Fitzmaurice, David M. Ong, Panos Merkouris (Cheltenham, Northampton, 2010), 161–181, 178.

the point of view of state sovereignty only.[83] This is not merely due to the transboundary nature of the problem, but also because environmental global health concerns the healthy interdependence among the elements of the environment that I have highlighted in the previous pages. CCHK is characterized by differential treatment provisions in terms of state responsibility.[84] The differentiation consists in CBDR and it is based on the ideas of justice[85] and solidarity. Solidarity "creates a context for meaningful cooperation that goes beyond the concept of a global welfare state."[86] This duty seems consolidated in environmental matters.[87] CBDR may not be a binding obligation, but it might be when coupled with other principles.[88] In the field of environmental global health, procedural obligations, including notification, along with environmental principles and an increasing practice – which has not been only state practice – might suggest that CBDR is the viable solution.[89] The IHR are not enough to prevent and respond to health emergencies because of their "state-centric nature."[90] In terms of response to epidemics, Sirleaf made a thorough study, long before the ongoing pandemic, on what CBDR would mean.[91] Without delving into all the details, she identified three forms of differentiation, namely on need, culpability, and capacity. She argued that the legal duty to "recognize and act upon the threats posed by epidemics," which states and non-state actors must abide by – could be based on "norms of international cooperation that already exist in international law."[92] She partly addressed environmental concerns, though.

As the reality has ruthlessly shown us, the prevention of pandemics cannot be merely based on WHO law. What we need is the sharing of responsibilities and liabilities for a plurality of actors:[93] not only states but also IOs,

83 Michael Bowman, "Environmental Protection and the Concept of Common Concern of Mankind," in *Research Handbook on International Environmental Law*, 493–518.

84 Werner Scholtz, "Greening Permanent Sovereignty through the Common Concern in the Climate Change Regime: Awake Custodial Sovereignty!" in *Climate Change: International Law and Global Governance*, II, eds. Oliver C. Ruppel, Christian Roschmann, Katharina Ruppel-Schlichting (Baden-Baden, 2013), 493–518, 494.

85 Cullet, "Common," 167.

86 Ronald St John MacDonald, "Solidarity in the Practice and Discourse of Public International Law," *Pace Int'l L. Rev.* 8 (1996): 259–302, 260.

87 Cullet, "Common," 178.

88 Ibid.

89 See the statement for collaboration of scientists for the production of vaccines www.who.int/news-room/detail/13-04-2020-public-statement-for-collaboration-on-covid-19-vaccine-development.

90 Sirleaf, "Responsibility," 293.

91 Ibid., 321–322.

92 Sirleaf, "Responsibility," 325.

93 Andre Nollkaemper and Dov Jacobs, "Shared Responsibility in International Law: A Conceptual Framework," *Michigan Journal of International Law* 34 (2013): 359–438.

transnational corporations, and even individuals. It is time to consider that the prevention and response to pandemics cannot be realized by states, as traditionally conceived in international law, only. In pragmatic terms, this would mean, for example, that the achievement of the cut of emissions of CO2 is a treaty obligation to counter climate change *and* an obligation states and non-state actors must abide by to guarantee the individual human right to health and environmental global health. It would entail a reconsideration of some elements of the human right to health, including, for example, accessibility: should human rights law be neutral with regard to the public or private nature of health services? In times of pandemics, this would mean that states and other actors have differentiated responsibility on the basis of their contribution to pollution, climate change, absence of adequate health services, and lack of appropriate plans to respond to emergencies. Economists might find the formula to weigh responsibility. International lawyers should theorize it. This would mean to conceive obligations for transnational corporations.[94] It would also lead to the identification of moral duties of solidarity of individuals.[95] How might this utopia reasonably turn into reality? I suggest that we go back to where we started, hence to the sanitary conferences of the nineteenth century. After the outbreak of the financial crisis in 2008, the "G" states established the Financial Stability Board to guarantee financial stability. Despite being an example of a soft organization, it proved to be able to exercise "hard" powers without replacing the International Monetary Fund.[96] Soft organizations are flexible, their mandate can quickly change, they endorse existing standards, and they adopt new ones. Most importantly, these bodies are represented not only by state organs but also by public authorities and private bodies. In the case of environmental global health, this would mean to endorse standards derived from a plurality of instruments, adopt new ones based on an eco-centric approach, and ensure the participation of a variety of actors, including pharmaceutical companies,

Scholtz, "Greening," identified the custodial element in cosmopolitan theory. See also Evan J. Criddle, "Fiduciary principles in international law", in *The Oxford Handbook of Fiduciary Law*, eds. Evan J. Criddle, Paul B. Miller, and Robert H. Sitkoff (Oxford, 2019), 343–364.

94 See the Report of the Special Rapporteur on the right to a healthy environment A/74/161, para. 71.

95 Tasioulas. Vayena, "The Place," 366, according to whom there are moral duties that are claimable as individual rights, but also moral duties that govern our conduct toward others, including the duties to preserve and promote the common good that may be not linked to the rights.

96 Sara De Vido, "The Financial Stability Board and Other New Modes of Governance," in *The Legal Implications of Global Financial Crises*, ed. Michael Waibel (Leiden Boston, 2020), 45–83.

and, indeed, natural objects.[97] This body can be shaped on already existing initiatives, such as the Global Health Security Agenda,[98] and have its secretariat at the WHO, which does not need to be replaced in my idea.[99] It might declare vaccines and essential medicines as a common heritage of humankind.[100] It might coordinate actions of solidarity that usually remain fragmented.[101] Soft law is a blessing and a curse, needless to say, but the current WHO law, despite the recent "manifesto" of 26. May 2020,[102] is not likely to allow the change of perspective I am encouraging.[103]

9.3 TOWARD A COSMOLOGICAL HEALTH LAW?

The eco-centric moves in international law that have been sketched in this chapter suggest the elaboration of what I call "cosmological health law," taking inspiration from Plato's cosmological medicine. Cosmology is the science of the *cosmos*, the universe as a well-ordered whole. It is the physical world studied by physics and astronomy. At least until 1960s, cosmology was widely regarded as a branch of philosophy, known since the pre-Socratics. Medicine has also been studied since ancient times. The Hippocratic Corpus is a noble example of this ancient medical thought and practice. Plato ascribed to Hippocrates the cosmological significance of medicine in the *Phaedrus*, where Phaedrus tells Socrates that the nature of body and soul can only be

97 On trustees for non-humans, see Stone, *Should Trees*, 57.

98 It is a voluntary initiative open to all countries.

99 On the possible reform of WHO law, including the IHR, for example including a compliance assessment mechanism, see Burci, "Health," 688.

100 See, for example, the Corona Global Response, to raise funds for the collaborative development and universal deployment of diagnostics, treatments and vaccines against coronavirus. https://ec.europa.eu/commission/presscorner/detail/en/IP_20_797, and the WHO Resolution A73/CONF./1 Rev.1, adopted on 19 May 2020. Criticisms on vaccines as common heritage in Roger Scarlin Chennels, *Equitable Access to Human Biological Resources in Developing Countries* (Heidelberg, 2016), 49 ff.

101 We have seen an unprecedented collaboration among scientists as response to the pandemic. www.nytimes.com/2020/04/01/world/europe/coronavirus-science-research-cooperation.html

102 The manifesto is a good starting point for reconsidering WHO law. It says: "Attempting to save money by neglecting environmental protection, emergency preparedness, health systems, and social safety nets, has proven to be a false economy – and the bill is now being paid many times over." WHO Manifesto for a healthy recovery from COVID-19, 26. May 2020, available at www.who.int/news-room/feature-stories/detail/who-manifesto-for-a-healthy-recovery-from-covid-19

103 Sharifah Sekalala, *Soft Law and Global Health Problems* (Cambridge, 2017). A similar, though very different proposal in nature, was launched by a group of scholars: The Right to Health Capacity Fund, conceived as a non-profit organization, modeled on existing funds, www.hhrjournal.org/2020/05/global-health-in-the-age-of-covid-19-responsive-health-systems-through-a-right-to-health-fund/.

known through the knowledge of the nature of the Whole.[104] Plato considered the Earth and the natural world as part of the *cosmos*, of which human beings constitute a "microcosmos" governed by the same principles of the whole.[105] Harmony and balance represent its natural state. The holism which characterizes the elements of the *cosmos* has been interpreted as constituting the roots of modern ecological thinking. Despite assuming a dualist conceptual framework, Plato developed an ecological consciousness and anticipated in his works, beyond the *Timaeus*,[106] how the well-being of the humans is embedded in the broader well-being of nature as a whole.[107] This argument was harshly criticized by a part of the scholarship that stressed the reason/nature dualism in Plato and his support for the human dominance upon nature.[108] However, it should be acknowledged that, in the same period, similar reflections flourished in China, where the *Inner Classic of the Yellow Thearch* of the third century B.C. revealed that the natural environment and human health are closely related,[109] starting a cosmological thinking that echoes the one in Plato's thought.

As a lawyer, I am fascinated by the idea of Plato's cosmological medicine, characterized by a holistic approach, "in the sense of considering the connection and the composition of the parts constituting the whole," where the whole is *holon*, *pan*, and *hen*,[110] hence the universe. Plato's cosmological medicine, can be read, following the point of view of Plato's scholarship, as a necessary "medical" practice of the philosopher against ethical and political disorder for the development of a "harmonic technê." I am not interested here in the

104 Laura Candiotto, "Plato's Cosmological Medicine in the Discourse of Eryximachus in the Symposium: The Responsibility of a Harmonic Technê," *Plato Journal* 15 (2015): 81–93, 88.

105 Anthony S. Kessel, *Air, the Environment and Public Health* (Cambridge, 2006), 26.

106 See for example the Discourse of Eryximachus in the Symposium (Candiotto, "Plato's"), and the first two books of the Republic (Mark Stone, "Plato, Environmental Sustainability, and Social Justice," *Athens Journal of Humanities & Arts* 5 (2018): 105–118).

107 Timothy Mahony, "Platonic Ecology. Deep Ecology," in *The Greeks and the Environment*, eds. Laura Westra, Thomas M. Robinson (Lanham, 1997): 45-54, 48.

108 See, in that sense, Plumwood, *The Mastery*, 70 ff. The debate continued between Plumwood and Mahony in the journal Ethics and the Environment. See Timothy Mahoney, "Platonic Ecology: A Response to Plumwood's Critique of Plato," *Ethics and the Environment* 2 (1997): 25–41; and Val Plumwood, "Prospecting for Ecological Gold Amongst the Platonic Forms: A Response to Timothy Mahoney," *Ethics and the Environment* 2 (1997): 149–168.

109 Florence Bretelle-Establet, "The Worst Environment in Which to Live in China," in *Making Sense of Health, Disease, and the Environment in Cross-Cultural History*, eds. Florence Bretelle-Establet, Marie Gaille, and Mehrnaz Katouzian-Safadi (Cham, 2019): 165–208, 168.

110 Laura Candiotto, "Plato's", 88, referring to the thought of Luc Brisson, "Is the World One? A New Interpretation of Plato *Parmenides*," *in Oxford Studies in Ancient Philosophy* 22 (2002): 1-20.

creation of this order, which Plato found in a superior "craftsman," but in the composition and the interactions among the constitutive parts of this whole. An author highlighted that one of the main problems of (Western in particular) medicine is to understand medicine as science and technology and to separate it from the arts.[111] That is also the problem of international law, which cannot appreciate the connections between global health, the human right to health, and the environment.

The *cosmos* of Plato's thought, in my understanding, is the environment as "us," the "everything-is-connected" of planetary health. A cosmological (international) health law considers environmental global health as a whole, in which all the parties are essential and intertwined, where the health of one part determines the health of all the others and where the health of each and every single element of the whole matters. It is an eco-centric law, which puts the environment, conceived as I did in the commitment, at the core of the system. A cosmological health law could be the theoretical backbone for a creative evolution of the legal system in force. It means, in pragmatic terms, to disrupt the pattern of domination human/nature and consider as subjects of international law a plurality of actors, including nature. It appreciates the right to a healthy environment in the interpretation provided by the Inter-American Court of Human Rights, which goes beyond the humans to pursue the integrity and the interconnections within the environment. It also leads to more flexible solutions, such as, as a first rough conceptualization suggests in the previous paragraph, the consideration of environmental global health as a CCHK entailing rights and responsibilities for all the subjects participating to the achievement of a harmonic and balanced environment. The law of state responsibility should be put into question because it no longer reflects the complexity of the contemporary world. Which actor is responsible for the attacks to environmental global health? How to assess this responsibility? How to demonstrate the link between – say – destruction of biodiversity and the outbreak of a pandemic? Which reparations should be conceived? A possible reconceptualization would lead to common but differentiated responsibilities, theorized in light of the contribution to the harm caused to the environment as "us." A cosmological health law also encourages the creation of a soft organization, where different actors have an equal voice and whose purpose would be to promote environmental global health putting emphasis on the importance of the planet as a whole.

[111] David Grease, "Reflections on a New Medical Cosmology," *J Med Ethics* 28 (2002): 81–85, 81.

9.4 CONCLUDING REMARKS

When the feeling of anxiety and claustrophobia are overwhelming, we search for a way out. We do not know what we are going to find when we cross the threshold, but we try anyway, guided by our knowledge and pushing it beyond what is imaginable. In this chapter, I considered health as part of a broader question of ecological planetary wellbeing, strongly supporting the shift to an eco-centric approach as the only possible way to make a significant change in the world and international law as well. This approach does not lead to deny differences between human beings on one hand, and non-human animals and natural objects on the other, but it is aimed at avoiding a mere anthropocentric and dominant approach, which, as we could see, leads to a legal reaction in a pandemic that is only based on the here and now and misses the scientifically demonstrated relationship between the destruction of the environment and health emergencies. It means to acknowledge different standards of protection, and different rights.

In all this, law – international law – must be characterized by the centrality of the environment meant as "us." It is law produced by humans, but if we put the environment at the center, we disrupt the traditional way to conceive international law and we see it as the product of interdependent bodies. This is my realized, but not impossible, utopia. Who would have ever imagined a treaty like the Whanganui agreement until some years ago? An unconditioned utopia would have probably imagined something more courageous, rooted in deep ecology, but I consider that what we can do as international legal scholars in this moment of global history is to change (at least) approach and mindset.

I also suggested that this eco-centric move might lead to the conceptualization of a cosmological health law, echoing Plato's thoughts, characterized by the holistic interactions among the different parties of the environment. What if the philosopher developing a "harmonic technê" in Plato's thought turns out to be the international lawyer who tries, though still navigating in the familiar waters of the discipline, to bring order in the chaos of an existing fragmented approach to health?

10

Human Rights

David M. Scott

The original critique of human rights is well known. Throughout the 1980s and 1990s, scholars drew attention to various blind spots in the human rights project. Feminists demonstrated its failure in representing and protecting women,[1] just as parallel limitations were targeted by queer[2] and disabled[3] activists, finding powerful institutional battlegrounds in the European Court of Human Rights and the United Nations. TWAIL and post-colonial scholars critiqued the colonial imagery of 'victims, savages and saviors' that

My thanks to the editors and the other workshop participants for invaluable comments on an earlier draft; Valentina Azarova, Yvonne McDermott Rees, and the students of Swansea University's Critical Transnational Lawyering module for discussion of a more polished version; and Eve-Anne Travers for final comments. Any mistakes remain entirely my own.

[1] For an overview see Karen Engle, 'International Human Rights and Feminism: When Discourses Meet', *Michigan Journal of International Law* 13 (1992): 517–610; see also Karen Knop, ed., *Gender and Human Rights* (Oxford, 2004).

[2] Eric Heinze, *Sexual Orientation – A Human Right: An Essay on International Human Rights Law* (Leiden, 1995); Alice M. Miller, 'Human Rights and Sexuality: First Steps Toward Articulating a Rights Framework for Claims to Sexual Rights and Freedoms', *American Society of International Law Proceedings* 93 (1999): 288–303; Kristen Walker, 'Capitalism, Gay Identity and International Human Rights Law', *Gay and Lesbian Law Journal* 9 (2000): 58–73; Kristen Walker, 'Moving Gaily Forward? Lesbian, Gay, and Transgender Human Rights in Europe', *Melbourne Journal of International Law* 2 (2001): 122–43. See also summaries in Emma Mittelstaedt, 'Safeguarding the Rights of Sexual Minorities: The Incremental and Legal Approaches to Enforcing International Human Rights Obligations', *Chicago Journal of International Law* 9 (2008): 353–86; Aeyal Gross, 'Post/Colonial Queer Globalisation and International Human Rights: Images of LGBT Rights', *Jindal Global Law Review* 4 (2013): 98–130, 98–101.

[3] For overviews, see the Symposium on 'International Human Rights Law and the Institutional Treatment of Persons with Mental Disabilities: The Case of Hungary', *New York School Journal of International and Comparative Law* 21 (2002): 339–592; Arlene S. Kanter, 'The Globalization of Disability Rights Law', *Syracuse Journal of International Law and Commerce* 30 (2003): 241–70, and, more recently, Arlene S. Kanter, *The Development of Disability Rights under International Law: From Charity to Human Rights* (London, 2012). My thanks to Richard Gibson for providing some of these references.

underpinned the movement,[4] and many critiques intersected multiple communities.[5] These blind spots, it was said, weakened human rights by reducing their claim to legitimacy and universality, and so correction – through either the creation of new rights, improvements in their enforcement, or a breaking open of the field's 'common sense' – was seen as a vital, although not limitless, horizon.[6]

At the same time, human rights was critiqued as a professional vocation. While offering 'solidarity and witness'[7] against unconscionable abuses like torture and forced disappearance, human rights risked bureaucratising the imagination (and resources) of humanitarian movements, foreclosing other strategies of resistance.[8] Additionally, as 'building the human rights movement' came to be seen as 'its own reward', critical reflection on the actual effect it was having was discouraged, particularly in its entanglement in military interventions abroad.[9] Worrying in this way was seen by the movement as unnecessary:

4 Makau Mutua, 'Savages, Victims, and Saviors – The Metaphor of Human Rights', *Harvard International Law Journal* 42 (2001): 201–45. See also Makau wa Mutua, 'The Ideology of Human Rights', *Virginia Journal of International Law* 36 (1996): 589–657; Makau Mutua, *Human Rights: A Political and Cultural Critique* (Philadelphia, 2008). On TWAIL's engagement with human rights more broadly, see William Twining, ed., *Human Rights, Southern Voices: Francis Deng, Abdullahi An-Na'im, Yash Ghai and Upendra Baxi* (Cambridge, 2009).

5 Anne Orford, 'Contesting Globalization: A Feminist Perspective on the Future of Human Rights', *Transnational Law and Contemporary Problems* 8 (1998): 171–98, critiques the spread of socio-economic inequality from a feminist perspective; feminism is critiqued from a post-colonial perspective in Ratna Kapur, 'The Tragedy of Victimization Rhetoric: Resurrecting the 'Native' Subject in International/Post-Colonial Feminist Legal Politics', *Harvard Human Rights Journal* 5 (2002): 1–38; and feminism is further problematised in Janet Halley, 'Take a Break from Feminism?', in *Gender and Human Rights*, 56–81.

6 Compare Abdullahi Ahmed An-Na'im, 'Introduction', in *Human Rights in Cross-Cultural Perspectives: A Quest for Consensus*, ed. Abdullahi Ahmed An-Na'im (Philadelphia, 1992), 2 ('Clearly, the credibility and practical efficacy of national and international human rights standards would be enhanced by increasing their legitimacy in the widest possible range of cultural traditions') and Heinze, *Sexual Orientation: A Human Right*, 22 ('Human rights law indeed loses credibility if 'everything' becomes a human right, if every malaise becomes elevated to the level of fundamental rights. However, it also loses credibility if, preferring issues that are safe and popular, it ceases to apply its own principles consistently.') with Walker, 'Moving Gaily Forward?,' 143 ('While the courts are important allies in the fight for transgender, gay and lesbian rights, they will not generally lead the way in the absence of some degree of wider social support. We thus need to pursue long term legislative and policy reform as well as judicial avenues in order to move forward in the protection of lesbian, gay and transgender rights.')

7 David Kennedy, 'Spring Break', *Texas Law Review* 63 (1985): 1377–1423, 1393.

8 David Kennedy, 'The International Human Rights Movement: Part of the Problem?', *European Human Rights Law Review* 2 (2001): 245–67. See also Wendy Brown, '"The Most We Can Hope for . . . ": Human Rights and the Politics of Fatalism', *South Atlantic Quarterly* 103 (2004): 451–63.

9 Kennedy, 'The International Human Rights Movement: Part of the Problem?', 260. On humanitarian intervention more specifically, see Anne Orford, *Reading Humanitarian Intervention: Human Rights and the Use of Force in International Law* (Cambridge, 2003).

the language of human rights rose above the bureaucratised violence of international law to speak, finally, in the name of all mankind. After all, who could possibly be *against* human rights?

Some people, apparently.[10] Drawing from strains of Marxism and continental philosophy,[11] scholars such as Costas Douzinas and China Miéville found the project as a whole to be insufficiently radical, at best a bourgeois salve over the deeper systemic violence of Western capitalism. Whatever ideals they may once have upheld, human rights had 'turned from a discourse of rebellion and dissent into that of state legitimacy'.[12] They were too abstract to avoid being 'reappropriated by those in power' and functioned only as a legitimation of the 'edifice of international law' as it continued to produce injustice worldwide.[13] Ultimately, they were a distraction from true emancipation.

By 2010, an entente had been reached. The movement was neither defeated nor perfected, but certain failings were acknowledged and their proponents promised to reflect and do better. 'Both beginners and seasoned veterans are far more savvy and pragmatic than any of us were when I started in the field almost thirty years ago', David Kennedy admitted in 2012. 'Painful lessons hard-learned have sown nagging doubts'.[14] Blind enthusiasm towards human rights was now 'so 90s'[15] and, with its original target gone, critiques against the movement's blindness were rendered kitsch, summarisable in 'eighteen vignettes'.[16] Yet critique has not vanished – on the contrary, critical

[10] Slavoj Žižek, 'Against Human Rights', New Left Review 34 (2005): 115–31.

[11] In Marxism see, classically, Karl Marx, 'On *The Jewish Question*', accessed 15 November 2019, www.marxists.org/archive/marx/works/1844/jewish-question/ and Steven Lukes, 'Can a Marxist Believe in Human Rights?', *Praxis International* 4 (1981): 334–45. From continental philosophy, see Jacques Rancière, 'Who Is the Subject of the Rights of Man?', *South Atlantic Quarterly* 103 (2004): 297–310; Alain Badiou, *Ethics: An Essay on the Understanding of Evil* (London, 2013). Not all Marxists were so convinced of its incommensurability with human rights, however. See Richard Nordahl, 'A Marxian Approach to Human Rights', in *Human Rights in Cross-Cultural Perspectives*, 162–88.

[12] Costas Douzinas, *The End of Human Rights: Critical Legal Thought at the Turn of the Century* (Oxford, 2000), 7.

[13] China Miéville, *Between Equal Rights: A Marxist Theory of International Law* (London, 2006), 304.

[14] David Kennedy, 'The International Human Rights Regime: Still Part of the Problem?', in *Examining Critical Perspectives on Human Rights*, eds. Rob Dickinson et al. (Cambridge, 2012), 19–34, 20.

[15] Martti Koskenniemi, 'Human Rights – So 90s', lecture given at Oxford University, 4 March 2014.

[16] Frédéric Mégret, 'Where Does the Critique of International Human Rights Stand? An Exploration in 18 Vignettes', in *New Approaches to International Law: The European and American Experiences*, eds. José Maria Beneyto and David Kennedy (The Hague, 2012), 3–40.

scholarship on human rights has steamed on ahead, over the past decade replacing its old tactics with new methods and approaches.

It is this relationship, the generational tipping point from the first to the second wave of human rights critique, that this chapter investigates. It aims at providing a broad overview of recent critical approaches to human rights in order to draw out its distinct features compared to previous decades. Like Mégret's vignettes, the chapter operates in 'a broad panoramic and strategic genre', bringing to the surface themes that recur across critique today.[17] I do not claim that every theme is present in every piece of critique written in the past ten years. These themes will be present in differing degrees of intensity in different types of scholarship. That said, my hope is that the chapter captures a broad, holistic picture of dominant trends: the kind of features one would pick out if asked 'what's new in critical human rights?'.

Section 1 begins by delineating four new forms human rights critique has taken over the past decade: an attention to human rights *practices*; an attention to the *history of human rights*; scholars seeking to *transform international law through rights*; and scholars pursuing what I call *'rightless human rights'* – human rights strategies translated into the logics of other legal regimes, notably private law. The tipping point between the two generations is then sketched in (only) nine vignettes. Section 2 identifies three criticisms of the previous generation that recur across today's scholarship: namely, that the first wave was *too pessimistic*, *too narcissistic*, and *too monolithic* in its treatment of the human rights movement. Six distinguishing commitments are then discussed in Section 3, finding in today's scholarship an overriding focus on *contextualism*, *pluralism*, *the temporality of rights*, *the need to tackle 'root causes'*, in particular inequality, *the need to protect human rights from populism*, and finally *the need to subject human rights critique to its own critique*. Section 4 closes with some suggestions as to where the next generation could go.

10.1 WHERE DOES THE CRITIQUE OF INTERNATIONAL HUMAN RIGHTS STAND TODAY?

Some preliminary ground-clearing first: what do I mean by the 'critique' of human rights? I take critique to mean scholarship that reflects on and contests the 'human rights movement', as an idea, culture, professional vocation, or intellectual current in international law.[18] This includes scholarship that

17 Ibid., 6.

18 I take this distinction from Susan Marks, 'Big Brother is Bleeping Us – With the Message that Ideology Doesn't Matter', *European Journal of International Law* 12 (2001): 109–23. See also Mégret, 'Where Does the Critique of International Human Rights Stand?', 4–6.

defends the human rights movement against critique, as rebuttal or refinement of critique implicitly retains an engagement with how the human rights movement should develop, but excludes scholarship that works from inside the parameters of the field to create or extend rights to meet 'new' challenges. So scholarship on environmental rights, the rights to water and food, business and human rights, the extension of rights to animals and rivers, the threat of big data and AI – while all fascinating – is not considered here.

With this in mind, four dominant methods or approaches can be identified as making up the field of critical human rights today. The first is scholarship that focuses on *human rights practices*. While not an entirely new field, the creation of a dedicated *Journal of Human Rights Practice* in 2009 serves as a blunt marker for the uptick in interest in the subject, publishing over the past decade theoretical reflections on methods of evaluation of human rights work,[19] case studies of non-traditional campaigns such as healthcare and housing struggles, particularly in the Global South,[20] and more practical coverage of cause célèbres such as Wikileaks and the Kony 2012 campaign.[21] Elsewhere, critical scholarship has engaged with the human rights practices of social movements – take the early example of Balakrishnan Rajagopal's study of the Narmada Valley struggle in India[22] or Paul O'Connell's and Catherine O'Rourke's recent work on the leveraging of human rights vocabularies by social movements in the UK and Ireland[23] – and the institutional implementation of rights.[24] Empirical studies of the human rights movement have

19 Robert Archer, 'Introduction to the Special Issue: Where is the Evidence?', *Journal of Human Rights Practice* 1 (2009): 333–8 and articles in that Special Issue.

20 Mark Heywood, 'South Africa's Treatment Action Campaign: Combining Law and Social Mobilization to Realize the Right to Health', *Journal of Human Rights Practice* 1 (2009): 14–36; Ludovic Langlois-Thérien, 'The Justiciability of Housing Rights: From Argument to Practice', *Journal of Human Rights Practice* 4 (2012): 213–32; Kristi Heather Kenyon and Regiane A. Garcia, 'Exploring Human Rights-Based Activism as a Social Determinant of Health: Insights from Brazil and South Africa', *Journal of Human Rights Practice* 8 (2016): 198–218.

21 Tom Sorell, 'Human Rights and Hacktivism: The Cases of Wikileaks and Anonymous', *Journal of Human Rights Practice* 7 (2015): 391–410; David Hickman, 'Jason and the Internauts', *Journal of Human Rights Practice* 4 (2012): 475–80.

22 Balakrishnan Rajagopal, 'The Role of Law in Counter-Hegemonic Globalization and Global Legal Pluralism: Lessons from the Narmada Valley Struggle in India', *Leiden Journal of International Law* 18 (2005): 345–87.

23 Paul O'Connell, 'Human Rights: Contesting the Displacement Thesis', *Northern Ireland Legal Quarterly* 69 (2018): 19–35; Catherine O'Rourke, 'Feminist Strategy in International Law: Understanding Its Legal, Normative and Political Dimensions', *European Journal of International Law* 28 (2017): 1019–45.

24 Makau Mutua, 'Standard Setting in Human Rights: Critique and Prognosis', *Human Rights Quarterly* 29 (2007): 547–630; Makau Mutua, *Human Rights Standards: Hegemony, Law, and Politics* (New York, 2016); David Kennedy, *A World of Struggle: How Power, Law, and Expertise Shape Global Political Economy* (Princeton, 2013). While Kennedy's book covers

become more common, too.[25] Uniting this scholarship is an interest in the often conflicting perspectives of those in the field – when, where, how, and to what ends human rights language is used, as opposed to a legalistic focus on treaties, texts, and the lawyers interpreting them.

The second form of critique is the field's much-vaunted *turn to history*. While Samuel Moyn's *The Last Utopia* is widely seen as the catalyser for this turn,[26] the history of human rights is incredibly broad, covering particular treaties,[27] institutions,[28] legal principles,[29] Global South perspectives,[30] and the relationship between rights and other moral traditions, notably religion.[31] The history of human rights was not completely uncharted territory before 2010[32] but has been given a much more critical edge in recent years, where

global governance and political economy more broadly, connections between this strand of Kennedy's work and his earlier human rights critique are drawn out in Stephen Hopgood, 'Law and Lawyers in a World after Virtue', *London Review of International Law* 4 (2016): 451–66.

25 Todd Landman, 'Measuring Human Rights: Principle, Practice, and Policy', *Human Rights Quarterly* 26 (2004): 906–31; Amanda M. Murdie and David R. Davis, 'Shaming and Blaming: Using Events Data to Assess the Impact of Human Rights INGOs', *International Studies Quarterly* 56 (2012): 1–16; Kathryn Sikkink, *Evidence for Hope: Making Human Rights Work in the 21st Century* (Princeton, 2017); Anna Arstein-Kerslake et al., 'Implementing a Participatory Human Rights-Based Research Methodology: The Unfitness to Plead Project', *Journal of Human Rights Practice* 11 (2019): 589–606.

26 Samuel Moyn, *The Last Utopia: Human Rights in History* (Cambridge, MT, 2010).

27 Christopher N. J. Roberts, *The Contentious History of the International Bill of Human Rights* (Cambridge, 2014); Marco Duranti, *The Conservative Human Rights Revolution: European Identity, Transnational Politics, and the Origins of the European Convention* (Oxford, 2017).

28 Stephen Hopgood, *Keepers of the Flame: Understanding Amnesty International* (Ithaca, 2006); Ron Dudai, 'The Long View: Human Rights Activism, Past and Present', *Journal of Human Rights* 7 (2008): 299–309.

29 On *jus cogens*, see Umut Ozsu, 'An Anti-Imperialist Universalism? *Jus Cogens*and the Politics of International Law', in *International Law and Empire: Historical Explorations*, eds. Martti Koskenniemi, Walter Rech, and Manuel Jimenez Fonseca (Oxford, 2017), 295–314; Felix Lange, 'Challenging the Paris Peace Treaties, State Sovereignty, and Western-Dominated International Law – The Multifaceted Genesis of the *Jus Cogens* Doctrine', *Leiden Journal of International Law* 31 (2018): 821–39. On human dignity, see Samuel Moyn, *Christian Human Rights* (Philadelphia, 2015).

30 Mutua, *Human Rights Standards: Hegemony, Law, and Politics*; Julia Dehm, 'Highlighting Inequalities in the Histories of Human Rights: Contestations over Justice, Needs and Rights in the 1970s', *Leiden Journal of International Law* 31 (2018): 871–95.

31 Moyn, *Christian Human Rights*; Pamela Slotte, '"Blessed are the Peacemakers": Christian Internationalism, Ecumenical Voices and the Quest for Human Rights', in *Revisiting the Origins of Human Rights*, eds. Pamela Slotte and Miia Halme-Tuomisaari (Cambridge, 2015), 293–329.

32 For precursors, see the Bibliographical Essay and Acknowledgments in Moyn, *The Last Utopia: Human Rights in History*, 311–26. See also Stefan-Ludwig Hoffmann, 'Introduction: Genealogies of Human Rights', in *Human Rights in the Twentieth Century*, ed. Stefan-Ludwig Hoffmann (Cambridge, 2010), 1–26.

history is investigated with the express purpose of demystifying human rights and unsettling narratives of their inevitability. Understanding how human rights ascended as both a normative and political vocabulary helps us appreciate their interrelation with other processes, as well as attenuating our expectations of the movement. As Moyn puts it: 'To know what to make of human rights in the future, the first step is to understand what they have made us'.[33]

In contrast to the above two approaches, a third group of scholars have reversed their critical attentions to argue for a *transformation of international law through human rights*. In their view, it is not that human rights have failed to live up to their promise but rather that public international law, in its traditional, state-centric form, has proven an intractable obstacle to their realisation. Arguments of this type can be found across many contemporary schools – global law,[34] global constitutionalism,[35] global administrative law[36] – but for ease I will group them under their most visibly human rights-y manifestation: that of humanity's law,[37] a movement that received its near-enough manifesto in Anne Peters' 2009 article 'Humanity as the A and Ω of Sovereignty':

33 Samuel Moyn, 'Epilogue: The Future of Human Rights', in *Human Rights and the Uses of History*, ed. Samuel Moyn (London, 2014), 135–47, 135.

34 Rafael Domingo, *The New Global Law* (Cambridge, 2010), 142, describing global law as the 'law of humanity' and human rights as the 'heart of global law;' see also Neil Walker, *Intimations of Global Law* (Cambridge, 2014), 71–7.

35 Samantha Besson, 'Human Rights as Transnational Constitutional Law', in *Handbook on Global Constitutionalism*, eds. Andrew F. Lang, Jr and Antje Wiener (Cheltenham, 2017), 234–47.

36 Lorenzo Casini, 'The Expansion of the Material Scope of Global Law', in *Research Handbook on Global Administrative Law*, ed. Sabino Cassese (Cheltenham, 2016), 29, describing the development of human rights law as a 'driver of the expansion of global law's material scope' and 'one of the sectors in which global law has developed most in recent decades'.

37 See, among other examples, Theodor Meron, 'International Law in the Age of Human Rights: General Course on Public International Law', *Receuil des Cours* 301 (2003): 1–489, revised and expanded as Thedor Meron, *The Humanization of International Law* (Leiden, 2006); Antônio Augusto Cançado Trindade, 'International Law for Humankind: Towards a New *Jus Gentium*', *Receuil des Cours* 317 (2005): 9–312; Antônio Augusto Cançado Trindade, *The Construction of a Humanized International Law: A Collection of Individual Opinions (1991–2013)*, Volume 1 & 2 (Leiden, 2014); Ruti G. Teitel, 'Humanity's Law: Rule of Law for the New Global Politics', *Cornell International Law Journal* 35 (2002): 355–87; Ruti G. Teitel, *Humanity's Law* (Oxford, 2011). Note that Teitel sees her project as distinct from and significantly more critical than Peters': Ruti Teitel, 'Author's Response to Martti Koskenniemi's Review of Humanity's Law', Ethics and International Affairs 27 (2013): 233–4. For invaluable summation and critical analysis of this school of thought, see Ukri Soirila, 'Humanity Discourse and the Disciplining of the State', *Chinese Journal of International Law* 17 (2018): 861–85; Ukri Soirila, 'Humanity', in *Concepts for International Law: Contributions to Disciplinary Thought*, eds. Jean d'Aspremont and Sahib Singh (Cheltenham, 2019), 361–78; and Ukri Soirila, *The Law of Humanity Project* (London, 2021);

> Humanity is the A and Ω of sovereignty. State sovereignty remains foundational only in a historical or ontological sense, to the extent that the states' mutual respect for each other's sovereignty constitutes the legal system of juxtaposed actors and governs law-making. State sovereignty is not only – as in the meanwhile canonical view – limited by human rights, but is from the outset determined and qualified by humanity, and has a legal value only to the extent that it respects human rights, interests, and needs. … Consequently, conflicts between state sovereignty and human rights should not be approached in a balancing process in which the former is played off against the latter on an equal footing, but should be tackled on the basis of a presumption in favour of humanity.[38]

The final form of critique is perhaps a bit of a cheat, for it covers scholarship that may not necessarily invoke human rights at all – a kind of '*rightless human rights*'.[39] The widespread turn to political economy in international law, for example, has been described as carrying a deep influence from 'the broader ethos of old-school liberal humanitarian movements', suggesting some overlap between the two projects.[40] Analysis of the role private law regimes play in both constituting human rights violations and offering strategies of resistance has also become common. Competition law has been elevated as a new frontier for reining in corporate power and economic inequality,[41] as has taxation, with UN Special Rapporteur on Extreme Poverty and Human Rights Philip Alston repeatedly stressing that 'tax policy is human rights policy'.[42] The focus of this work is the

[38] Anne Peters, 'Humanity as the A and Ω of Sovereignty', *European Journal of International Law* 20 (2009): 513–44, 515.

[39] This section draws in part on personal experience working with the Global Legal Action Network, a team of lawyers, academics, activists, and journalists who work to creatively leverage transnational legal fora for progressive ends. See Global Legal Action Network website, accessed 14 November 2019, for information on the network's activities; and Valentina Azarova and David Scott, 'Transnational Public Interest Lawyering: A Clinical Project – GLAN Manchester reading list [2018–19]', accessed 15 November 2019, for pedagogical reflection.

[40] Akbar Rasulov and John Haskell, 'International Law and the Turn to Political Economy', *Leiden Journal of International Law* 31 (2018): 243–50, 246 and 247.

[41] Tomaso Ferrando and Claudio Lombardi, 'EU Competition Law and Sustainability in Food Systems: Addressing the Broken Links' (Report for Fair Trade Advocacy Office, February 2019) https://fairtrade-advocacy.org/ftao-publications/publications-statements/ (accessed 15 November 2019); Ioannis Lianos and Amber Darr, 'Hunger Games: Connecting the Right to Food and Competition Law', UCL Centre for Law, Economics, and Society Research Paper Series: 2/2019.

[42] See, inter alia, Philip Alston, 'Tax Policy is Human Rights Policy: The Irish Debate', Keynote Address at Christian Aid conference on The Human Rights Impact of Tax and Fiscal Policy, Dublin, 12 February 2015, available at www.ohchr.org; Zak Manfredi, 'Tax Policy is Human Rights Policy', Law and Political Economy Blog, 1 February 2018, https://lpeblog.org/2018/02/01/tax-policy-is-human-rights-policy/; Philip Alston and Nikki Reisch, eds., *Tax, Inequality, and Human Rights* (Oxford, 2019). See also Felix Lange, 'Review of Samuel Moyn. *Not*

same as 'normal' human rights work – seeking an end to impunity, injustice, violations of physical integrity, and so on – but it does so by reaching beyond the movement's traditional sources and forums to appropriate previously alien regimes as new legal strategies. As such, this migration of human rights energies contests the future direction of the movement as much as any explicitly human rights-oriented approach. Who says human rights law is the only way to secure human rights?

10.2 THREE CRITICISMS

With these critical approaches mapped out, this section surveys the common criticisms made against the previous generation. I resist taking a stance on what has produced this generational shift – likely an indeterminate mix of changes in the 'outside world' and the internal dynamics of scholarly production[43] – and focus only on how the previous generation of critique is represented in today's scholarship: an almost trope-like function where its failures are cited as justifying the new methodologies taken up over the past decade.[44] Needless to say, not every second wave critique will demonstrate all three criticisms, but together they capture the broad-brush treatment given to the first wave of critique.

10.2.1 *The First Wave Was too Pessimistic*

The first generational break is in the expectations of the human rights movement. While never against rights completely, first wave critique was not overly positive about its capacity to lead emancipatory projects. At the more modest end of the scale, there was uncertainty as to how far rights could go in incorporating the concerns of marginalised communities.[45] At the other end

Enough: Human Rights in an Unequal World. Cambridge, Massachusetts: Belknap Press', *European Journal of International Law* 29 (2018): 1427–31, 1430–1, who interestingly asks the same question in relation to the critical turn to history: 'should we all become tax lawyers now' that we know the ways in which the human rights movement has failed?

43 On these scholarly dynamics, see Jean d'Apremont, 'Wording in International Law', *Leiden Journal of International Law* 25 (2012): 575–602; Maria Aristodemou, 'A Constant Craving for Fresh Brains and a Taste for Decaffeinated Neighbours', *European Journal of International Law* 25 (2014): 35–58.

44 Note that 'generational' is not understood in a biographical sense, as a set of 'old' versus 'young' academics. David Kennedy and Makau Mutua, for example, appear in both the first and second wave. The idea is rather about mutations to the concept of critique itself: what 'doing' critique meant in the 1980s–2000s versus 'doing' critique now.

45 See, for example, Engle, 'International Human Rights and Feminism: When Discourses Meet', 600: 'Through my own experience learning about and working in the human rights field, I have felt many of the tensions and ambivalences that seem to guide much of women's

of the scale was a clearer distrust: Kennedy's worry was, after all, that the movement is 'more part of the problem in today's world than part of the solution'.[46]

This pessimism is a target of many second wave critiques. O'Connell describes its criticisms as 'overbroad' and 'fundamentally mistaken', using his study of two social movements in London and Ireland to demonstrate how human rights can be leveraged without sacrificing attention to broader injustice.[47] Katheryn Sikkink – in her appropriately titled book *Evidence for Hope* – similarly poses her empirical history of human rights in opposition to 'pessimistic literature'.[48] Among humanity lawyers, Peters finds the 'legal nihilism' of the first wave to be 'exaggerated, confused, or flawed',[49] a summation Ruti Teitel and Robert Howse agree with.[50] And even rightless rights scholarship finds new opportunities in the vocabulary of human rights, leveraging its tools to transform other regimes such as in Tomaso Ferrando and Claudio Lombardi's suggestion to make human rights violations a sanctionable market distortion under competition law.[51]

Perhaps most notably, hardcore anti-rights stances have almost entirely disappeared.[52] This does not mean that the human rights movement has

human rights advocacy. I have wondered whether human rights law and discourse have much to offer women, and I have therefore been uncertain about how to combine my work in feminism and human rights. Sometimes it has seemed as though they comprise two different fields altogether'.

46 Kennedy, 'The International Human Rights Movement: Part of the Problem?', 245.

47 O'Connell, 'Human Rights: Contesting the Displacement Thesis', 24, 25.

48 Sikkink, *Evidence for Hope*, 11.

49 Peters, *Beyond Human Rights*, 532.

50 Robert Howse and Ruti Teitel, 'Does Humanity-Law Require (or Imply) a Progressive Theory of History? (And Other Questions for Martti Koskenniemi)', *Temple International and Comparative Law Journal* 27 (2013): 377–97, 378: 'None of the historical facts or phenomena raised by Koskenniemi have the effect of rendering the humanity-orientation in international law, or the goals of social and political change associated with it, unreasonable or incoherent. … When advocates of human rights speak of a world that is free and just, they are usually not making a claim of messianism or historical determinism, but rather they are simply expressing the ideal outcome implied by their underlying normative commitments'.

51 Ferrando and Lombardi, 'EU Competition Law and Sustainability in Food Systems', 45: 'If a low purchasing price may not be considered a form of dumping per se, the existence of child labour, environmental degradation and violations of human rights could be considered as distortions of the market to be redressed by means of competition law'. See also ibid., 6, which explicitly cites the obligations of member states under the European Convention on Human Rights.

52 One notable exception is Ben Golder's 'pragmatism of refusal': 'an initial step in beginning to weigh the costs and benefits of … other submerged political and legal possibilities is that we have to refuse human rights as the default framework through which we render global injustice intelligible'. See Ben Golder, 'Theorizing Human Rights', in *The Oxford*

won over its sceptics, necessarily – the decline may as easily be a result of the broader decline in interest in postmodern and continental philosophy within legal academia,[53] just as renewed interest in political economy may have redirected the energies of this generation's Marxists[54] – but the dominant mood is to see these anti-rights stances as unfounded.[55] Rights may well be flawed but, in the end, they are as imperfect as any other vocabulary: '[j]ust as democracy and equality are impoverished under capitalism, so too are human rights, but this is no reason to abandon any of these emancipatory languages'.[56]

10.2.2 *The First Wave Was Too Narcissistic*

The second generational break is in who is seen to make up the human rights movement. While scattered references would be made to other actors in the introductory sections of first wave scholarship, actual critique was reserved for the law: 'the machinery, the texts, the profession, the institution'.[57] Accordingly, when first wave critics looked into the movement's future they saw only themselves, and set about either pushing for legal solutions to the movement's problems – more norms, more institutions, more mechanisms of enforcement – or threw themselves into existential crises over the law's indeterminacy.[58] Ironically, this also led them to bemoan their own depoliticising effect: rights strengthened 'lawyers at the expense of priests, engineers, politicians, soothsayers and citizens who might otherwise play a more central role in emancipatory efforts'.[59]

Handbook of the Theory of International Law, eds. Anne Orford and Florian Hoffmann (Oxford, 2016), 684–700, 700.

53 Although cf., again, Ben Golder, *Foucault and the Politics of Rights (Stanford, 2015)*.

54 For two recent Marxist defences of rights, however, see Christopher M. J. Boyd, 'Can a Marxist Believe in Human Rights?', *Critique* 37 (2009): 579–600; Paul O'Connell, 'On the Human Rights Question', *Human Rights Quarterly* 40 (2018): 962–88.

55 Moyn, *Not Enough*, xi, for example, describes his recent historical work as '[staking] out a moderate position between those who claim that human rights are unrelated to political economy and distributive injustice (except of course to provide the essential tools for reining them in) and those who think the human rights revolution has been a mere sham masking inhumane domination'.

56 O'Connell, 'Human Rights: Contesting the Displacement Thesis', 25, citing Prabhat Patnaik, 'A Left Approach to Development', *Economic and Political Weekly* 45 (30) (2010): 33–7.

57 Kennedy, 'The International Human Rights Movement: Part of the Problem?', 259.

58 Kennedy, 'The International Human Rights Movement: Part of the Problem?', 258–60; Martti Koskenniemi, 'The Effect of Rights on Political Culture', in *The European Union and Human Rights*, ed. Philip Alston (Oxford, 1999), 99–116; Martti Koskenniemi, 'Human Rights Mainstreaming as a Strategy for Institutional Power', *Humanity: An International Journal of Human Rights, Humanitarianism, and Development* 1 (2010): 47–58.

59 Kennedy, 'The International Human Rights Movement: Part of the Problem?', 262.

Yet nothing required the human rights movement to be construed in this way. As second wave writers repeatedly make clear, the first wave's legalistic focus excluded large swathes of day-to-day practice, producing a limited picture of how the movement actually worked. If 'tax policy is human rights policy', for example, then critique must grapple with the role of tax lawyers, economic policy advisors, and central bankers in the construction of the human rights movement, just as right to health frameworks require input from medical doctors and development specialists. To gain an accurate picture of how human rights work in a particular struggle, legal strategies have to be situated within the full spread of the movement: 'non-governmental organizations, citizens' initiatives, government bureaus, international institutions, private foundations, military staffs, specialised journalists, authors, and media – all in one or another way "doing" human rights'.[60]

The second wave has thus also pushed back against any presumed link between the legal enforceability of a right and its importance. Rights are not only legal instruments: they can serve as tools for activist mobilisation, alliance-building, policy influence, and so on. 'While it is often assumed that the key benefit of human rights activism is "accountability" and some form of remedy for human rights violations', Christine Bell writes, 'there are often further instrumental benefits to human rights interventions, particularly in deeply divided societies, which are little commented on or factored into legal analysis'.[61] Rajagopal, too, notes that social movements often have a much more 'ambivalent relationship' with the law: it is not immediately clear, in any situation, 'how victim groups perceive the "law" or even to what extent "law" (and what law?) is relevant to the goals of victims themselves'.[62] To presume that legal enforcement is the primary task of human rights activism, then, is false, and so second wave scholarship has criticised the narrow scope of the previous generation, 'on how the great and the good engage with human rights'.[63]

10.2.3 *The First Wave Was Too Monolithic*

Alongside its legalism, the first wave had a habit of describing and critiquing human rights as a single, univocal entity: the movement developed or

60 Kennedy, 'The International Human Rights Movement: Still Part of the Problem?', 20.

61 Christine Bell, 'Human Rights and the Struggle for Change: A Study in Self-Critical Thought', in *Examining Critical Perspectives on Human Rights*, 217–46, 225.

62 Rajagopal, 'The Role of Law in Counter-Hegemonic Globalization and Global Legal Pluralism', 347.

63 O'Connell, 'Human Rights: Contesting the Displacement Thesis', 24.

stagnated at an equal pace, and criticism against one segment could be extended to the whole with little alteration. Where internal conflict was noted, resolution was deferred until after the general tensions of the movement were formulated. Engle, for example, describes her delineation of the different styles of feminist engagement with international human rights law as '[creating] *the possibility* for forthright discussions about the difficult task of applying human rights law to women's issues',[64] while Kennedy similarly hoped to '*encourage* other well meaning legal professionals to adopt a more pragmatic attitude towards human rights' and to '*develop* a stronger practice of weighing the costs and benefits of their articulation, institutionalisation and enforcement'.[65] The articulation of any substantive commitments, as Hilary Charlesworth noted at the time, was visibly absent.[66]

In contrast, the second wave has demonstrated an overriding focus on understanding the discrete and conflicting contexts in which rights are invoked. They may open up legal strategies previously unavailable to activists[67] or clear a space for political discussion.[68] They may pose a radical transformation of disciplinary foundations, as in humanity law and rightless human rights scholarship; or they may entrench a state of affairs, as in Aeyal Gross's studies of the 'pinkwashing' of Israel's occupation of Palestine.[69]

64 Engle, 'International Human Rights and Feminism: When Discourses Meet', 524 [emphasis added]. A similar stopping point occurs in Mutua, 'Savages, Victims, and Saviors', 245: 'The purpose of this Article is not to raise or validate the idea of an original, pure, or a superior Third World society or culture. Nor is it to provide a normative blueprint for another human rights corpus, although such a project must be pursued with urgency. Rather, the Article is a plea for a genuine cross-contamination of cultures to create a new multicultural human rights corpus ... [but the human rights movement] will not do so unless it stops working within the [Savages, Victims, and Saviors] metaphor'.

65 Kennedy, 'The International Human Rights Movement: Part of the Problem?', 246 [emphasis added].

66 Hilary Charlesworth, 'Author! Author! A Response to David Kennedy', *Harvard Human Rights Journal* 15 (2002): 127–32.

67 Rajagopal, 'The Role of Law in Counter-Hegemonic Globalization and Global Legal Pluralism'.

68 Bell, 'Human Rights and the Struggle for Change', 228: 'Human rights standards, for all their vagueness and difficulties of application, are external to particular conflicts and can play a role in moving people towards a conversation about common values *versus* particularistic clientelism. In Northern Ireland, the legal formulation of human rights as international law binding the state also assisted the involvement of the Protestant community on issues that were seen as 'for Nationalists,' by appealing to a broader set of values that had acceptance beyond our shores and were indeed ultimately statist and conservative'.

69 Aeyal Gross, 'Gay Governance: A Queer Critique', in *Governance Feminism: An Introduction*, eds. Janet Halley et al. (Minneapolis, 2018), 344–74; Aeyal Gross, 'Homoglobalism: The Emergence of Global Gay Governance', in *Queering International Law*, ed. Dianne Otto (New York, 2017), 148–70. See also Ron Dudai, 'Entryism, Mimicry and Victimhood Work:

Human rights may well depoliticise, but sometimes – such as in cases of armed conflict and civil war – such depoliticisation may be beneficial. As Christine Bell summarises, 'when translated into a local context, there is a need to question not just the politics of human rights activism, but the politics of the alternatives'.[70] Rights strategies cannot be abstractly theorised. When undertaking critique today, the focus has shifted 'from debates about the intellectual validity of human rights as a way of framing the world towards an exploration of implementation', with implementation to be taken on its own terms.[71]

10.3 THREE COMMITMENTS

At this point, we can turn to commitments. What follows are some common themes of contemporary critique. Some are large questions – existential threats to the future of the movement. Others are smaller, almost rhetorical flourishes. Cumulatively, however, these features give contemporary critique its distinct flavour: a sense of what it means to engage in critique or to 'be' a critical human rights scholar today in contrast to previous decades.

10.3.1 Human Rights Must Be Contextualised

As already discussed, second wave critique places significant weight on the perspectives of the actors using human rights: what their goals and tactics were within a particular struggle, rather than their measurement against some external standard of the critic's choosing. In some cases, this turn is practical. A focus on context gives a better picture of the decision-making practices of institutions, social movements, and NGOs, as a window into the way expertise and governance are exercised in a human rights context.[72] But contextualism is also frequently presented as a commitment to – even solidarity with – those actors who still use the vocabulary. O'Connell, for example, frames his engagement with social movements as a corrective to the previous generation's tendency 'to neglect, or undervalue, the role of social struggles in articulating and contesting formulations of human rights'.[73] Similarly, Sikkink sees her

The Adoption of Human Rights Discourse by Right-Wing Groups in Israel', *International Journal of Human Rights* 21 (2017): 866–88.

70 Bell, 'Human Rights and the Struggle for Change', 224.

71 Richard Carver, Ron Dudai, and Paul Gready, 'Preface to the Anniversary Issue', *Journal of Human Rights Practice* 11 (2019): 271–2, 271.

72 Elizabeth M. Bruch, 'Researching Human Rights Professionals: Tracing the Networks of Human Rights Practice', *Journal of Human Rights Practice* 11 (2019): 116–31.

73 O'Connell, 'Human Rights: Contesting the Displacement Thesis', 25.

work as carrying 'a more positive message that could help sustain [activists] in the context of their current struggles'.[74] Placing the viewpoints of human rights actors front and center works to dispel the pessimism of the prior generation by changing the standard of critical evaluation. Rights strategies are to be evaluated in light of the goals, limitations, and resources of a particular movement, so that outcomes – even if imperfect – are measured against pragmatic expectations. When judging the strategic possibilities of human rights, then, the first people we should ask are those who use them.[75]

10.3.2 *Human Rights Must Be Pluralised*

Packaged with this contextualisation is a commitment to expanding the concept of the human rights movement. Sometimes this is a disciplinary question: '[c]ross-fertilization' within the movement will 'challenge conventional ways of working, stimulate innovation, and encourage reflective practice'.[76] Other times, the focus is on traditionally excluded actors, such as those in the Global South. But notice how this marks a shift from the previous generation's focus on discursive blind spots. Contemporary critique has not abandoned this kind of analysis, but supplements it with an assessment of the actual representativeness of human rights processes: who, in practice, is excluded from shaping that discourse, in which fora, and at which stages of implementation. A human rights movement that takes seriously the viewpoints of social movements or Global South actors as the starting point of human rights practice will look very different to one operating in a legalist mode.[77] The commitment of second wave critique, then, is to making those

74 Sikkink, *Evidence for Hope*, 7.

75 Note, in this light, the increasing reliance on participant interviews as a form of human rights data: see Bruch, 'Researching Human Rights Professionals'; Eitan Felner, 'Human Rights Leaders in Conflict Situations: A Case Study of the Politics of "Moral Entrepreneurs,"' *Journal of Human Rights Practice* 4 (2012): 57–81; Tanya Notley, Sam Gregory, and Andrew Lowenthal, 'Video for Change: Creating and Measuring Ethical Impact', *Journal of Human Rights Practice* 9 (2017): 223–46.

76 Gready and Philips, 'An Unfinished Enterprise', 3. See similarly Philip Alston, 'The Populist Challenge to Human Rights', *Journal of Human Rights Practice* 9 (2017): 1–15, 4: 'Going forward, it will be highly desirable for the movement to ... involve a broader range of interlocutors in its reflections than has been the case in the past'.

77 See variously O'Connell, 'Human Rights: Contesting the Displacement Thesis', 24 ('A failure to understand human rights as grounded in antagonistic social struggles and, as such, reflecting such antagonisms, results in a one-sided, negative understanding of human rights, and leads, readily, to their dismissal'.); Sikkink, *Evidence for Hope*, 10 (distinguishing her approach from the traditional debate over 'global pessimism and optimism' about human rights by focusing 'instead on the impact of a long series of human rights struggles, often led by

voices heard. As Mutua puts clearly: 'It is not that I doubt the ability of my colleagues in the North to exercise the skepticism that is necessary; rather, the voices that have been shut out are the only ones that are likely to say something really new'.[78]

10.3.3 *Human Rights Must Be Temporalised*

If first wave critique was frustrated with the 'end-of-History trumpeting' of the human rights movement of the 1980s and 1990s,[79] the second wave has become obsessed with how to place it in history. This isn't only in the field's historical turn. Humanity scholars, for example, frequently refer to globalisation as a kind of historical rupture that both necessitates and empowers the expansion of human rights,[80] and elsewhere, the debate is on how we characterise our present: is it neoliberal?[81] populist?[82] post-human?[83] an age or austerity?[84] Or are these simply euphemisms for the longer history of capitalism?[85]

oppressed people, inspired by human rights ideas, and targeting powerful institutions and practices, including colonialism and deep exclusion and repression'); Dehm, 'Highlighting Inequalities in the Histories of Human Rights', 873 (contrasting between 'a particular vision and form of human rights as an internationally authorized claim of the individual against the state, rather than recognizing that this configuration of rights is itself historically contingent and the product of social struggles').

78 Mutua, *Human Rights Standards: Hegemony, Law, and Politics*, ix.

79 Mégret, 'Where Does the Critique of International Human Rights Stand?', 6.

80 See, for example, Anne Peters, 'The Merits of Global Constitutionalism', *Indiana Journal of Global Legal Studies* 16 (2009): 397–411, 405: 'Globalization puts the state and state constitutions under strain. … What were typically governmental functions, such as guaranteeing human security, freedom, and equality, are in part transferred to "higher" levels'.

81 Samuel Moyn, 'A Powerless Companion: Human Rights in the Age of Neoliberalism', *Law and Contemporary Problems* 77 (2014) 147–69; Jessica Whyte, *The Morals of the Market: Human Rights and the Rise of Neoliberalism* (London, 2019); and the Legal Form symposium on the latter, available at https://legalform.blog/archive/.

82 Ron Dudai, 'Human Rights in the Populist Era: Mourn then (Re)Organize', *Journal of Human Rights Practice* 9 (2017) 16–21; Gerald L. Neuman, ed., *Human Rights in a Time of Populism: Challenges and Responses* (Cambridge, 2020). For critical discussion, see Christine Schwöbel-Patel, 'Populism, International Law and the End of *Keep Calm and Carry on Lawyering*', *Netherlands Yearbook of International Law* 49 (2018): 97–121.

83 Upendra Baxi, *Human Rights in a Posthuman World* (Oxford, 2009).

84 Paul O'Connell, 'Let Them Eat Cake: Socio-Economic Rights in an Age of Austerity', in *Human Rights and Public Finance: Budgets and the Promotion of Economic and Social Rights*, eds. Aoife Nolan, Rory O'Connell, and Colin Harvey (Oxford, 2013), 59–76.

85 Susan Marks notes that 'the talk in human rights reports, as well as in the academic literature, is of how human rights stand with respect to "the market" or to "globalisation," "economic liberalisation," or "neo-liberalism"' rather than in relation to capitalism: Susan Marks, 'Four

These framings are important for how contemporary critique is carried out. They foreground different actors, traditions, processes, events, and measurements of significance that all shape the way human rights are understood and shaped. Once aware of these time phrases, in fact, you find them everywhere. The genre is now cluttered with human rights 'futures'[86] and 'endtimes'[87] and a pervasive sense that human rights are 'out of time', both in the closing of the 'age of rights'[88] and their anachronistic survival in some new, hostile epoch. Rarely, if ever, will you find the kind of ahistorical treatment that was common in the previous generation, where the movement could be generically improved by changing its understanding of human rights to be more inclusive, effective, pragmatic, and so on. For that reason, it seems better to talk not of the historicisation but of their *temporalisation*: the ways in which contemporary critique instinctively situates human rights in time, providing them with a past, present, and future that sharpens our diagnosis of their operation.[89]

Human Rights Myths', in *Human Rights: Old Problems, New Possibilities*, eds. David Kinley, Wojciech Sadurski, and Kevin Walton (Cheltenham, 2013), 217–35, 232. These terms all have different temporalities: 'neoliberalism' is rooted in the 1980s, 'globalization' in the 1990s, but 'capitalism' back to the 1800s.

86 Upendra Baxi, *The Future of Human Rights* (Oxford, 2000); Samuel Moyn, 'Epilogue: The Future of Human Rights', in Samuel Moyn, *Human Rights and the Uses of History*, 135–48; Stephen Hopgood, Jack Snyder, and Leslie Vinjamuri, eds., *Human Rights Futures* (Cambridge, 2017); James Loeffler and Mila Versteeg, 'Foreword: The Future of Human Rights Scholarship', *Law and Contemporary Problems* 81 (2018): i–xi. See also Oxford University's 'Oxford Martin Programme on Human Rights for Future Generations', accessed 28 October 2019.

87 Stephen Hopgood, *The Endtimes of Human Rights* (Ithaca, 2013); Eric Posner, *The Twilight of Human Rights Law* (Oxford, 2014).

88 Makau Mutua, 'Is the Age of Human Rights Over?', in *The Routledge Companion to Literature and Human Rights*, eds. Sophia A. McClennen and Alexandra Schultheis Moore (London, 2016), 450–8; Ingrid Wuerth, 'International Law in the Age of Trump: A Post-Human Rights Agenda', Lawfare, 14 November 2016.

89 My thinking here is influenced by the work of German historian Reinhart Koselleck. See, in particular, Reinhart Koselleck, '"Space of Experience" and "Horizon of Expectation": Two Historical Categories', in *Futures Past: On the Semantics of Historical Time*, ed. Reinhart Koselleck (New York, 2004), 255–75; and Reinhart Koselleck, 'Constancy and Change of All Contemporary Histories: Conceptual-Historical Notes', in *Sediments of Time: On Possible Histories*, ed. Reinhart Koselleck (Stanford, 2018), 100–16. Cf. Fleur Johns, 'The Temporal Rivalries of Human Rights', *Indiana Journal of Global Legal Studies* 23 (2016): 39–60, 42, who uses temporality in a different sense, looking not at changing perceptions in the time-consciousness of scholarship but on the ways human rights practice '[engenders] regular temporal rhythms more or less of its own production'.

10.3.4 *Human Rights Must Tackle Root Causes, In Particular Inequality*

In 2011, Susan Marks wrote of the newfound interest in the 'root causes' of human rights violations: 'not just about what human rights abuse causes; [but] also about what causes human rights abuse'.[90] Critique has followed this turn, with economic inequality becoming a particular focal point.[91] Moyn, for example, has been vocal in calling for the human rights movement to rethink its strategies in the face of rising inequality, lest it become 'a casualty of a justifiable revolt against the rich'.[92] Anne Peters, too, characterises 'debates on poverty, inequality, and social exclusion' as 'global concerns', connecting these concerns to the emergence of humanity law-oriented frameworks.[93] And much of the impetus behind rightless human rights is an attempt to grasp at these economic inequalities through the realm of private rather than public law. 'Gone are the days when it was thought sufficient to expose killings, torture, arbitrary detention', Alston states in his speech on tax policy. 'We now realize that such policies are rooted in broader societal structures and that they too need to be addressed'.[94]

10.3.5 *Human Rights Must Be Protected from Populism*

The other commonly identified threat to the human rights movement is populism.[95] Alston characterises populist leaders 'as explicitly antagonistic to all or much of the human rights agenda', posing a challenge for the human rights movement 'fundamentally different from much of what has gone before'.[96] Global constitutionalists, too, have cast populism as 'an attack on the three foundational features of the global constitution – democracy, human

90 Susan Marks, 'Human Rights and Root Causes', *Modern Law Review* 74 (2011): 57–78, 61.

91 Cf. Dehm, 'Highlighting Inequalities in the Histories of Human Rights', who explores how debates on inequality were already occurring between states and international institutions in the 1970s. The focus here is on critique's (re)integration of inequality as a structural concern, rather than an assertion that human rights have never encountered inequality before (a distinction Dehm similarly draws: ibid., 873).

92 Samuel Moyn, 'How the Human Rights Movement Failed', New York Times, 23 April 2018.

93 Anne Peters, 'Global Constitutionalism: The Social Dimension', in *Global Constitutionalism from European and East Asian Perspectives*, eds. Takao Suami et al. (Cambridge, 2018), 275–350, 290.

94 Alston, 'The Populist Challenge to Human Rights', 1.

95 The two are often linked, in fact, with rising inequality eroding support for the 'system', including human rights, and thus setting the scene for anti-systemic populists. See Alston, 'The Populist Challenge to Human Rights', 6; Dudai, 'Human Rights in the Populist Era', 19; Moyn, 'How the Human Rights Movement Failed'.

96 Alston, 'The Populist Challenge to Human Rights', 1–2.

rights, and the rule of law'.[97] Yet the populist moment, scholars stress, is not the end of human rights. Rather, it offers 'an opportunity for revitalizing' them,[98] provided that the movement responds with 'innovative thinking and creative strategising'.[99] Populism poses deep questions about why the movement has lost popular support, why 'the majority in society feel that they have no stake in the human rights enterprise, and that human rights groups really are just working for "asylum seekers," "felons," "terrorists," and the like'.[100] In this way, populism calls for recommitment to the movement to stop the very spread of authoritarian populism. If rights can be made worthy of popular support again, they also provide a frontier for protecting the rest of the system.

10.3.6 Human Rights Critique Must Be Critiqued

In his discussion of populism, Alston makes a number of comments about the role of scholarship at the present juncture. 'It has become fashionable, especially at elite universities in the West, to disparage human rights', Alston writes. Much critical scholarship is 'formulaic, and unfocused in meaningful or instructive ways on the real challenges that confront us and on the challenges that are becoming more and more real by the day in our world'. Alston thus asks scholars to reflect on the 'unintended consequences' of their critique: the transmission to students 'that the human rights enterprise is largely an illusion, that it is not something that they really should be putting their time into, that it is built on sand, and that it has no future'. Facing populism's real hostility to the human rights project, Alston suggests that now is not the time for cynicism.[101]

We can quibble over the connections drawn here between populism and critique, but it does signal a broader self-reflexivity that can be found across critical scholarship today. In previous generations the critic was placed firmly outside the field: the human rights movement was something 'over there', to

97 Jonathan Havercroft et al., 'Editorial: Donald Trump as Global Constitutional Breaching Experiment', *Global Constitutionalism* 7 (2018): 1–13, 4. See similarly Mattias Kumm et al., 'Editorial: The End of 'the West' and the Future of Global Constitutionalism', *Global Constitutionalism* 6 (2017): 1–11, 2 (describing the success of populist parties as signaling 'the decay of "the West" as a relatively cohesive geopolitical configuration anchoring a normative model of global order in which commitments to human rights, democracy and the rule of law are central'); Anthony F. Lang, Jr and Antje Wiener, 'A Constitutionalising Global Order: An Introduction', in *Handbook on Global Constitutionalism*, eds. Anthony F. Lang, Jr and Antje Wiener (Cheltenham, 2017), 1–20.

98 Dudai, 'Human Rights in the Populist Era', 16.

99 Alston, 'The Populist Challenge to Human Rights', 2.

100 Ibid., 6.

101 Ibid., 13.

be studied and critiqued in a detached manner. Now, however, the 'critical human rights scholar' is a character in the story: the academic 'sitting in Harvard applying critical thought to concepts in a cool and rational way' contrasted with the activist in the field.[102] This dichotomy raises real questions about the relationship critique should maintain with practice, as Lynn Welchman captures in a telling anecdote:

> In the spring of 2014, getting ready for my flight home from a meeting in Tunis, I put the book I was going to read on the plane down on the breakfast table I was sharing with some friends from the Arab human rights movement. Its title caught their attention: *The Endtimes of Human Rights*. 'End times?' one exclaimed in mock horror, 'we've hardly had a chance to get started and it's already over?'[103]

Cynicism is out of fashion. When scholars reflect on why they participate in critique, the distancing of the movement from critique has been replaced with a more closely drawn relationship, aiming to ensure that critique is 'doing something' in the 'real world'. As Dustin Sharp writes: 'It is not too much to expect us to answer questions such as: What would satisfy us? What should come next? What is it about a particular critique that might open up space for hope, dialogue, and change? In sum, when David Kennedy asks whether the human rights movement has become "part of the problem," I think this question needs to include the entire travelling circus of professionals and commentators'.[104]

10.4 CONCLUSION

Let me try and draw this all together into a coherent picture. The tipping point of human rights critique has both expanded and detailed its scope. Rejecting the generalised pessimism of the previous generation, critical approaches over the past decade have situated human rights in their actual practice,

102 Bell, 'Human Rights and the Struggle for Change', 219.

103 Lynn Welchman, 'Human Rights, Law and Politics: A Reflection on Human Rights Work in the Middle East and North Africa', in *Routledge Handbook on Human Rights and the Middle East and North Africa*, ed. Anthony Tirado Chase (Abingdon, 2016), 502–11, 502.

104 Dustin N. Sharp, 'Through a Glass, Darkly: Three Important Conversations for Human Rights Professionals', *Journal of Human Rights Practice* 11 (2019): 296–304, 300. See similarly Bell, 'Human Rights and the Struggle for Change', 245: 'Just as Kennedy sees a loss in the legalisation and "expertisation" of humanitarian enterprises, so I feel a loss that I think is related to his, revolving around the "academicisation" of the activism of movements. I wonder whether we can stop our critique of the deadening hand of legal analysis of human rights at the movement or whether we need to include academic voices and even critical discourse as a part of the overall tapestry'.

determining on a more day-to-day level who is and is not able to wield them to particular ends. Yet this reorientation has also broadened the horizons of its demands: critique is no longer an inward-facing, intellectual judgment of the human rights movement, but an outward positioning of the movement in relation to structural questions: of time/history, of inequality, and of (re) surgent populism. In this way, contemporary scholarship shows both a recommitment to the human rights movement and a raising of our expectations of it.

Where, then, will the critique of international human rights stand tomorrow? One prevalent theme of contemporary scholarship has been to treat the field no longer as a unified movement but an overlapping and often contradictory set of struggles, actors, perspectives, histories, 'worlds', times, expectations, and anxieties.[105] Reading critical scholarship across the past decade, one starts to wonder if scholars are even talking about the same topic anymore. At what stage do 'human rights' cease to be a useful lens for viewing this work? Is there a point where we would be better talking about 'activist legal strategy', perhaps, or 'NGO studies?'

There's a sense of déjà vu here for anyone who remembers the handwringing that happened over international law's fragmentation not so long ago.[106] In posing the fracturing of the human rights movement as a loss or a gain, one unveils a predisposition towards that movement in the first place. Nevertheless, it is important to think about the effect this could have on the power of human rights critique. The worst outcome would be for critical energies to dissipate into an infinite number of foxholes. If critical scholarship wants to maintain its renewed commitment to human rights as a tool against

105 I take this phrase from Upendra Baxi, 'Concepts of Human Rights: The Three Worlds of Human Rights', in People's Movement for Human Rights Learning, *Human Rights Learning: A Peoples' Report* (New York, 2006), 17–23, who distinguishes between the production of human rights standards at the international level, their translation (and transgression) through national implementation, and their rearticulation in activist struggle.

106 Compare Anne Peters, 'The Refinement of International Law: From Fragmentation to Regime Interaction and Politicization', *International Journal of Constitutional Law* 15 (2017): 671–704, 680, describing the fragmentation debate as 'a concern for a loss of legitimacy of international law, a loss which will ultimately threaten that law's very existence'; Sahib Singh, 'The Potential of International Law: Fragmentation and Ethics', *Leiden Journal of International Law* 24 (2011): 23–43, 23, who saw fragmentation as 'a rare opportunity for international lawyers to review what has gone and what is to come: . . . in short, a chance to learn lessons of the past'; and Eyal Benvenisti and George W. Downs, 'The Empire's New Clothes: Political Economy and the Fragmentation of International Law', *Stanford Law Review* 60 (2007): 595–631, who saw the debate as a strategy of disempowerment, bogging everyone down while real power worked smoothly across these divisions. More ambivalently, see Martti Koskenniemi and Paivi Leino, 'Fragmentation of International Law? Postmodern Anxieties', *Leiden Journal of International Law* 15 (2002): 553–79.

inequality, populism, and the like, then an open conversation about how to balance contextualism with coherence is worthwhile.

With this in mind, let me close by sketching some possibilities as to how this conversation could start. The first option would be to make critique more goal-oriented.[107] Second wave scholarship has made much of its decoupling of the human rights movement from human rights law, as well as its renewed focus on structural inequality, but in terms of strategy it remains shy in outlining the actual policies human rights should be placed in support of. Thinking more explicitly about how human rights could contribute to concrete demands like universal healthcare, climate justice, or a job guarantee would be one way of bridging between the structural and the contextual, to attach rights more overtly to particular causes.[108] To be clear, this is not a suggestion to return to the old vocabulary of inventing new rights – rights 'to' the environment or social security. Rather, it would mark an extension of the contextual lessons of second wave scholarship in a more programmatic fashion: to provide a better sense of the contribution human rights can make in a particular struggle, for particular classes of actors, at a particular juncture, in contrast to or in collaboration with other approaches.

Alternatively, one could think less about finding new banners under which to organise human rights practices and think instead about techniques of reconstitution and translation: how best to connect the insights of an activist with the mechanisms of an international institution, or how a neoliberal account can be made to speak to a populist one. I'm not suggesting a total erasure of difference – many differences, of course, reflect important political distinctions that should rightly be fought over – but reflection on the deeper reasons why we continue to critically engage with human rights at all, despite the wide variances in approach and perspective, may produce common ground for new avenues of research. Somewhat obliquely, what I have in mind is the work of anthropologist Anna Tsing and her concept of translation as 'the drawing of one world-making project into another'.[109] What different frameworks of translation can we conceive of to bridge across faultlines?

107 My thanks to John Haskell for this suggestion.

108 I am thinking here in a similar direction to Barrie Sander, 'The Expressive Turn of International Criminal Justice: A Field in Search of Meaning', *Leiden Journal of International Law* 32 (2019): 851–72, particularly 866–71, where international criminal courts are instrumentalised for non-traditional and extra-legal purposes, for example by lodging a complaint with the International Criminal Court to draw attention to the ill-treatment of refugees by the Australian government, regardless of the actual legal success of that complaint.

109 Anna Lowenhaupt Tsing, *The Mushroom at the End of the World: On the Possibility of Life in Capitalist Ruins* (Princeton, 2015), 62.

Tsing's work – which focuses specifically on the 'world-making' of capitalist supply chains – points us to one suggestion, which would be to take seriously the materiality of human rights practices: how these practices are facilitated, how long they take, how much they cost, where that money comes from, and who is or is not able to access it. Thinking about the human rights 'supply chain', where energy (and money) are entered at one end with the hope of some tangible outcome at the other, may in turn unveil other frontiers for improving the effectiveness of human rights work – questions like the availability of legal aid for claimants, the importance of human rights education, or the role law clinics can play in bridging between academia and practice.[110] Thinking of human rights as a process, with spaces of varying opportunity and limitation, allows us to identify non-traditional pressure points and 'chokeholds' that can be analysed, targeted, and struggled over.[111] One might even loosely call this – with all the fuzziness already noted in international law's appropriation of the term[112] – a kind of *political economy* of human rights practices.[113]

If scholars can contribute a more accurate image of the diverse ways activists, practitioners, and institutions interface within human rights, however conceived, they can help bring to light the constraints and opportunities that structure those interactions – structures that may be less visible from the trenches of the movement. Once armed with that knowledge, practitioners

110 On law clinics, see Lynn Welchman, 'The International Human Rights Clinic at SOAS', in *Reinventing Legal Education: How Clinical Education is Reforming the Teaching and Practice of Law in Europe*, eds. Alberto Alemanno and Lamin Khadar (Cambridge, 2018), 247–71. For a more significant university involvement in human rights struggle, see Rajan Hoole, 'Sri Lanka: Ethnic Strife, Fratricide, and the Peace vs. Human Rights Dilemma', *Journal of Human Rights Practice* 1 (2009): 120–39, covering the role the University Teachers for Human Rights (Jaffna) group played during the Sri Lankan civil war. On human rights education outside the university, see Alison E. C. Struthers, 'The Underdeveloped Transformative Potential of Human Rights Education: English Primary Education as a Case Study', *Journal of Human Rights Practice* 9 (2017): 68–84.

111 On this idea, see Tomaso Ferrando, 'Land Rights at the Time of Global Production: Leveraging Multi-Spatiality and "Legal Chokeholds,"' *Business and Human Rights Journal* 2 (2017): 275–95; and more generally The IGLP Law and Global Production Working Group, 'The Role of Law in Global Value Chains: A Research Manifesto', *London Review of International Law* 4 (2016): 57–79.

112 Rasulov and Haskell, 'International Law and the Turn to Political Economy'.

113 For one example – albeit not framed in these terms – see the *Journal of Human Rights Practice* special issue on funding: Victoria Forbes Adam and Ingrid Massagé, 'Funding Effective Human Rights Work', *Journal of Human Rights Practice* 8 (2016): 311–5 and following articles, particularly Elizabeth A. Wilson, 'Restrictive National Laws Affecting Human Rights Civil Society Organizations: A Legal Analysis', *Journal of Human Rights Practice* 8 (2016): 329–57, which explores the kind of non-traditional limitations on human rights work that seem ripe for further exploration.

will be given new avenues for making human rights work more effective. None of these ideas are fully fleshed out; nor do they preclude the pursuit of other avenues. But a critical project that places some or all of these questions front and center, in my mind, will be better equipped to continue forging connections between critical scholarship and the actual practice of rights, recommitting the movement to its fight against structural injustice.

11

Labor

Raúl Carrillo

Labor has seen better days. The early twenty-first century has witnessed a worldwide decline in the power of unions and labor movements generally.[1] "Rights talk" is understandably the last discourse many labor scholars want to revisit. After all, labor rarely receives a fair hearing in the courts. Historically, the "most utopian elements of the labor movement" have avoided judiciaries as anti-democratic sites of agitation.[2] And yet, without arguing for rights beyond workplace bargaining power, unions and labor movements have consistently been defeated by arguments for "negative" individual rights.[3] As a result, we should contemplate rights-based reforms beyond labor union empowerment, including guaranteed jobs.[4] Such reforms need not (and should not) be won through the courts. Nor should they be treated as ends unto themselves. But they should be won.

The stakes are staggering. Labor injustice has become ecocidal.[5] Since the industrial revolution, economic growth, development, and poverty reduction have depended on the exploitation of natural resources, but particularly from

Thanks to Dr. John Haskell for inviting me to participate in this series, and for his insightful comments. Additional thanks to the Modern Money, Job Guarantee, and Law and Political economy communities. I would not have these thoughts without them.

1 *See* Jedidiah J. Kroncke, *The False Hope of Union Democracy*, 39 U. PA. J. INT'L L. 615 (2018) (going on to survey union development and decline in the United States, Brazil, and China).

2 Kate Andrias, *Building Labor's Constitution*, 94 TEX. L. REV. 1591, 1594 (2016).

3 *See* Kroncke, *supra* note 1, at 622 (describing this process as "near completion" in the United Kingdom and "well in progress" in the United States).

4 *Id.* at 703.

5 *See generally* INTERGOVERNMENTAL PANEL ON CLIMATE CHANGE, GLOBAL WARMING OF 1.5°C at 177–283 (Valérie Masson-Delmotte et al. eds., 2019), https://www.ipcc.ch/sr15/ (detailing the risks of global warming of 1.5°C or more, including ecosystem and species loss; increased drought, heatwaves, and flooding; declining ocean and agricultural productivity; decreased water and food security; and continuing sea-level rise into the next century).

the global south.[6] Fossil fuels have driven access to energy, transportation, and quality of life improvements for many workers. Yet with a perpetual lack of bargaining power *as a class* – and for many, additional disadvantages due to other identities – workers around the globe are locked into the perpetuation of a climate catastrophe that will destroy our homes and terminate the species.

This chapter argues that the full realization of the "right to work," found in several treaties in international law, would require, on its own terms,"true full employment", wherein everyone who wants a job is entitled to one-vis-a-vis a state party. Moreover, whereas some courts and scholars have argued that true full employment is economically impossible for most states or all states due to lack of fiscal resources, advances in monetary theory (and critical legal theories of money, public finance, and macroeconomics) suggest this is not the case. Indeed, although there exists a *spectrum of monetary sovereignty* and different states face different geopolitical and financial pressures, many of the assumptions that suggest the "right to work" is economically impractical to realize in full effect should now be discarded. Public monetary and financial systems can be reconfigured to directly create jobs and full employment, as well as other collective workers' rights, to say nothing of preserving human life on this planet.

11.1 THE RIGHT TO WORK UNDER INTERNATIONAL HUMAN RIGHTS LAW

The right to work – generally conceived as an individual entitlement to a job paying wages capable of supporting a dignified existence – has a long history across the globe, within liberalism, socialism, and other traditions.[7] Although the right to work may not have figured prominently in the politics leading to the French Revolution, it was the "first right in importance" for the new Jacobin state.[8] Indeed, the right to work was first encoded as a human right in the French Constitution of 1793.[9] Over the next 150 years, right to work claims featured in the programmatic goals of both revolutionary and reformist

6 Special Rapporteur on Extreme Poverty and Human Rights, *Climate Change and Poverty, Rep. of the Special Rapporteur on Extreme Poverty and Human Rights*, ¶10, Human Rights Council, UN A/HRC/41/39 (July 17, 2019).

7 *See, e.g.*, Philip Harvey, *Human Rights and Economic Policy Discourse: Taking Economic and Social Rights Seriously*, 33 Colum. Hum. Rts. L. Rev. 363, 371 (2002) (discussing the history of the right to work in broad strokes).

8 Samuel Moyn, Not Enough: Human Rights in an Unequal World 28 (2018).

9 1793 Const. 21 (Fr.) (declaring that "[p]ublic relief is a sacred debt. Society owes maintenance to the unfortunate, either by procuring them work, or by providing the means of existence to those who are unable to labor."). The general "right to work" is maintained in the current

political, social, and religious movements (though just as often ignored).[10] In the aftermath of World War II and the birth of the United Nations (UN), the right to work finally attracted significant enough attention to be recognized in numerous human rights agreements.[11] Over the following decades, it has also been recognized in several national constitutions to various degrees, even among countries with markedly different labor systems.[12]

Today, Article 23A of the Universal Declaration of Human Rights (UDHR) declares that "everyone has the right to work, to free choice of employment, to just and favourable conditions of work and to protection against unemployment."[13] The drafters understood the obligation required the state to at least *strive* to achieve full employment as recognized in Articles 55 and 56 of the UN Charter.[14] Although the UDHR is not a treaty, it has arguably evolved into a "statement of customary international law."[15] The UN Millenium Development Goals also include the objective of "full and productive employment for all, including women and young people."[16]

The preambles of several International Labor Organization (ILO) treaties similarly point to the right to work. As a general matter, the ILO maintains the

French Constitution, but is not construed as having any enforceable duties. *See* Sophie Robin-Olivier, *The French Approach to The Right to Work: The Potential of a Constitutional Right in Ordinary Courts* in THE RIGHT TO WORK: LEGAL AND PHILOSOPHICAL PERSPECTIVES at 195 (Virginia Mantouvalou ed., 2015).

10 *See* Harvey, *supra* note 7.

11 *Id.*

12 For instance, communist countries have historically established both rights to work and duties to work. *See* Amir Paz-Fuchs, *The Right to Work and the Duty to Work* in THE RIGHT TO WORK, SUPRA NOTE 9, at 177, 182–189 (Virginia Mantouvalou ed., 2015) [Hereinafter THE RIGHT TO WORK]. *But see also* Article 27, paragraph 1 of the current Constitution of Japan also includes a right to work and obligation to work. *See* Kenji Arita, *The Development of Right to Work Theories of Labour Law in Japan* in THE RIGHT TO WORK at 177, 182–189 (Virginia Mantouvalou ed., 2015). Overall, 138 national constitutions have recognized the "right to work" in some form or another. CONSTITUTE PROJECT, www.constituteproject.org/search?lang=en&key=provwork (last visited July 1, 2020).

13 Universal Declaration of Human Rights, G.A. Res. 217A (III), U.N. GAOR, 3d Sess., Resolutions, Part I, U.N. Doc. A/810 (1948).

14 *See* Harvey, *supra* note 7, at 376–377.

15 *Id.* at 375–376. Some scholars argue the UDHR is fundamentally imperialist in construction and impact and the very point of demanding rights under its banner is to cause crises of legitimacy. *See*, e.g., Jeena Shah, UDHR: Our North Star for Global Social Justice or an Imperial and Settler-Colonial Tool to Limit Our Conception of Freedom?, 31 Pace Int'l L. Rev. 569, 570 (2019). See also Makau wa Mutua, Savages, Victims, and Saviors: The Metaphor of Human Rights 42 HARV. INT'L L. J. (2001); Makau wa Mutua, The Ideology of Human Rights, 36 VA. J. INT'L L. 589 (1996) (arguing human rights law is rooted in a Eurocentric rhetoric and corpus).

16 *See* U.N. STATISTICS DIVISION MILLENNIUM DEVELOPMENT GOALS INDICATORS, http://mdgs.un.org/unsd/mdg/default.aspx.

1940s definition of "full employment" as a "situation where all persons seeking employment have been provided with paid positions."[17] However, only a few ILO conventions deal with employment creation, much less direct job creation by state parties.[18] For instance, Article 1 of ILO Convention 122 calls for member states to declare and pursue an active policy designed to promote "full, productive and freely chosen employment."[19] ILO Convention 168 on Employment and Protection against Unemployment requires "[e]ach Member shall declare as a priority objective a policy designed to promote full, productive and freely chosen employment by all appropriate means … "[20] Moreover, it requires that each member "shall endeavour to establish, subject to national law and practice, special programmes to promote additional job opportunities and employment assistance … for identified categories of disadvantaged persons … such as women, young workers, disabled persons, older workers, the long-term unemployed, migrant workers lawfully resident in the country and *workers affected by structural change* (emphasis added)."[21]

In some fashion, the right to work is also found in Article 6 of the International Covenant on Economic, Social, and Cultural Rights (ICESCR),[22] Article 11(1)(a) of the Convention on Elimination of All Forms of Discrimination against Women (CEDAW),[23] Article 5(e)(i) of the Convention on Elimination of All Forms of Racial Discrimination (CERD),[24] Article 15 of the African Charter on Human and People's Rights

17 *See* Philip Harvey, *Benchmarking the Right to Work* in ECONOMIC RIGHTS: CONCEPTUAL, MEASUREMENT, AND POLICY ISSUES 120–122 (Shareen Hertel & Lanse Minkler eds., 2007) (arguing most jurisdictions now consider four percent to six percent unemployment to be "full employment").

18 *See* G. Mundlak, Working Out the Right to Work in a Global Labour Market in THE RIGHT TO WORK, supra note 9, at 291, 308–309 (Virginia Mantouvalou ed., 2015).

19 ILO Employment Policy Convention, No. 122, *adopted* July 9, 1964, 569 U.N.T.S. 65 (entered into force July 9, 1965).

20 *See* C168 – Employment Promotion and Protection against Unemployment Convention, 1988 (No. 168), at art 7, June 21, 1988.

21 *Id.* at art. 8.

22 International Covenant on Economic, Social and Cultural Rights art. 6, *opened for signature* December 19, 1966, 993 U.N.T.S. 3 [hereinafter ICESCR]. *See also* Ulrike Davy, *How Human Rights Shape Social Citizenship: On Citizenship and the Understanding of Economic and Social Rights*, 13 WASH. U. GLOBAL STUD. L. REV. 201, 228 (2014) (describing the human rights debates preceding the signing of ICESCR … "In April 1952, the Soviet Union tabled an amendment explicitly stating that the right to work "should be guaranteed by the State, with the object of creating conditions precluding the threat of death from hunger or inanition. The United States and France objected instantaneously.").

23 International Convention on the Elimination of All Forms of Discrimination against Women art. 11(1)(a), *opened for signature* March 1, 1980, 1249 U.N.T.S. 13 [hereinafter CEDAW].

24 International Convention on the Elimination of All Forms of Racial Discrimination art. 5(e)(i), *opened for signature* March 7, 1966, 660 U.N.T.S. 195 [hereinafter CERD].

(the African Charter),[25] Article 1 of the European Social Charter (the European Charter),[26] Article 6 of the Additional Protocol to the American Convention on Human Rights in the Area of Economic, Social, and Cultural Rights (the San Salvador Protocol),[27] the 1951 Convention Relating to the Status of Refugees (Refugee Convention),[28] and several other international treaties.[29]

These treaties have not been interpreted to provide individuals an administratively or judicially enforceable right to a job. Neither, of course, have they been interpreted to invoke a collective right to true full employment (obviating the proverbial "reserve army of labor").[30] As a first-order matter, not all of the treaty interpretations agree that a right to a job should serve as the positive instantiation of the right to work,[31] nor do they tend to impose an obligation on party states to guarantee an immediate right to work but importantly, they do adopt policies that are meant specifically to gradually secure such right.[32]

[25] African Charter on Human and Peoples' Rights art. 15, June 27, 1981, 21 I.L.M. 59 (1982) (entered into force October 21, 1986) [hereinafter African Charter].

[26] European Social Charter (revised) art. 1, *opened for signature* May 3, 1996, E.T.S. No. 163. [hereinafter European Charter].

[27] Additional Protocol to the American Convention on Human Rights in the Area of Economic, Social, and Cultural Rights art. 6, *adopted in San Salvador* November 17, 1988 [hereinafter San Salvador Protocol].

[28] United Nations Convention Relating to the Status of Refugees, July 28, 1951, 189 U.N.T.S. 137 [hereinafter Refugee Convention].

[29] As a note on continental agreements, "...Europe, Africa, and the Americas have had regional legal systems for human rights enforcement for years, but Asia has yet to establish a concrete and legally binding regional mechanism to redress human rights violations." This may change as the Association of Southeast Asian Nations (ASEAN) adopted a human rights declaration in 2012. Mariam Sarwar, *Human Rights the "ASEAN Way": Exploring the Possibilities for A Regional ADR and Adjudicative Body in Southeast Asia*, 52 Loy. L.A. L. Rev. 27, 27–28 (2018).

[30] The economist Michal Kalecki was the first to clearly state, in a chapter entitled, "Political Aspects of Full Employment" that a capitalist economy can be sustained at full employment only if challenges to capitalists' social and political hegemony could be contained by means of public policy. Michal Kalecki, SELECTED ESSAYS ON THE DYNAMICS OF THE CAPITALIST ECONOMY 1933–1970, 138–45 (1971). See also, Tayyab Mahmud, PRECARIOUS EXISTENCE AND CAPITALISM: A PERMANENT STATE OF EXCEPTION, 44 SW. L. REV. 699, 705–08 (2015) (analyzing the changing role of the reserve army of labor within neoliberalism).

[31] *See* H. Collins, *Is There a Human Right to Work?* in The Right to Work *supra* note 9, at 16, 24 (arguing the right to work is a human right and "should contain the positive right to a job at its centre.").

[32] CESCR, General Comment No. 3, The Nature of States Parties Obligations under Article 2(1), ¶ 9, U.N. Doc. E/1991/23 (December 14, 1990) [hereinafter General Comment No. 3] (declaring that the progressive realization principle imposes the obligation on State Parties to "move as expeditiously and effectively as possible" toward the full implementation of

For instance, the right to work is predictably the first right mentioned in the ICESCR. In 2005, the Committee on Economic, Social, and Cultural Rights (CESCR) published General Comment 18 on the Right to Work,[33] affirming that the right to work is inherent to human dignity and essential for realizing other human rights. The guidance even notes that Article 6 is interdependent with Article 7, which recognizes the universal right of everyone to "the enjoyment of just and favourable conditions of work," and adopts a principle of nondiscrimination.[34] And furthermore, it indicates that special measures should be taken to reduce the unemployment rate among disadvantaged groups, including women, younger people, older people, migrants, and disabled people.[35] Yet General Comment 18 also clarifies that in order to fill the Article 6 obligation – to recognize "the right of everyone to the opportunity to gain his living by work which he freely choose or accepts" – the state party to the covenant need only adopt "policies and techniques to achieve steady economic, social and cultural development under safeguarding fundamental political and economic freedoms to the individual."[36]

Moreover, General Comment 18 fails to delineate what constitutes a programmatic failure to comply with Article 6. States are only required to develop a "national employment strategy,"[37] including job training programs geared toward private sector employment.[38] The capacity to do more for full employment is not demanded, even of states with sufficient financial resources. James W. Nickel has described this absence of any requirement for a ratifying government to serve as the "employer of last resort" as the "most striking" thing about ICESCR's approach to the right to work.[39] General Comment No. 18 states that any person whose right to work has been violated

economic, social, and cultural rights). At least one scholar has argued that the duty of progressive realization should be interpreted as a "duty to design public budgets and to implement macro-economic policies with a view toward fulfilling economic, social, and cultural rights…"Olivier de Schutter, Public Budget Analysis for the Realization of Economic, Social, and Cultural Rights, in THE FUTURE OF ECONOMIC AND SOCIAL RIGHTS 527, 528 (Katharine G. Young ed., 2019).

33 *See* CESCR, General Comment No. 18, The Right to Work: Article 6 of the International Covenant on Economic, Social and Cultural Rights, ¶ 1, U.N. Doc. E/C.12/GC/18 (February 6, 2006) [hereinafter General Comment No. 18].

34 *Id. See also*, Gillian MacNaughton & Diane F. Frey, *Decent Work, Human Rights, and the Millennium Development Goals*, 7 HASTINGS RACE & POVERTY L. J. 303, 326 (2010).

35 *See* General Comment No. 18, *supra* note 33, at ¶ 31.

36 ICESCR art. 6, *supra* note 22.

37 General Comment No. 18, *supra* note 33, at ¶ 19.

38 *See* Colm O'Cinneide, *The Right to Work in International Human Rights Law* in THE RIGHT TO WORK, *supra* note 9, at 99, 109–11.

39 James W. Nickel, *Giving Up on the Right to Work* in THE RIGHT TO WORK, *supra* note9, at 137, 144–145.

should have full access to judicial or similar remedies, but thus far, the failure of a ratifying state to provide employment to everyone who wants to work has not been deemed a violation of the right to work.[40] One cannot claim a right to work against a state under ICESCR simply because one wants a job.[41]

11.2 FULL EMPLOYMENT & JUS COGENS

When one examines the need for full employment in the context of other labor rights under these treaties, and the realities of existing labor systems, the absence of a mandate for full employment makes little sense. Above all, this is because the international treaties discussed in this chapter generally bar labor discrimination.[42] For example, Article 2(2) of the ICESCR requires that the rights set out in the Covenant "will be executed without discrimination."[43] Even during times of financial crisis or hardship, state parties are not permitted to apply "retrogressive policies" in a discriminatory manner.[44]

There can be no doubt that today's labor systems feature all sorts of discrimination.[45] One might argue this is why these international treaties exist. One might also argue this is why the United States has not ratified many of them. But simple prohibitions against discrimination in labor practices have not tended to bring about equal treatment at the nation-state level. In her recent essay, *Inequity as a Legal Principle,* Lua Kamál Yuille examines employment law to demonstrate that inequity is law's "leitmotif."[46] Statutes like the US Civil Rights Act of 1964 are intended to prevent the failure or refusal to hire individuals because of their "race, color, religion, sex, or national origin."[47] And yet, decades of legal history demonstrate that systematic and systemic discrimination and unfairness – labor "injustice" as Yuille

40 General Comment No. 18, *supra* note 33, at ¶ 48.

41 *See* Davy, *supra* note 22at 227. Davy discusses how Eastern European countries fought for the ICESCR to include a right to work that specified state duties concerning employment. Latin American, Arab, and Asian delegates also pushed for duties on the states to various degrees against the objections of the United States and Western European delegates.

42 *See, e.g.*, ICESCR, *supra* note 22, art. 2(1).

43 *Id.*, art. 2(2).

44 *See* Ignacio Saiz, *Rights in Recession? Challenges for Economic and Social Rights Enforcement in Times of Crisis*, 1 J. OF HUM. RTS. PRAC. 283 (2009).

45 Indeed, some economists argue that intergroup conflict is endogenous to the social space of economic settings. *See, e.g.*, William Darity Jr., *Stratification Economics: Context Versus Culture and the Reparations Controversy*, 57 U. KAN. L. REV. 795, 803 (2009) (going on to discuss stratified labor and wealth in Latin America and the United States).

46 Lua Kamál Yuille, *Inequity as a Legal Principle*, 66 U. KAN. L. REV. 859, 860 (2018).

47 *Id.*

distinguishes it – permeates the law (and thus legal constructions like the labor system).[48]

Indeed, most labor systems today are defined not merely by discrimination, but segregation and rampant inequality – within states and between states. Most developing countries have abundant natural resources, but all have unemployed, underemployed, or under-qualified domestic labor.[49] Making matters worse, the geo-financial architecture is such that job creation in developing countries often relies on imports of intermediate and capital goods, rather than the creation of domestic substitutes. Many workers in developing countries produce raw materials and "low-value-added" goods for developed countries. Many of the firms producing such goods are involved in "dirty supply chains." In this condition, industrial giants reap the fruits of productive processes that involve unsafe and unsanitary conditions, long working hours, forced overtime, discrimination, sexual harassment, and other forms of workplace violence.[50] Many workers trapped in low-wage sectors often find themselves trapped within firms promoting war, incarceration, deportation, in addition to climate change and other forces that threaten the very communities from whence the workers come.

One could argue that states have an obligation to provide employment in order to satisfy other labor rights, especially a right to nondiscrimination. Indeed, true full employment becomes fundamentally necessary when one looks at the right to work via the peremptory, non-derogable norm against certain forms of nondiscrimination recognized by the international community. For instance, a prohibition on racial discrimination is well-established as *jus cogens*.[51] The Inter-American Court of Human Rights (IACtHR) has recognized nondiscrimination and equality before the law, in general, as *jus cogens* in nature: "any discriminatory treatment with regard to the protection and exercise of human rights entails the international responsibility of the State."[52] The IACtHR argued that in order to comply with *jus cogens*

48 *Id.*

49 *See generally*, Fadhel Kaboub, *Elements of a Radical Counter-Movement to Neoliberalism: Employment-Led Development*, 40 Rev. of Radical Pol. Econ. 223 (2008).

50 Committee on Decent Work in Global Supply Chains, Reports of the Committee on Decent Work in Global Supply Chains: Resolution and Conclusions Submitted for Adoption by the Conference, ILC PR 14–1/2 (2016), www.ilo.org/wcmsp5/groups/public/–ed_norm/–relconf/documents/meetingdocument/wcms_489115.pdf.

51 Special Rapporteur on Peremptory Norms of General International Law (Jus Cogens), *Fourth Rep. on Peremptory Norms of General International Law (Jus Cogens)*, ¶60, Int'l Law Comm'n, U.N. Doc. A/CN.4/727 (January 31, 2019) (by Dire Tladi).

52 *Juridical Condition and Rights of the Undocumented Migrants*, Advisory Op. OC-18/03, Inter-Am. Ct. H.R. (ser. A) ¶ 96–101, (September 17, 2003), www.corteidh.or.cr/docs/opiniones/seriea_18_ing.pdf [hereinafter Advisory Opinion OC-18/03].

principles of equality and nondiscrimination, states are obligated to take *affirmative action* to reverse or otherwise change discriminatory situations, including with respect to third parties who maintain these discriminatory situations.[53]

Some scholars argue that socio-economic rights are a necessary condition for the realization of *jus cogens* human rights (for example, the right to life), and should thus also receive the status of *jus cogens* norms.[54] Such a case can be made for the right to work given the stratification and structural discrimination within labor systems. If a norm qualifies as *jus cogens* then an executive, legislative, or judicial act does not excuse a state's violation of that norm.[55] Full employment is a prerequisite for fair employment overall.[56]

11.3 MODERN MONEY AND THE RIGHT TO WORK

Narrow interpretations of the right to work do not merely suffer from a failure to synthesize rights concerns. They are also plagued by the precarious assumptions of orthodox economics. For instance, the CESCR guidance makes clear that the duty of a state party is to demonstrate they are making measurable progress toward the realization of the right to work, notwithstanding their level of development and resources.[57] But it does not provide a rubric for what this actually means. Paragraph 19 clarifies that "the Covenant provides for progressive realization and acknowledges the constraints due to the limits of available resources " What sorts of resources are they talking about? Financial resources? Biophysical resources? Human labor itself? All of the above?

Equally opaque, Paragraph 26 indicates that the major obligation on states is the formulation and implementation of an employment policy "with a view to stimulating economic growth and development, raising levels of living, meeting manpower requirements and overcoming unemployment and

53 *Id.* at ¶104.

54 *See, e.g.*, Elena Pribytkova, *What Global Human Rights Obligations Do We Have?*, 20 CHI. J. INT'L L. 384, 417 (2020) (identifying a tension in the human rights discourse).

55 Vienna Convention on the Law of Treaties art. 53, *opened for signature* May 23, 1969, 115 U.N. T.S. 331 (entered into force January 27, 1980). *See also*, David Weissbrodt, *Remedies for Undocumented Noncitizens in the Workplace: Using International Law to Narrow the Holding of Hoffman Plastic Compounds, Inc. v. NLRB*, 92 MINN. L. REV. 1424, 1435 (2008).

56 See, e.g., Pauli Murray, *The Right to Equal Opportunity in Employment*, 33 Cal. L. Rev. 388, 432 (1945) (arguing that when jobs are plentiful all kinds of discrimination, including racial discrimination, is minimized, rendering full employment the "basic problem to be solved").

57 Katerina Housos, *Austerity and Human Rights Law: Towards A Rights-Based Approach to Austerity Policy, A Case Study of Greece*, 39 FORDHAM INT'L L.J. 425, 437–438 (2015) (discussing the principles of "progressive realization" and "non-retrogression").

underemployment."[58] It also requires that states take "effective measures to increase the resources allocated to reducing the unemployment rate, in particular among women, the disadvantaged and marginalized "[59] In essence, the ICESCR is interpreted as simply requiring states to have an employment policy that gradually, generally improves a state's macroeconomic condition based on conventional indicators. And it requires the state, to somehow, in some way, *increase resources* for reducing unemployment, but not necessarily succeed in reducing it.

Paragraph 30 states that parties that are unwilling to use the "maximum of their available resources" for the realization of the right to work are in violation of their obligations under ICESCR Article 6.[60] And Comment No. 18 goes on to state that "[v]iolations of the right to work can occur through the direct action of States or State entities, or through the lack of adequate measures to promote employment."[61] Perhaps most interestingly for our instant purposes, Paragraph 36 offers, as an example of a violation of the right to work, "the insufficient expenditure or misallocation of public funds which results in the non-enjoyment of the right to work by individuals or groups, particularly the disadvantaged and marginalized."[62] While the guidance does not mandate specific macroeconomic policies be adopted, it does suggest that states "identify the resources available to States parties for achieving their objectives as well as the most *cost-effective* ways of using them (emphasis added)."[63] But here again, these passages fail to clarify what sort of resources should be considered (General Comment No. 3 likewise fails to substantiate the term "resources").[64]

In general, both advocates and critics of an enforceable right to work assume that true full employment – a job for everyone who wants one – is beyond the economic and technical capacity of states.[65] Perhaps even more importantly, they assume that a duty not to interfere with workers' right to earn living, such as the principle imposed under ICESCR Article 1(2), merely imposes

58 *See* General Comment No. 18, *supra* note 33, at ¶ 31.

59 *Id.*

60 *Id.* at ¶ 30. For an extended discussion of the scattered treatment of the term "maximum of their available resources" in doctrine, see Rodrigo Uprimny, Sergio Chaparro Hernández, and Andrés Castro Araújo, Bridging the Gap: The Evolving Doctrine on ESCR and Maximum Available Resources, in THE FUTURE OF ECONOMIC AND SOCIAL RIGHTS, supra note 32, at 624–654 (Katharine G. Young ed., 2019).

61 *Id.* at ¶ 31.

62 *Id.* at ¶ 30.

63 *Id.* at ¶ 41.

64 See generally General Comment No. 3, *supra* note 32.

65 *See, e.g.*, Collins, *supra* note 31at 19.

"negative" obligations on the government, as if the state were not responsible for the status of the labor system in general or incapable of promoting a discriminatory labor system specifically. CESCR Comment No. 18 even clarifies that nondiscrimination and equal protection of employment are "core obligations" of ratifying states,[66] but does not connect this obligation to any responsibility for the state to employ workers directly.

As a school of interdisciplinary thought, Neochartalism – or as it is known colloquially, Modern Monetary Theory (MMT) – provides a rich, deep framework for thinking about this set of issues through an alternative prism.[67] Fundamentally, the paradigm asks us to look at the connection between money and labor differently, and reassess our conception of the constraints of states' financial versus biophysical resources (including labor power). MMT has added an important dimension to our understanding of unemployment as a product of monetary design and thus public law.[68] From a legal standpoint, by tracing the historical origins of money to law and public institutions, it demonstrates that the imposition of non-reciprocal obligations on the population (e.g., taxes, tribute, fees, dues), payable in a specific type of money (or currency), creates and drives demand for that currency. The tax in effect creates a certain type of unemployment – people must seek work for *legal tender* to satisfy the tax obligation.[69] Work to provide in-kind resources would not satisfy most governments in the modern era.

Anthropological evidence supports the foundational story that money begins with public authority as an administrative tool for public authorities to command labor and manage the distribution of real resources.[70] From the outset, money has been a collective, public enterprise that reflects the social hierarchies of the polity from which it emerged. Another way to say this: money is itself a legal institution and within the domain of the public international law lexicon.

66 *See generally* General Comment No. 3, *supra* note 32, at ¶ 31.

67 *See* Rohan Grey & Raúl Carrillo, *A Memo from MMT's Legal Department*, New Econ. Persps. (July 15, 2017), http://neweconomicperspectives.org/2017/07/memo-mmts-legal-department.html (describing the legal foundations and dexterity of MMT relative to other bodies of economic thought).

68 See generally Raúl Carrillo, *Unemployment Isn't Natural, It's a Creature of Legal Design*, 37 Law & Ineq. 128, 130 (2019).

69 For another iteration of this thesis, see Duncan Kennedy, *The Stakes of Law, or Hale and Foucault!*, 15 Legal Stud. F. 327, 351 (1991). Interestingly, Article 29(6) of the African Charter states that "the individual shall also have the duty . . . to work to the best of his abilities and competence, and to pay taxes imposed by law." This establishes a direct link between work and taxation. *See* African Charter art. 29(6), *supra* note 25.

70 *See* Rohan Grey, *Monetary Resilience*, 41 W. New Eng. L. Rev. 505, 509–510 (2019).

It is incumbent upon currency issuers to design viable macroeconomic policies to secure true full employment over the long run. From an MMT-informed human rights view, a monetary system is an extension of a state's powers over the currency and it is incumbent on the state to design policies that would attain and maintain true full employment over the long run.

MMT analysis links monetary systems & labor systems together, under the color of public law. When MMT economist Stephanie Kelton continually repeats "money doesn't grow on rich people" (or taxpayers), she is referencing a legal argument.[71] From a critical legal perspective, "monetary sovereigns" can never run out of money in the same way political sovereigns can never run out of "property" "contract," or "corporations." An entity can be said to have monetary sovereignty when it can not only issue its own currency, but float its exchange rates, denominate its debts in its own currency, and most importantly, collect taxes, fines, and fees in its own currency (maintaining the currency circuit).[72] Most monetary sovereigns are political states, but not all political states are monetary sovereigns.[73] For every nation seeking political independence, the process of acquiring sovereignty is never complete until it is accompanied by monetary sovereignty – in other words, until it establishes its own national currency (some exceptions notwithstanding).[74]

MMT does not consider monetary sovereignty to be something you simply have or you do not have. On the contrary, we have long recognized a *spectrum of monetary sovereignty*, within which some countries have more and others less.[75] Entities with minimal monetary sovereignty or agency do not generate

[71] Zach Carter, *Stephanie Kelton Has the Biggest Idea in Washington*, THE HUFFINGTON POST, www.huffpost.com/entry/stephanie-kelton-economy-washington_n_5afee5eae4b0463cdba15121 (May 20, 2018).

[72] See, e.g., Christine Desan, *Money as a Legal Institution*, in MONEY IN THE WESTERN LEGAL TRADITION: MIDDLE AGES TO BRETTON WOODS 18, 24 (David Fox & Wolfgang Ernst eds., 2016); Pavlina Tcherneva, *Chartalism and the Tax-Driven Approach to Money*, in A HANDBOOK OF ALTERNATIVE MONETARY ECONOMICS 69, 72–73 (Philip Arestis & Malcolm Sawyer eds., 2006).

[73] For example, Greece, which uses the Euro, has little monetary sovereignty. The European Central Bank ultimately controls money in Greece. Senegal, which uses the CFA Franc, which is controlled by the French Treasury, which is also subordinate to the European Central Bank, also lacks monetary sovereignty. *See* Ndongo Samba Sylla, *The CFA Franc: French Monetary Imperialism in Africa*, LONDON SCH. OF ECON. BLOG (July 12, 2017), https://blogs.lse.ac.uk/africaatlse/2017/07/12/the-cfa-franc-french-monetary-imperialism-in-africa/.

[74] Pavlina R. Tcherneva, *Money, Power, and Monetary Regimes* 6–8 (LEVY ECON. INST. OF BARD COLL., Working Paper No. 861, 2016), www.levyinstitute.org/pubs/wp_861.pdf [https://perma.cc/L522-EV5C].

[75] *Id. See also* Nathan Tankus, Monetary Sovereigns, Monetary Subjects And Monetary Vassals: A Spectrum Approach to Monetary Sovereignty and Our Dollar World, Lecture,

money; we are forced master a system that routes tradeable legal claims on real resources that we collectively produce (i.e. "money") to ourselves however we can.[76] Beyond the monetary sovereign, there can be said to be "monetary subjects" and "monetary vassals," who must use a sovereign's currency to survive.[77] As Christine Desan says, monetary design "can bring people together or set them at each other's throats."[78] Historically, international monetary design has been used to subjugate states and peoples in the global south – predictably, the places most in need of Job Guarantee.[79]

As MMT economist Fadhel Kaboub, among others, has noted, Job Guarantees can be difficult in developing countries, but they also provide an avenue away from post-colonial economic dependency on other states.[80] In other words, a movement for "right to work" would necessarily challenge the international financial architecture that many argue precludes its realization. The demand for true fulfillment of the right would render the right a site of political struggle rather than stasis.

States with little monetary sovereignty often face trade deficits due to very fundamental economic problems, many of them arising from colonization itself. They may also arise from neocolonialism. Comment No. 18 may require state parties to endeavor to promote the right to work in other countries via bilateral and multilateral negotiations and protect the right to work in negotiations with international financial institutions,[81] but it is difficult to claim this occurs in practice.

MANCHESTER INT'L LAW CTR., YOUTUBE (June 11, 2018), www.youtube.com/watch?v=xZnEDrVfcHU.

76 *See, e.g*, KATHARINA PISTOR, THE CODE OF CAPITAL 77–107 (2019) (discussing money as debt and thus power). Heterodox economists claim currency users as facing a deeper "survival constraint" than currency issuers. See Hyman P. Minsky, STABILIZING AN UNSTABLE ECONOMY (1986) (discussing capitalist economic systems as financial systems based on credit finance originated by entities exercising power within monetary hierarchies).

77 *See* Tankus, *supra* note 75.

78 Christine Desan, *The Impact and Malleability of Money Design*, LPE BLOG (March 25, 2019), https://lpeblog.org/2019/03/25/the-impact-and-malleability-of-money-design/.

79 *See e.g.*, Mathew Forstater, Taxation and Primitive Accumulation: The Case of Colonial Africa, in THE CAPITALIST STATE AND ITS ECONOMY: DEMOCRACY IN SOCIALISM RESEARCH IN POLITICAL ECONOMY, VOL. 22, 51–65. https://modernmoneynetwork.org/sites/default/files/biblio/RiPE%20Forstater.pdf.

80 *See, e.g.*, Joe Weisenthal & Tracy Alloway, *This Is How MMT Applies To Emerging Markets*, BLOOMBERG (April 8, 2018), hwww.bloomberg.com/news/articles/2019–04-08/this-is-how-mmt-applies-to-emerging-markets (interviewing Dr. Kaboub); Scott Ferguson et al., *The New Postcolonial Economics with Fadhel Kaboub*, MONTHLY REVIEW ONLINE (July 7, 2018), https://mronline.org/2018/07/07/the-new-postcolonial-economics-with-fadhel-kaboub/ (interview of Dr. Kaboub for "Money on the Left," a podcast by the Modern Money Network Humanities Division).

81 *See* General Comment No. 18, *supra* note 33, at ¶ 30.

For myriad reasons, many developing countries lack the ability – or have been told they don't have the ability – to produce enough food, energy, and medicine to meet their own domestic demand. So, they import food, energy, and medicine from more developed countries – and pay for those crucial imports with foreign currency. Twistedly, the ongoing trade deficits cause these countries' currencies to depreciate relative to foreign currencies and thus make the critical imports even more expensive. This can cause inflation and even political turmoil, as recently occurred in Kaboub's native Tunisia.[82] Countries that could theoretically control their own economies are forced to renegotiate debt denominated in foreign currency, ask for more aid, hat-in-hand, or simply default.[83]

MMT recognizes that this sort of "export-led growth" is often a trap.[84] Despite how often people in developed countries like to repeat the talking point, developing countries are not simply mismanaging policy. The existing international system of money, trade, and labor undermines their generative capacity to actually achieve human rights goals. In part, this could be addressed by Kaboub's recommended South–South trade partnerships that help developing countries to grow complementary industries and escape the position in the global production chain where they are stuck selling incomplete goods to developed countries and buying back finished products, importing finished goods, and exporting intermediate goods.[85] As long as most developing countries rely on importing basic necessities, they will remain "developing" – trapped in a desperate scramble to acquire the currencies of the rich world. For most developing countries, a domestic Job Guarantee based on cultivating sustainable food and renewable energy sovereignty is sorely needed.[86] So long as the program itself does not become the ultimate goal, it can also destabilize the broader international trade architecture. Many arguments for marshalling the "maximum available resources" for rights

82 *See* Noureddine Taboubi, Secretary-General, Tunisian General Labour Union, *Strikes overturn wage cuts, but IMF blindness risks ruining Tunisia*, BRETTON WOODS PROJECT (April 4, 2019), www.brettonwoodsproject.org/2019/04/strikes-overturn-wage-bill-but-imf-blindness-risks-ruining-tunisia/.

83 *See, e.g.*, William Mitchell, *Modern monetary theory in an open economy*, ECON. OUTLOOK (October 13, 2009), http://bilbo.economicoutlook.net/blog/?p=5402.

84 *See* STEPHANIE KELTON, THE DEFICIT MYTH 127–155 (2020) (discussing the MMT view of international trade).

85 *Id.* at 154–155.

86 Fadhel Kaboub & Fadil Aliriza, *Modern Monetary Theory: A Tool for the Global South?*, ROSA LUXEMBURG STIFTUNG (November 2019) www.rosalux.de/en/publication/id/41284/modern-monetary-theory-a-tool-for-the-global-south. Energy sovereignty has long been a goal of international egalitarian movements. *See, e.g.*, Karuna Mantena, *Getting the NIEO Right*, LPE BLOG (May 21, 2018), https://lpeblog.org/2018/05/21/getting-the-nieo-right.

fulfillment focus exclusively on debt financing, tax collection, and international development assistance, using inappropriate metrics like "diminishing marginal returns to investment" for private parties, when they should be focused on increasing the monetary and fiscal agency of state parties to satisfy the requirements of international human rights law.[87]

11.3.1 *Designing Job Guarantees*

Recent political developments suggest that legal systems should be reconfigured to provide both an individual and collective right to employment at a living wage with benefits. Most labor reforms do not address fundamental roots of inequity with labor systems – especially the utter necessity for individuals and workers as a class to work for *money*, and to not only survive, but to settle debts to the state.[88] Insofar as we are committed to the notion that societies must reproduce themselves through labor, then it seems that the only possible counter to what economist Michal Kalecki dubbed the "threat of the sack" is a legal commitment to a full employment economy, wherein workers may gain not only "self-assurance and class-consciousness," but increased power over the conditions of the labor system as a whole.[89]

Although there exist several iterations of Job Guarantee programs across political, intellectual, and historical traditions, they should be publicly funded, locally driven, and commit the state to guaranteeing a living wage job with good benefits, including healthcare, to anyone who wants or needs it, as a matter of right.[90] The program is universal and permanent, and does not demand that employees withdraw from transfer-based social programs (save unemployment insurance programs). In this way the program is not only intended to eliminate involuntary employment, but to provide an opening to change the nature of work itself.

The core of the Job Guarantee is the individual and collective right to remunerative employment, but while recognition of a legal right to work is necessary, it is by itself insufficient. As Philip Harvey, a predominant scholar of the "law and economics of the right to work" argues, the right is necessarily

[87] For extended discussion of CESCR doctrine concerning "maximum available resources", see Uprimny et al., supra note 60.

[88] *See* Carrillo, *supra* note 68.

[89] KALECKI, SUPRA NOTE 80.

[90] *See, e.g.*, L. Randall Wray et al., *Public Service Employment: A Path to Full Employment*, LEVY ECON. INST. OF BARD COLL., Research Project Report, (April 2018), www.levyinstitute.org/pubs/rpr_4_18.pdf; Angela Glover Blackwell et al., *10 Principles for a Federal Job Guarantee*, POLICYLINK, www.policylink.org/blog/ten-principles-federal-job-guarantee (articulating consensus principles among Job Guarantee advocates in the United States).

aspirational, contingent, and evolutionary.[91] Successful rights enforcement requires administrative support from courts and agencies,political support from the public, and fiscal support from currency issuers (typically legislatures and central banks, mechanically speaking).

Under the Washington Consensus, most central banks use a reservoir of unemployed workers to stabilize the business cycle.[92] When the economy grows and inflationary pressures are expected to emerge, the central bank often responds by attempting to create more unemployment. Consequently, unemployment insurance and other non-wage income support rise to boost aggregate demand, tax revenues from people who have lost their jobs decline, and the business cycle recovers from the downturn. By contrast, the Job Guarantee proposal uses employment to stabilize the business cycle. As workers lose their private sector jobs, they enter the public sector. Spending on the program increases to provide the necessary countercyclical spending and recover the economy from recession. Once the private sector recovers, it begins to hire away workers from the public program back into private sector employment, thereby naturally shrinking government spending on the program, providing an automatic stabiliser in the opposite direction.

Beyond serving as an automatic macroeconomic stabilizer for the real economy, the Job Guarantee can ideally secure a space for work focused on dignity, self-actualization and public purpose, divorced from concerns of profiteers. In no state or jurisdiction is there a shortage of meaningful labor, from infrastructure repair to care work to artistic revitalization. Combating climate change alone requires massive public mobilization to transform energy and food production, restore ecosystems and defend frontline communities.

Thankfully, as a result of the international popularization of the movement for a "Green New Deal" (GND), as well as economic justice movements in general, there is some international consciousness around the necessity of green full employment. For instance, even former UN Special Rapporteur on extreme poverty and human rights Philip Alston, has not only argued that climate change presents an opportunity for "decoupling economic growth from emissions and resource extraction," but for wholesale reform of labor systems.[93] Alston reports from the field that "unavoidable changes to the economy and the workforce make a strong case for universal job guarantee

[91] Philip Harvey, *Aspirational Law*, 52 Buffalo L. Rev. 717, *passim*, (2004).

[92] For a description of this process and its implications, see e.g., Kelton, *supra* note 84, at 243–254.

[93] Special Rapporteur, *supra* note 6, at 13.

programmes that provide rights-based work, creating the assets, services and infrastructure for a green transition and disaster mitigation in exchange for a stable income."[94] While Alston's Job Guarantee advocacy is neither particularly bold nor rooted in a new legal or macroeconomic paradigm, it serves as a barometer for systemic change.

The US Green New Deal is a rights-based program: the original resolution promises guaranteed healthcare, housing, education, and employment.[95] Proposals in other countries, as well as arguments for a Global Green New Deal, maintain rights at their center. Due to its focus on a Just Transition,[96] the GND requires a federally funded, locally driven Job Guarantee, committing the federal government to provide a living wage job with good benefits, including healthcare, to anyone who wants or needs one. For the program to change the way we work, we also need income protections to support workers who leave emission-intensive sectors, and workforce development programs to supplement Job Guarantee wages in GND-critical sectors.

By becoming the public option for employment, full-fledged Job Guarantee programs put pressure on the "private" sector to raise labor standards. Jurisdictions could "effectively set a wage that would obviate the most routine aspects of degrading life conditions by moving the price of marginal labor," as every private sector employer would have to compete with the Job Guarantee wage.[97] It would also provide qualitative benchmarks, such as improved conditions and new legal safeguards. In this sense, struggles for higher minimum wages are baked into the political power of the Job Guarantee. Whether people ultimately choose to stay in Job Guarantee jobs or not, the policy offers millions of workers a pathway into sectors where certain workers, especially those who have been historically discriminated against could build skills and credentials to pursue other endeavors.

94 *Id.*

95 Recognizing the Duty of the Federal Government to Create a Green New Deal, H.R. Res. 109, 116th Cong. (2019), www.congress.gov/116/bills/hres109/BILLS-116hres109ih.pdf.

96 *See, e.g.*, Ann M. Eisenberg, *Just Transitions*, 92 S. Cal. L. Rev. 273, 285–289 (2019) (discussing a history of the concept, beginning with labor activism on environmental issues). *See also Just Transition: A Framework for Change*, Climate Justice Alliance, https://climatejusticealliance.org/just-transition/ (describing a Just Transition as a "vision-led, unifying and place-based set of principles, processes, and practices that build economic and political power to shift from an extractive economy to a regenerative economy.")

97 Robert C. Hockett & Roy Kreitner, *Just Prices*, 27 Cornell J.L. & Pub. Pol'y 771, 793 (2018).

MMT also helps us think about how to provide proper fiscal support for rights enforcement in general. Over the past few years, one of the most ambitious rights-based direct job creation programs, the Mahatma Gandhi National Rural Employment Guarantee Act (MGNREGA), has been starved by the Indian Parliament. As Rajendran Narayanan has been chronicling, "instead of sufficiently funding MGNREGA, a legal right, in times of severe drought," the government has attempted to create an overly complex financial and administrative infrastructure to patch up the program without spending more public money (or more cynically, to eliminate the program's political viability).[98] This is anathema to the Modern Money perspective, which recognizes the symbiosis between effective funding and effective enforcement. Job Guarantee programs can only succeed and become powerful if we *pull* money from public coffers, and away from the central banks and other technocrats who stingily *push* funding under status quo models. This is, ultimately, a political contest of labor.

But with sufficient financing, a legal right to a job and a Job Guarantee program can also address other structural inequalities within the labor system and potential repair past wrongs. For instance, women around the world currently perform the majority of care work without formal remuneration. A Job Guarantee program could assist child and elder care professionals, moving familial burdens off the backs of women and into the public sphere, thereby formalizing and valorizing existing care work.[99]

If this sort of program seems too bold or utopian, it is precisely what happened in Argentina. At the time of an inflationary crisis in 2001, Buenos Aires dramatically shifted to a domestically oriented growth strategy.[100] The government stopped pegging its exchange rate and hoarding dollars. Policymakers chose to default on foreign debt and instead invest in their own economy. President Kirchner then created a massive direct job creation program that guaranteed work for poor heads of households by right. As MMT economists Randy Wray and Pavlina Tcherneva reported, *Plan Jefes y Jefas de Hogar* (Head of Households

98 Rajendran Narayanan & Rakshita Swamy, *Six reasons why the Economic Survey's presentation of MGNREGA is misleading*, The Hindu (July 23, 2019), www.thehindu.com/opinion/op-ed/a-misleading-presentation-of-a-labour-programme/article28660814.ece

99 *See, e.g.*, Vicki Schultz, *Life's Work*, 100 Colum. L. Rev. 1881, 1928 (2000) ("What would it take to make available to everyone full and equal participation in decently-paid, life-sustaining, participatory forms of work in which women and men from all walks of life can stand together as equals?")

100 *See* Mitchell, *supra* note 83.

Plan) created jobs for 2 million participants – roughly 13 percent of the labor force.[101] Mostly women, the participants focused on community-based projects like gardening, renovation of social centers, running food kitchens, and teaching classes on public health. And from a macroeconomic standpoint, the program helped Argentina avoid many of the problems associated with reliance on foreign capital; individuals and the state regained meaningful self-determination over their futures.

Imagine this approach scaled out globally, tethered to demands for international human rights law to actually support a "right to work". Full employment economies undergirded by a Job Guarantee would have workers at their disposal to assist with guarantees of housing, healthcare, education, family, and disability support, as well as reparations. Through the Job Guarantee, public grant funding for the arts and innovation could be allocated to loose associations and individual workers as a replacement of inherently hierarchical equity liability funding.[102] Overall, we could reduce our dependence on mega-corporations and money managers and direct future governance toward alternative systems of workplace democracy and community-oriented production.[103] In other words, we might fulfill the promise of universal human dignity.

11.4 DEMOCRATIZING JOB GUARANTEES

Job Guarantee programs can themselves contain more democratic elements. For instance, Kaboub has proposed a tiered-wage Job Guarantee of unionized employment caring for people, community, and the planet.[104] For purposes of democracy and inclusion, it is also important that the Job Guarantee maintain a space for employment in collective enterprises chosen directly by the

101 Pavlina Tcherneva & L. Randall Wray, *Employer of Last Resort Program: A case study of Argentina's Jefes de Hogar program*, Ctr. for Full Employment & Price Stability, Univ. of Missouri-Kansas City (April 2005), www.cfeps.org/pubs/wp-pdf/WP41-Tcherneva-Wray-all.pdf.

102 *See* Rohan Grey, *Who Owns the Intellectual Fruits of Job Guarantee Labor?*, in The Job Guarantee and Modern Money: Realizing Keynes Labor Standard 207, 212–217 (Mathew Forstater et al. eds., 2017).

103 *See* Mathew Forstater, *The Job Guarantee and Municipal Confederalism: Exploring the National and Local Levels of Program Operation*, in Employment Guarantee Schemes 145, 145-154 (M. J. Murray & Mathew Forstater eds., 2013).

104 *See generally*, Fadhel Kaboub, *The Fiscal Cliff Mythology and the Full Employment Alternative: An Affordable and Productive Plan*, Rev. of Radical Pol. Econ. (2013), https://journals.sagepub.com/doi/abs/10.1177/0486613413487162.

community. This commitment is already reflected in human rights literature. For instance, CESCR guidance states "the right of individuals and groups to participate in decision-making should be an integral part of all policies, programmes and strategies intended to implement the obligations of States parties under article 6."[105] And CEDAW Article 14 states that women in rural areas should have the right to organize co-operatives in order to obtain access to opportunities via employment *or* self-employment.[106] The sources for this effort are available to public international law if we choose to observe them.

Historically, many communities have created complementary currencies to fund democratically chosen projects based on volunteer labor.[107] In more democratic Job Guarantee programs, the community in neighbourhoods could create its own jobs and dictate how funds should be spent, as in Argentina's *Jefes y Jefas* program.[108] The official MMT Job Guarantee proposal explicitly includes funding for worker cooperatives.[109] Community-led job programs, rooted in the right to work, are natural complements to participatory budgeting in general and are better structured to satisfy anti-discrimination principles.[110]

If international law truly aims for universality, it might begin to more seriously learn from actors and efforts traditionally pushed to the margins of global governance. Participatory budgeting, for instance, could make direct job creation programs less corrupt and closer to the immediate needs of local communities.[111] These processes, developed in Porto Alegre, Brazil, have in fact been increasingly replicated and used by localities around the world.[112] In participatory budgeting, communities determine a ranking of the priority issues they want city or local budgets

105 *See* General Comment No. 18, *supra* note 33, at ¶42.

106 CEDAW, *supra* note 23, at art. 14.

107 *See* Alexander Kolokotronis, *Three Ways to Design a Democratic Job Guarantee*, TRUTHOUT (MAY 20, 2018), https://truthout.org/articles/three-ways-to-design-a-democratic-job-guarantee/.

108 *Id.*

109 *See* Wray et al., *supra* note 90 at 35.

110 *See* Pavlina R. Tcherneva, *The Job Guarantee: Design, Jobs, and Implementation* 16–17 (LEVY ECON. INST. OF BARD COLL., Working Paper No. 902, 2018), www.levyinstitute.org/pubs/wp_902.pdf.

111 *See, e.g*, John Ackerman, *Co-Governance for Accountability: Beyond "Exit" and "Voice"*, 32 WORLD DEV. 450–451, 457 (2004).

112 *See* Tara J. Melish, *Maximum Feasible Participation of the Poor: New Governance, New Accountability, and A 21st Century War on the Sources of Poverty*, 13 YALE HUM. RTS. & DEV. 1, 88–89 (2010).

to focus on, which is considered binding on city or local officials.[113] Priorities are then monitored by citizens' groups over the budgetary cycle.[114]

Citizens assemblies, wherein a randomly selected group of people, advised by technical experts, make binding votes on legislation, could also find a place in Job Guarantee programs.[115] Icelanders famously used a citizens' assembly to draft a new constitution following the global financial crisis.[116] The random selection meant this was the first time in modern human history that a constitution was drafted with 50 percent representation by women (and not just elite women of means).[117] Similarly, the recent Irish Constitutional Convention, conducted in 2012, is also lauded for deepening democracy in similar ways.[118] Overall, citizen assemblies, paired with a rights-centered Job Guarantee, could provide space to redefine what sort of labor is actually necessary in a given community and to do so on intersectional grounds.[119]

MMT could have transformative implications for human rights, international law, and development. When we consider what should be an obvious point – that each polity should have sufficient control over its currency to actually fulfill human rights objectives like the right to work – we expand the policy imagination at a critical time for labor. A deeper and more nuanced understanding of a state's "maximum available resources," in the context of monetary hierarchy, could have tremendous implications for the working people of the world.[120] MMT transforms technocratic budgetary problems into questions about public

[113] *Id.*

[114] *Id.*

[115] *See* Jonathan Crock, *The Human Right to Democratic Control of Money*, Presentation, HARVARD L. SCH., "Money as a Democratic Medium" Conference, YOUTUBE (2018), www.youtube.com/watch?v=hXAuK2LCjt4.

[116] *See* Jonathan Crock, *The Job Guarantee Design and Human Rights*, Presentation, UNIV. OF MISSOURI-KANSAS CITY, 1st Annual MMT Conference, YOUTUBE (October 24, 2017) (publicly connecting MMT and the Job Guarantee to participatory budgeting for the first time), www.youtube.com/watch?v=YFbrJWLSSpY/.

[117] *Id.*

[118] *See* Silvia Suteu, *Constitutional Conventions in the Digital Era: Lessons from Iceland and Ireland*, 38 B.C. INT'L & COMP. L. REV. 251, 264–268 (2015).

[119] *See, e.g.*, Allegra M. McLeod, *Envisioning Abolition Democracy*, 132 HARV. L. REV. 1613, 1646 (2019) (arguing participatory budgeting is a key tool for abolitionist justice and the redefining of public safety).

[120] For an appraisal of other methodological perspectives on "MAR", see Uprimny et al., supra note 60, at 641-649.

law and democratic control of money as a public good.[121] It strikes at a conception of false scarcity that belies human rights implementation generally.[122] It problematizes the international monetary architecture and casts its contradictions with the fulfillment of international human rights law into relief. And in doing so, it could help re-envision a new role for international labor law in increasing labor's power.

[121] Indeed, it "insists that money is an inalienable public utility that can always be mobilized to meet social and ecological needs." Scott Ferguson, *The Shape of Law*, ARCADE (STANFORD) (based on an oral presentation delivered at Law in Global Political Economy: Heterodoxy Now, a conference organized by the Institute for Global Law and Policy at Harvard Univ., June 2–3, 2018), https://arcade.stanford.edu/blogs/shape-law.

[122] For another example of false scarcity in human rights law, see generally, Carmen G. Gonzalez, International Economic Law and the Right to Food, in RETHINKING FOOD SYSTEMS: STRUCTURAL CHALLENGES, NEW STRATEGIES, AND THE LAW 165-193 (Nadia Lambek, et al., eds., 2014).

12

Liberation

Alberto Rinaldi

International law loves stories of liberation. The idea of an emancipatory path humanity is constantly about to undertake and which will eventually lead to peace and prosperity is one that has long fascinated international lawyers too, and still keeps fascinating some.[1] Yet, in the last three decades, international law has also come under the fierce attack of various kind of critiques – from postcolonial scholars to feminist studies and the historiographical 'turn' – which in different ways have called for a re-assessment of its ambiguous role in not-so-much emancipatory projects across times and spaces.[2]

The result is that a bit less is believed now of the fairy tale of a discipline that was portrayed to have always been there in order to take humanity by the hand and to fulfil its emancipatory potentials.[3] International law was indeed utilised as a tool to colonise, subjugate and delegitimise peoples and cultures outside of the Western tradition.[4] Celebrated and thrilling times of 'liberation' for some resulted in harsh repression for others at the very same moment.[5] With this in mind, it is difficult today to spend enthusiastic words on the theme of 'liberation' without actually feeling a cramp to the stomach. Who was indeed

1 Cf. Malcom Shaw, *International Law: 6th edition* (Cambridge: Cambridge University Press, 2008), 1–42.

2 For a non-exhaustive list: Anthony Anghie, *Imperialism, Sovereignty and International Law* (Cambridge: Cambridge University Press, 2005), Martti Koskenniemi, Walter Rech and Manuel Jiménez Fonseca, ed., *International Law and Empire: Historical Explorations* (Oxford: Oxford University Press, 2017) and Hilary Charlesworth and Christine Chinkin, ed., *Boundaries of International Law: A Feminist Analysis* (Manchester: Manchester University Press, 2000).

3 Cf. Martti Koskenniemi, *From Apology to Utopia: The Structure of International Legal Argument* (Cambridge: Cambridge University Press, 2006).

4 *See* Emmanuelle Jouannet, 'Universalism and Imperialism: The True-False Paradox of International Law?', *European Journal of International Law* 18:3 (June 2007): 379–407. *See* also Anne Orford, ed., International Law and Its Others (Cambridge: Cambridge University Press, 2009).

5 Nathaniel Berman, 'In the Wake of Empire', *American University International Law Review* 14 (1998–1999): 1515–1569.

'liberated', and how? From whom, and at what cost? While the force of rights-language and formal inclusion continue to catalyse the attention of many, the strenuous battle fought by the colonial subjects for a place among the 'civilised nations' still echoes in the corridors as one of the most important achievements of the post-World War II international venture.

In December 1960, General Assembly Resolution 1514 granted independence to colonial countries and peoples, marking a milestone in how 'liberation' has come to be envisioned in the contemporary discourse and in the practice of international law.[6] At that time, the struggle for the self-determination of territories still under Western ruling was enflaming the United Nations, with the old colonial powers being rapidly outnumbered by their former subjects.

With the arrival of national liberation movements on the international stage, the question over the legitimacy of guerrilla warfare became a heated topic, broadly reflecting the East–West blocs' confrontation, and eventually culminating in the recognition of wars of national liberation with Protocol I to the Geneva Conventions.[7] Those revolutionary years have gone down in history as a fundamental turning point in the trajectory of 'national liberation', with new sovereign states granted a voice in presiding over the fate of world's affairs. and it is indisputable that new players have been granted a voice in presiding over the fate of world's affairs.

And yet, if 'liberation' has cut through the progressive but troubled routes of the modern project of international law – from colonialism to protectorate to self-determination and formal independence – this very idea has reached a sort of end point in a particular form of liberating arrangement: state sovereignty. While other formulations are not really envisaged (the usual case cited is that of Western Sahara), perhaps one of the heaviest legacies of national liberation movements is precisely their confinement within the limits of the nation-state, with all that this 'confinement' entails. After all, for some that emancipatory moment indeed coincided with a new form of dependence.[8] And so, one feels back at square one: the former colonies 'liberated' themselves from their masters, but at what price? And what were the contours of this emancipatory

6 Declaration on the Granting of Independence to Colonial Countries and Peoples, A/RES/1514 (XV), 14 December 1960.

7 International Committee of the Red Cross (ICRC), Protocol Additional to the Geneva Conventions of 12 August 1949, and relating to the Protection of Victims of International Armed Conflicts (Protocol I), 8 June 1977.

8 Bhupinder S. Chimni, 'Third World Approaches to International Law: A Manifesto', *International Community Law Review* 8 (April 2006): 3–27.

venture – the dressing code, so-to-speak – to be able to sit at the negotiating table and converse with their newly acquired colleagues?

As one too soon recognises, this uncomfortable heritage is not easily escapable. Not even in present times, an age celebrated for the end of political ideologies, and in which global, transnational processes – we are told – should have paved new ways of imagining the architecture of international relations.[9] Naturally, the so-called decolonising process has taken many different shapes, and it has included a variety of stories and trajectories.[10] The purpose is not to unpack further *this kind* of critique. Precisely because that stance found itself in an impasse, and the object of criticism becomes the flip side of its own discontent, the price to pay for reaching sovereign freedom remains a stumbling block of the counter-discourse surrounding 'liberation'. How can one venture into such an enterprise without falling into the usual suspects then, while reflecting on the commitments that come with the very act of critique? Couldn't we change perspective for once?

In order to do so, I invite the reader to take a step out of the traditional actors of national liberation struggles, their overloaded legacy and related assessments, to focus on a less obvious player which generally lingers at the back of the same 'liberating' story. I want in fact to draw attention to an 'other' perspective, with the aim to enlarge the lens of the usual conversation about 'liberation'. The actors I have in mind (I shall rather use the plural from now on) are 'foreign fighters'.

Generally understood as 'individuals leaving their countries of nationality to fight in wars overseas', foreign fighters tend in fact to be attracted by violent armed struggles abroad, struggles which are posited at the hedge of emancipatory projects of various kinds.[11] Their recent history, I claim, can shed some

9 Cf. Francis Fukuyama, *The End of History and the Last Man* (New York: Free Press, 1992). *See* also Anne-Marie Slaughter, A *New World Order* (Princeton: Princeton University Press, 2005).

10 Which of course include looking at 'liberation' as a hybrid process, and not studied only by remaining on one side or the other of the barricade. The point is unpacked further along this article. For main reference: Sundhya Pahuja, *Decolonizing International Law: Development, Economic Growth and the Politics of Universality* (Cambridge: Cambridge University Press, 2011).

11 *See* David Malet, *Foreign Fighters: Transnational Identity in Civil Conflicts* (Oxford: Oxford University Press, 2013) and Nir Arielli, *From Byron to Bin Laden. A History of Foreign War Volunteers* (Harvard: Harvard University Press, 2018). For Malet, there is always a 'transnational identity' that reconnects these individuals to certain groups and struggles abroad. For Arielli, the decision to fight abroad is inexorably linked with forms of ideological struggles which determine the volunteers' choice to leave, and at the same time define their historical contingencies. Arielli divides those ideological motivations in three grand-moments, or 'waves': (1) the liberty vs. tyranny wave (nineteenth century); (2) the leftwing vs. rightwing wave (1917–1980); (3) and the so called clashes of civilisations wave (1980-present).

light over the ambivalences permeating the traditional story of 'liberation', and can help us reassess our own utopias connected with it.

To begin with, let me however put some caveats. First on the very terminology utilised here. The so-called foreign fighter is rather a novel invention, appearing in international discourse and in the academic literature only with the involvement of the 'Arab mujahideen' during the Soviet–Afghan War (1979–1989).[12] Recently, the issue has witnessed a global resurgence when the Security Council, in an effort to stop individuals flooding in the Syrian civil conflict, unanimously adopted Res.2178 criminalising 'foreign-terrorist-fighters'.[13] Historians have generally referred to the broader phenomenon of 'foreign volunteering', and scholarship has today recognised the involvement of these volunteers in many conflicts over the last two centuries.[14] Some famous examples include the wars of independence in Latin America during the early nineteenth century, where a significant number of British citizens fought under various guises;[15] or the Greek war of independence (1821–1832), which saw many volunteers driven by philhellenic sentiments joining the ranks of the Greek insurgents against the Ottoman empire (including the famous poet Lord Byron).[16] The list continues with the American Civil War (1861–1865), the Second Boers War (1899–1902), and as one ventures into the last century, the Spanish Civil War (1936–39), the Israeli War of Independence (1947–1949) and the Yugoslav wars (1992–1995) – all civil strifes where the presence of foreign individuals on the battlefield was recorded.[17] For the purpose of this chapter, the two terms (foreign fighters/volunteers) will be used interchangeably.

12 Cf. Daniel Byman, *Road Warriors: Foreign Fighters in The Armies of Jihad* (Oxford: Oxford University Press, 2019). The term 'Muslim foreign fighter' was coined by the political scientist and specialist in Islamic studies Thomas Hegghammer. Thomas Hegghammer, 'The Rise of the Muslim Foreign Fighters: Islam and the Globalization of Jihad', *International Security* 35:3 (Winter 2010/11): 53–94.

13 Addressing the Growing Issue of Foreign Terrorist Fighters, S/RES/2178, 24 September 2014.

14 Christine G. Kruger and Sonja Levesen, ed., *War Volunteering in Modern Times: From the French Revolution to the Second World War* (London: Palgrave Macmillan, 2013) and Nir Arielli and Bruce Collins, ed., *Transnational Soldiers: Foreign Military Enlistment in The Modern Era* (London: Palgrave Macmillan, 2013).

15 Moises Enriquez Rodriguez, *Freedom's Mercenaries: British Volunteers in the Wars of Independence of Latin America. Vol I: Northern South America and Vol II: Southern South America* (Lanham: Rowman & Littlefield, 2006).

16 William St. Clair, *That Greece Might Still Be Free: The Philhellenes in The War of Independence* (Oxford: Oxford University Press, 1972).

17 On the Yugoslav case: Jennifer Mustapha, 'The Mujahideen in Bosnia: The foreign fighter as cosmopolitan citizen and/or terrorist', Citizenship Studies 17:6–7 (February 2013): 742–755.

As it is easy to guess, my second point is about history. Precisely for what I have just pointed out, one should not mistake this move as a sort of an anachronistic operation.[18] If I utilise the examples of different 'foreign fighters' in the long durée, the aim is certainly not to throw concepts, actors and a whole set of diverse chronological trajectories in the same box uncritically.[19] I am aware of the risks one can incur in taking for granted current categories to search for their meaning in the past, and my intent is not meant to legitimise any political stance specifically related with this actor in the present.

But history is indeed a very interesting place to look in order to better understand how these 'individuals travelling abroad to fight in wars overseas' were characterised in different ways throughout the last two centuries: at times being described as 'idealistic volunteers', 'racist mercenaries' and only recently as 'enemies of humanity'. What is even more captivating, is that the actor 'foreign fighter' is a very ambivalent figure which has always posed serious problems to any straight-cut systematisation into the formal categories of law. As by their very definition they move from national to international settings (without usually belonging to a regular army), and as their motivations to rejoin wars abroad are extremely mixed, there is a fascinating ambiguity permeating their choices to participate in 'liberating' struggles of various kinds.[20]

18 In recent years, the methodological quarrel between historians and international lawyers on the use of 'history' has given way to a vibrant debate on the theme of 'contextualism' and on the risks arising from using present concepts by resorting to them uncritically in the past. Here, I side with Anne Orford as she describes the (international) legal method as necessarily 'anachronistic'. This is to say that, unlike historians, international legal scholars might be more interested in how concepts move across time and space, rather than seeking for a 'pure' contextualisation of the so-called historical material. Anne Orford, 'On International Legal Method', *London Review of International Law* 1:1 (September 2013): 166–197.

19 Robert W. Gordon, 'Critical Legal Histories', *Stanford Law Review* 36 (January 1984): 56–125. For important scholarly work on critical historical methodologies, please refer to: Keith Jenkins, Re-Thinking History (London: Routledge, 2003) and Joan Scott, *Theorie Critique de l'Histoire: Identites, Experiences, Politiques* (Paris: Fayard, 2009). *See* also Michel Foucault, 'Nietzsche, Genealogy, History', *in Nietzsche*, eds. Brian Leiter and John Richardson (Oxford: Oxford University Press, 1978), 139–164.

20 For instance, one can find among their ranks romantic adventurers (like Lord Byron), ex-army mercenaries (like the famous British naval officer Lord Cochrane, who was employed respectively by the Chilean, the Brazilian and the Greek navies during their wars of independence), political adviser (like the Marquise of Lafayette during the American Civil War), revolutionaries (like Garibaldi in the Ragamuffin war), diplomats fulfilling the role of 'secret agents' (like Lawrence of Arabia during the Arab Revolt of 1916–1919), committed intellectuals (like Hemingway, Orwell, or Malraux – among many others – in the Spanish civil war), etc. Thus, if 'foreign fighters' are today mainly conflated with individuals leaving for Syria and Iraq, this is only the most recent categorisation of a not-so-new phenomenon.

That very ambiguity is reflected in the way legal actors have framed (and continue to frame) foreign fighters by employing a strict 'good/bad' dichotomy in order to categorise their presence in the battlefield. A net moral distinction is in fact operating each time between the 'lawful' and the 'unlawful' foreign volunteer (both at the national and at the international level), the status of foreign fighters being de facto dependent on the political affiliations, the passions, the desires and even the fantasies of the various players in the legal arena in a given historical period.[21] Without venturing too far, the point I wish to make is that foreign fighters mirror a whole set of 'liberating/emancipatory' stances, which can help enrich the traditional way of understanding 'liberation' as an heritage of the decolonisation period, rather than simply situating this figure in relation to the traditional self-determination stories we have been accustomed to. It is thus by looking at their recent history that this narrative can actually be problematised and, along with that, our own criticism and commitments to it.

During the Spanish Civil War (1936–1939), foreign volunteers flooded in the Iberian Peninsula from all corners of the world.[22] Relevant to contextualise the political climate of the time, the whole civil war was presented in Europe as a conflict between communist and fascist ideologies. As a matter of fact, with the help of volunteers sent by Mussolini and Hitler, General Francisco Franco had been able to fuel his rebellion against the 'legitimate' Republican government.[23] What began as a sort of a mutiny soon resulted in a civil war, also thanks to the aid furnished by foreign powers to both sides of the trench in the form of weapons, supplies and troops.[24] Interestingly, a clear differentiation between 'good' and 'bad' foreign volunteers marked the heated

[21] Nathaniel Berman has showed in its seminal work how 'rules' remain essentially a human product, and likewise how human beings tend to put their own 'passions and ambivalences' into the categories of law. Following the same methodological path, the point I want to make is that the 'foreign fighters' as a legal category is an example to show how 'status' cannot explain their whole story. Or rather, it can, only in function of a precise context, culture and time. Nathaniel Berman, *Passions and Ambivalence: Colonialism, Nationalism, and International Law* (Leiden: Brill, 2011).

[22] For a detailed account: Hugh Thomas, *The Spanish Civil War: Third Edition* (London: Penguin, 1977).

[23] For a legal account of the war Ann Van Wynen Thomas and A. J. Thomas Jr., 'International Legal Aspects of the Civil War in Spain, 1936–39', *in The International Law of Civil War*, ed. Richard Falk (Baltimore: The John Hopkins University Press, 1971), 111–175.

[24] The Russian Comintern (also known as the Communist International or Third International) was the organisation which was recognised as the main promoter and organiser of the dispatch of 'leftist' volunteers in Spain for instance. While both Hitler and Mussolini dispatched their troops on the Spanish soil at different moments.

discussions at the League of Nations, where the Spanish minister of foreign affairs Julio Álvarez del Vayo pleaded the case for his country:

> [i]t is painful for the Spanish Government to accept the use of the title 'volunteers' for two different categories of men; on the one hand, those who are sent from countries where every free expression of will is crushed by the iron tyranny of the totalitarian regimes and who are not even volunteers in name [. . .] On the other hand, those who came of their own free will to fight side by side with us [. . .] A clear and noble ideal brought these volunteers into the struggle in Spain because of its universal aspect.[25]

This idea is reiterated in many Parliamentary discussions of the same period. In order to distinguish the 'totalitarian volunteers' sent by Germany and Italy and the 'true volunteers' fighting for freedom, a clear moral line is demarcated, putting the accent on the noble ideals underlying the cause of those men rejoining the International Brigades, vis-à-vis 'the hired levies from Italy and Germany'.[26] Both the British Houses and the French National Assembly will become the principal stages for two clashing views over the presence of 'volunteers' in the civil struggle happening in Spain.[27] As such, the supporters of the 'idealistic' volunteers will be opposed by those who firmly believed there was nothing unlawful in backing the 'legitimate' side of the Spanish rebellion, and who welcomed the volunteer troops sent by Italy and Germany. The one on the Iberian Peninsula represented a larger struggle between 'civilization' and 'barbarity', revolving around two very different ideas of what a liberating venture should look like. As we step out of the decolonisation period, perhaps we start to recognise that the idea of what a 'liberation' should be or represent might have actually taken different shapes. Weren't those fascist troops also supporting a liberating stance, that is freeing Spain from a communist take-over? Naturally, if read with today's eyes, this may well appear as a reactionary argument, to say the least. History has indeed judged the rise of nazi-fascism and of radical right-wing ideologies, and there is no need to repeat that story here. However, it suffices to take a glance at our contemporary political landscape, to realise that those stances are not exactly dormant. Conversely, they tend to reappear quite abruptly from time to time. What I want to emphasise here is that the idea of 'liberation' to which we are accustomed to

[25] League of Nations, Official Journal 18, 97th Session of the Council. Fifth meeting (May–June 1937), 319.

[26] Particularly the speech of Philip Noel-Baker, representative of the Labour Party, in March of 1937. HC Deb, 17 March 1937, Vol. 321, c2143.

[27] In France, a law for the interdiction of volunteers is discussed at the Chamber of Deputies (today's National Assembly) in January 1937. Journal officiel de la République française. Débats parlementaires. Chambre des députés. Séance du vendredi 15 Janvier 1937, at 42.

is perhaps more ambivalent than we might think. Those supporting Franco's 'emancipatory' project to free Spain from the communist threat have stood on some valuable moral ground. Franco's project to free Spain from the communist threat had its supporters among the most conservative European forces, and this was reflected in how foreign volunteers were differently understood on one side or the other of the ideological barricade.

In the very same period in which national liberation movements were conducting fierce battles for freeing themselves from their old rulers, some 'other' foreign nationals were also descending on the African continent to fight on the very opposite front. Their presence on the battlefield was epitomised by the Luanda Trial (June 1976), in which ten Britons and three Americans were tried by the People's Revolutionary Court of Angola with the accusation of being 'mercenaries'.[28]

At the time, Angola represented one of the terrains where the new battle between communism and imperialism was raging – battle epitomised by the Cold War years.[29] However, with an interesting shift of the political landscape seen in the Spanish case. This time, countries such as Russia and Cuba were in fact sponsoring their own 'foreign volunteers/advisors' as a legitimate form of aid to African states, while deploring the presence of white mercenaries and especially their connivance with Western, 'imperialistic' countries.

Precisely this inversion of perspective is quite fascinating not only to understand the bigger geo-political context of the Luanda trial, but also to better characterise those foreigners involved in the battlefield on the side of the old colonial powers. Many of the so-called mercenaries going to fight in various parts of the third world were in fact Western citizens adhering to an open anti-communist and right-wing political ideology.[30] As the story goes, third world states did everything in their power to highlight the fundamental

28 The trial has been recounted by a variety of authors, as well as by the international press. For a selection: Mike J. Hoover, 'The Laws of War and the Angolan Trial of Mercenaries: Death to the Dogs of War', *Case Western Reserve Journal of International Law* 9:2 (Spring 1977): 323–406. George H. Lockwood, 'Report on the Trial of Mercenaries: Luanda, Angola – June, 1976', *Manitoba Law Journal* 7:3 (1977): 183–202. Wilfred Burchett and Derek Roebuck, *The Whores of War: Mercenaries Today* (London: Penguin Books, 1977).

29 *See* John Stockwell, *In Search of Enemies. A CIA Story* (New York: Norton, 1978) and Jiri Valenta, 'The Soviet-Cuban Intervention in Angola, 1975', *Studies in Comparative Communism Vol.* XI *(Spring/Summer* 1978): 3–33.

30 *See* Sarah Percy, *Mercenaries: The History of a Norm in International Relations* (Oxford: Oxford University Press, 2007). Interesting also are the autobiographical accounts of some famous European mercenaries: Jean Schramme, *Le Bataillon Leopard: Souvenirs d'un Africain Blanc* (Paris: Robert Laffont, 1969). Mike Hoare, *The Road to Kalamata: A Congo Mercenary's Personal Memoir* (Lexington: Lexington Books, 1989). Rolf Steiner, *Carre Rouge: du Biafra au Soudan, Le Dernier Condottiere* (Paris: Robert Laffont, 1976). The writing of

difference that seemed to separate these foreign individuals from the idealistic volunteers of the Spanish civil war, that is, fighting for mere personal profit as opposed to fighting for a noble ideology.[31] And yet, not everyone was agreeing to the negative portrait made of the 'mercenaries', and especially to their delegitimisation as some sort of unlawful combatants. Almost a decade before the Luanda trial, the Congo crisis (1960–1967) had already inflamed the discussions at the United Nations between newly independent countries and the old colonial rulers on this very issue.[32] As recalled by the Belgian delegate Paul-Henri Spaak in a famous speech at the Security Council in November 1961:

> You seem to forget all history and to believe this is the first time that people have gone to fight in foreign armies. Have you forgotten certain events which took place before the Second World War, when men from all countries went to defend *freedom* [emphasis added] in other countries? What would have happened then, if those men who had gone to fight in another country had been punished when they returned home. It is easy to laugh, but this is history.[33]

And so, it turned out that white 'mercenaries' were perhaps fighting also under some political agenda: keeping Africa out of a communist invasion. Was that a liberating project as well? And are we able to accept *that* history when assessing the ways of doing critique, while reflecting on the commitments that inevitably come with it?

these famous soldiers of fortune show how they all professed a strong attachment to the 'old and virtuous' military values and how they generally shared an ideal of white supremacy.

31 This particular vision concretised in the codification of art. 47 of Additional Protocol I, which outlawed mercenaries in international armed conflicts.

32 For an excellent summary of the background of the Congo crisis as well as the main legal issues at stake: Donald W. McNemar, *The Postindependence War in the Congo*, in Falk, *supra* note 23, 244–302.

33 UN Security Council Official Records, 976th Meeting (17 November 1961). Spaak's speech at 44. The very same line of argumentation will be found in national political debates happening in England and in the United States in the aftermath of the Luanda court's sentence. The debates (both dating August 1976) are found in the 'Report of the Committee of Privy Counsellors appointed to inquire into the recruitment of mercenaries' (commonly known as the 'Diplock Report') for Great Britain; and the 'Hearing before the Special Subcommittee on Investigations of the Committee on International Relations' (titled 'Mercenaries in Africa') at the House of Representatives for the United States. As well resumed by a representative of the British conservative party: 'We must not deprecate mercenaries too much. Lord Byron was a mercenary. I should have thought that many people in the Labour Party would take a pride in the record of the Attlee battalion in the International Brigade [...] Of course, they were mercenaries [...] The Gurkhas have done tremendous service for this country. They are mercenaries too'. The speech of Julien Amery on February 9th at the Foreign Policy and Morality Commons Sitting. HC Deb, 9 February 1976, Vol. 905, c47.

At least, that history would explain the *laissez-faire* and ambiguous attitude showed by many Western states when deciding which legal responses to adopt to stop their 'mercenaries' from reaching the African continent. An attitude that has certainly changed in today's political landscape, when in a rush to stop the influx of foreign nationals joining the ranks of the Islamic State and other jihadist groups, the UN Security Council has unequivocally criminalised these individuals as 'foreign-terrorist-fighter', urging all member states to pass severe legislation to face the problem.[34] Yet, the very same confrontation between 'good' and 'bad' foreign fighters is once again revived by the presence in the battlefield of two seemingly different types of volunteers: the ruthless criminals joining 'terrorist groups' and those 'freedom fighters' fighting instead on the 'good' side of the trench.[35] Although there are no surprises with regards to which volunteers usually receive harsher sentences, it is significant to note that even among the ranks of those terrible 'enemies of humanity', there might be idealists fighting for a noble cause:

> the young men and women who go [to Syria] are *idealists* [emphasis added]. After all, young men and women went to fight in the Spanish Civil War; they were doing a similar thing [. . .] we have to understand the dynamics of what these young men and women are doing and not just say immediately, 'They are all terrorists and when they come back we will put them all in jail'.[36]

There is a question which can no longer be avoided at this point: what liberating stances are we able to contemplate as valid? And how do we understand the claims made by present-day non-state armed groups, especially those pointing beyond the contours of the nation-state?[37] If after the revolutionary years of decolonisation the fight against colonial and racist regimes has taken over the discourse of 'liberation' and has confined the right to self-determination to the political boundaries of state sovereignty, liberating claims of various kinds are certainly not dormant, especially today. The three examples presented along this paper wanted to step out of the traditional

34 S/RES/2178, 24 September 2014, *supra* note 13.

35 In the not-so abundant literature concerning Western foreign fighters present in the Syrian territory, and particularly those fighting against the Islamic State, see specifically: Kyle Orton, 'The Secular Foreign Fighters of the West in Syria', *Insight Turkey* 20:3 (July 2018): 157–177. Henry Tuck, Tanya Silverman and Candace Smalley, '"Shooting in the right direction": Anti-ISIS Foreign Fighters in Syria &; Iraq', *The Institute for Strategic Dialogue* | Horizons Series No. 1 (August 2016).

36 HD Deb, 26 September 2014, Vol. 755, cc1676-1746. Lord Desai intervention, c1716.

37 See the response to Lord Desai intervention by Lord Privy Seal (Baroness Stowell of Beeston): 'the Spanish Civil War was an issue that we could understand in our terms. The caliphate is not like that. It is different from the Spanish Civil War in legitimising people going there'. *Id.* cc1676-1680.

narrative of the decolonisation period, as well as to provide with a different standpoint of critique.

Read this way, the recent history of 'foreign fighters' could be taken as a mirror of states' responses to foreign conflicts, advancing the argument that these actors have always epitomised positions, ideas and values about intervening in foreign wars – of course in very different legal and political contexts – precisely not through the lens of national liberation armies or movements. From there, we could ask how the presence of foreign volunteers is contributing to shape our own perception of 'wars of national liberation', and consequently, think about the moral values and the underlying assumptions we resort to when we unpack any critique of the 'traditional' liberation narrative.

As I have tried to sketch in this condensed story, foreign volunteers' choices to rejoin people and struggles abroad point indeed to the ambivalent landscape of political commitments related with various kinds of 'liberation'. Their presence in the battlefield being marked by a strict good/bad dichotomy, this dichotomy gets normally translated into normative responses and, most importantly, tends to reflect moral–political stances related with emancipatory projects of different kinds. We then come to the conclusion that 'liberation' has in fact taken many shapes and has attracted different political visions and passions, pushing the most diverse range of 'foreign volunteers' to intervene abroad.

But shouldn't this urge also be ours, when doing critical work and – by doing so – when committing to the utopias that underlie it? Rather than shutting the door to the apparent impossibility of certain claims, shouldn't we take a more intermediate position to begin with? This is not to suggest a post-modern relativisation of radically different struggles, nor to subtly push for any 'civilising mission' in order to subsume 'others' into 'us'. But rather, to re-start by posing questions: what liberating stances is international law able to accept? During the decolonisation period some groups were certainly seen as 'illegitimate', 'unlawful' and even posing a terrorist threat. If allowing some players while disallowing others is a normal business for international law, what is perhaps more interesting to reflect upon, is the tendency to consent only to some of the competing voices. Here one is forced to go back to the commitments, and their ambiguity: do we want to create more space? For whom? And in what tone should these 'others' be allowed to speak? 'Liberation' is certainly a murky enterprise, precisely because no one agrees on what an emancipatory path should really look like. What I want to suggest, is that we should remain vigilant about the possibilities out there, even where the terrain seems particularly rough, or impassable. There are options to be considered when looking at non-state actors' claims, even if at first, they seem intolerable to attain. If the risk of reproducing the well-known vision of things (sovereignty), only sweetened by a one size-fits all narrative (more rights), is always around the corner, should one fall into despair? Or shouldn't this be an occasion to become more receptive, especially in a period which seems to disavow any real alternative? Perhaps it is more about beginning a serious work of criticism, rather than accommodating claims along the usual axes. The recent history of foreign volunteering points indeed to the ambivalence of liberating projects (and of its supporters), an ambiguity always out there for consideration. To leave space to *that* imagination should thus be our commitment. Making this kind of an effort, is perhaps the most genuine emancipatory project one can hope for, in the routinely times that come after the fall of utopias.

13

Multilateralism

Christine Schwöbel-Patel

In the famous Faust tale, Faust (or Faustus) makes a pact with the devil. Depending on the retelling of the tale, the pact is one in which the scholar Faust trades his soul for unlimited knowledge or some other kind of superhuman power. In the seventeenth century Christopher Marlowe retelling, Faustus buys the services of Mephistopheles (a demon of Lucifer's) for twenty-four years of living in 'voluptuousness' with his soul.[1] Johann Wolfgang von Goethe's Faust makes a pact with Mephistopheles in which the devil serves him on earth and he promises to serve the devil in hell.[2] In the twentieth century retelling by Thomas Mann, Doktor Faustus is a composer who exchanges his soul for twenty-four years of living as a 'musical genius'.[3] In most versions, Faust's years of voluptuousness are followed by suffering – either by him being carried off to hell or death by more earthly maladies.[4] The corruption of his mind caused by his ambitions for greater power means that Faust must face consequences. Marlowe references Icarus in the Greek myth about hubris: 'His waxen wings did mount above his reach. And melting heavens conspired his overthrow'.[5] In the present chapter, I suggest that international law's pact with capitalism after the end of the Cold War – an important consolidating moment of the neoliberal order – can be interpreted as the beginning of its twenty-four years of voluptuousness. Taking a little license with the precise number of years, the rise of nationalist populism,

1 Christopher Marlowe, *Doctor Faustus*, ed. David Scott Kastan (New York 2005) A-Text, para 90 (p. 17).

2 Johann Wolfgang von Goethe, Faust I und II (Hamburg 2011).

3 Thomas Mann, *Doctor Faustus: The Life of the German Composer Adrian Leverkühn as Told by a Friend*, trans. John E. Woods (New York 1999) 5.

4 In Thomas Mann's Doktor Faustus, he dies of syphilis. Although one might argue about whether this is really such an earthly malady, given its associations with genius. In Goethe's tale (his latest version), Faust is saved and is carried off to heaven by angels.

5 Marlowe (note 1) 6.

associated with 2016 and subsequent years, marked the end of the years of voluptuousness. The absence of a sustained multilateral response to the 2020 pandemic caused by COVID-19 is the latest in a list of global crises prompting national and regional responses over multilateral responses.

Indeed, multilateral responses to the most pressing contemporary global crises – whether climate catastrophe, income inequality, mass migration, or the coronavirus pandemic – have mostly been notable only through their absence or failures. The Paris Agreement, the multilateral agreement signed by most states to limit global temperature increases, is binding only as to its reporting provisions, and not actually in regard to carbon emissions.[6] Neither the United Nations Millennium Goals nor their more recent incarnation as Sustainable Development Goals have been able to halt the increasing disparity between rich and poor.[7] Responses to the 'refugee crisis' have been notable mainly through national and regional punitive measures against people crossing borders – and their tragic consequences – rather than through protective multilateral agreements. And, finally, the response to the coronavirus pandemic has highlighted how fragile multilateral institutions such as the World Health Organisation (WHO) are when faced with ethno-nationalism. The hijacking of Personal Protective Equipment shipments as well as US President Trump invoking the Defense Protection Act to prevent US exports of key medical gear have illustrated the prevalence of a nationalist competitive mindset over a multilateral co-operative one. Responses to crises indicate, then, that instead of multilateral approaches, there is an increasing prevalence of nationalist and bilateral approaches to cross-border agreement. Meanwhile, the United Nations' calls for more multilateralism drift into the abyss, with the occasional sound bite amplified through the vague buzzes of liberal international lawyers on their exclusive sound waves.

What has happened to multilateralism in the past years, and why are there seemingly so few remaining champions of it (bar international lawyers)? As a starting point, I propose a consideration of the immediate years following the end of the Cold War – this is international law's 'Mephistopheles moment'. After having sought influence as a discipline for many years, the post-1989 'new world order' of liberal internationalism promised great improvements for the discipline of international law and its professionals: success, resources, and influence. The condition for the

6 Paris Agreement to the United Nations Framework Convention on Climate Change (adopted 22 April 2016, entered into force 4 November 2016) https://unfccc.int/files/essential_background/convention/application/pdf/english_paris_agreement.pdf.

7 www.un.org/millenniumgoals/; https://sdgs.un.org/goals.

success, resources, and influence – the pact entered into – was that international law was obligated to protect and uphold capitalism. International law was required to play an active part in constituting a neoliberal order in which law guaranteed and legitimised global financialisation, privatisation, and more generally the freedom of capital to move across borders. Competition as the *logos* of capitalism was to be foregrounded as the central paradigm conducting the relations between states. After considering moments of acceleration during the years of voluptuousness (namely the global financial crisis and fragmentation), I consider the tipping point of multilateralism next. What were the conditions under which there was a backlash? Here, I mention the two dominant views on why multilateralism has receded, namely the 'strongman' perspective and the 'new Cold War' perspective. Neither fully answer the question of 'why now?', and neither pay sufficient attention to the question of multilateral agreements that remain in place. I therefore suggest a structural approach, which takes seriously that the post-Cold War period was a time when multilateralism facilitated the expansion of capital into previously socialist and planned economy states. To put it crudely: Since the geographic expansion has come to an end, there is no longer a need for certain types of cooperative multilateralism. This may explain the move away from multilateralism (although some multilateral agreements remain strong), but it does not yet reveal what is next for international law. There are several variations of the ending of the Faust tale: Faust dies, Faust is redeemed, or Faust lives, but ends up serving the devil. What will be the fate of international law?

13.1 THE MEPHISTOPHELES MOMENT FOR INTERNATIONAL LAW

All analogies, including this one, have their limitations. International law can only to a limited extent be anthropomorphised as the 'Faust' in this account. The discipline cannot have agency in the way Faust in the tale can. Not only is the discipline constituted of multiple interests, institutions, and partly conflicting norms, it is also a site of struggle over what the 'international' means and whom it protects. And yet, its hegemonic expressions give it certain contours. Individuals, institutions, and other actors, have shaped a 'mainstream' or dominant liberal legal approach. It is this mainstream idea of liberal internationalism that is the object of this study. A further limitation of the analogy with the Faust tale is that it would be difficult to argue that it was really international law's 'soul' that was at stake in the post-Cold War period. International law was no innocent discipline pre 1989. Arguably it had no 'soul' to trade. The international law of 1989 had a long history of protecting private property over the interests of a Commons,[8] of co-creating the colonial world from the sixteenth century onwards,[9] and of organising and legitimising the imperial powers of the nineteenth century onwards. It was this international law that enabled the repression of a colonial insurgency in the mid-twentieth century, and tempered the radical potential of a New International Economic Order and democratisation of the United Nations in the 1970s.[10] Overall, the post-Cold War period was less of a significant break than it would seem in a Faustian analogy of before-and-after the encounter with the devil or the devil's apprentices. And yet, despite these limitations of the analogy, international law stood at a crossroads in 1989: It could be shaped to facilitate the needs of global capital *or* the needs of a form of global justice that placed emphasis on redistribution, environmental protection, and protection of the vulnerable. The former prevailed.

Following its Mephistopheles moment, the 1990s certainly saw the fortunes of international law change. The 'End of History' presented opportunities for significant expansion and influence.[11] The UN General Assembly declared the period 1990–1999 as the 'United Nations Decade of International Law',[12] and the 'new tribunalism' saw the establishment of many new institutions of international law.[13] More institutions required more international lawyers, increasing the influence of international lawyers in new and existing power structures. At the same time as gaining greater power and influence, international lawyers attained a reputation as 'humanitarians' – heroic individuals fighting for global peace, security, and prosperity. With the nationalist and anti-imperialist voices of the former communist and socialist bloc subdued or even muted, international lawyers saw an opportunity to move, as Philippe Sands put it, from the 'corridors of foreign ministries', into 'the boardrooms of businesses, the lobbying newsletters of non-governmental organizations (NGOs), and the front pages of newspapers'.[14] This in turn fostered a new

8 Susan Marks, *A False Tree of Liberty: Human Rights in Radical Thought* (Oxford 2019).

9 Antony Anghie, *Imperialism, Sovereignty and the Making of International Law* (Cambridge 2012); Kate Miles, *The Origins of International Investment Law: Empire, Environment and the Safeguarding of Capital* (Cambridge, 2013).

10 Adom Getachew, *Worldmaking after Empire: The Rise and Fall of Self-Determination* (Princeton 2019); Priyamvada Gopal, *Insurgent Empire* (London, 2019).

11 Francis Fukuyama, 'The End of History?', *The National Interest* 16 (1989): 3–18.

12 United Nations General Assembly Resolution 44/23, 'United Nations Decade of International Law', 60th plenary meeting at the 44th session (17 November 2019) UN Doc A/RES/44/23.

13 Thomas Skouteris, *The Notion of Progress in International Law Discourse* (The Hague 2010) 164–179.

14 Philippe Sands, *Lawless World: Making and Breaking Global Rules* (London 2006) 15.

generation of international lawyers ready to fight the good fight. During the 1990s, then, securing multilateral agreements came to be regarded as the main tool of global cooperation and stability. Whilst in international law, multilateralism can refer simply to three or more states being a party to a treaty, it is mostly thought of more broadly as 'global cooperative action'.[15] This emphasis on cooperation has however arguably obscured the emphasis on *competition* in the global neoliberal order.

13.2 THE PACT

In Marlowe's tale, Faustus asks: 'Stay, Mephistopheles, and tell me what good will my soul do thy lord [Lucifer]?' Mephistopheles answers simply: 'Enlarge his kingdom'.[16] International law's alliance with capitalism too had the effect of enlarging capital's kingdom. But, it does more than that; it also legitimises and reproduces capitalism in the form of the global neoliberal order. Whilst a systematic analysis of multilateralism in the 1990s is impossible in this short contribution, it is worth highlighting three sub-disciplines of international law that utilised multilateralism in favour of capital: International economic law, international criminal law, and international human rights law. It was in 1995 that the World Trade Organisation (WTO) was created to gradually eliminate trade barriers between member states. With the WTO, the link between free trade and development politics was institutionalised, forging one of the key rationales for the discipline of international economic law.[17] But, problems of legalised globalisation soon emerged. The era of the WTO de facto prompted the loss of political power for states in the Global South – states that had been lured through the promise of the 'neutrality' of the market for development. The imposition of free trade rules and open markets of economies in the Global South caused what Nicolas M. Perrone and David Schneiderman have recently referred to as 'international economic law's wreckage'.[18] Opening up economies to foreign goods, services and capital presented opportunities for the states of the Global North to exploit resources (natural resources as well as labour), depressing their value and binding states of the Global South to punitive trade agreements. The further inequality caused by

[15] André Nollkaemper, 'Unilateralism/Multilateralism', Max Planck Encyclopedia of International Law 10 (2012): 179–185.

[16] Marlowe (note 1), para. 35, p. 21.

[17] www.wto.org/english/thewto_e/history_e/history_e.htm.

[18] Nicolás M. Perrone and David Schneidermann, 'International Economic Law's Wreckage: Depoliticization, Inequality, Precarity', in *Research Handbook on Critical Legal Theory* (Cheltenham 2019) 446–472.

the policies of the International Monetary Fund (IMF) to release debt only on condition of structural adjustment reforms that opened up national markets to global competition are well documented – not least by the IMF itself.[19] Not only were international lawyers drafting these treaties, they were also on hand to enforce and protect them. Once the multilateral landscape had been secured, the path was cleared for bilateral investment treaties that protected foreign capital, very often at the expense of domestic working conditions and the environment. Today, the system of international trade (and investment) rules set up in the 1990s determines where raw materials are produced, where goods are manufactured, and how foreign investors are protected abroad. International lawyers have been at the epicenter of creating 'a world of winners and losers'.[20] Despite this, multilateralism is and was often portrayed by liberal internationalists as the 'good bit' in globalisation.[21] By and large, then, international lawyers were simultaneously protecting capital and thought of as standing above the messiness of international politics or of the market, embodying instead the cool and measured voice of reason. This moral story of multilateralism is rhetorically mostly connected to the post-World War II period, rather than the post-Cold War period.[22]

The strong appeal of the narrative link of multilateralism with the 1940s can be observed with another emerging sub-discipline of international law of the 1990s, namely international criminal law. The ad hoc tribunals for Yugoslavia and Rwanda drew the world's attention to individual criminal accountability of international crimes, cemented through the establishment of the permanent International Criminal Court in 1998, and morally justified with a strong narrative link to the Nuremberg trials. In the enthusiasm for making individuals accountable for mass killings (arguably the main preoccupation), international criminal law, however, became an instrument to effectively turn the gaze away from structural violence. Attention was arrested on the designated core crimes: genocide, crimes against humanity, war crimes, and the crime of aggression. This individualised approach to accountability has shielded hegemonic states, as well as corporations, from sustained accountability for structures of inequality, including poverty and exploitation through capital's search

[19] Jonathan D. Ostry, Prakash Loungani, and Davide Furceri, 'Neoliberalism: Oversold?', Finance & Development 53:2 (2016): 38–41 at: www.imf.org/external/pubs/ft/fandd/2016/06/ostry.htm.

[20] Perrone and Schneidermann (note 18).

[21] Mary Robinson, interviewed in 'Global Governance: Former World Leaders on Collective Responsibility, The Future of Multilateralism and The United Nations', *Finding Humanity* podcast, Series 1, Episode 9 (24 June 2020).

[22] For example, see James Crawford, 'The Current Political Discourse Concerning International Law', *Modern Law Review* 81:1 (2018): 1–22.

for profit. Arguably, the structuring and institutionalising of stereotypes of who global justice 'dispensers' and who global justice 'receivers' are has widened rather than narrowed the divisions between the Global North and the Global South. Indeed, there was no group that was living in more voluptuousness (whether in material terms or in terms of their perceived moral superiority) than the ever specialising international legal group of 'tribunal hoppers' who benefited from the 'rise and rise' of their field.[23] International criminal law, similarly to international human rights law, is generally understood as existing outside of the market and is therefore mostly thought of as commensurate with a moral higher good. Its protection of capital, and capital*ism*, has therefore remained vastly under-researched.

A related debate on an imagined depoliticised system that protects the status quo and omits redistribution of wealth has emerged in the field of international human rights law. Similarly to its sister sub-discipline just mentioned, human rights law is often considered as separate from the market and economy, or simply its 'powerless companion'.[24] However, as Jessica Whyte has argued, the separation of morals from the market and the market from a legalistic moral regime misses the analysis as to why 'human rights have often proved more useful in protecting the wealthy and legitimising the interventions of the most powerful states than in protecting the powerless'.[25] The deepest connection between human rights and sustaining rights of the wealthy can be found in rights to defend property, market access rights, and other rights that defend capital.[26] It is telling that precisely these inflections of human rights debates were emerging in the 1990s. Although multilateralism *appeared* to favour collaboration over competition, it in fact centered competition, making both multilateralism and international law simultaneously popular and fragile.

13.3 ACCELERATION POINTS RATHER THAN TIPPING POINTS

During its years of voluptuousness, international law accommodated for changes to capital's demands, one might say even to the point of absurdity. The Faust analogy stretches to these periods of acceleration as periods of

23 Elena Baylis, 'Tribunal-Hopping with the Post-Conflict Justice Junkies', *Oregan Review of International Law* 10 (2008): 361–390.

24 Samuel Moyn, 'A Powerless Companion: Human Rights in the Age of Neoliberalism', *Law and Contemporary Problems* 77 (2015): 147–169.

25 Jessica Whyte, *The Morals of the Market* (London 2019) 3.

26 Ernst-Ulrich Petersmann, 'The WTO Constitution and Human Rights', *Journal of International Economic Law* 3 (2000): 19.

giddiness brought on through initial success: In Marlowe's telling, Doctor Faustus travels to Rome to play pranks on the Pope; in Goethe's darker version, Faust gives Gretchen, whom he intends to seduce, a sleeping potion for her mother – the potion turns out to be poison. Among the crises of the End of History years, the perhaps most unexpected continuation of the giddy years of voluptuousness occurred during the financial crisis from 2007–2008. This was not to be the tipping point for multilateralism as a support system for the neoliberal order. Quite the contrary, this was the time that saw the further consolidation of financialisation and privatisation facilitated through multilateralism and legitimised through international law. In international economic law, the principle of free trade continued to be viewed as the natural means of globalisation, and economic growth the indisputable end. Despite notable attempts of inhibiting the acceleration and consolidation of the neoliberal order (notably through the Occupy Movements), the global financial institutions such as the IMF and the World Bank fortified their impermeability to democratic processes. If anything, then, this period saw a deepening of depoliticisation in the separation of politics and markets. Such deepening is perhaps most identifiable in the defiant literature on global constitutionalism that sought harmonisation and consolidation on the basis of human rights, democracy and the rule of law – whilst largely neglecting mention of their distributive effects.[27] The literature on global constitutionalism was, of course, in part a response to the discipline's supposed fragmentation. However, although described as in opposition, both global constitutionalism and fragmentation shared their commitment to capital. Perhaps paradoxically, fragmentation is *caused* through multilateralism. While global constitutionalism inadvertently separates questions of the market from democratic contestation, fragmentation generates competition among institutions and experts. In their study on the political economy of fragmentation in international law, Eyal Benvenisti and George W. Downs describe how fragmentation allows powerful states to preserve their dominance and opportunistically break the rules.[28] Only the powerful states can enact the privilege of forum-shopping and sabotage a more egalitarian system. States from the Global South are further marginalised in this market-system, and are forced to undermine any solidarity in South–South relations for the purposes of short-term gains. The argument is somewhat akin to David Kennedy's argument in *World of Struggle* where he

[27] In 2009, just a year after the financial crisis, Anne Peters published here piece 'On the Merits of Global Constitutionalism', *Indiana Journal of Global Legal Studies* 16 (2009): 397–411.

[28] Eyal Benvenisti and George W. Downs, 'The Empire's New Clothes: Political Economy and the Fragmentation of International Law', *Stanford Law Review* 70 (2007): 595–631.

describes the elite experts who retain an overview over their areas of specialism whilst global governance as a whole remains a mystery.[29] This does not only mean a 'loss of overview', as suggested in the International Law Commission's report on fragmentation, it also blunts the tools of structural critique. Such critique is made more difficult when the discipline requires expertise of tiny eco-systems of institutions, norms, and experts.

Although the global financial crisis and the onset of fragmentation were points of acceleration for international law's protection of capital (via multilateralism), it is crucial to note that critics and scholars of Third World Approaches to International Law contested the blanket benevolence of multilateralism. One particular critical counter-narrative stands out, not least for its description of multilateralism as 'terror'.[30] China Mieville notes how in international law, instead of questioning the structural issues, problems have always been deemed as the *exception*. Whether torture at Guantanamo Bay, or the blatant aggression of the Iraq War, these are events that are portrayed as occurring *despite* a benevolent international law. Mieville contrasts this lamenting by international lawyers with their silence in regard to the UN-sanctioned coup in Haiti in 2004. Here, multilateralism adopts an imperial form, and international lawyers ignore it or fail to critically interrogate it in their commentary. The bias of outrage for what is deemed as the violent exception hides the violent norm.

13.4 THE TIPPING POINT

Critics of multilateralism found themselves in strange company when isolated threats of withdrawal from multilateral organisations became a trend in 2016. A growing body of literature is accumulating that aims to pinpoint causes of 'The End' of the multilateral fairytale (where no one lives happily ever after). This literature is divided into two dominant narratives,: First, the 'strongman' perspective; and second, the hegemonic state perspective. I propose a third narrative of the end of multilateralism: the structural perspective. The 'strongman' perspective explains the move away from multilateralism as tied to its leaders and their macho leadership styles. President Modi of India, Orban of Hungary, Erdoğan of Turkey, and Bolsonaro of Brazil, have all been described in these ways, and have all expressed their dislike of multilateralism to conduct foreign affairs. Their appeal

[29] David Kennedy, *A World of Struggle: How Power, Law, and Expertise Shape Global Political Economy* (Oxford 2016).

[30] China Mieville, 'Multilateralism as Terror: International Law, Haiti and Imperialism', *Finnish Yearbook of International Law* 19 (2008): 63–92.

is generally explained through a mistrust of democratic institutions, an anti-elitism and attendant populism. US President Trump often topped the dubious machismo politician's list. Trump famously announced withdrawal of the USA from multilateral agreements such as the Paris (climate) Agreement and the Trans Pacific Partnership (TPP), and more recently the WHO. The 'strongman' perspective as a means of explaining the turn away from multilateralism, whilst appealing for its easy 'fix' of replacing the incumbent, places too great an emphasis on the power of the individual. Certainly, leaders have great power, but even policy proposals of authoritarian leaders must be 'heard', they still require supporters, and their actions must be implemented. Without these conditions, the individual has only limited power. That is to say that a view on individual leaders is not sufficient for explaining global trends.

A variation of the 'strongman' thesis is to consider strong states rather than strong leaders. This view most closely aligns with arguments referring to a 'new Cold War' between states. The focus here tends to be on the USA, and more recently, China and Russia. Central to this narrative is the US–China trade war, which has seen both states imposing tariffs, thereby countering the WTO's ethos of eliminating trade barriers. Pointing out China's lack of enthusiasm for multilateralism, in contrast to that of the US perhaps, is not new. Russia too is noted as using its greater influence to move away from multilateral commitments from the twentieth century. The move away from multilateralism here is presented as a condition of what Eyal Benvenisti recently referred to as 'fading hegemonic support' for multilateralism.[31] An additional nuance on this fading hegemonic support argument considers questions of legitimacy of national policies. The nationalist populist lens presents legitimacy as conferred on the representatives of states from within the state – from popular assent. Mostly, this is associated with populism on the Right, but not exclusively. Whilst the fading hegemonic support argument is important for understanding imperial rivalries, it misses the simultaneous turn away from multilateralism of non-hegemonic actors. Take, for example, the withdrawal of Additional Declarations permitting individuals and NGOs to submit cases to the African Court of Human and Peoples Rights. Declarations were recently withdrawn by Tanzania, Benin, and Cote d'Ivoire.[32] Or, going back to 2016, the withdrawal declarations from the ICC's Rome Statute made

[31] Eyal Benvinisti, 'International Law in the Age of Bilateralism' (2018) working paper available at: www.law.nyu.edu/sites/default/files/International%20Law%20in%20the%20Age%20of%20Bilateralism.pdf.

[32] Nicole de Silva and Misha Plagis, 'A Court in Crisis: African States' Increasing Resistance to Africa's Human Rights Court' *Opinio Juris* (19 May 2020), http://opiniojuris.org/2020/05/19/a-court-in-crisis-african-states-increasing-resistance-to-africas-human-rights-court/.

by Burundi, The Gambia, and South Africa. In addition to overlooking withdrawals from non-hegemonic states of multilateral treaties, the narrative often simplifies state action to a realist perspective. This underestimates the ways in which state decision-making is tied to capital. This perspective therefore also tends to downplay the *multilateralism* employed. For example, to set up the Asian Infrastructure Investment Bank, China used the tried and tested tools of multilateral treaty negotiations.[33] In contrast to its bilateral financing deals, China has established a new multilateral financial institution with the AIIB.

The view that is most persuasive in making sense of the loss of appetite for (certain types of) multilateralism is a structural view. This view takes into account a general preference for competition over collaboration that can at times be facilitated through multilateralism. The diagnosis of the structural view is rooted in changed material conditions. In the immediate aftermath of the Cold War, the circulation of capital was enabled through the many contracts and treaties that 'opened up' economies, in particular former socialist states like those of Eastern Europe. These states were reimagined as new markets, besides offering a new consumer base, they also offered resources and labour to be extracted. 'Capital strives to produce a geographical landscape favourable to its own reproduction and subsequent evolution', states David Harvey.[34] These new economies also became each other's competitors, competing in particular on the basis of cheap labour and other conditions conducive to capital growth (but often damaging to the health and environment of these new markets). This geographical space was, after several years of assimilation, exhausted. Arguably, *this* is the tipping point for multilateralism: As soon as sufficient spaces and places were produced to ground capitalist activity, there was no longer a real need for multilateralism, at least in the form of cooperation. Capital now needed to search for new means and methods of accumulation.

It is therefore important to study which *types* of multilateralism continue to find support and which types have become redundant. As a general rule, the type of multilateralism that stabilises capital flow remains important. Whilst the WTO dispute settlement system may no longer fully operational, the WTO's rationale of development through (free) trade and its emphasis on protecting private actors remains. Critically, this regards the movement of capital, *not* labour. As global value chains have stabilised, the need to 'import' and assimilate new labourers becomes less urgent. To illustrate this, we might think of how the UK has recently approached multilateralism. The British exit

[33] www.aiib.org/en/index.html.

[34] David Harvey, Seventeen Contradictions and the End of Capitalism (London 2014) 146.

from the regional multilateral system of the European Union (Brexit) has primarily been rhetorically played out in relation to restrictions on immigration. For its supporters, Brexit means to restrict or disempower institutions that protect the free movement of people across borders. As British manufacturing was dismantled in favour of establishing the UK as a financial services nation, a labour excess became apparent. Labourers from the EU (who could move between EU countries due to the freedom of movement arrangements), were consequently regarded as a threat to the fragile low-wage economy. The working class areas of the UK, in particular the former mining and manufacturing locations, became seduced by the idea of 'taking back control'. Whilst rhetorically the free movement multilateralism of the EU was dismissed, the free trade multilateralism of the World Trade Organisation was meanwhile glorified.[35] The rejection of (low-skilled) migration occurred at the same time as mass migration caused by the so-called refugee crisis appeared to place pressure on Western states. The protection of jobs has consequently taken on a distinctly ethno-nationalist tone.

The British example goes some way to explaining worries about the emergence of fascism in place of multilateralism. So long as capital is permitted to flow but not people, the 'Other' is framed as a threat to the prosperity of the nationalist state. But, it is not a lack of multilateralism that is to blame (but if it were!); the root of the problem is the financialisation of the British economy – the decision by the Thatcher government to be at the heart of global banking – which has led to the erosion of its labour market. 'Strongman' politics and the new Cold War remain challenges, but they are correctly classified as symptoms, not causes, of the tipping point for multilateralism.

13.5 THE 'SOUL' OF INTERNATIONAL LAW

Although slightly dismissed earlier, we might now (re)consider the notion of international law's 'soul'. Thomas Mann's Dr. Faustus is widely believed to encompass a warning about the danger of ethno-nationalism sliding into fascism. The 'original' Faust tale was celebrated by the German national socialists as a distinctly 'German' tale. They saw in it a superior combination of enlightenment thinking and mysticism. Doctor Faustus in Mann's version (notably written in the mid-1940s), strives in his musical compositions for the 'pure', focusing on how to overcome impurities through exclusion. Seeking the 'pure' as a higher order in art was no doubt a reference by Mann to

[35] David Collins, 'Why a No-Deal Brexit is Nothing to Fear', *The Spectator* (4 August 2018), www.spectator.co.uk/article/why-a-no-deal-brexit-is-nothing-to-fear.

delusions of pure art in Nazi Germany. In the Third Reich, art that was modern, socially critical, that came from a Marxist tradition and/or was produced by Jews, was referred to as *entartete Kunst* – translated into English as 'degenerate art'. The warning emanating from Mann's Dr. Faustus is that the search for the 'pure', not only homogenises, but also excludes peoples, cultures, and dissent, leading ultimately to fascism.

As competition for capital growth increases, states have reimagined themselves as competing in a global market, where market interests override social interests. Powerful states look for opportunities of greater growth, while weaker states are often self-disciplining in order not to violate international investment and trade norms. Economic power collapses into political power.[36] Political pressures of migration are a contemporary element of this dynamic: Whilst people from the Global South are forced to leave their homes due to the fallout caused by war, climate catastrophe, and planned underdevelopment, treaties and agreements protecting capital over people have prevailed.

The COVID-19 pandemic too has highlighted inequalities arising from competitive over collaborative approaches. States that had most enthusiastically embraced the neoliberal order – like the UK and the US in the Global North and Brazil in the Global South – have experienced deepening of inequalities in terms of health and income. People who were already marginalised, particularly those who were racialised, have suffered most in terms of negative impacts of the pandemic. Not only have black and brown people had a far higher death toll in prosperous Western states, these people and communities have also disproportionately lost their jobs. Such are the consequences of a systemic marginalisation of people of colour, through (international) laws that encourage and legitimise national policies of austerity and privatisation.

The tale of Faust who sells his soul resonates with international law's commitments to protecting the market over social justice. Does, then, international law 'die', like in some Faust tales? So far, the signs are that backlashes against multilateralism have prompted international law simply to shift its focus. International law is moving its normative influence more exclusively to finance and trade – and therefore a whole host of bilateral and regional arrangements. This is not so much the demise of international law as it is its restructuring. Perhaps, in reference to Faust, it is the place where international law must now repent for enabling inequality during its years of voluptuousness. Perhaps, like Faust in Marlowe's version is damned to serve Lucifer for eternity, international law is forever damned to serve capital(ism) in its self-constructed hell.

36 Peronne and Schneiderman (note 18).

13.6 CONCLUSION

Late-twentieth century multilateralism appears to have reached its tipping point. As I have suggested with the Faust analogy, multilateralism was mainly operationalised in the service of capital after the end of the Cold War. As capital no longer requires multilateralism to 'expand its kingdom', this type of multilateralism has become mostly, although not entirely, obsolete. International law, though, has not come to its demise. Its eulogies can be saved for another day. It is important to remember, though, that international law is not static. Social justice is a site of struggle. If we have learned anything from 2020, it is that what comes next is difficult to predict. Nevertheless, if there is a space for international law to step in for social justice, then it must lose the chains of capitalism.

It should be stressed that contemporary associations with tipping points often, correctly, refer to climate emergency.[37] The UN's Intergovernmental Panel on Climate Change warned in a special report in 2018 that there were only twelve more years left until the tipping point of irreversible climate change with catastrophic environmental breakdown.[38] In light of the urgency of climate catastrophe work concerning the wiping out of entire species, climate refugees, and more extreme weather, it may seem almost frivolous to turn attention to anything but considerations of the environment. However, although I have not written directly about it here, international law's relationship with neoliberalism is critically connected with climate catastrophe: It is through the tireless expansionism of capital that climate change is being propelled towards a tipping point. Indeed, the coinciding of climate and multilateralism tipping points are of particular interest: Climate catastrophe by its very nature is a global problem that requires global, cross-border solutions. An understanding of neoliberalism and climate catastrophe as being *caused* by the current multilateral international legal architecture, rather than something to be addressed through multilateralism, requires a deeper rethinking of multilateralism as a tool for progressive change. Once multilateralism is more widely accepted as also a form of 'terror', its relationship with competition (and capitalism) can more robustly be examined. The question remains therefore whether international law is able to extricate itself from the clutches of capitalism. Building its success on capitalism has been the cause of its current predicament and pushback, and yet, it so far remains unrepentant. We are reminded again of Marlowe's Faust: International law's waxen wings may be melting, but it continues to seek the sun.

37 www.ipcc.ch/site/assets/uploads/sites/2/2019/06/SR15_Chapter3_Low_Res.pdf.

38 www.ipcc.ch/sr15/.

14

Race

Adrien K. Wing

During spring and summer of 2020, there was an increased emphasis in the United States on racial issues due to the tragic death of African American George Floyd by members of the Minneapolis, Minnesota police force.[1] Protests that began in the United States in more than 140 cities expanded to many other countries in the world, with denunciations of racism in those nations being trumpeted as well.[2] In addition to the refrain "Black Lives Matter" and "I can't breathe" coming from the global streets, numerous businesses, universities, sports teams, governments, and nongovernmental organizations issued statements pledging antiracist behavior, new programs, and sometimes additional resources.[3] In June 2020, the United Nations Human Rights Council (UNHRC) condemned systemic racism against people of African descent. Members of families affected by police violence testified and more than 600 groups were involved.[4]

Do these recent events mean that the discussion of race and racism has reached a tipping point in international law? Are the majority of societies banding together to demand that something must be done against racism, xenophobia, or anti-

[1] Holly Bailey, *New Police Video Reveals George Floyd's Desperate Pleas before his Death*, WASH. POST., July 15, 2020, www.washingtonpost.com/national/new-video-reveals-george-floyds-desperate-pleas-before-his-death/2020/07/15/c81e9d3c-c6b4-11ea-b037-f9711f89ee46_story.html.

[2] Javier Hernandez & Benjamin Mueller, *Global Anger Grows over George Floyd Death, and Becomes an Anti-Trump Cudgel*, NY TIMES, June 1, 2020, www.nytimes.com/2020/06/01/world/asia/george-floyd-protest-global.html.

[3] Chauncey Alcorn, *Analysis: Five Things Corporate America can do besides tweeting to combat Racism*, CNN, June 3, 2020, www.cnn.com/2020/06/03/business/corporate-america-racism/index.html.

[4] Jamey Keaten, *UN to Commission Report on Systemic Racism, Discrimination after George Floyd's Killing*, WUSA9, June 19, 2020, www.wusa9.com/article/news/nation-world/un-body-to-report-on-racism-after-floyd-killing/507-33a9e867-d720-4d45-97d1-4ca9f7523cf1.

immigrant sentiment much as some are now doing for climate change or sexual harassment/assault? I fear the answer is "no" despite the unprecedented recent attention. As a matter of fact, the reverse may be true. Forces of reaction are in ascendance in many countries, some calling themselves "populists" or "(white) nationalists." While some people are stating "Black Lives Matter," others are defending Confederate flags and statues while spewing vicious racist language, running over protestors, and perhaps engaging in modern-day lynching.[5]

Global attention has focused on the racist treatment of African Americans in the past. In 1947, the NAACP submitted a 96-page petition to the newly established United Nations demanding accountability for human rights violations against African Americans in the United States. That petition, edited by W. E. B. DuBois, covered topics ranging from slavery and Jim Crow to voting rights, criminal justice, education, employment, and access to health care.[6] In 1951, the Civil Rights Congress presented a petition to the United Nations, charging that the US violated Article II of the UN Genocide Convention by failing to prevent the lynching of African Americans.[7]

Global attention occurred during the Civil Rights movement,[8] Black Power movement, the beating of Rodney King, and the tragic deaths of Trayvon Martin and Michael Brown, among others. Even having a Black President in the United States, Barack Obama, did not result in a post-racial era. The white backlash against him instead might have contributed to the 2016 Trump victory.[9]

This chapter first briefly discusses the notion of a tipping point, as delineated in this volume. Then, it offers a critique of how international law currently approaches the problem of race and racism. Next, the chapter explores the commitments we should consider in our search for solutions. The piece concludes with a call to theoretically demarginalize critical jurisprudence and embrace it within the dominant mainstream. There is a need for a critical praxis that designs specific solutions to contemporary and future problems. There is much work to be done.

5 Democracy Now, *Fear Grows of Modern Day Lynchings as Five People of Color are Found Hanged*, June 18, 2020, www.democracynow.org/2020/6/18/headlines/fear_grows_of_modern_day_lynchings_as_six_people_of_color_are_found_hanged.

6 Jamil Dakwar, *WEB DuBois's Historic UN Petition Continues to Inspire Human Rights Advocacy*, ACLU, October 25, 2017, www.aclu.org/blog/human-rights/human-rights-and-racial-justice/web-du-boiss-historic-un-petition-continues.

7 *Id.*

8 Mary Dudziak, Cold War Civil Rights: Race and the Image of American Democracy (2000).

9 Vann Newkirk II, *Five Decades of White Backlash*, The Atlantic, Jan. 15, 2018, www.theatlantic.com/politics/archive/2018/01/trump-massive-resistance-history-mlk/550544.

14.1 TIPPING POINT

The term "tipping point" was used in the 1950s by University of Chicago political science professor Morton Grodzins, when he adopted it from the field of physics. In that latter discipline, it referred to adding weight to a balanced object until it toppled or tipped over. Grodzins studied residential segregation in US urban settings. He noted the fact that when a few black families lived in an area, the racial demographics stayed the same. At some point, if the white community perceived that one too many black families had moved into an area, it would trigger white flight en masse. That moment was then defined as the tipping point for that community.[10] The use of the term can now be found in a wide variety of fields.

In 2000, Malcolm Gladwell brought the term to popular culture when he wrote *The Tipping Point: How Little Things Can Make a Big Difference*. He defined it as "the moment of critical mass, the threshold, the boiling point."[11] Very recently, the term has been described with respect to sexual harassment/assault allegations, and the #metoo movement. Societal views have evolved and it is now much less inclined to tolerate such behavior by powerful men like former Hollywood mogul Harvey Weinstein and others.[12]

Pollster Daniel Yankelovich addressed the use of tipping points in foreign affairs with respect to the Iraq war, as "the moment at which a large portion of the public begins to demand that the government address its concerns."[13] Events in the 2011 Arab spring were categorized as reaching a tipping point in some of the countries of that region.[14] China's recent trade war with the United States has been characterized as a potential tipping point for the Chinese economy.[15] Swedish environmental rights activist teenager Greta Thunberg has indicated

10 Morton Grodzins , Metropolitan Segregation (1957); Morton Grodzins, The Metropolitan Area as a Racial Problem (1958).

11 Malcolm Gladwell , The Tipping Point: How Little Things can Make a Big Difference 12 (2000).

12 *See* Megan Twohey, *Harvey Weinstein Is Fired after Sexual Harassment Reports*, NY Times, October 8, 2017, www.nytimes.com/2017/10/08/business/harvey-weinstein-fired.html.

13 Daniel Yankelovich, *The Tipping Points*, Foreign Affairs (May/June 2006), www.foreignaffairs.com/articles/2006–05-01/tipping-points.

14 Leila Hudson & Matt Flannes, *The Arab Spring: Anatomy of a Tipping Point*, The Nation, September 3, 2011, https://nation.com.pk/03-Sep-2011/the-arab-spring-anatomy-of-a-tipping-point.

15 Bryan Borzykowski, *Trade War with US could be the Tipping Point for China's $14 Trillion Debt-ridden Economy*, CNBC.COM, April 24, 2018, www.cnbc.com/2018/04/24/trade-war-with-us-may-be-tipping-point-for-chinas-debt-ridden-economy.html.

that she hoped the global Friday climate protests would be a "social tipping point" in the fight for environmental rights progress.[16]

The time is ripe for this volume.[17] As the above discussion illustrates, there are many ways to characterize the term. In the context of this book, tipping point means a collective feeling of dread or anxiety in reference to the ongoing global issues involving race and racism.

While the title of this chapter focuses on race, I will expand my coverage to feature ethnicity as well as race, as these categories often intertwine or overlap.[18] Race was historically linked to biology, but this concept has been discarded as racist, and it is acknowledged that there are now potentially more biological differences within so-called races than between them. Yet, some fear that the biological notions about race never died or are resurgent in the twenty-first century.[19]

Ethnicity is linked to cultural characteristics such as clothing, food, music, holidays, religion, language, clothes, etc.[20] These can be the hyphenated umbrella identities such as Asian-American, Arab-American, African-American, etc. Hyphenated umbrella groups can also be broken down into more specific ethnicities such as Chinese-American or Vietnamese-American. A Chinese-American may be very different culturally from a Chinese national. Even the Chinese-American group may be broken down into those from China, Taiwan, or Hong Kong, with many distinctions between them. For some ethnic groups, they may all be considered to be in one race, whereas others can be in multiple races. For instance, Nigerian Americans might all be considered "black." Puerto Ricans can be black, white, or something in between.

Race and ethnicity today can also be viewed as "social constructions."[21] Thus in the US, I am viewed as an African American, although I have also been mistaken for Latina, Arab, Indian, mulatto, mixed, or something else,

16 Greta Thunberg Hopes Climate Strikes will be "Social Tipping Point," FRANCE24.COM, September 20, 2019, www.france24.com/en/20190920-greta-thunberg-hopes-climatestrikes-wil l-be-social-tipping-point-1.

17 This book is the result of a May 2019 symposium held at the American Society of International Law Tillar House.

18 *See* The Sage Handbook of Race and Ethnic Studies (Patricia Hill Collins & John Solomos eds., 2010).

19 *See* Angela Saini , Superior: The Return of Race Science (2019).

20 *See* Mohammad Shahabuddin, Ethnicity and International Law: Histories, Politics and Practices 13–14 (2016).

21 For an analysis of the social construction of race in the American context, see Ian Haney Lopez , White by Law (1997).

due to my relatively light skin and curly hair. Some of my relatives are white skinned with blue eyes and light hair, and have passed as white. When I taught in Cape Town for six summers, my characteristics caused me to be regarded as "Coloured" according to the former discredited South African legal hierarchy. Coloureds were above blacks, but below whites in the pecking order, and even though the legal categories no longer exist, stratifications still occur based on these categories.[22] In South Africa, my partner and I were considered an interracial couple because his skin was dark brown. In the US, we are considered a same-race couple. In Brazil, my features have caused me to be considered white, with only dark brown people being considered Black.[23] In each instance, whoever is classified as white gets the most societal privileging – legally in the past, but now still de facto economically and educationally.

14.2 CRITIQUE: MASTER'S TOOLS

As the late Critical Race Theory founder professor Derrick Bell said, quoting a verse from Jeremiah in the Bible, "The harvest is past, the summer is ended, and we are not saved."[24] Bell cited this verse in his 1987 book *And We are Not Saved: the elusive quest for racial justice*, after a career as a civil rights lawyer and then a Harvard law professor. It is equally true today more than thirty years later. Bell was often viewed as very pessimistic as he considered that racism might be permanent and racial progress might be cyclical in nature. In his 1992 book FACES AT THE BOTTOM OF THE WELL: THE PERMANENCE OF RACISM, he stated, "even those herculean efforts we hail as successful will produce no more than temporary 'peaks of progress,' short-lived victories that slide into irrelevance as racial patterns adapt in ways that maintain white dominance."[25]

Why does the quest for racial justice remain so elusive, whether on the national level that Bell mainly dealt with, or on the global level with which this volume is concerned? Why has a tipping point not been reached where the

[22] *Race in South Africa: Still an Issue*, ECONOMIST, Feb. 4, 2012, www.economist.com/middle-east-and-africa/2012/02/04/still-an-issue.

[23] For more about my own racial characterisation, see INTRODUCTION TO GLOBAL CRITICAL RACE FEMINISM 8 (Adrien K. Wing ed., 2000) [hereinafter GCRF].

[24] DERRICK BELL , AND WE ARE NOT SAVED: THE ELUSIVE QUEST FOR RACIAL JUSTICE (1987), quoting Jeremiah 8:20.

[25] *See* DERRICK BELL, FACES AT THE BOTTOM OF THE WELL: THE PERMANENCE OF RACISM 12 (1992).

nations of the world would shun the centuries of racism and come to embrace an anti-racist perspective suitable for the twenty-first century?

One part of the problem is that most areas of law, whether domestic or international, have developed in a "race neutral" manner. Course materials and the majority of scholarship may not mention race, ethnicity, or racism at all. In actuality, "race neutral" may mean that white capitalist Christian heteropatriarchy is the given "neutral." Much as with sex or gender, if a reader wants a mention of race and racism, you may find it only in articles specifically about that topic, rather than incorporated into all subject matter.

Is a part of the problem illustrated in the words of the late African American lesbian feminist Audre Lorde, who once stated:

> For the master's tools will never dismantle the master's house. They may allow us temporarily to beat him at his own game, but they will never enable us to bring about genuine change.[26]

Let us examine the words more closely. Who is the master? What is the master's house? What are the tools of the master? Can the tools destroy the house? Should we destroy the house?

For our example, let us posit that the master is not a particular person, but white, capitalist, Christian heteropatriarchy that dominates the globe, emanating in particular from the global North, but followed by many others not in the north. The field of international law generally has been dominated by the views of elite, white male Christian westerners. The views of the majority of the population, including women and people of color around the world, are often marginalized or invisible to the master. Thus, one reason that racial justice globally is elusive is that the masters do not hear the voices of those affected by racism and other-isms, and think that the status quo, which privileges them, is normal and objective.

So then, what is the master's house? It could be classified as the entire global North. Alternatively, it could be seen as the more privileged parts of the global North, how the top 1 percent or 10 percent live above the situation of the majority of the population of the global North. Is the master's house therefore a shining city on a hill as referred to by numerous politicians or in the Bible? "You are the light of the world. A city set on a hill cannot be hidden."[27] Do the masters recognize that the developed countries became shining lights only

[26] Audre Lorde, *The Master's Tools Will Never Dismantle the Master's House*, *in* SISTER OUTSIDER: ESSAYS AND SPEECHES 110 (1984).

[27] Bible, Mathew 5:14. *See, e.g.*, Barack Obama, Remarks at the University of Nebraska Omaha in Omaha, Nebraska, January 13, 2016, The American Presidency Project, www.presidency.ucsb.edu/documents/remarks-the-university-nebraska-omaha-omaha-nebraska.

based upon centuries of colonialism and exploitation of people and land from the global South, but also including a number of people living within the global North? The master's house continues to be cleaned by the same people who have been exploited and ignored. Some of them may literally live within the house, but are restricted to the basement or to undesirable parts of the property. They may be restricted by glass or cement ceilings. Those exploited may include the women of the master, often doing multiple jobs, one unpaid who keeps the master's house and family functioning. They may include women of color who assist the woman of the master, while their own families are neglected. Some people must travel long ways and even immigrate to the master's house to try to find relatively well-paid work to support their families back home in the global South or poor parts of the global North. Racial justice remains elusive because the racist/sexist foundations of the master's house are not recognized as unjust, but as normal or essential to the functioning of the house.

Next, what are the master's tools? The master's tools can be almost anything: shovel, ladder, paint, pen, propaganda, education, theory, state/private violence, white privileging, the prison industrial complex, affirmative action, racism, sexism, or homophobia, for example.[28] Some of the oppressed minority have attended the same elite schools as the master and have learned how to use his tools well. Some may have even married his women. Some would not rock a system they have been indoctrinated to respect and defend, hoping that they or their children will join the masters one day. Tools can certainly help renovate or protect the house. Racism, sexism, and other isms can help ensure that the master's house does not get too crowded, that only certain kinds of people will get the full privileges of the house, with others believing that the exclusionary status quo is how things must be. Can there be racial justice if racism and white privileging are part of the tools of the house?

Assuming the master's house is highly problematic and deeply embedded in racist soil, can the master's tools destroy the house? One reading of Lorde is that the tools cannot destroy the house. One implication might be that if you try to use his tools to destroy his house, you will be coopted in the process. Thus, ending racism with his tools is not possible. For example, affirmative action may be one of the master's tools, and yet forty years of such programs have not resulted in true integration of most workplaces, wherever they are in the world. The big change over time is that the Diversity Equity and Inclusion

28 *See* Peggy McIntosh, *White Privilege: Unpacking the Invisible Knapsack*, www.racialequitytools.org/resourcefiles/mcintosh.pdf; White Privilege conference, www.whiteprivilegeconference.com.

program in a particular institution may be headed by a person of color, yet that office lacks power to create real institutional change.

Another reading could be that you could design and use your own tools that you wield to fight against the master. The next line of the famous Lorde quote is rarely mentioned. "And this fact is only threatening to those women who still define the master's house as their only source of support."[29] Thus, you are only threatened if your worldview is so narrow as to only see the master's house and the master's tools as your salvation. You can build your own house. You could sabotage or at least undercut the master's house with your tools or his tools. There is the old saying that "the pen is mightier than the sword."[30] While the master may have his pen, you may have yours that you use for your own purposes. If you free your mind from its miseducation about the status quo, then perhaps what you think is impossible, is possible. Racism/sexism could end or at least be controlled, much as AIDS or alcoholism can be controlled.

A final question could be, should we destroy the house even if we could? A lot of time and effort went into building the house, and these efforts were unpaid or underpaid with respect to the majority of the global population, who may have contributed willingly or unwillingly to construction of the house. Blowing up the master's house with his tools might create a lot of destruction physically and psychologically, that might undercut gains that need to be made for the majority.

One of the most vivid examples of societal destruction would be the Khmer Rouge's efforts to take Cambodian society back to year zero, killing 25 percent of the population, almost everyone with education.[31] Instead of such a horrific result, maybe you can use your tools to renovate or salvage the house on other principles or build more rooms in the house in an ecologically sustainable way. The house will still need walls, windows, bathrooms, and floors, so perhaps some parts can be repurposed in a progressive way.

14.3 COMMITMENTS: REVISED TOOLS

The remainder of the chapter discusses tools, that is, commitments that might help achieve a tipping point in finding global racial justice. These tools have been adopted by those of us educated in the master's schools and who teach in his institutions. Assuming the master's house will not be totally blown up, these tools may be useful for renovation. We can use the lens of race and

29 Lorde, *supra* note 26.

30 Adage by Edward Bulwer-Lytton (1839) discussed in Alison Gee, *Who Said the Pen is Mightier than the Sword*, BBC.COM, Jan. 9, 2015, www.bbc.com/news/magazine-30729480.

31 *See* Cambodia Tribunal Monitor, www.cambodiatribunal.org/history/cambodian-history/khmer-rouge-history/.

ethnicity to illustrate how international norms need to be examined from a more complex perspective, taking into account a wider array of views. In other words, theory may be part of the master's tools, but we can design theory that goes beyond the master's understanding or is used in ways the master would not have thought about or intended. It might be that we must use tools the master could be made to understand so that we can try to get him to be more amenable to sharing within the house in a more egalitarian manner. It might be that we could renovate or build a house that he would recognize as a house, but its underpinnings would not be based on exploitation of people or the environment to thrive.

The section below discusses some tools from several jurisprudential trends: TWAIL (Third World Approaches to International Law); feminist jurisprudence; Critical Race Theory (CRT); and Critical Race Feminism (CRF).

14.3.1 TWAIL

In 1995, TWAIL held its first conference at Harvard Law School. It was an exciting time as the topics included post-colonialism, Critical Race Theory, and law and development, subjects not part of the standard international law conference. The attendees included predominantly male professors and graduate students who were teaching or studying or had graduated from elite schools in the global North, specializing in international law. A significant number of those attending were people of color.

Post World War II decolonization efforts in the Third World inspired the participants. Some of the first generation scholars they admired were men from the developing world, including: R. P. Anand, Upendra Baxi, Mohammed Bedjaoui, Keba M'baye, and Christopher Weeramantry.[32] For example, former Algerian diplomat and International Court of Justice Judge Bedjaoui analyzed traditional international law that had Europe as its center, Christianity as its religion, capitalism as its economy, and imperialism as a necessity.[33]

In the twenty-five years since the 1995 conference was held, there have been numerous scholars, still mainly male, who have developed the tools of TWAIL. They include: Antony Anghie, Balakrishnan Rajagopal, Bhupinder Chimni, Celestine Nyamu, Usha Natarajan, James Thuo Gathii, Joel Ngugi,

[32] LEGAL VISIONS OF THE 21ST CENTURY: ESSAYS IN HONOUR OF JUDGE CHRISTOPHER WEERAMANTRY (Anthony Anghie & Gary Sturgess eds., 1997).

[33] *See* Mohamed Bedjaoui, Poverty of the International Order, *in* INTERNATIONAL LAW: A CONTEMPORARY PERSPECTIVE 153 (Richard Falk, et al. eds., 1985).

Makau Mutua, Mohsen Al Attar, Obiora Chinedu Okafor, Sylvia Tamale, and Vasuki Nesiah.[34] While there is no agreed upon canon, the authors critique white elite male dominant notions of international law that marginalize all other groups, "teasing out encounters of difference along many axes – race, class, gender, sex, ethnicity, economics, trade, etc. – and in inter-disciplinary ways – social, theoretical, epistemological, ontological and so on."[35] They are concerned with the past, present, and future. For example, Okafor has stated:

> Current and future international law is unlikely to help African people. It has played a significant role in maintaining conditions of poverty. The future is not likely to promote the exercise of more African agency. It is also not likely to permit space to allow Africans to resist their global circumstance and will remain insensitive. Change will continue to be administered *on* Africa and not really *by* Africans.[36]

The participants have included those that may ally themselves with Critical Legal Studies, Critical Race theory, postcolonial theory,[37] literary theory, modernism, and Marxism as well as feminism. Some authors have been more radical in their approach to international law and some more reformist. In other words, some may be more oriented toward using the master's tools in his house to renovate it, rather than in a manner to blow it up. Everyone from either approach would acknowledge that the development of international law was racist.[38] Everyone would be supportive of including the voices of those in the developing world.[39]

One of TWAIL's central goals has been to push for international law's transformation into a tool of emancipation to achieve global justice.[40] Can the master's

34 *See, e.g.*, ANTHONY ANGIE , IMPERIALISM, SOVEREIGNTY AND THE MAKING OF INTERNATIONAL LAW (2005); Makau Mutua, *What is Twail?*, 94 AMERICAN SOC. INT'L LAW PROC. 31, 33 (2000); THE THIRD WORLD AND INTERNATIONAL LEGAL ORDER: LAW, POLITICS AND GLOBALIZATION (Anthony Anghie, B. S. Chimni, Karin Mickelson & Obiora Okafor eds., 2003).

35 James Thuo Gathii, *TWAIL: A Brief History of Its Origins, Its Decentralized Network, and a Tentative Bibliography*, 3 TRADE L. & DEV. 26, 37 (2011).

36 Obiora Chinedu Okafor , *Poverty, Agency and Resistance in the Future of International Law: An African Perspective, in* INTERNATIONAL LAW AND THE THIRD WORLD: RESHAPING JUSTICE 95 (Richard Falk, et al. eds., 2008).

37 *See, e.g.*, LEELA GANDHI, POSTCOLONIAL THEORY: A CRITICAL INTRODUCTION (2nd ed. 2019).

38 Martti Koskenniemi, *Race, Hierarchy and International Law: Lorimer's Legal Science*, 27 EUROPEAN JOURNAL OF INTERNATIONAL LAW 415 (2016).

39 Additionally, there are critiques of TWAIL. *See, e.g.*, John D. Haskell, *TRAIL-ing TWAIL: Arguments and Blind Spots in Third World Approaches to International Law*, 27 CAN. J. L. & JURISPRUDENCE 383 (2014).

40 *See* Antony Anghie & Bhupinder S. Chimni, *Third World Approaches to International Law and Individual Responsibility in Internal Conflicts*, 2 CHINESE J. INT'L L. 77 (2003).

tools include emancipation for justice? It is possible if one considers the American and French revolutions and the tools advocated in those upheavals. Those tools, unfortunately, were not designed to serve the majority of the population. Therefore, some potential tools have existed for a long time. The challenge now is how to apply them to everyone, rather than only for elite white males.

A number of women have written feminist analyses from a TWAIL perspective. Besides the women previously mentioned, these include: Penelope Andrews, Hope Lewis, Lama Abu-Odeh, Paulina Garcia Del Moral, Athena Mutua, Leslye Obiora, Diane Otto, Mosepe Fagbongbe, and this author, Adrien Wing. Some are critical of the "arrogance" of various Western feminist approaches to addressing women's human rights issues in the developing world.[41] They are also trying to fill in gaps in the analysis of their male TWAIL peers, who do not consider gender.

TWAIL has also inspired Fourth World Approaches to International Law (FWAIL). University of California at Santa Cruz professor Hiroshi Fukurai was the incoming president of the Asian Law and Society Association in 2018. He wrote an article mentioning FWAIL. It seeks to examine the nature of panethnic indigenous people's struggles for independence in Asia as well as sociopolitical and historical roots of regional conflicts.[42] Some TWAIL followers might expect that this sort of emphasis could be accommodated within TWAIL. It remains to be seen if over the next decade, FWAIL will evolve separately as a new offshoot from the various forms of critical jurisprudence.

14.3.2 *Feminist Jurisprudence*

I will discuss Critical Race Feminism later in this chapter. Additionally, I have written on international law and feminism myself.[43] Feminism has developed within various international law subfields. These areas include: Public International Law; Use of Force (*Jus ad Bellum*); Self-Determination, State Sovereignty and State Responsibility; Peacemaking, Peacekeeping and Peacebuilding; Law and Development; International Institutions; International Humanitarian Law (*Jus in Bello*); International Criminal Law; International

41 Adrien K. Wing, International Law and Feminism, *in* Research Handbook on Feminist Jurisprudence 466, 477 (Robin West & Cynthia Bowman eds., 2019) (hereinafter *International Law*).

42 Hiroshi Fukurai, *Fourth World Approaches to International Law (FWAIL) and Asia's Indigenous Struggles and Quests for Recognition under International Law*, 5 Asian J. of Law and Society 221 (2018).

43 *See International Law*, *supra* note 41.

Human Rights Law; International Refugee Law, Female Migration and Trafficking; International Labor Law; and International Economic/Trade Law.[44]

For the purposes of this chapter, my limited inquiry constitutes several questions. Are the mainly white women that developed these feminist interventions now masters or still just part of the master's house? Do they not benefit to a certain degree from white heteropatriarchy privilege, even if they are not male? Are they using the master's tools of theory in a slightly different way to do some relatively minor renovations in the house? Alternatively, are these efforts not the master's tools at all, but potentially radical ways to blow up at least some parts of the house?

It is quite clear that most white women benefit from white privileging even while being suppressed by sexist behavior. Some benefit even though they may be working-class single parents. Thus, for many of them based in the Global North, they might seek some reform in the master's house, but it is still their house as well. Very few may be likely to advocate a more radical view that would blow up the house, a house where much of the unpaid and underpaid labor has been due to their work.

A recent New York case got global attention where an elite white woman Amy Cooper, a liberal Democrat, called the police and lied about an African American male threatening her. Birdwatcher Christian Cooper had told her to leash her dog in Central Park as required by law. It is fortunate that the incident was taped and the parties left the area before the police came. Mr. Cooper could have lost his life or liberty if the police attacked him based on the lies of the white woman.[45] Ms. Cooper might be a feminist, who may have faced sexism in her career, but she wrapped herself in her white privileging on this occasion. She is not likely to want to blow up the house. On the other hand, feminist Catharine MacKinnon who has radical views on pornography, marriage, and other domestic and international issues, is more likely to be viewed as wanting to blow up parts of the house.

14.3.3 *Critical Race Theory*

Critical Legal Studies (CLS),[46] which began in the 1970s, influenced the development of CRT in the 1980s.[47] Predominantly white male Ivy League

[44] *Id.*

[45] Sarah Nir, *White Woman Is Fired after Calling Police on Black Man in Central Park*, NYTimes, June 1, 2020, www.nytimes.com/2020/06/01/world/asia/george-floyd-protest-global.html.

[46] *See* comprehensive bibliography, Duncan Kennedy & Karl E. Klare, A *Bibliography of Critical Legal Studies*, 94 Yale L. J. 461 (1984).

[47] For works on CRT, see, e.g., Critical Race Theory: An Introduction (Richard Delgado & Jean Stefancic eds., 2017); Critical Race Theory: The Key Writings that Formed the Movement xix (Kimberlé Crenshaw et al. eds., 1996).

professors created CLS and they had been influenced in part by European postmodernists and other US-based radical movements. These CLS sons of privilege developed intellectual tools that some could view as being capable of destroying the master's house, but they were doing so while ensconced in some of the cushiest rooms at Harvard and similar institutions. They deconstructed the master's canon that asserted that law was neutral and objective. Instead, law was indeterminate and reactionary. Some might have viewed the Critters as using the master's inaccessible tools of high theory, which were not comprehensible even to some professors, much less the general public. To some, the Critters may have been perceived as spoiled children playing intellectual war games. Most of them would not be hurt, as their own tenured status would be relatively unaffected. Some scholars viewed Harvard then as a Beirut war zone because of the conflicts between Critters and their intellectual opponents.[48]

CLS attracted some scholars of color, some of whom were teaching in the elite schools. These scholars were interested in class analysis, but felt it was insufficient as a tool to fully deconstruct the plight of people of color. Even elite people of color were not immune to racism, and any jurisprudence that ignored that reality, was insufficient. Thus, the scholars developed CRT as an expansion centering race/ethnicity into their analysis. CRT developed as a race intervention in leftist/postmodern theory since CLS lacked that perspective.

Simultaneously, the 1960s US civil rights movement influenced the development of CRT as well. CRT founders like Derrick Bell had even been civil rights lawyers before becoming professors. Civil rights frameworks had achieved certain legal successes with the passage of new laws and individual court victories, but had many limitations. The pace of change was very slow and racism was not vanquished. Thus, CRT evolved as a progressive intervention into race discourse, focused on anti-subordination and the deconstructing of white privilege. It is color conscious, not color blind, emphasizing the plight of the oppressed, especially people of color. It endorses real-world praxis as well as theory and may use narrative as methodology. UCLA Law School has even developed a Critical Race Studies program, which is dedicated to racial justice advocacy, and is the only program of its kind.[49] Several preeminent scholars

[48] *See* Jennifer Kingson, *Harvard Tenure Battle Puts 'Critical Legal Studies' on Trial*, NY TIMES, Aug. 30, 1987, www.nytimes.com/1987/08/30/weekinreview/harvard-tenure-battle-puts-critical-legal-studies-on-trial.html.

[49] *See* Critical Race Studies, UCLA LAW https://law.ucla.edu/academics/areas-of-focus/critical-race-studies/overview/. For lists of CRS symposia, see https://law.ucla.edu/centers/social-policy/critical-race-studies/events/annual-symposium/.

anchor this program including: Kimberlé Crenshaw, Devon Carbado, Cheryl Harris, and Tendayi Achiume.

CRT spawned many offshoots as various overlapping subordinated groups and those allied with them developed their own interrelated multidisciplinary theories. These offshoots include: Latino Critical Theory (LATCRIT);[50] AsianCrit; IndianCrit; Critical White Studies; QueerCrit; Queer Race Crit; Ecrit (empirical);[51] DisCrit (disability); DesiCrit (South Asians); and ClassCrit.[52]

Some CRT scholars such as Penelope Andrews, Ruth Gordon, Henry Richardson, and Makau Mutua, have tackled international and comparative law questions, with all the approaches deconstructing mythologies of objectivity and neutrality.[53] Their efforts could be seen as GlobalCrit. For instance, Andrews has assessed "the pertinence of critical race theory in unmasking international law's colonial, racist and patriarchal underpinnings," as well as suggested "practical ways in which a critical race theory approach can enrich the international legal system, by giving a voice to the voiceless and by addressing the conditions of marginality in which much of the developing world is trapped."[54] Some scholars like Mutua, have been affiliated with TWAIL as well.[55]

Can the CRT tools of theory and praxis do more than other tools previously mentioned to help achieve transformative racial justice? Are the authors, with their pedigrees mainly from the elite institutions of the master, able to do more than merely try to renovate small pieces of the house? After all, they have lived in relative comfort within the house, even if they do not own it. Have any of these authors become masters themselves or do they delude themselves if they think that can be the case? Another generation has grown up with these authors as parents and many of their children may also live in relatively wonderful rooms in the master's house. Do the tools of CRT actually distance

50 *See* LATCRIT, http://www.latcrit.org/index/.

51 *See, e.g., Critical Race Theory and Empirical methods conference*, 83 Fordham L. Rev. (2016).

52 For further discussion of some of these offshoots, see Adrien K. Wing, *Is There a Future for Critical Race Theory*, 66 J. Legal Ed. 44 (2016).

53 *See, e.g., Critical Race theory and International law symposium issue of* 45 Vill. L. Rev. (2000); Henry Richardson, *Excluding Race Strategies from International Legal History: The Self-Executing Treaty Doctrine and the Southern Africa Tripartite Agreement*, 45 Vill. L. Rev. 1091 (2000); Ruth Gordon, *Critical Race Theory and International Law: Convergence and Divergence: Racing American Foreign Policy*, 94 Am. Soc'y Int'l L. Proc. 260 (2000); Mathias Möschel, Law, Lawyers and Race: Critical Race Theory from the United States to Europe (2014).

54 Penelope E. Andrews, *Making Room for Critical Race Theory in International Law: Some Practical Pointers*, 45 Vill. L. Rev. 855, 857 (2000).

55 Mutua, *supra* note 34.

its adherents from the masses of oppressed people who will never read their law review articles or even the popular press books some may write? Few lawyers, judges, or law students have time separate from their day jobs to read such literature. Is effort spent on law review footnotes wasted when it might be spent in more direct actions?

14.3.4 *Critical Race Feminism*

The last potential tool discussed is CRF.[56] Women of color have remained marginal within law generally. Their issues and perspectives have been subsumed under the rubric of all people, all women, or all people of color. These women are disproportionately stalled at the bottom of every society – economically, socially, and politically. CRF emphasizes the legal status of women of color both domestically and internationally, intersecting with CLS, CRT, and feminist jurisprudence. CRF also resonates with womanist theory, which developed outside of the legal discipline by scholars and authors such as Toni Morrison, Patricia Collins, belle hooks, Angela Y. Davis, and Alice Walker.[57] CRF is a gender intervention with CRT and a race intervention in feminist theories. On the international level, CRF intersects with TWAIL and global feminist jurisprudence as well. Global CRF extends some concepts into the realms of international and comparative law.[58]

CRF also introduces its own distinct analytical contributions. Very notable is the concept of anti-essentialism.[59] CRF counters the traditional feminist ideology of the "essential female voice" and exposes that as really a white female voice that subsumes women of color. Perhaps the most major CRF contribution is the theory of intersectionality, which Kimberle Crenshaw is most known for espousing. CRF demarginalizes the anti-essentialist plight of women of color by analyzing the intersection of their race and gender identities.[60] A related term

56 *See* Critical Race Feminism: A Reader (Adrien Wing ed., 2nd ed. 2003) [hereinafter CRF].

57 *See* The Womanist Reader (Layli Phillips ed., 2006); Patricia Hill Collins, Black Feminist Thought: Knowledge, Consciousness, and the Politics of Empowerment(2nd ed. 1990); belle hooks, Feminist Theory: From Margin to Center (1984); Toni Morrison, Beloved (1987); Alice Walker , The Color Purple (1982); Angela Y. Davis, Women, Race & Class (1981).

58 *See* Wing, *supra* note 24.

59 *See* Angela P. Harris, *Race and Essentialism in Feminist Legal Theory*, 42 Stan. L. Rev. 581 (1990).

60 *See* Kimberlé Crenshaw, *Demarginalizing the Intersection of Race & Sex: A Black Feminist Critique of Antidiscrimination Doctrine, Feminist Theory and Antiracist Politics*, 1989 U. Chi. L. For. 139 (1989).

is "multiple consciousness," which Mari Matsuda used to describe the intersectional identities of women of color.[61] Matsuda also called for scholars to "look to the bottom," to the lives of women themselves.[62] In earlier scholarship, I have chosen to use the word "multiplicative" to configure identity that can also include class, age, disability, religion, sexual orientation, parental status, marital status, nationality, and disability, among others.[63] The denial of women's rights in the domestic and public spheres results in "spirit injuries," a critical race feminist term that contemplates the psychological, spiritual, and cultural effects of multiple assaults upon women. Spirit injuries can lead to spirit or literal murder.[64] Legal scholars authoring some CRF publications include: Kimberlé Crenshaw, Angela Harris, Lani Guiner, Mari Matsuda, Patricia Williams, Cheryl Harris, Dorothy Roberts, Berta Hernandez, Margaret Montoya, Celina Romany, and myself Adrien Wing.[65]

Intersectionality theory is being used by scholars in various countries. For example, Queen's University Belfast professor Dagmar Schiek critiqued the analysis of the European Court of Justice in the 2018 *Achbita* and *Bougnaoui* cases. The court sided with employers who dismissed Muslim women for wearing hijabs. The author asserted that European Union antidiscrimination law should recognize intersectional discrimination on the grounds of gender, ascribed race, and religion. The law should increase in complexity to provide these women with justice instead of simplistic analysis that leaves them unprotected.[66]

61 Mari Matsuda, *When the First Quail Calls: Multiple Consciousness as Jurisprudential Method*, 11 Women's Rts. L. Rep. 7 (1989).

62 Mari Matsuda, *Looking to the Bottom: Critical Legal Studies and Reparations*, 22 Harv. Civ. Rts. Civ. L. L. Rev. 323 (1987).

63 *See* Adrien K. Wing, *Brief Reflections towards a Multiplicative Theory and Praxis of Being*, 6 Berk. Women's L. J. 181 (1990–91).

64 *See Id.* for more on the concept of spirit injury. For more on spirit murder, see Patricia Williams, *Spirit-Murdering the Messenger: The Discourse of Fingerpointing as the Law's Response to Racism*, 42 U. Miami L. Rev. 127 (1987).

65 See articles in CRF, *supra* note 56.

66 Dagmar Schiek, *On Uses, Mis-uses and Non-uses of Intersectionality before the Court of Justice (EU)*, 18 (2–3) Int'l J. of Discrimination and the Law 82 (2018). For more articles on international intersectionality, *see, e.g.*, Shreya Atrey, *Women's Human Rights: From Progress to Transformation, An Intersectional Response to Martha Nussbaum*, 40 Hum. Rts. Q. 859 (November 2018); Ana Martin Beringola, *Intersectionality: A Tool for the Gender Analysis of Sexual Violence at the ICC*, 9 Amsterdam L. Forum 84 (2017); Gauthier de Beco, *Protecting the Invisible: An Intersectional Approach to International Human Rights Law*, 17 Hum. Rts. L. Rev. 633 (2017); Pok Yin S. Chow, *Has Intersectionality Reached its Limits? Intersectionality in the UN Human Rights Treaty Body Practice and the Issue of Ambivalence*, 16 Hum. Rts. L. Rev. 453 (2016); Shreya Atrey, *Lifting as We Climb: Recognizing Intersectional Gender Violence in Law*, 5 Onati Socio-leg. Series (Online) 1512 (2015); Aisha Nicole Davis, *Intersectionality and International Law: Recognizing Complex Identities on the Global Stage*, 28 Harv. Hum. Rts. J. 205 (2015).

Intersectionality theory has reached the United Nations. The Committee on the Elimination of All Forms of Racial Discrimination, which is the treaty body for the Convention on Elimination of All Forms of Racial Discrimination (CERD) passed General Recommendation No. 25 on the gender-related dimensions of racial discrimination.[67] African women influenced the adoption of this recommendation. The CERD Committee recognized that women of color may face specific harms on the basis of gender, such as sexual violence, forced sterilization, abuse in informal sectors or as domestic workers abroad, and inability to access complaint mechanisms due to the gender-biased nature of those systems. The Committee requested that states disaggregate their data so that the situation of women will not be subsumed, and thus the Committee and states will be able to target assistance for women specifically. Unfortunately, like all treaty bodies, the Committee has no police power to follow up on states violating CERD or any of the General Recommendations.[68]

So what are the commitments that are to be gleaned from the critiques of race discourse (or the lack of it) raised in TWAIL, Feminist Jurisprudence, CRT, and CRF. Are anti-essentialism, intersectionality, multiple consciousness, multiplicative identity, or spirit injury just part of the master's toolkit? I would say "no!" They are potential commitments developed by those of us educated in his institutions, but intended to help us analyze and benefit those living in the bowels of the master's house or outside the house. These jurisprudential trends indicate that we must have an intersectional approach to "shifting bottoms and rotating centers."[69] In other words, we should no longer unconsciously or consciously use the terms of objectivity or neutrality, when we are actually centering white Christian heteropatriarchal norms. Within one analytical framework, we must be prepared to put the needs of those at the bottom, those who are not masters, at the center, rather than at the periphery or omitted altogether.

Additionally, a commitment to critical praxis that designs specific solutions to contemporary and future problems will be needed. Theory alone cannot make the changes required in the master's house. Moreover, when the master

67 CERD Committee. General Recommendation No. 25: Gender Related Dimensions of Racial Discrimination, www.peacewomen.org/sites/default/files/ohchr_generalrec25_march2000_0.pdf.

68 For more discussion of CERD Recommendation 25, see Adrien Wing, The International Human Rights of Black Women: Justice or Just Us, in BLACK WOMEN AND INTERNATIONAL LAW: DELIBERATE, INTERACTIONS, MOVEMENTS AND ACTIONS (Essays in Honor of Gabrielle Kirk McDonald) 37 (Jeremy Levitt ed., 2015).

69 Athena Mutua, *Shifting Bottoms and Rotating Centers: Reflections on LatCrit III and the Black/White Paradigm*, 53 U. MIAMI L. REV. 1177 (1999).

feels that unwanted and unauthorized renovation is being attempted in his house, there may be a literal or figurative backlash or a squashing of those efforts. Thus, this kind of praxis could take centuries, and we may find as Professor Bell posited, that racism is permanent.

Right now, commitments like these are not incorporated into the master's theories learned in most standard law courses, legislation, or cases. Nevertheless, these tools may help those of us who are not masters develop future policies that can renovate or maybe even theoretically blow up parts of the house. For instance, some US cities and states are now passing laws that forbid people from being fired on the basis of their natural hairstyles, something that disproportionally affects black women.[70] A number of scholars had focused on the hair problems dating back to the 1980s and Drexel Professor Wendy Greene was involved with the recent efforts.[71] While these hair issues are being discussed in the United States, a commitment to free one's hair would be relevant around the world, and it might be relevant for men as well as women, for people of all races and ethnicities, and not only Blacks. For example, there are white men who wear dreadlocks. If legal protections could be extended out to Black women and then Black men to wear their hair in dreads, should it be extended to these white men as well? Perhaps, their situation is fundamentally different as dreads would not be their natural hair. In addition to domestic law, could CERD[72] be invoked as well as the International Covenant on Civil and Political Rights (ICCPR)[73] and the Women's Convention (CEDAW)?[74]

14.4 CONCLUSION

TWAIL, feminist jurisprudence, CRT, and CRF may each include tools that can renovate the master's house in the areas of race and ethnicity. If they remain marginal, only known to a small group of adherents however, there may not be much that will be done within the house. It certainly may not be

[70] *California becomes First State to Ban Discrimination against Natural Hair*, CBS News, July 4, 2019, www.cbsnews.com/news/crown-act-california-becomes-first-state-to-ban-discrimination-against-natural-hair.

[71] *See* Paulette Caldwell, *A Hair Piece, Perspectives on the Intersection of Race and Gender*, 1991 Duke L. J. 365 (1991); D. Wendy Greene, *Splitting Hairs: The Eleventh Circuit's Take on Workplace Bans against Black Women's Natural Hair in EEOC v. Catastrophe Management Solutions*, 71 U. Miami L. Rev. 987 (2017).

[72] Convention on Elimination of All Forms of Racial Discrimination, December 21, 1965, 660 U.N.T.S. 195.

[73] International Convention on Civil and Political Rights, March 23, 1976, 999 U.N.T.S. 171.

[74] Convention on the Elimination of Discrimination against Women, December 18, 1979, 1249 U.N.T.S. 13.

enough to constitute the tipping point necessary to make substantial progress in achieving global racial justice. Thus, there is a need to attempt to theoretically demarginalize these forms of critical jurisprudence and incorporate them within the dominant mainstream, that is, the heart of the master's house.

Assuming that blowing up the house will not happen, an alternative may be trying to build a new house. This house would be conceptualized by all members in the society, and everyone could afford to live there. The house would be in harmony with the environment, rather than exploiting it. It would be inviting, as everyone would have a key, rather than exclusionary. If most people, however, including the people of color, are still living in the master's house or aspire to live in it, they may not feel it is worth the tremendous effort to invest in such fundamental change as a new house. Perhaps, some would be open to a reformist approach with a new wing to the house.

My oldest grandson is about to finish college. When he is a grandparent, what kind of house will he live in? Will he accept the same status quo of the Boomer generation with houses built based on privileging and exploitation? Will his contribution be to constitute an additional Black face among those oppressing others? Will things be even worse with his family hoping to achieve as much as the Boomers did while global economic and environmental conditions plummet? Perhaps, he and others of his generation will be the Greta Thunbergs with respect to eliminating racism. Perhaps, they will make commitments to design houses that are transcendent and inclusive and that we would all be proud to live in.

15

Religion

Mark Weston Janis

Religion was an important stimulus for the emergence of modern international law. It may well be one of the discipline's most serious challenges. A religion is generally founded on a certainty that it is the one, and only one, true faith. It rejects other paths to God and eternal bliss. What can international law or international lawyers possibly say or do to moderate religious certainties and to quiet religious hostilities that threaten inter-state relations and the international order?

Although the stories of religious animosities go back thousands of years, as international lawyers, we need go back only so far as the paradigm-setting work of the Dutch jurist, Hugo de Groot. Grotius' book, *The Law of War and Peace,*[1] was penned in the midst of Europe's bloody Thirty Years War (1618–1648). This battle between the Roman Catholic Church and its secular allies, notably the Holy Roman Empire, and the rising Lutherans and Calvinists along with rebel Protestant princes, was curiously aided by the anti-Imperial but nonetheless Roman Catholic French monarchy. Perhaps more than half of Germany's population perished in the conflict, as Catholics and Protestants slaughtered each other.[2] Grotius, a brilliant and tolerant Protestant Arminian, a statesman, theologian, and lawyer, with a belief in the possibility of universal salvation for godly people, was imprisoned by a conservative Dutch regime, but escaped to France, where he was supported in Paris by the French Crown. His ambition was to find a way in law to reconcile the warring faiths.[3] The product of this ambition, *The Law of War and Peace,* was destined to be one of the foundational books of modern International Law.

1 H. Grotius, *De Jure Belli Ac Libri Tres* (Carnegie Classics of International Law, 1925, Kelsey trans. 1646 ed.).

2 E. A. Ryan, 'Catholics and the Peace of Westphalia', 9 *Theological Studies* 590, 591 (1948).

3 M. W. Janis, 'Sovereignty and International Law: Hobbes and Grotius', *Essays in Honour of Wang Tiega* 391 (Ronald St. John Macdonald ed. 1994).

Nothing excited Grotius more than the hope that conflicting absolutist religions – not only Christian, but Jewish, Muslim, and Eastern – might share common principles of law. Properly reconciled and promoted, such legal commonalities could prescribe rules that would be observed in inter-state relations. These commonalities Grotius saw as either natural and God-given or positive and set out in treaties or custom. Grotius' paradigm of a law of nations built on foundations of natural and positive law he proved almost exclusively by reference to religious and philosophical doctrines.[4] While his legal–philosophical legacy continues to be celebrated by generations of international lawyers, Grotius' law of nations was also conceived to reconcile religious hostilities: how well has it done with religion over time?

Grotius' scholarly masterpiece was almost immediately fruitful in practice. In 1648 at Münster and Osnabrück, the Catholic and Protestant princes negotiated a pair of agreements called the Treaties of Westphalia,[5] and ended what was by then the Thirty Years War. Interestingly, the Roman Church, or at least the Vatican, refused to accept the Treaties of Westphalia until the 1960s, more than three hundred years later. This was perhaps for good reason; the 1648 Peace of Westphalia formalised the legal and moral equivalence of the Protestant and Catholic faiths, seriously undermining the claim of Rome to be the one and only universal church. Instead, the Westphalian treaties assigned to each European sovereignty the international legal right to establish whatever each decided was the right religion for itself: Catholic, Lutheran, or Calvinist. Included in the treaties were some minimal protections for minority religions in each state, notably the right to worship, albeit perhaps only in private. The great triumph of the new Grotian system of international law meant that henceforth no state had the right to intervene in another state to impose a religion. So, some states – Italy, Austria, France, Spain, and Portugal – were safely Catholic. Other states – the Netherlands, Sweden, Denmark, and England – were Protestant. Still other states – Germany and Switzerland – had distinct political entities that were sometimes Catholic and sometimes Protestant.

This largely North–South religious divide still characterises Europe. The rest of the world has largely followed suit. Latin America is largely Catholic; the United States and Canada a mix of Catholic and Protestant; North Africa and the Middle East largely Muslim; South Asia Hindu and Muslim; East Asia Buddhist and Confucian. The Westphalian international legal arrangement,

4 Mark W. Janis , 'Religion and the Literature of International Law', *The Influence of Religion on the Development of International Law* 61 (Mark W. Janis ed. 1991).

5 Consolidated Treaty Series 198 (1648).

insofar as it prohibits inter-state imposition of religion, has been generally viewed by many within the international legal community as a success over four centuries.

However, this Grotian system of inter-state live-and-let-live religion was never designed to deal with three religious challenges, one ancient, the other two relatively modern. The traditional challenge is the protection of religious minorities, a challenge that has more or less defeated international law time and time again. The second and third challenges are recent, but equally troublesome: protecting religious proselytism and dealing with the large-scale migration of diverse religious populations. Taken together, these three challenges may pose a tipping point, upsetting the apple cart of the traditional international legal order. Let us look at the three in turn and then finally consider how international law and international lawyers might best meet these religious challenges.

The settlement of Westphalia was successful in two important respects. First, the Peace put an end to religious wars and the invasions by Catholic and Protestant princes that had vexed Europe for more than a century. No longer would sovereigns be legally allowed to attempt to impose their religious preferences on other states. Second, the Treaties enunciated the international legal norm that each sovereign was permitted to establish by its own choice its own religion. Both accomplishments have endured for more than three centuries, no mean feat. However, the first problem was and is that Westphalia left minority religions mostly out in the cold.[6] Whether they be Catholics in England and Ireland, Protestants in France, Austria, and Spain, or Jews throughout Europe, minority religions were to suffer centuries of abuse by national governments. Indeed, the Westphalian settlement itself contributed to the oppression faced by minority religions. The new international legal rule against religious intervention discouraged sovereigns from protecting co-religionists in foreign countries. In the case of the Jews, there was no Jewish sovereign anywhere in any case to plead their cause. The Holocaust bears grim witness to the failure of the state-centric religious posture of post-1648 international law.

The legal obstacle of non-intervention has been partially moderated by the emergence of international human rights law in the middle twentieth Century. International instruments like the 1948 UN Declaration on Human Rights and the 1950 European Convention on Human Rights and Fundamental Freedoms explicitly provide for religious freedom for all men

[6] M. W. Janis, 'The Shadow of Westphalia: Majoritarian Religions and Strasbourg Law', 4 *Oxford Journal of Law and Religion* 75 (2015).

and women, even those who are not adherents to a majoritarian faith. However, the weakness of the traditional system persists.[7]

Strikingly, the European Court of Human Rights, an institution dedicated to the protection of individual human rights, has turned the European Human Rights Convention on its head when dealing with minority rights. It took the Court decades to summon up the courage to hear a case, *Kokkinakis v. Greece*, brought under Article 9, the religious freedom article of the Convention.[8] In *Kokkinakis*, a Jehovah's witness was protected against Greece and the Greek Orthodox Church. Since then however, in far too many instances, the Strasbourg Court has interpreted Article 9 as protecting majoritarian rights against minority religions. This for the sake of social harmony. So, the Court has protected majoritarian Catholics in Austria,[9] Ireland[10], Italy,[11] and France.[12] Only when non-Catholic established religions are challenged, for example, in Orthodox Greece in *Kokkinakis* or in Muslim Turkey,[13] has the Court been inclined to protect a religious minority. Thus, it seems the spirit of the Westphalian religious settlement carries on. As I have written elsewhere: '[M]odern Europe, still in its Westphalian shadow, promotes intra-European peace by permitting states to establish their own distinct national visions of the role of religion in society. Protecting minority religious challenges to such national visions is, despite *Kokkinakis*, usually a step too far out of the shadow of Westphalia for the Strasbourg Court'.[14]

The second major religious challenge to modern international law is posed by proselytism. Given the belief of many religious adherents that theirs is the one and only true faith, there is an incentive for the faithful to strive to convert non-believers. Although the urge to proselytise is not common to all religions, it is a feature of many. There are, for example, strong missionary movements among many Western religions, for example Catholics, Evangelicals, Jehovah's Witnesses, Seventh Day Adventists, Protestant Fundamentalists, and Mormons. Outside of the West, proselytism may also be an important religious characteristic, for example among Muslims.

After Westphalia, post-1648 international law did prohibit state-sponsored interventions to impose religious preferences. However, privately sponsored

7 Bernadette Meyler, 'The Limits of Group Rights: Religious Institutions and Religious Minorities in International Law', 22 *St. John's Journal of Legal Commentary* 535 (2007).
8 European Court of Human Rights, Application no. 14307/88 (25 May 1993).
9 Otto-Preminger-Institut v. Austria, Application no. 13470/87 (20 September 1994).
10 Murphy v. Ireland, Application no. 44179/98 (10 July 2003).
11 Lautsi v. Italy, Application no. 30814/06 (Grand Chamber, 18 March 2011).
12 SAS v. France, Application no. 43835/11 (1 July 2014).
13 Sahin v. Turkey, Judgement of 10 November 2005 (Grand Chamber).
14 Shadow, *supra* note 6, at 93.

missionary efforts are not so regulated by international legal rules. Albeit, there was a melding of the state and private actors in the nineteenth Century when European empire-building and colonialism marched alongside missionary zeal, in Africa and East and South Asia. This triggered a good deal of international conflict, but nowadays states are rarely so outwardly active in promoting religious conversions. However, private proselytism carries on.

Does international law have a role to play respecting religious proselytism? As one observer put the problem: '[The] most controversial issue concerns the balance between the freedom to maintain a religion without interference and the freedom to proselytize'.[15] International legal claims are made on both sides of the divide. The proselytisers promote the development of international rules that will protect their missionary activities. Those being proselytised propose rules that strive to protect their peoples and distinctive cultures from foreign missionaries and influence. Notably, Saudi Arabia and other Muslims states have long objected in international fora to the development of any international law that would recognise the right of individuals to change their religions or beliefs.[16] Some states want it both ways: the right to vigorously propagate their faith and the right to isolate their own populations from foreign religions. The field of proselytism is relatively poorly addressed both in state diplomacy and in scholarly studies, probably because of the emotions involved. Proselytism is apparently dangerous territory for meddling international law and international lawyers.[17]

A third significant religious challenge for international law is posed by the mass migration of millions of refugees from their native lands by the strife of war and the misery of poverty. Most often, this movement of peoples is from South to North: from Africa, the Middle East, and Latin America to Europe and North America. Albeit the migrants from Latin America share a Christian culture with their northern neighbours, most of the refugees from Africa and the Middle East do not. Many are Muslim, a religious faith which, until recently, was not part of most European and American nations. World-wide, there are today more than 800 million people who are migrants living outside their native country, about 12.5 per cent of the world's total population.[18]

15 Moshe Hirsche, 'The Freedom of Proselytizm under the International Agreement and International Law', 47 *Catholic University Law Review* 407, 425 (1998).

16 Id. at 411–425.

17 See Natan Lerner, 'Proselytism, Change of Religion, and International Human Rights', 12 *Emory International Law Review* 477 (1998).

18 Todd M. Johnson and Gina A. Bellofatto , 'Migration, Religious Diasporas, and Religious Diversity: A Global Survey', 29 *Missions Studies* 3, 8 (2012). Of these, some 47.4 per cent are Christian and 25.4 per cent Muslim. Id. at 8–9.

International law since the Second World War has laid great store on a distinction between political refugees and economic migrants. Political refugees, who in fact suffer from political, religious, or ethnic prejudice and violence, generally have a legal right to be given new homes in destination countries. Economic migrants, who seek a better standard of living, may be accepted or rejected by destination countries more or less by volition. The problem comes in that international rules also prescribe the right of all refugees/migrants to be given administrative due process to legally determine their political/economic status. Determining such status has become harder and more time and cost consuming each decade, each year. So, there are long delays and bad holding places, along with tremendous costs for the destination countries and heavy hardship on the migrants.

Adding to these anxieties comes a popular sentiment that there are simply too many immigrants and that, if accepted, these new migrants are too different in culture and religion to successfully integrate in more developed and peaceful countries. This fear has contributed to the growth of populist sentiment, parties, and governments, which reject, not only liberal migration policies, but international law and international institutions. The phenomenon of populist rejection of international law and organisation is probably the most serious threat today to the legitimacy of the traditional Westphalian international legal system.

Faced with these three religious challenges, what can be done by international law and international lawyers? Such challenges are at least partly caused by the absolutist character of most religions and most religious adherents. There is always going to be an absolutist and emotional faith that one's own religion is the one and only true faith. Intolerance of other faiths is a built-in feature of most religions. This is as much a given in our times as it was in the era of Grotius.

The Westphalian settlement was hugely successful in prohibiting state imposition of religious preference on other states. However, Westphalia did not put an end to religious intolerance, as evidenced by the centuries-old problem of the persecution of religious minorities. Today, intolerance towards religious minorities is joined by the new challenges posed by the perceived threats of proselytism and the mass migration of non-co-religionists. These three challenges may well crack the foundation of the Grotian international legal order.

Modern international lawyers must tackle the same problem of religious intolerance that Grotius faced long ago. It will probably be difficult and uncomfortable to do so, but it is well worth the try. What might be done both in the academy and on the diplomatic front? For the academic international lawyer, the time has come to take religion seriously. There is relatively little attention paid by scholars to the nature and differences among the various religions. This should be done. Why not follow in the footsteps of Grotius and search for commonalities among the different faiths? Why not propose common grounds for religious tolerance? This calls for more in-depth studies, not only of substantive international law and national law, but also of religious beliefs. We need to identify what divides religions and what there is in them all that will help us to live together in harmony.

For national diplomacy and international institutions, the time may have come to treat different religions differently. Why not identify those aspects of religions that are intolerant and strive to make religious antagonisms just as unacceptable in world politics and law as do comparable political and economic antagonisms? This will be very difficult indeed, since religious sentiment is taken so very seriously by national populations and governments and hence by international institutions. As theologian Martin Marty wrote about religion and religious rights, 'what is it about religion that leads partisans to adduce it with such passion and self-assurance … ? Certainly some answers to that question would include the fact that most religions regard themselves as rooted in the transcendent, the super mundane, the extraordinary realms of existence'.[19] There is no nation that is untouched by the problem of religious certainty and its consequences.

What can international diplomacy and international instruments do? We need to find common ground to face all three of the challenges. We should provide effective international guarantees for minority religions within all countries, even within those nations passionately devoted to a single national faith. All nations should be legally and politically bound to protect minority religious and their rights to gather and to worship openly. There should be commonly accepted metes and bounds to the right to proselytise, enough to protect outside religions when they strive to convert, but within reasonable limits when needed to protect national cultures and sensibilities. There should be internationally protected standards respecting the rights of immigrants to practice their faiths, while permitting governments to maintain and promote accepted national cultures and majoritarian religions that help define that character.

[19] Marten E. Marty , 'Religious Dimensions of Human Rights', in *Religious Human Rights in Global Perspectives: Religious Perpectives* 1, 7 (John Witte Jr. and Johan D. Van de Vyve eds. 1996).

None of this will be easy or straightforward. Much of it may well be unattainable. But it should be the job of international law and international lawyers to try. We must seek out facts, enunciate what counts as reasonable possibilities, and promote equitable solutions. No set of tasks is likely to be harder for the discipline and its practitioners, but nothing is more essential. The modern challenge of religion is our new Grotian moment. Let us seize it.

16

Rule of Law

Justin Desautels-Stein

Consider the well-travelled question, 'What is international law?' Unlike its confident counterparts in fields like constitutional law, administrative law, criminal law, and the like, the field of international law is downright famous for not really being sure of what it is.[1] In its search for some closure, this uncertainty tends to flow in one of three directions. First, we have the issue of whether international law is really law at all, and so, we want to know, well then what *is* 'international law' if we cannot take its name seriously? Relying upon philosophers like John Austin or H. L. A. Hart as a starting point, the interrogation builds a particular conception of what law requires to be law qua law: something about an enforceable command issued from a superior to an inferior, or something about primary and secondary rules.[2] With one of these or some other related conception in place, the analysis goes comparative, asking whether 'international law' meets the predefined criteria of the selected philosopher of law.[3] Over the years, I think it is fair to say that international legal theorists have made the argument for good comparisons with some success.[4] That said, the comparative exercise haunts the public imagination, continuously reminding that international law cannot possibility meet the criteria for real law, since international law is unenforceable. This ontological debate over international law's existence as law per se is likely the most well-known in popular conversations about international law's legality.

[1] For a recent treatment in this vein, *see* JEAN D'ASPREMONT , INTERNATIONAL LAW AS A BELIEF SYSTEM (2017); JOHN HASKELL , POLITICAL THEOLOGY AND INTERNATIONAL LAW (2018).

[2] JOHN AUSTIN , THE PROVINCE OF LAW DETERMINED AND THE USES OF THE STUDY OF JURISPRUDENCE (1998); H. L. A. HART , THE CONCEPT OF LAW (1997).

[3] For a representative discussion, *see* DAVID BEDERMAN , THE SPIRIT OF INTERNATIONAL LAW (2006).

[4] *See, e.g.*, Oona Hathaway and Scott Shapiro, *Outcasting: Enforcement in Domestic and International Law*, 121 YALE LAW JOURNAL 252 (2011).

A second way in which the question gets answered is to focus on the identity of international law's concepts, rather than a question about the concept of international law. Indeed, the whole debate over the concept of international law seems, from this second point of view, beside the point. What international lawyers need to know are the rules, rules for making agreements between sovereigns and between citizens, rules for governing disputes, and rules for solving problems and getting things done. Here, the question of what international law *is* gets answered by way of a doctrinal survey of the field's more or less fundamental and peripheral concepts, from sovereignty to state responsibility, from human rights to the powers of international organisations, from the high seas to war and trade, and so on. When this doctrinal or professional form of an answer is contrasted with the 'philosophical' approach, the conversation seems to split in two: the first discussion no longer looks like it is so much about the 'what' of international law as it is about the 'whether'. And the 'whether it exists' question just seems silly to salaried lawyers and judges, quite literally in the business of doing international law on a day-to-day basis. Ultimately, the doctrinal answer is the answer of today's sophisticated course books and treatises: a true and practical description of the field's legal concepts, as understood and worked out by the profession for professionals.[5]

A third and rather different way to approach international law's identity crisis is to join the 'professional' approach in its dismissal of the 'philosophical' problem as useless, but at the same time attack the professional approach as inadequate in its feeble construction of the 'what'. In this third and 'socio-legal' approach, the question of what international law *is* turns out to be deeply entangled with the question of how international law works at a level beyond doctrine, and a focus on international law's concepts is never going to be very helpful here.[6] Indeed, if international lawyers want to solve problems and get things done, knowing the profession's rules is only scratching the surface. What you really need to understand, if you want to understand international law, is the social process in which international law is ceaselessly realised.[7]

This socio-legal approach to the question of international law's identity manifests in multiple dimensions. For example, it may be that one form or another of rational choice theory best explains what international law really is,

[5] *See, e.g.*, Lori Damrosch , et. al., International Law: Cases and Materials (2009).

[6] *See, e.g.*, Friedrich Kratochwil , The Status of Law in World Society: Meditations on the Role and Rule of Law (2014).

[7] *See, e.g.*, Moshe Hirsch , Invitation to the Sociology of International Law (2015).

how it works, why it does this and never does that.[8] Or it could be the study of international politics that sheds the best light on international law,[9] or it could be social theory,[10] or the idea that there are really two or three or seven different international legal orders,[11] or that the constitution of international law is produced through the works of non-state actors like multinational corporations or nongovernmental organizations,[12] or culture[13] or nationalism[14] or gender[15] or class.[16] Whatever the social context you choose, and whatever the context that will most helpfully explain the 'reality' of international law, what every version of the socio-legal approach has in common is a belief in the lack of utility in the philosophical approach, and the lack of sophistication in the professional approach. Beyond that, and the general assumption that the reality of international law will only be disclosed by way of 'situating' international law in some 'external' social context, there are, quite obviously, many ways to go here.[17]

All together, we have three distinctive and, I would think, entirely valid perspectives on the question, 'What is international law?' We have the philosophical, the professional, and the socio-legal. However, if each perspective is valid, which one is *right*? Which should we promote? Or at least, even if the three perspectives are each valid in a way, can we at least say that one perspective is superior? The problem, of course, is that on their own terms each perspective is logical with respect to its premises, or at least, with a bit more time we could certainly flesh them out to be so. The problem seems to boil down into an uncomfortable (or is it comforting?) situation of methodological anarchy. Perhaps this eclecticism is a sign of analytical maturity, or

8 *See, e.g.*, Andrew Guzman, How International Law Works: A Rational Choice Theory (2010).

9 *See, e.g.*, Anne-Marie Slaughter, A New World Order (2005).

10 *See, e.g.*, Alexander Wendt, Social Theory of International Politics (1999).

11 *See, e.g.*, Paul Schiff Berman, Global Legal Pluralism: A Jurisprudence of Law Beyond Borders (2014).

12 *See, e.g.*, Jose Alvarez, The Impact of International Organizations on International Law (2016).

13 *See, e.g.*, Antony Anghie, Imperialism, Sovereignty, and the Making of International Law (2007).

14 *See, e.g.*, James Summers, Peoples and International Law: How Nationalism and Self-Determination Shape a Contemporary Law of Nations (2007).

15 *See, e.g.*, Hillary Charlesworth and Christine Chinkin , The Boundaries of International Law: A Feminist Analysis (2000).

16 *See, e.g.*, China Mieville, Between Equal Rights: A Marxist Theory of International Law (2006).

17 According to Andrea Bianchi, the answer is 14. *See* Andrea Bianchi , International Law Theories: An Inquiry into Different Ways of Thinking (2016).

a kind of professional equipoise. Or perhaps it is a sign that we are on the edge of some disciplinary tipping point.

Before offering my own view of the tipping point, however, I want to ask another question. If we are familiar with the conventional debates surrounding the question of international law's identity, what of the international *rule* of law?[18] Is this question any different from 'What is international law?' As philosophers like Jeremy Waldron and Joseph Raz have suggested in the context of domestic law, the distinction may reference on the one hand our concept of law – what law *is* and what it *does in fact* – and on the other hand what we see as law's aspiration and purpose – what law *must do if it is to achieve its goals*.[19] But does this distinction have any meaning in the international legal order? James Crawford put it this way: 'So the question we need to ask is whether in engaging this broader range of activities, international law itself should observe the standards it sets for national systems. Or is it substantially exempt from them, embodying the idea that the rule of law is a virtue for national systems which international law can enforce without having to comply with it itself'.[20] Crawford's response was in favour of the former, arguing for the necessity of holding international law to the same rule of law standards as any national legal system. As for what those standards entailed, Crawford borrowed from Raz, who in turn borrowed from Dicey, Fuller, and Hayek. If international law abides by the rule of law, Crawford explained, we ought to expect the absence of arbitrary power, laws that are always prospective, a generality of application, and the independence of the judiciary. Crawford's assessment from twenty years ago was that the results were mixed.[21] Query how, if we join in the pursuit of this checklist view of the rule of law, international law ranks today.

This is all fair enough, and in principle the questions of international law's existence and international law's commitment to the rule of law seem analytically distinct. The better approach, I think, is to view the two questions together, though this depends entirely on the context in which we view the relation of the questions. As I shall suggest in the next few pages, I offer the

[18] *See generally*, Tom Bingham, *The Rule of Law in the International Legal Order*, *in* THE RULE OF LAW IN INTERNATIONAL AND COMPARATIVE CONTEXT (Robert McCorquodale, ed., 2010); Kratochwil, *supra* note 6.

[19] *See, e.g.*, Jeremy Waldron, *The Concept and the Rule of Law*, 43 GEORGIA LAW REVIEW 1 (2008); Joseph Raz, *The Rule of Law and its Virtue*, 93 LAW QUARTERLY REVIEW 195 (1977). *See also*, HANDBOOK ON THE RULE OF LAW (Christopher May and Adam Winchester, eds., 2018).

[20] James Crawford, *International Law and the Rule of Law*, 24 ADELAIDE LAW REVIEW 3, 8 (2003).

[21] *Id.* at 12.

context of 'liberal legal thought' for understanding the entwined relation between international law's identity and fidelity. When viewed from this vantage point, the three answers to the question of whether international law exists turn out to also be three separate arguments for international law's fidelity to 'the rule of law'.

As I argue below, when viewed in the context of liberal legal thought, the identity of the international rule of law turns on whether jurists are generally capable of providing legal justifications that appear free of political or moral capture. Whether the international rule of law is closing in on a tipping point depends – again, in the context of liberal theory – on whether these three justifications persuasively *naturalise* the relevant field. 'Naturalising the field' means crafting a form of apolitical justification that persuades as law. If the justification fails to naturalise, or seems on the edge of losing its suasion, the rule of law is either at or past the tipping point. The act of naturalising the relevant field in the service of the rule of law is, of course, an ideological operation. The extent to which a jurist understands their legal justifications as natural is a measure of their immersion in that ideology, and ultimately, their deeper political commitments. As a result, the question of whether the rule of law is at or past a tipping point has everything to do with an individual jurist's relation with ideological mystification. That is, if viewed in the context of liberal legal thought, the question of the tipping point will always be in the eye of the beholder.

As I have just suggested, the problem of knowing whether international law is really law, or if international law is consistent with the rule of law, is a problem of context. That is, our answers depend entirely on the context that comes ready to hand. We might prefer the context of doctrinal problem-solving, the context of social process, or the context of political or moral theory. Interestingly, when cast as a problem of context, the questions seem to rearrange themselves. The socio-legal approach takes law and puts 'it' in some externalised vision of reality. The professional approach is also interested in an extra-legal context, but only in micro-doses: just enough to see how our professional expertise helps solve this local problem or that local problem, just enough so that it works. The philosophical approach, in contrast, has less interest in demanding that law conform to a social or doctrinal context than it does in requiring law to abide by certain theoretical commitments. One might say that this is a demand 'internal' to law, though it would be easy enough to spin it as a relation between 'law' on the one side and an 'external' political or moral theory on the other. In any event, what I now want to suggest is that the professional, socio-legal, and philosophical contexts do not monopolise the field. A fourth, and highly productive context for analysing the international rule of law, is what I call the *legal context.*

To build a legal context, we first presume that law is like a language, and more, that there are several languages of law. Thus we must begin with a choice of a target language system. Of course, one might choose instead to ask whether all legal languages find a common heritage in some proto-language, and attempt to reconstruct that proto-language. That said, the prospect of rounding together everything that might ostensibly pass as 'international' and 'legal' hardly seems worth the candle. Even if we could identify a plausible collection of American, British, French, German, Swiss, Russian, Spanish, Indian, Japanese, Chinese, Christian, Muslim, Jewish, Buddhist, and Baha'i understandings of international law, we would hardly have scratched the surface. The whole continent of Africa is missing, for example, as are so many religious systems. And just consider how hierarchical the list already is, and how difficult it would be to say what any of these labels are 'really' about, or why these and no other traditions that surely inform the universe of material that constitutes the entirety of 'international legal thought' are included. What's more, the challenge in showing all of these traditions as a part of a single and unified language of law might very well be insurmountable.[22]

As all of this suggests, my preference is to target a more discrete language system, and my choice is what I call 'liberal legalism', or 'liberal legal thought'.[23] I choose liberal legalism for at least four reasons. First, in the context of liberal legalism, the questions of whether law is law and whether law is abiding by the rule of law, are entirely fungible. Second, liberal theory is relatively conspicuous and easy to differentiate. Third, my hypothesis is that the international manifestation of liberal legalism is both widely known and influential. Fourth, I choose liberalism because it is spectacularly strange in its blending of aspiring ideal and deadening prejudice. What's more, choosing liberal legalism as the legal context for international legal thought means that I am choosing nothing else: not US international law, Chinese international law, Jewish international law, or any other system of thought. If there is coincidence or overlap, it is unintended.

To build the legal context of liberal legal thought, I begin with its three master theses. These are (1) the thesis of free competition (2) the thesis of social

[22] For discussion, *see* Anthea Roberts, Is International Law International? (2017).

[23] Here I am borrowing from the discussion of liberalism in Justin Desautels-Stein , The Jurisprudence of Style: A Structuralist Legal History of American Pragmatism and Liberal Legal Thought (2018).

control, and (3) the thesis of naturalising juridical science. Next, I select a legal concept in the field of international law, and examine the tensions between the theses of free competition and social control that constitute that concept, and the availability of naturalising juridical science for resolving that tension. To the extent we find available means for *legally* harmonising the contest between the two theses, the rule of law in this area is – in the context of liberal legal thought – secure. The concept that I will use as an exemplary vehicle is that of international migration.[24] As Tendayi Achiume has defined it, international migration refers to 'the act of leaving one's place of birth and moving across national borders in pursuit of greater capacity to self-determine through territorial admission and political inclusion'.[25] If migration is properly characterised as a legal concept – in addition to its identity as a social phenomenon – then migration is both constituted and regulated by legal rules. Or, to put this another way, if migration is a legal concept, and not only a social or political activity, then we should be able to speak of migration in the register of the 'rule of law'. Can we?

In the liberal structure of international legal thought, the thesis of free competition holds that international society is entirely artificial, and that the true supports of the international architecture are sovereign states. These sovereigns are autonomous and rights-bearing, and if international society happens at all, it happens as a result of the exercise of sovereign will. There is no a priori definition of international society that might precede the exercise of sovereign will. It is only through the contest of these sovereign wills that borders come into being, and individual human beings decide to remain domiciled where they are or take their chances in the global migration market. Thus, in the light of this first thesis, we would expect sovereigns to exercise full authority over the question of which persons are allowed to migrate, and which are excluded. The extent to which migrants are able to select new residences in this global marketplace of sovereign prerogatives is left to individual abilities to compete and prove their worth as potential citizens/residents. While citizens might potentially exert political influence on the sovereign's decisions regarding its right to exclude, foreign participants in the global migration marketplace remain objects of consumption.

[24] *See* Vincent Chetail, *The Transnational Movement of Persons Under General International Law – Mapping the Customary Law Foundations of International Migration Law*, *in* Research Handbook on International Law and Migration (Vincent Chetail and Celine Bauloz, eds., 2014); Chantal Thomas, *What Does the Emerging International Law of Migration Mean for Sovereignty?*, 14 Melb. J. Int'l L. 392 (2013).

[25] E. Tendayi Achiume, *Migration as Decolonization*, 71 Stanford Law Review 1509 (2019).

In the liberal structure of international legal thought, the thesis of social control holds that if left unchecked, the thesis of free competition yields an anarchical society. Not only will the thesis of free competition make it ultimately impossible for sovereigns to freely exercise their own wills, the potential goods we expect from competition and cooperation remain unrealised in the absence of meaningful regulation. As a result, the second thesis of social control holds that some form of international police power must exist, defining the proper scope of sovereign right and obligation. International society remains artificial, but if we are to realise the goods we expect from a world in which sovereigns freely exercise their rights, sovereigns must be subject to social control. Thus, in the light of this second thesis, we would expect a legal regime for regulating and protecting the passage of citizens across borders – a legal regime irreducible to the mere exercise of sovereign caprice. In this view, it is unacceptable to leave the question of successful migration entirely in the hands of sovereign choices about which kinds of migrants make 'successful' citizens. Nevertheless, migrants in the global marketplace remain objects, not subjects.

There is an ongoing dissonance in the contesting demands of the first two master theses in liberal legal thought – here it is the tension between the sovereign's right to exclude the world from its territory, and the sovereign's duty to yield in favour of certain rules regulating the sovereign's right to exclude. These contrasting theses govern the forms in which the legal concept of migration takes shape in its various doctrinal manifestations. What we have thus far, however, is only tension and paradox without consonance and coherence: sovereigns have the authority to exclude all migrants, and yet, if the rights of sovereigns writ large are to be guaranteed, we need international controls that limit what sovereigns can and cannot do. It is this dissonance between the demands of the first two theses which gives rise to the third thesis in liberal legal thought. This is the harmonising thesis of naturalising juridical science.

The thesis of naturalising juridical science has a very different task than either of the first two, and it is this task that brings us back to our questions of whether international law is really law, or whether there is an international rule of law. It is also this third thesis that highlights the location of the tipping point. Here's how. The task of naturalising juridical science is to ensure that the tension between the theses of free competition and social control is resolved harmoniously, objectively, in *law*. The resolution must be legal, it cannot be merely political, and it cannot be merely moral. That is, the task of naturalising juridical science is about both law's identity as something other than politics or morality, and law's fidelity to an order that is justifiable in 'objective' registers. If naturalising juridical science fails in its task, the international law of migration fades into raw politics, therefore failing to be law, or consistent with the rule of law, which in liberalism now amounts to the same thing. For example, if the field of international migration law does nothing other than codify the rights of sovereigns to enjoy a plenary power of exclusion in the reserved domain of domestic jurisdiction, we fail in the effort to talk of an international *legal* concept of migration: we have tipped passed the space of law and are just talking about national politics. In the other direction, if the field of international migration law does nothing other than talk of a cosmopolitan human right to migrate across open borders, we have tipped beyond the space of law and now seem to be just talking about a free-floating morality. In the context of liberal legal thought, what we need to justify the rule of law – migration as a *legal* concept – is naturalising juridical science.

In liberal legal thought, naturalising juridical science may take many forms in resolving the dissonance between the rights of sovereigns to exclude and what is required to establish a global rule of law. Here, I very briefly survey three of those forms, the same three I mentioned at the start: the pragmatic professional, the socio-legal, and the philosophical. In their own way, each form attempts to ground an argument for resolving the tension between the theses of free competition and social control, without falling into politics on the one side or morality on the other. After reviewing exemplary work from David Martin, Harold Laswell, Myres McDougal, Arash Abizadeh, and Tendayi Achiume, I conclude with a comparative summary that makes explicit how each of the three forms supports the idea of migration as a distinctively legal concept.

First, consider David Martin's example of what I am calling the pragmatic professional's approach.[26] In a chapter from the turn of the century titled 'The Authority and Responsibility of States', Martin argued for an understanding of the sovereign's right to exclude under the heavy influence of the thesis of free competition.[27] As Martin explained at the outset, 'the starting point' is 'broad state authority' in 'setting the standards for admission to and exclusion from national territory ... '[28] This starting point is a 'basic assumption' of our 'international system',[29] and all restrictions on and attempts to regulate this

[26] I want to make clear at the outset that the professional approach is not necessarily conservative. It can have more left or more right orientations. Nevertheless, it is true that the professional approach tends to gravitate toward what it understands as the status quo, and so in this sense it may be sensible to call it "conservative" with respect to an attitude toward social change.

[27] David Martin, *The Authority and Responsibility of States*, *in* MIGRATION AND INTERNATIONAL LEGAL NORMS (T. Alexander Aleinikoff and Vincent Chetail, eds. 2003).

[28] *Id.* at 33.

[29] *Id.* at 31.

fundamental right to exclude are exceptional.[30] Nevertheless, Martin explained that 'it has been exceedingly rare for any state to exercise the maximum of its theoretical power by halting virtually all migration'.[31] Why do states not exercise the full extent of this power, and not just close down their borders altogether? The answer is that, in this professional approach, it would be impractical to do so. Closing down national borders would cause problems; perhaps not as many problems as a policy of open borders would create. But neither approach makes sense in light of the need to mitigate the sovereign's right to exclude in the light of practical considerations.

For example, Martin suggests that states actually end up constrained in their decisions about admission and exclusion on a problem-by-problem, field-by-field basis. As international law relates to national security, international trade, development, investment, employment and labour, education policies, public health concerns, forced migrants, and the threat of returning would-be refugees to hostile territory, international legal rules may affect and regulate sovereign rights of exclusion in the form of bilateral treaties, like consular treaties, investment treaties, friendship, navigation, and commerce treaties, and the like. International law may also pose restrictions in the form of regional agreements and multinational conventions, like NAFTA on the one side or the Refugees Convention on the other.

From this point of view, broad statements about the state's 'plenary power' are too generalised when analysed beyond the context of some particular problem. As Martin recently argued, we do not believe in the broad authority of the state to fashion its own immigration controls because we have faith in the sovereign's right to exclude and the thesis of free competition. Rather, the plenary power *persuades* because the plenary power *works*. In a treatment of classic US Supreme Court decisions like *Chae Chan Ping* and *Fong Yu Ting*, Martin argued that the Court had never intended to raise a sovereignty claim in order to trump competing visions of social justice and human rights, that is, the thesis of social control. Rather, these decisions helped articulate the relation between federal and state power in the distinctive context of the American constitutional system. If the Supreme Court had deemed the United States unable to decide matters concerning migration control, then the role would have fallen to the states in their exercise of the police power. Not finding a natural home in any of the constitution's enumerated powers, the United States would have only been able to speak to border controls with

[30] *Id.* at 32. The most obvious and yet still relatively weak such restriction is the anti-discrimination norm.

[31] *Id.* at 33.

the plural voices of the individual states. However, as Martin explained, without a unified voice about how or who to exclude from the national political community, the very coherence of a national polis might dissolve. Thus, Martin concluded, 'Asserting jurisdiction over a territory, which includes authority to choose which noncitizens to admit or exclude, is simply part of what it means to be a sovereign nation'.[32]

Perhaps, however, the problems of the late nineteenth century are not the problems of the early Twenty-First? Maybe the need to immunise the federal government's decisions about migration and exclusion are no longer necessary due to the pressing needs of national coherence – needs that 'made sense' earlier in the nation's life, but make less sense for today? For Martin, the problem has indeed changed, but its solution presses in the same direction. 'Failed states are more common, and well-armed insurgencies have proliferated. The march of democracy has slowed and, in several countries, reversed. Climate change and even plague-like diseases presage more complicated foreign policy challenges, many of which will have a migration dimension … I do not foresee the Supreme Court retreating significantly from the strong deference doctrines derived from *Chae Chan Ping*'.[33] The upshot: privileging the sovereign's right to exclude provides concrete solutions to real problems, both domestic and international. To understand why, or in what ways the right to exclude ought to be extended or diminished, we need to look at the problem at hand and the expertise we will need to solve it.

The socio-legal approach provides a second mode of argument about the relation between free competition and social control. As mentioned at the start, a socio-legal approach suggests that we can know international law's identity through a search for law's process in social life. This perspective has been a part of the landscape in international legal thought for generations, dating at the very least to the post-war work of the New Haven School.[34] Broadly speaking, socio-legal scholars have long believed that if international law was to be 'real', to show fidelity to the international rule of law, it would have to actually serve the real needs of states and international society.[35] To do that, international law must be effective, and in order to be effective,

32 *Id.* at 36.
33 *Id.* at 49–50.
34 *See, e.g.*, Harold Koh, *Is There a 'New' New Haven School in International Law?*, 32 Yale Journal International Law 559 (2007).
35 *See, e.g.*, Hersch Lauterpacht, The Function of Law in the International Community (2011); Phillip Marshal Brown, *International Lawlessness*, 32 Am. J. Int'l L. 775 (1938). Hans Morgenthau, *Positivism, Functionalism, and International Law*, 34 Am. J. Int'l L. 260, 273 (1940).

international law needed a conceptual basis for explaining how it could change and adapt to new social demands.

A key insight in the new socio-legal approach was borrowed from legal realism, suggesting a relativity of the various rights and relationships in the international legal order. Most prominently, this 'relativity' suggested a new system in which the rights of sovereigns were contextualised among the rights of non-state actors, especially individuals and international institutions, as well as against the world's 'real' social problems. Few rights, in this view, could achieve a kind of natural or basic status, and for those that could, they were considered the rights of individual human beings, and not sovereign rulers. Further, the relativity of rights was contextualised in a complex process of international society, in which the old boundaries between states, between domestic and the international, and between disciplines, became increasingly suspect. In the work of New Haven scholars like Harold Lasswell and Myers McDougal, for example, the more sophisticated our empirical understandings of the global process in which law met social needs, the better would be our ability to make more effective reforms.[36] The operating assumption was that the realist critiques of abstract, static, archaic forms of law had been right, and that what needed to happen next was a transformation of those insights – through more sophisticated empiricism – into a concrete policy platform.

Like many others of their generation,[37] Lasswell and McDougal were post-realists in the sense that they were deeply informed by early twentieth century attacks on the classic conception of the sovereign's right to exclude. Lasswell and McDougal's 'Policy Perspective' steadily developed in parallel with the work of Hart and Sacks, producing what is probably best understood as an international variant of the legal process school.[38] This new institutionalism would be guided by the freshest of cutting edge thinking about the functional nature of law, an understanding of the deeply political nature of law, and a process-oriented program in which a legal regime was best considered in its social contexts.[39] The basic goals of the regime were very broad – in their case, it was 'human dignity' – and the actual meaning of the goal could only be discovered in practice, and not before it. The goal values were targeted

[36] *See, e.g.*, Myres McDougal and Harold Lasswell, *The Identification and Appraisal of Diverse Systems of Public Order*, 53 AM. J. INT' L. 19 (1959).

[37] *See generally* MORTON HORWITZ, THE TRANSFORMATION OF AMERICAN LAW, 1870–1960: THE CRISIS OF LEGAL ORTHODOXY (1979).

[38] On legal process in the United States, *see* Charles Barzun, *The Forgotten Foundations of Hart and Sacks*, 99 VA. L. REV. 1 (2013).

[39] *See* Justin Desautels-Stein, *At War with the Eclectics: Mapping Pragmatism in Contemporary Legal Analysis*, 2007 MICH. ST. L. REV. 565 (2007).

through 'continuous reappraisal of the circumstances in which specific institutional combinations can make the greatest net contribution to the overarching goal'.[40] To the extent that the goal might find itself manifested differently in the specifics of various local contexts, these 'varying detailed practices by which the overriding goals are sought need not necessarily be fatal ... but can be made creative in promoting [our goals]'.[41]

The ongoing process of relativising the sovereign's right to exclude developed into a vast array of fields that today fills out the contemporary terrain of international law. With respect to my focus on migration as a legal concept, Lasswell and McDougal's study of the 'contemporary emerging world society, with its ever-increasing personal mobility and transnational interactions ... ',[42] the starting point was *not* the thesis of free competition. Rather, their approach began with a concession to the relativity of rights between sovereigns and non-state actors, and in particular, the rights of individuals. On their view, the traditional distinction between citizen and alien is already a mistake, since 'every individual is a potential alien in relation to all the states of which he is not a national'.[43]

To be clear, Lasswell and McDougal had no interest in making an argument for open borders; there will be rational forms of exclusion.[44] But the rationality of the regime that intended to keep certain individuals out of a sovereign's territory ought to be guided by two pillars: the common interests of international society in servicing the principle of human dignity, and the complexity of a world system in which concepts like 'sovereigns' and 'owners' are best analysed as bundles of rights and relationships,[45] rather than 'reified pseudoabsolutes'.[46] As Lasswell and McDougal concluded:

> The fact of alienage does not change the fundamental demands and interests of the individual as a human being; its only relevance must be to the organized interests of a territorial community, which, in various contexts, his activities may affect. It is widely recognized today that many, if not most, 'national' boundaries are highly artificial and anachronistic from any functional perspective, impeding a rational regional organization of the world,

40 Myres S. McDougal and Harold D. Lasswell, *The Identification and Appraisal of Diverse Systems of Public Order*, 53 AM. J. INT'L L. 1, 5 (1959).

41 *Id.* at 6.

42 Myres McDougal, Harold Lasswell , and Lung-chu Chen, *The Protection of Aliens from Discrimination and World Public Order: Responsibility of States Conjoined with Human Rights*, 70 AM. J. INT'L L.432, 433 (1976).

43 *Id.* at 437.

44 *Id.*

45 *Id.* at 439.

46 *Id.* at 432.

> and, as suggested above, that the grounds commonly employed by states in making their characterizations of 'nationality' may bear only an accidental relation to the facts of community membership. In this context, the necessities of an aggregate common interest in a global community and society, requiring a more rational relation of peoples to resources, should be made to yield as little as possible to the demands and practices of an outmoded and destructive nationalism. A clear consciousness of interdependence offers more hope even for shared exclusive interests than the amnesia of parochialism.[47]

Ultimately, it was simply unrealistic to adhere to a rigid and mechanical view of the sovereign's right to exclude through the implementation of xenophobic and increasingly militarised immigration regimes. It was unrealistic on the one hand for its prioritisation of a sovereign's rights over other rights in the system, and it was unrealistic on the other as a matter of capturing the complexities of international society.

As demonstrated in the pragmatic and socio-legal approaches, the law of human rights is often seen as a constraint upon the sovereign right to exclude foreigners. In this particular sense, human rights operate from the thesis of social control, offering obligations and constraints on the thesis of free competition and the sovereign right to exclude. The work to be done for the pragmatic and socio-legal approaches goes to the means for balancing the conflict, and hopefully, naturalising the scene in such a way that the legal concept of international migration is free of contradiction.

From a third and philosophical perspective we see yet another way in which to resolve the tensions at work in the concept of international migration. In the work of Arash Abizadeh, for example, the sovereign's right to exclude is indeed constrained by the rights of foreigners, but rather than think of the constraints as externally imposed as forms of social control, Abizadeh suggests that if the sovereign's right to exclude is to be considered legitimate, the exercise of that right must be informed by the consent of foreigners. His argument, however, is not the cosmopolitan one that assumes a vision of humanity that ought to guide the decision-making of sovereigns. Abizadeh's claim is rather that, when sovereigns exercise a right to exclude foreigners, and these foreigners have not had a say about it, such a 'unilateral' exercise of exclusion violates the very concept of sovereignty itself because such exercise is *undemocratic*.

In his 'Democratic Theory and Border Coercion', Abizadeh begins with a familiar articulation of the contest between the theses of free competition

[47] *Id.* at 439.

and social control.[48] This contest shows itself differently, depending on whether it is viewed as a matter of justifying a restriction on sovereign freedom by tracing the justification to that freedom's conditions of possibility, or whether the justification must instead be traced to the actual participation of all those human beings over which the sovereign's right extends. That is, in the first view of the contest, what we require is a justification that shows the balance of sovereign right and social control to be just – just with respect to the reduction of freedom enjoyed by the *sovereign*. On the second view, we require a justification that traces the *construction* of sovereign rights to the participation of citizens that are subject to the sovereign's decisions. This second justification is not so much about justice as it is about the legitimacy of state regulation. As Abizedeh put it, the first version of the tension between freedom and control requires a hypothetical justification about the justice of the particular balance, while the second version 'demands actual, institutionalized discursive political processes dependent on mobilizing citizens' participation as a democratic people'.[49]

For the pragmatic and socio-legal approaches, the debate is squarely in the first version of the contest – about how to justify restrictions on sovereign rights. For Abizadeh and the philosophical approach, it is this second version of the contest and the requirement of a justification meeting the demands of democratic legitimacy that fortifies a sovereign's right to unilaterally control its borders. The reason being, if there is to be legitimacy in sovereign decision-making, it needs be democratically accountable, and a proper construction of the relevant demos must be defined by a distinction between who counts in the process, and who does not. The sovereign's right to exclude non-members of the demos is, on this view, necessary in order to ground the relevant political community. This, in other words, is the argument from liberal democracy shoring up 'the starting point' of sovereign authority common to both the professional and socio-legal approaches.

Abizadeh's point of intervention, however, is that this is simply a mistaken view of liberal democratic theory. He explains,

> The initial question is whether there are any considerations intrinsic to democratic theory that create a presumption either in favour of unilateral domestic border control or in favour of joint control by citizens and foreigners. The answer depends on to whom democratic justification is owed.

[48] Arash Abizadeh, *Democratic Theory and Border Control: No Right to Unilaterally Control Your Own Borders*, 36 Political Theory 37, 40 (2008). Abizadeh uses the more familiar vocabulary of freedom and coercion.

[49] *Id.* at 43.

> Whether a closed border entry policy under the unilateral control of citizens is democratically legitimate cannot be known until we first know to whom the justification of a regime of control is owed. My thesis is that, according to democratic theory, *the democratic justification for a regime of border control is ultimately owed to both members and nonmembers*.[50]

Abizadeh's reasoning rests upon the idea that, in order for the sovereign's exercise of exclusionary rights to be legitimate, that exercise must be justified to all persons subject to the sovereign's social control, regardless of whether they are citizens or not. Sovereign coercion must be justified to all *persons* that are made its object, not only to citizens. The reason, in liberal democratic theory, is that justifications for restrictions on human freedom are owed to every person so restricted; liberal democratic theory does not, on its own terms, make any specifications about scope. Thus, whenever a sovereign limits the freedom of a person by coercive means, that coercion must be justified, including when it is a person beyond the border that is coerced. The result is a picture of what Abizadeh calls a borderless demos. A borderless demos is not a political community delimited by territorial borders, but rather one that takes shape by way of the scope of the sovereign's social control. If you're coerced, you're in the demos, and if you're in the demos, restrictions on your autonomy must be justified by way of your participation in the democratic process.

Even if this is right, might it still be a mistake to give equal weight to the views of these coerced non-members, at the expense of the territorially delimited political community? It is the latter, after all, which is the home of the nation, the people, the 'self' in the right of self-determination. Abizadeh's claim is that there is indeed a mistake here, but the mistake lies in thinking that we can speak coherently of a territorially conspicuous people or nation or other such 'self', the will of which is meant to guide the sovereign. The decision about where to set borders and how to enforce those borders can never be generated from within a theory of liberal democracy, but must instead presume the existence of a prepolitical national will. To the extent we lack faith in the pre-democratic, pre-political existence of such a 'really existing corporate entity', Abizadeh argues that the only meaningful way to conceptualise the 'borders' of legitimised sovereign authority is to define those borders by the justifications (consistent with personal freedom and equality) the sovereign delivers to those persons subject to the sovereign's social control. The truest political community that we can conceive is the community of

50 *Id.* at 44.

persons subjected to the sovereign's sovereign control. Abizadeh frames this view of the borderless demos along the following:

> I take it that democracy is better understood as an attempt to legitimise the collective and political exercise of power, on terms respecting the equality and freedom of those over whom power is exercised, via participatory political practices of expression, contestation, discursive justification, and decision-making. Democracy represents an attempt to replace relations of force, coercion, or domination with relations governed by fair negotiation, argumentation, and decision-making, and to legitimise the remaining uses of coercion by subjecting them to terms set via such democratic practices. So the answer to the question of why the *fact* that something happens to be the expressed 'will of the people' should provide a ground for legitimising the exercise of political power over them is this: Because (and insofar as) grounding political rule in this way serves the *freedom* and *equality* of those over whom power is exercised; it makes collective self-rule, on terms respecting the freedom and equality of the objects of power, possible. And *that* justification itself imposes constitutive normative constraints on the kinds of procedures and processes required to articulate a democratic will qua legitimising ground of power.

In her recent article 'Migration as Decolonization', Tendayi Achiume explicitly follows Abizadeh's account in an effort to reconceptualise migration as a legal concept. In this philosophical approach, it remains appropriate to begin with sovereignty as a starting point of analysis. Furthermore, sovereigns enjoy various rights and duties in the international legal order. However, these rights and duties do not flow from a magical metaphor about the sovereign as a rights-bearing individual in an international state of nature. In a more faithful view of democratic theory, sovereign rights and duties are sourced directly in the wills and interests of individuals. Which individuals? Following Abizadeh, Achiume suggests that we misread democratic theory if we take the answer to be exclusively citizens. The relevant political community is 'unbounded', and a sovereign's borders do violence to the *fact* of this unboundedness, this truly borderless political community. Neither Abizadeh nor Achiume suggest that this yields a case for an international legal rule of open borders. For Abizadeh, sovereign choices about admission and exclusion must be informed by the views of the all persons subject to sovereign coercion. For Achiume, however, the democratic body consists of those tied together due to an imperial past. As she explains, 'For any given First World country X, the nature of its de-colonial admission and inclusion obligations to any given Third World migrant from country Y will depend on the extent of exploitative benefit or advantage that country X derives from neocolonial empire, and the extent of subordination or disadvantage that a given migrant endures by virtue of being a national of country Y'.[51]

The takeaway is an effort to redefine basic international legal ideas like sovereignty and self-determination from an anticolonial view of distributive justice. Achiume argues that legal conceptions of migration must be articulated from a position of 'co-sovereignty', by which she means the rights of third world migrants to share in the democratic processes of first world states. To exclude these 'co-sovereigns' from deliberations about border controls is to violate their rights of 'self-determination'. Not, however, the rights of *peoples* to self-determination, but the rights of *persons*.[52] Like sovereignty, self-determination undergoes some level-shifting: it is not the state that is sovereign, nor the people that have a right to self-determination; or at least, it is not *only* these entities that enjoy such rights. Individual migrants are barred the right to self-determination when they are excluded from entry in a first world state with which they are interconnected through an imperial past and neoimperial present. They are so barred because the existence of exclusive border control robs them of a chance to exercise their co-sovereign rights in the democratic process. As Achiume concludes, imperialism remains unjust, decolonisation as the self-determination of *peoples* has run out of steam, and a better understanding of democratic theory illuminates the ethically desirable conclusion that international migration *is* a form of decolonisation – and perhaps the best game in town. What's more, our own legal conceptions of sovereignty and democracy require it. This is not an argument for the social control of sovereignty. It is an argument for redefining the scope of what sovereignty means at all.

In an effort to demonstrate whether or when the international rule of law might approach a tipping point, I began with a reorientation of the question. Rather than ask of international law's fidelity to a 'rule of law' standard, or ask of international law's 'reality', I argued that the phenomenology of our experience of a pending tipping point depends entirely on the contexts with which we choose to approach these questions. The preference in this chapter is to begin the analysis with the context of legal thought, which necessitates viewing law as a language system. In this context, one must next select a particular language to study, and relying upon previous work, I chose the context of *liberal* legal thought. In liberal legal thought, the interplay of three master theses shapes the structure of legal argument. These are the thesis of free competition, the thesis of social control, and the thesis of naturalising juridical

51 Achiume, *supra* note 25, at 1560.
52 *Id.* at 1566.

science. It is this third thesis in liberal legalism – the thesis of naturalising juridical science – that is crucial for assessing the international rule of law, which determines our experience of a point at which we have moved beyond law and into politics or morality. In this light, the rule of law depends on the phenomenological availability of legal arguments serving to naturalise what would otherwise be contradictions between the theses of free competition and social control. These contradictions jeopardise the rule of law because they jeopardise the very project of legality. When we encounter the structure of liberal legal thought, the task of naturalising juridical science is to provide the jurist an experience of particular legal concepts as just that – *legal*. If the presentation feels all too political, all too moral, we have hit a tipping point, perhaps gone past it. We know we are at a tipping point when the thesis of naturalising juridical science fails to naturalise, fails to legitimise, fails to justify. If the legal justification fails to persuade, fails to give you the experience of legal necessity, so goes the rule of law.

In the foregoing pages I surveyed three examples of the effort to naturalise the conflicts that constitute the legal concept of migration. In the context of liberal legal thought, we will expect the language of a legal concept to be shaped by the theses of free competition (i.e., the sovereign's right to exclude) and social control (i.e., the applicability of certain restrictions on the right to exclude). We will also expect the thesis of naturalising juridical science to mediate that relation, *legally*. This means that we hope for the availability of legal arguments intended to 'make sense' of that tension, resolving dissonance into consonance. If we hear the consonance, we hear the rule of law. So what did we hear? Dissonance or consonance?

In the register of the pragmatic professional, Martin began the argument with a rooting in the sovereign's right to exclude the world. This rooting, however, was less due to a metaphysical belief in the sanctity of sovereign equality than it was due to a belief in the reality of sovereign right. Sovereigns have the right to admit and reject economic migrants, not because it is just, but because it makes sense. What's more, sovereigns nevertheless allow migration, and take part in various treaty regimes that restrict their choices. Why? What justifies limits on the right to exclude foreigners? Sovereigns participate in these architectures of social control because it makes sense to do so. It works. If sovereigns are to realise their many goals, they have to work with the cards they have been dealt with. To do otherwise is simply impractical, and all 'modern' nations at least aspire towards a degree of rationality, of making 'it work'. Ultimately, the concept of international migration is legal and consistent with the rule of law because its argumentative claims are not arbitrary or so politically malleable as to make the concept into a farce. The concept is shaped by the practical reality of sovereign right, and the practical reality of real-world problems that *demand* the technical expertise of legal professionals, yielding objective legal conclusions. Pragmatic problem-solving resolves the tension between free competition and social control on an ad-hoc, case-by-case basis.

In the register of the socio-legal scholar, Lasswell and McDougal began the argument with the necessity of international interdependence. This necessity, however, had less to do with a natural view of a global community than it was due to a belief in the reality of a global social process in which both sovereigns and economic migrants make their way. True, sovereigns retain a right to admit and reject these migrants, but it is no longer a right that orients the system because it somehow 'makes sense to do so'. Rather, the socio-legal counsel for the field of international migration law is motivated by a concern for functionality and effectiveness. The questions that matter are about the international reality of migration, who is coming from where, in what numbers, when, and why. These are empirical questions, and international migration law must track the empirical data, both in terms of the world's most pressing needs, and in terms of the best answers social science can provide. To do otherwise is to relegate international law to an irrelevant morality out of touch with the real needs of international society. Ultimately, the concept of international migration is legal and consistent with the rule of law because its argumentative claims are not arbitrary and so ethically malleable as to make the concept into a politically impotent cluster of beliefs. The concept of international migration is shaped by the reality of rights – both those of sovereigns and individuals – but also and probably more importantly, by an empirical understanding of the global social system, with its various problems, needs, and interests. These problems, needs, and interests *demand* the application of social science expertise, yielding objective legal conclusions. A functionalist, socio-legal view of global social process in which international migration takes place resolves the tension between free competition and social control at the level of the international system.

In the register of the political theorist, Abizadeh and Achiume began the argument with a reorientation of the relation between sovereign exclusion and international migration. The reason for doing so is that we misread the scope of sovereign rights when we mistakenly conflate the relevant democratic body with a regime of territorial borders. In the pragmatic and socio-legal registers, sovereigns enjoy rights to exclude the world, and these sovereign rights are restricted due to beliefs about solving particular problems or beliefs about the international system. But these sovereign rights exist in the calculus as rights pertaining to what states can and cannot do with respect to territorially defined borders. The relevant considerations there were 'bounded' by particular communities engaged in a larger social system.

In the register of the political theorist, however, what must be seen is that this 'bounded' sense of community is neither explained nor justified by the grammar of liberal legal thought. That is, the grammar provides no clues as to the scope of a relevant community. All we can say for sure is that, in the terms of liberal democracy, the sovereign's exercise of the right to exclude, or make any decisions at all, must trace its authority back to the individuals who are subject to the sovereign's social control. What this means in the case of international migration law is that sovereign rights to exclude the world may or may not be justifiably restricted in the ways offered by the pragmatic professional and the socio-legal scholar. The political theorist is operating on a different level.

In this register, we don't go outside of the sovereign right to exclude in a search for social control, but rather open up the category of the sovereign and build social control from within. Thus, *every* person subject to the coercive control of the sovereign – most especially including the right to exclude foreigners at the border – has the right to participate in the democratically available means of governance, and the right to make the sovereign accountable. On this view of the unbounded demos, restrictions on the 'unilateral' right to exclude come from the people made subject to sovereign control; the restrictions come from within, not from without. Ultimately, the concept of international migration is legal and consistent with the rule of law because its argumentative claims are neither arbitrary nor subject to cosmopolitan beliefs in open borders or utopian ideals. The concept of international migration is shaped by the reality of rights – primarily the rights of individuals – but also a view of rights wielded by a far more heterogeneous and inclusive demos than the one typically limited to a set of arbitrary borders. Despite consistent misunderstandings, this view of rights is actually *demanded* by our reigning conception of sovereignty, which is itself the fundamental lynchpin of the international legal order. A view of international migration from the vantage of political theory resolves the tension between free competition and social control at the level of sovereign right.

In the context of liberal legal thought, is the field of international migration law consistent with the international rule of law? In three registers we hear that the answer is yes, but the forms of naturalising juridical science vary. In the first instance we are meant to hear the consonance because of the objectivity of pragmatic problem-solving, the objectivity of doing things when 'it works'. In the second instance we are meant to hear a consonance due to the objective quality of conforming our rules of migration to the expertise of social science. In the third instance, dissonance yields to consonance by shifting away from the contradiction between sovereign right and social control, and turning instead to what makes the exercise of sovereign right legitimate at all.

Is the international rule of law at a tipping point, at least here in the local context of migration, and in the larger context of liberal legalism? It depends. It depends on the extent to which a proffered justification has generated a sense of legal necessity, a sense that law is on the scene, that law is not only politics. It depends on the jurist's political commitments, and the extent to which they are caught up in any among many of liberalism's mystifications. It depends on whether out of the clang of dissonant notes you come away from the experience with a sense of comfort. Do you?

17

Russia

Boris N. Mamlyuk

Who *really* gets to decide sovereignty claims? Who assumes state sovereignty and who has the right and power to abrogate or limit the said sovereignty rights? Who is the collective "we" in Haskell's framing that is practicing *law-faith*: "*belief* in the rule of law as a neutral process of adjudication [of sovereignty questions]?" Is "we" just a form of "surreptitious conscription," a politically loaded "attempt to smuggle tribalism through customs?"[1]

Yet again, Russia offers a useful prism for refracting and reframing these questions into more discrete analytical themes, with relevance far beyond Russia. Analyzing Russian sovereignty forces us to acknowledge that the theoretical and methodological questions concerning sovereignty are far from settled. In fact, these questions remain central battlegrounds in ongoing geopolitical contests. This shows no sign of trend reversal. What, for instance, are the limits on Russian sovereignty under international law?

Surveying Russia's doctrinal approach to (and experience with) sovereignty allows us to split the compound doctrine of sovereignty into more discrete constituent streams, such as political, economic or legal sovereignty, and to study the interplay between these constituent forms and modalities within supposedly self-contained formal *lawgics*.[2] This exercise offers a deeper appreciation of the complex ways that state actors deploy sovereignty-based lines of argumentation to achieve both familiar and novel geopolitical objectives along legal and extra-legal lines.

To unpack Russian sovereignty under international law, Part I begins by fragmenting the doctrine of sovereignty into several non-exhaustive parts, sourcing from Anglo-American (aka "Western") international law currents.

[1] Christopher Hitchens, *Letters to a Young Contrarian* (2009), 103–104.

[2] See, e.g., Jean d'Aspremont, *International Law as a Belief System* (Cambridge 2017), 45–48 (describing what can be styled self-referentialism in international law).

Part II then analyzes sovereignty from a so-called Russian perspective. Armed with Western and Russian approaches to sovereignty, Part III considers potential lacunae and incongruity within (and across) both sets of doctrines and assesses shared, divergent, and implicit normative commitments that animate sovereignty discourse and sovereign anxiety among Western, Russian, and ostensibly neutral observers. The desired takeaway is a deeper understanding of the persistence, multi-dimensionality, and fragility of legal frameworks as default modes of argumentation about power relations between states, including self-proclaimed Great States[3] whose sovereignty is rarely questioned in foundational terms.

The key thesis this chapter seeks to explore is this: in contrast to Schmitt's aphorism that "Sovereign is he who decides on the exception,"[4] could it be that one is *truly* sovereign only when one finds ways to transcend one's "sovereign anxiety?" What does it mean to be truly sovereign, and can we answer this question in strictly formal legal terms? If not, what does this say about the continuing relevance and limitations of our formal *lawgics*?

17.1 SOVEREIGNTY AND SOVEREIGNTIES

Derived from the Vulgar Latin term *superanus* (leader or chief), the term "sovereignty" refers to a body's power to rule over someone or something. The power to rule evokes supreme authority and the broad freedom to take measures without the interference or coercion of another. In this sense, state sovereignty is the power to rule over persons within a given state, to the exclusion of other states.

Despite lying at the foundation of international law, sovereignty does not have a single broadly accepted definition within the discipline. Consider Brownlie's introduction to sovereignty:

> The sovereignty of states represents the basic constitutional doctrine of the law of nations[.] If international law exists [!], then the dynamics of state sovereignty can be expressed in terms of law. If states (and only states) are conceived of as sovereign, then in this respect at least they are equal, and their sovereignty is in a major aspect a relation to other states (and to organizations of states) defined by law.[5]

3 Gerry Simpson, *Great Powers and Outlaw States: Unequal Sovereigns in the International Legal Order* (2004).

4 Carl Schmitt, *Political Theology: Four Chapters on the Concept of Sovereignty* (George Schwab, trans., U. Chicago 1985).

5 Brownlie (2012), at 447.

To distinguish sovereignty (from, say, jurisdiction), Brownlie suggests we view sovereignty as "shorthand for legal personality of a certain kind, that of statehood."[6] In this sense, sovereignty is both a defining substantive right and standard for determination of statehood. If a State, then *ipso facto*, a sovereign state.

This binary conception of sovereignty (and of statehood, by extension) is open to multiple critiques. Defining sovereignty by reference to statehood, and vice versa, is circular.[7] Even in linguistic terms and common usage, sovereignty has so many different noun and adjectival forms that sovereignty is often implicitly framed by non-lawyers as a gradient, rather than some absolute quality: an actor may have more or less sovereignty, different degrees of sovereignty, and which varies with respect to certain persons, conduct, territories, and/or related legal rights.[8]

Of course, every international lawyer knows that sovereignty, like virtually every other doctrine, contains multitudes of definitions, interpretations, and postures.[9] Western treatises teach us that sovereignty has many subsidiary forms under international law, including concepts like shared sovereignty,[10] residual sovereignty,[11] and sovereign rights beyond territory. This is not a new trend. As gentle civilizers, European international lawyers have had centuries of experience expanding and exploiting the gray area between, say, formal sovereignty,[12] informal sovereignty, effective sovereignty,[13] national sovereignty, transferred sovereignty,[14] company sovereignty,[15] limited sovereignty, and so forth. Today, the gray area includes many other potentially antecedent

6 Brownlie (2012), at 204.

7 Antony Anghie, Imperialism, *Sovereignty and the Making of International Law* (2004) 100 ("Once constituted [...] the sovereign asserts supremacy by presenting itself as the means by which society operates and comes into being. It is through recognition doctrine that *sovereignty doctrine is reconstructed and presents itself as self-contained, coherent, comprehensive and all-encompassing*. A structure of power and decision making is implicit in the doctrine because the power to 'recognise' new states is vested in the states that are already sovereign.") (emphasis added).

8 Lauren Benton, *A Search for Sovereignty: Law and Geography in European Empires, 1400–1900* (Cambridge University Press 2010), 236–237 (describing various sovereignty classification continuums).

9 Koskenniemi (2005) 228–233.

10 Brownlie (2012), at 209–210.

11 Brownlie (2012), at 207.

12 Martti Koskenniemi, *The Gentle Civilizer of Nations: The Rise and Fall of International Law* (2002) 148–150.

13 Koskenniemi (2002) 144.

14 Koskenniemi (2002) 141.

15 Sovereignty claims through corporate forms operating pursuant to state-issued charters, licenses, and grants. Koskenniemi (2002) 144.

and derivative forms: individual sovereignty,[16] fiscal sovereignty, economic sovereignty, monetary sovereignty,[17] cyber sovereignty ... The list is only as exhaustive as our professional imagination.

In intellectual provenance, each of these is influenced and informed by liberal Enlightenment notions of popular sovereignty, dating back to Jean-Jacques Rousseau, John Locke and peers. The genesis block for each of these sovereignty forms is the conception of the sovereign individual.[18] It is the putatively sovereign individual who chooses to group with other putatively sovereign individuals to form sovereign tribes that then transform into sovereign nations and sovereign states in relation and opposition to other tribes, nations, and states.

Leading Anglo-American international law treatises rarely deconstruct the origins and transformation of sovereignty in the Western philosophical canon. While one encounters occasional coverage of exceptional or *sui generis* approaches to sovereignty (for example, Soviet limited sovereignty postures in the context of Brezhnev Doctrine;[19] special status sovereignty of Hong Kong, Macau, and so forth), the robust theoretical, comparative, and critical alternative accounts of sovereignty are often dismissed or relegated to the fringe as heterodox scholarly traditions.[20]

16 See e.g., James Dale Davidson, William Rees-Mogg, Mastering the Transition to the Information Age (1999).

17 Geoffrey Ingham, *The Nature of Money*, Economic Sociology: European Electronic Newsletter, ISSN 1871–3351, Max Planck Institute for the Study of Societies (MPIfG), Cologne, Vol. 5, Iss. 2, pp. 18–28 (at 20) (arguing that in the "most general terms, as Weber, contended, money is a weapon in the struggle for economic existence"); William N. Goetzmann, Money Changes Everything: How Finance Made Civilization Possible (2016).

18 Larry Siedentop, *Inventing the Individual: The Origins of Western Liberalism* (Harvard University Press 2014) (tracing the birth of individual moral and legal personality, and related doctrines like equality between individuals, to early Christian Church doctrine and pre-Renaissance theologians and canon lawyers working to advance church fiscal interests); Duncan Kennedy, "Form and Substance in Private Law Adjudication," *Harvard Law Review* 89 (1976) 1685, 1717 (observing that the "rhetoric of individualism so thoroughly dominates legal discourse at present that it is difficult even to identify a counter-ethic").

19 The Brezhnev Doctrine of "limited sovereignty" described the USSR's claimed right to intervene in the internal affairs of other socialist states. The doctrine was first articulated by Soviet Foreign Minister Gromyko at the June 27, 1968 session of the Supreme Soviet, where he asserted that the "Socialist commonwealth" would not tolerate the withdrawal of any of its constituent parts. The doctrine was used to rationalize Soviet military intervention in Warsaw Pact states like Czechoslovakia. See Julius Varsańyi, "Limited Sovereignty or Regional Integration for East-Central Europe?" *International & Comparative Law Quarterly* 23:3 (1974), 657–666; Leon Romaniecki, "Sources of the Brezhnev Doctrine of Limited Sovereignty and Intervention," *Israel Law Review* 5 (1970) 527–554.

20 See, e.g., Damrosch (2009), XV–XXX.

While orthodox narratives openly acknowledge the plurality of doctrinal meanings attached to sovereignty within the mainstream,[21] mapping inconsistent usage across legal sources allows orthodox narratives to frame sovereignty questions as discrete legal problems for which international law provides a menu of disciplinarily autarchic solutions.[22] In their search for coherence from supposedly axiomatic first principles, jurists like Brownlie and Crawford often reduce multidimensional and inherently fluid sovereignty doctrines to rigid positivistic dogmas; to the extent such dogmas admit pluralism, the pluralism is dogmatically bound and disciplinarily constrained. The key point is that the "most highly qualified publicists" must maintain rigid discipline over doctrinal pluralism to preserve the appearance of a coherent international legal order, thus cementing and advancing their role as literal sources of law within this order.[23] This is how we get dogmas like sovereignty as a legal form that is a "complement of state rights,"[24] akin to a bundle of property rights in, say, private law.[25]

Sovereignty is as sovereign states do.[26]

But whose interests do these frameworks serve? What normative commitments are hardwired into these supposedly settled doctrinal motherboards? We might consider this through the concepts of Dogma and Catma.

> Dogma: sovereignty is a basic legal doctrine; sovereignty is a positive legal right; sovereign right = the right to act "*as sovereign*, as of right and independently of the consent of any state;"[27] sovereignty is relational; sovereign states = equal states, before the law. Its commitments: individualism, uniformity, coherence, universality, law.
>
> Catma: sovereignty is inherently conflictual;[28] sovereignty is (legal) – culturally contingent; sovereignty is political; sovereignty is axiomatically unequal ('strong' sovereigns prefer their sovereign rights relative to 'weak' sovereigns). Its commitments: tribalism, relativism, agency, pluralism, politics.

21 Brownlie (2012), at 204.
22 d'Aspremont (2017).
23 Statute of the International Court of Justice, Article 38(1)(d).
24 Brownlie (2012), at 204.
25 Domestic legal analogies to international legal forms are themselves open to critique. See Akbar Rasulov, Why It Is Not a Good Idea to Think of Treaties as Contracts: A Critique of the Domestic Analogy, available on SSRN https://papers.ssrn.com/sol3/papers.cfm?abstract_id=2361753&download=yes
26 Subject to exceptions, limitations, terms and conditions. For the scope of those limitations, please see Brownlie (2012), et al.
27 Brownlie (2012), at 204.
28 Antony Anghie, Imperialism, Sovereignty and the Making of International Law (2004); Koskenniemi (2002) 148–150.

At this point, there is no need to prefer one view over the other, except to take note of the indeterminacy at play. Rather, we should appreciate how the dogma and catma are actually mutually reinforcing: both represent the basic grammar behind the complex vocabulary of sovereign rights-speak in international legal discourse. As a bookmark, we should also note how one's choice to present sovereignty as both a (1) legal right, and (2) Hohfeldian bundle of opposite and correlative rights, powers, privileges, liabilities, and so forth[29] may itself be viewed as a (thinly veiled) attempt to occlude or elide the expression of a normative commitment.

We will unpack these commitments after our voyage to Russia.

Before we pack our bags, though, we may benefit from two additional heuristics to describe sovereignty in more functional terms along our imagined continuum, something like *nominal sovereignty* as distinguished from *true sovereignty*.[30] *Nominal sovereignty* will be a placeholder for the dogmatic (Anglo-American/Continental) view of sovereignty as a positive legal right and chief attribute of statehood.[31] *True sovereignty* will refer to something like state practice with respect to sovereignty, or how states "experience the law of sovereignty" in their affairs.

Like the familiar legal realist split and interplay between "law on the books" and "law in action," *nominal sovereignty* reflects a textbook legal positivist conception of sovereignty-as-[legal]-right(s). *True sovereignty* reflects the realist expectation that one cannot understand sovereignty-as-right unless and until one understands how sovereignty-rights (e.g., sovereignty claims, arguments, and exceptions) are actually practiced and performed by state actors and agents.

Nominal sovereignty and *true sovereignty* are both relational: a given state's sovereignty is always defined by multiple actors within and outside that state who project differing views of where that state falls along our theoretical sovereignty spectrum. *True sovereignty* presupposes a claim of *nominal sovereignty* (at least from the perspective of the aspiring sovereign). But a nominally sovereign state may have little, or no, *true sovereignty*. In Hohfeldian terms,

29 Hohfeld, Wesley Newcomb, Fundamental Legal Conceptions as Applied in Judicial Reasoning: and Other Legal Essays 14 (Walter Wheeler Cook, ed., Yale 1920).

30 Jean Bodin, Six Books of the Commonwealth, Book VIII: Concerning Sovereignty (1576; M. J. Tooley, transl., 1955) ("The true sovereign remains always seized of his power.").

31 See, e.g., Manley O. Hudson, Separate Opinion, Lighthouses in Crete and Samos Case, PCIJ, Series A/B, No. 71, 1937, 127 (describing situations where a State may consent to so many limitations on its independence that only nominal sovereignty remains, "shorn of the last vestige of power," such that a "ghost of a hollow [theoretical] sovereignty cannot be permitted to obscure the realities of [the] situation.").

nominal sovereignty and *true sovereignty* may be jural opposites and/or correlatives, depending on the specific configuration of sovereignty claims at issue.

For example, Iraq in 2004 under military occupation and CPA government may claim to have *nominal sovereignty*, but most observers would likely concede that Iraq, at that time, had little or no *true sovereignty*. We can and should expand that query to the present for every state and non-state actor in the international community. These surveys remind us that sovereignty – standing alone – is not only an exceedingly difficult concept to describe, but it is virtually impossible to measure, both theoretically and empirically. This may help us develop more granular models for sovereignty, or to replace the abstraction with something more useful altogether, thereby finally shedding sovereignty's colonial yoke.[32]

Apart from serving as a methodological aide, the heuristic split between *nominal sovereignty* and *true sovereignty* is also useful in an immediate instrumentalist sense. Among other things, the realist move gives us methodological cover to analyze an allied and/or rival international legal tradition on its own terms, anticipating and minimizing the chance that our scholarship gets misread as partisanship. Applying critical realism and various comparative international law methodologies can help mitigate political risk in highly adversarial intellectual and policymaking settings. We might think of this as an intellectual sovereignty.

Piercing veils of sovereignty and questioning the sovereignty of Great States is, in a sense, tantamount to an attack on those sovereigns. The more anxious the sovereign, the higher the chance they may feel attacked. So in both immediate and more abstract psychological terms, methodological moves like this are palpably liberating: they may reduce false-affiliation and other types of anxiety, including sovereign anxiety. These postures may help states perform basic sovereignty self-audits: how sovereign are we, really?

Faith in the robustness of one's methodology serves as a type of "freedom of thought" insurance. This encourages intellectual risk-taking even if the hoped-for insurance benefits never materialize. The incantation of realist methodological traditions is also a faith signal to communities of peers and readers at large. Faith does not mean the unilateral assertion of scholarly good faith by the author, which is presumptuous and, in any event, only raises suspicion. On the contrary, the leap of faith here is merely the expectation of intellectual curiosity and, yes, sovereignty – the sincere desire by readers to pack their doctrinal bags for a research trip to Russia, only to leave those bags at the gate before getting on the plane.

32 Anghie (2004); Benton (2010).

17.2 суверенитет & суверенность

Like the word "constitution" (*конституция*), "sovereignty" (*суверенитет*) is a loaned word in Russian. Transplanted from Germanic (*souveränität*) and French (*souveraineté*) legal and linguistic traditions, the term usually refers to state sovereignty. As in other traditions, *суверенитет* is used in multiple other contexts. Related to *суверенитет* is the noun *суверенность*, describing the quality of sovereign existence across a broad range of domains, from political sovereignty to the subjective feeling of, say, spiritual sovereignty.

Like their Western parallels, Russian international law and jurisprudence treatises begin by acknowledging the plurality of legal and colloquial meanings attached to sovereignty, including *national sovereignty*, *sovereignty of law*, and related political theories from European philosophical traditions.[33] But focusing analysis on purely formal/doctrinal or even meta-discursive ways that sovereignty is used and taught in contemporary Russian international law settings is to miss the forest for the trees. To appreciate the evolution of sovereignty in Russian international law and the persistence of sovereign anxiety among Russian international lawyers, we must refresh our recollection of Soviet approaches to sovereignty.

As a self-professed revolutionary state of a qualitatively new type (socialist state), the Soviet Union embodies both the emancipatory potential of each of the aforementioned conceptions of sovereignty, as well as their individual and collective limitations. The literature on Soviet sovereignty doctrines, theories, and claims is vast,[34] so our introduction will be necessarily brief although sufficiently deep to identify at least several fundamental tensions.

The leading Soviet legal theorist on sovereignty is Josef Davidovich Levin (1901–1984), the author of the definitive treatise, *Sovereignty* (published in 1948 and republished in 2003).[35] According to Levin, sovereignty cannot be understood in purely legal terms: "to explain law, we must exit law's bounds."[36] In

[33] *Теория государства и права* (Мартышина О.В., ред. 2007) [Theory of State and Law (Martishina, O. V., ed., 2007)].

[34] One of the best English-language introductions to Soviet conceptions of state, international law and sovereignty is a 1949 article in the *American Journal of International Law* by Mintauts Chakste, a former justice of the Supreme Court of Latvia. Mintauts Chakste, "Soviet Concepts of the State, International Law and Sovereignty," 43 *AJIL* 21 (1949).

[35] Иосиф Давыдович Левин, Суверенитет (1948; 2003) [Josef Davidovich Levin, *Sovereignty* (1948; 2003)], available at https://kartaslov.ru/книги/Левин_И_Д_Суверенитет [page references are to eBook edition]. In addition to his reissued monograph, Levin's corpus of scholarly work remains foundational to contemporary Russian theories of state and sovereignty. See e.g., Теория государства и права (Мартышина О.В., ред. 2007) [Theory of State and Law (Martishina, O.V., ed., 2007)].

[36] Levin, *Sovereignty* at 35.

Soviet Marxian terms, the only way to understand sovereignty is to view it through the prism of class struggle and the demands of class rule.[37] "Class rule," according to Levin, "is the 'main norm' [...] that determines the substance of law, the process of state law-making, state structure, and so-called legal constraints [on, between, and within] states."[38] Dominant class interests and expressions of "class will" constrain both law, states, and governments. Class interests determine and structure the function and scope of these constraints.[39]

"Class power is the highest law."[40] The sovereign is the dominant social class. "Class," per Levin, is that "social force that holds the state within its hands as a weapon of domination."[41] The nature of sovereignty, according to Levin, "stems from a conception of the state as a weapon of class rule, which arose under exploitative social conditions to rein in the exploited majority so as to serve the interests of the exploiting minority."[42] States, governments, and their subsidiary organs are the juridical expressions and forms of class rule; class rule and class interests determine the nature and scope of separation of powers, and respective legal, institutional, and normative hierarchies.[43]

Levin was very conscious that this class conception of sovereignty presents obvious logical conundrums: what does it mean to "hold a state" within one's hands? How does a class transmute its sovereignty to the state? How does a class exercise constraints on a state? To resolve these apparent ambiguities and paradoxes, Levin emphasizes the need for "meta-juridical" socio-political approaches to sovereignty, a dynamic dialectical conception of the interplay between sovereignty's form and substance.

To answer *who* is actually sovereign and *how* said sovereigns exercise their sovereign power, Levin offers the following heuristics: the bearer of substantive socio-political sovereignty (*political sovereignty*) is the dominant class within a given state, whereas the bearer of sovereignty in terms of legal form (*juridical sovereignty*) is the combination of state (administrative) organs and weapons of state "as the organizations of the dictatorship of a given class."[44] As the dominant economic power in society, the dominant class controls the form and substance of its own sovereignty; the dominant class determines the

37 *Id.*
38 *Id.*
39 *Id.*
40 *Id.* at 36.
41
42 *Id.* at 39.
43 *Id.* at 39.
44 *Id.* at 40.

desired form and substance of the law. "The power of the ruling class," Levin urges, "cannot be fully defined by legal forms. In this sense the sovereign can truly be said to be above the law."[45]

Political sovereignty is objectively supreme to juridical/legal sovereignty. "Political sovereignty" writes Levin, "is the highest power of the dominant class within a state, acting as the foundation of law, and in this sense, standing *above* the law, given that it is the source of all law."[46] However, Levin shortly contradicts himself when describing the four requisite characteristics of sovereignty, in formal legal terms.[47] In terms of the content of sovereignty, this means that the ruling class is free from outside interference with its goals and interests, and in terms of the legal form, it expresses the absence of external legal restrictions on such freedom, *aside from norms of international law generally binding on all states*.[48] We will unpack the analytical tensions here shortly, but only after noting the anxiety that informs Levin's theory: "Our split between *political sovereignty* and *legal sovereignty* helps us realize genuine *popular sovereignty*, whereas in bourgeois theories this split is only intended to limit the rights of the people."[49]

Levin's emphasis on "genuine" sovereignty is highly revealing, echoing the earlier heuristic split between *nominal sovereignty* and *true sovereignty*. This split between something like authentic or effective sovereignty versus merely asserted or formal sovereignty underlines the centrality of the arbiter, circling back to our first question: who *really* gets to decide sovereignty claims? Like Haskell's "we," please also note Levin's "us." The doctrinal/theoretical split between *political sovereignty* and *legal sovereignty* "helps *us* realize genuine [sovereignty]" – but is "us" the Soviet Union, Soviet international lawyers, Soviet apparatchiks, or is it the working class on whose behalf Levin purports to speak? The key point here is that it would be a fatal mistake to conflate these

45 *Id.* at 43.

46 *Id.* (emphasis in original)

47 They include: (1) unitary power (2) monopoly or concentration of coercive power (3) unlimited state power (4) independence from external control. Levin (1948), 49. There is a deliberate ambiguity and tension here. After listing the third characteristic, Levin writes: "These three characteristics represent state sovereignty." After introducing the fourth characteristic, quoted above, Levin writes: "There is no sovereignty without the union of all of these characteristics[.]" The likely intended effect is to leave the reader unsure of whether international law is normatively supreme to a specific, say, sovereignty claim by a socialist revolutionary state, and if so, which principles of international law are thus normatively supreme.

48 *Id.* at 49; Brownlie (2012), at 204 (a sovereign state is one that can act as sovereign, "as of right and independently of the consent of any state.").

49 *Id.*; see also Mintauts Chakste, *Soviet Concepts of the State, International Law and Sovereignty* 43:1 *AJIL* (1949), 21–36 (emphasis added).

discrete actors into some corporeal "Soviet" whole, as though the interests of these actors were somehow aligned.[50]

Crucially, we should also note how the Soviets describe law as a governance requisite. Per Levin, governance necessitates promulgation of plural *legal sovereignty* forms (legal institutions) to effectuate lawful and orderly functioning of the state and state machine.[51] We will analyze why Levin deems plural sovereignty forms essential here and how they are instrumentalized in Russian and Western legal discourse and practice in Part III. For now, however, we must unpack another fascinating nuance of Soviet sovereignty theory: its explicitly propertarian roots.

According to Levin, the "real foundation of sovereignty is property."[52] Sovereignty is not equivalent to property, but property systems constitute the real and material basis of state sovereignty insofar as property defines the place of the ruling class in production and property serves as the economic and political source of the power of the governing class.[53] Per Levin, "Sovereignty depends on property, and simultaneously, political sovereignty and legal sovereignty is used by the governing class to define and defend existing systems of property."[54]

In this propertarian sense, sovereignty is meant to reflect the "dialectic nature of social life, the internal contradictions, the contest between the old and new."[55] Levin does not develop this property theory further, but the core thesis is that "the class which possesses the tools and means of production" holds economic power, which serves as the basis for political power, and ultimately, legal power.[56] This propertarian sensibility reappears in Levin's core doctrinal definition of sovereignty: "Sovereignty is unconditional state power over *its* territory and its independence from other states."[57]

50 Levin's repeated need to assert commonality of interests between urban and rural workers, "led by the Soviet proletarian class," underscores this point. Levin (1948), 42.

51 *Id.* Levin emphasizes that "lawfulness" is determined from the perspective of the governing class.

52 Levin (1948), 41.

53 Mintauts Chakste, "Soviet Concepts of the State, International Law and Sovereignty," *American Journal of International Law* 43:1 (1949), 21–36(emphasis added).

54 Levin (1948), 42.

55 *Id.*

56 *Id.*; for background on Soviet property law theory, including the evolution of Pashukanis' commodity-form theory of law in relation to then-contemporary Soviet theories of state and law, please see, Boris N. Mamlyuk, "Early Soviet Property Law in Comparison with Western Legal Traditions," in *Research Handbook on Political Economy and Law*, eds. Ugo Mattei, John Haskell (2015), 462–465.

57 Levin (1948), 48 (emphasis added).

Were Soviet workers – as a class – really property owners who steered the fate of the Soviet state?[58] If not, to what extent did Soviet [state] sovereignty really represent the interests of the Soviet working class(es)? Levin answers this indirectly in a historical note:

> In 1917, workers and peasants of Russia, under the leadership of the working class and its party [Bolsheviks] juxtaposed *their* right to sovereignty against the existing order and asserted their sovereignty in the form of the Soviet state.[59]

The most important part of this passage – the '*their*' (*свое*) emphasized by Levin – is extremely difficult to translate, but it is critical because it contains a glaring, and likely deliberate, ambiguity. Grammatically, there are several distinct subjects in this passage who we know may have the "right to sovereignty" per Levin: (1) workers (2) peasants (3) the working class, and (4) the party of the workers. The verb "juxtaposed" (*противопоставили*) is conjugated to denote the union of the four subjects, an intent that is confirmed by the conjugation of the second active verb "asserted" (*утвердили*). In the Russian original, it is clear that the juxtaposition and assertion are done collectively, but the sentence structure is unusually awkward: Levin's emphasis on *свое* potentially signals a desire to have readers labor through the syntax and meaning, to analyze precisely *whose* sovereignty rights are being asserted (as between the four groups of potential sovereigns and/or mutually) and *how* these rights are merged in the process of claim construction/assertion, just as we are doing here.

But the awkward way in which Levin joins workers, peasants, the working class, and the Bolshevik party distracts from yet another potentially deliberate rhetorical sleight of hand, one with historic implications: the casually hegemonic way in which *Russians* (specifically, *Russian* workers and *Russian* peasants) are described as the actual sovereign rights bearers who went on to assert and constitute the Soviet state.

This is not cherry-picked analysis, designed to distort and malign acts of genuine solidarity between Russian and other Soviet tribes in their emancipatory struggle against Tsarist oppression. We are merely reading Levin at his word – in Russian – in order to understand and reconstruct Soviet sovereignty politics from the definitive Soviet treatise on sovereignty. As a vocal critic of

[58] Mamlyuk (2015) (describing how Soviet property law reified property relations, and how formal Soviet property regimes contributed to the collapse of the Soviet Union and the subsequent disenfranchisement of Soviet workers).

[59] Levin (1948), 47 ("В 1917 г. рабочие и крестьяне России под руководством рабочего класса и его партии противопоставили *свое* право на суверенитет существующему порядку и утвердили свой суверенитет в форме советского государства.") (emphasis in original).

"bourgeois imperialism," Levin should have been mindful of the way that latent chauvinism manifests in doctrinal postures.[60] Therefore, it is reasonable to infer an intent to conflate Russian and Soviet interests from textual passages in an authoritative treatise whose main goal was to dissect and articulate said interests in direct contraposition to the "bourgeois imperialist" mainstream of the day.[61] In other words, passages like the one above *are* sovereignty claims. Levin is both claimant and arbiter, simultaneously asserting and affirming the supposed equivalence of *Russian* popular/proletarian sovereignty with *Soviet* sovereignty. "Georgian, Ukrainian, 'Transcaucasian' ... workers need not worry, the Great *Russians* are boldly juxtaposing and asserting Soviet sovereignty, on behalf of the proletariat of all 'nationalities'," Levin assures his readers, "[S]o numerous are they that they need not even be listed. Unlike the *Russian* workers and peasants, of course, ... the bearers of sovereignty."

This is a key passage in Levin's *Sovereignty*, gives a rare but revealing glimpse into the subtle way that *Russian* nationalism, imperialism, and moral/cultural leadership (read: superiority) crept into and colonized the supposedly a-national *Soviet* "historical mission of creating a new social order, a new type of state," and, in so doing, invested the "principle of

60 *Id.* at 53.

61 Russia features only occasionally in Levin's *Sovereignty*, but when it does, Russophilia and Russocentrism are striking. For example, in a long excerpt from Lenin's exchange with Rosa Luxemburg, Lenin (and Levin, via direct quotation) points out how, "not only small states, but even [Great] Russia, for instance, wholly depend economically from the might of imperialist financial capital of "wealthy" bourgeois states. Not only miniature Balkan states, but even [Great] America in the nineteenth century was, economically, a colony of Europe, as Marx points out in Kapital." The suggestion here is that Marxists (seeped in critiques of nationalism and imperialism [Labor > Nations]) had the intellectual means to recognize their own latent nationalism/chauvinism; they possessed the critical toolkit for understanding how even rhetorical preference for, say, Russia as a Great State exacerbated the "nationalities questions," because they *personally* developed and deployed those lines of critique against the *other* imperialists. Levin's inability to see the latent imperialist in the mirror is traceable directly to Lenin. Compare V. Lenin, *The Right of Nations to Self-Determination* (1914) (quoting Engels letter to Marx on May 23, 1851, "The role of the Poles in history was one of 'bold (hotheaded) foolishness'. 'And one cannot point to a single instance in which Poland has successfully represented progress, even in relation to Russia, or done anything at all of historical importance.' Russia contains more of civilisation, education, industry and the bourgeoisie than 'the Poland of the indolent gentry' ... all these thoughts [opines Lenin] show[] the deep insight of genius") with id. ("the working class should be the last to make a fetish of the national question, since the development of capitalism does, not necessarily awaken all nations to independent life. But to brush aside the mass national movements once they have started, and to refuse to support what is progressive in them means, in effect, pandering to nationalistic prejudices, that is, recognising 'one's own nation' as a model nation (or, we would add, one possessing the exclusive privilege of forming a state).").

sovereignty with new substance."[62] Seen in this light, is the "new substance" really new or is the affirmation of the "principle of sovereignty" (bounded by "norms of international law generally binding on all states") just another mechanism for effectuating preexisting Russian imperial goals? Please note how Levin's propertarian theory of sovereignty and statehood is also smuggling [Russian] tribalism through [indigenous] customs; by asserting *Russian* workers' sovereignty claims as the basis for Soviet sovereignty, and depicting sovereignty as unconditional state power over its territory, Russia appropriates non-Russian Soviet territory as "*its* territory." The absence of Soviet Others in Levin's *Sovereignty* further engorges the presence of the Russian self.

One of the best ways to appreciate Russian "sovereign anxiety" – that is, Russia's ambivalent, inconsistent, and fraught lived experience with sovereignty claims – is to analyze Soviet sovereignty practice with respect to both constituent Soviet republics and the late-Soviet doctrinal innovation of limited sovereignty with respect to non-Soviet socialist states.

The 1924 Soviet constitution formally guaranteed the sovereignty of Soviet Republics.[63] The republics did not lose sovereignty when joining the union and retained the right to secede.[64] Indeed, upon the dissolution of the USSR, the Republics did so pursuant to these guarantees. However, much as with the formation of the United States of America, the republics did lose the right to conduct their own foreign relations, execute treaties and to control their armed forces.[65] Article 3 of the constitution granted to the republics residual foreign policy powers. Like the Tenth Amendment of the US Constitution, the provision retained to the states those powers not delegated to the central government.[66]

Prior to 1923, Ukraine, Belarus, Georgia, Armenia, and Azerbaijan had each negotiated treaties independently.[67] From 1924, these rights were severely

62 Levin (1948), 47; Lenin (1914) (quoting Marx: "by the negation of nationalities [it is possible], quite unconsciously, to understand their absorption by the model [in this case, French] nation.").

63 The constitution was drafted in December 1922 and officially came into force on July 6, 1923, though the Soviet Union was established pursuant to the constitution on January 1, 1923. The constitution consisted of two parts, the (1) Declaration on the Formation of the USSR (declaring to the world the formation of the Soviet state); and, (2) Convention on the Formation of the USSR (containing the substantive provisions for unification).

64 Декларация об Образовании Союза Советских Социалистических Республик – Договор об образовании СССР (Конституция СССР 1924) [Declaration on Formation of the USSR – Convention on Formation of the USSR (1924 USSR Constitution), adopted July 6, 1923], Ch. 2, art. 4, *available at* www.hist.msu.ru/ER/Etext/cnst1924.htm#i (last accessed July 7, 2008) [*hereafter* 1924 USSR Constitution].

65 1924 USSR Constitution, Ch. 8, arts. 51–52.

66 *See* US Const., Amend. 10.

67 *See* Margolis, *supra*, at 106.

curtailed, as the foreign relations powers were centralized into the hands of one All-Soviet Commissariat of Foreign Affairs.[68] Most importantly, aside from centralizing foreign relations powers, the constitution centralized the economic means of production of the constituent states. In fact, foreign relations and foreign trade were given the same primacy. In addition, the constitution required Union-wide management and planning of the economy and budget. To implement these policies, the constitution also mandated the development of general legal and legislative principles (an all-Union justice system [общесоюзная юстиция]).

Pashukanis wrote at some length on the formation of the Soviet federal state and on federalism more broadly. After reviewing the federalist of confederate forms of government of the US, Switzerland, Austria, Mexico, and several other states, he began his analysis with the observation that only in a non-capitalist regime was true "brotherly" federalism possible.[69] This is one of many platitudes that began to appear in his later work. Nonetheless, his analysis of Soviet federalism is instructive. He stresses that during the Revolution, the Bolsheviks opposed federalism, instead advocating a centralized unitary state with maximum protection of national minorities.[70] From the outset, however, the "national question" presented a formidable obstacle to unification, as national minorities demanded the right to self-determination and economic sovereignty. The solution was a compromise position whereby regions would retain their autonomy while ceding economic and foreign policy powers.[71] The right of secession had special significance for Pashukanis because it symbolized the freedom with which each state had joined the union.[72] In the event of secession, each republic would return to being a sovereign state under international law. Pashukanis also distinguished the Soviet federation from the "bourgeois federations" on the basis that "bourgeois states retained the right to send military excursions against member states" whereas such right was absent from the Soviet constitution.[73] Prophetically, Pashukanis wrote, "because [the Soviet constitution does not contain the right of military force against members] it is far stronger and indestructible than any capitalist federation."[74]

68 1924 USSR Constitution, Ch. 8, arts. 51–52.

69 е. пашуканис, очерки по международному праву 91 (Гос. Изд. Сов. Законодательство, 1935) [E. Pashukanis, Essays on International Law 91 (State Publ. Soviet Jurisprudence, 1935)].

70 *Id.* at 93.

71 *Id.*

72 *Id.* at 94.

73 *Id.* at 94.

74 *Id.* This incorrect statement is one of many in Pashukanis' *Essays*, and has little to do with the political pressures on him at the time; the sloppy analysis does indicate a sharp departure from his earlier methodical work.

Foreign authors analyzing Soviet federalism rightly focused on the convergence and centralization of power. Hazard, in his comparative outline of Soviet and American legal systems, pointed out that the tenor of Soviet rhetoric on questions of federalism was highly suspicious, in fact, antagonistic, toward centrifugal forces.[75] Margolis, analyzing Soviet federalism, observed that the guarantees of the constitution resembled the contract theories of Althusius, Locke, and Rousseau.[76] Margolis, citing Schuman, wrote that "Soviet federalism was halfway between the U.S. and the British Commonwealth."[77] Indeed, the only remarkable feature of Soviet federalism was the successful way it temporarily defused the "national question" with the appeal to Marxist proletarian brotherhood, force, and the grant of far-reaching autonomous powers over internal matters.[78]

In 1933, an article on Soviet federalism was published in the journal *Sovetskoe Gosudarstvo*,[79] where the authors restated Lenin's expansive view of Soviet federalism and the goal of further expansion as being in the interests of all workers and the only way to accomplish the amalgamation of nations.[80] This principle was reflected in the formal recognition of sovereign national rights with consolidated political and economic rights, exactly as formulated in the 1922 Soviet constitution.[81] Soviet federalism, it was stressed, guaranteed complete autonomy and was unique among the world's federal states. The authors took special note that the uniqueness of the Soviet form was even recognized as such by a German jurist, K. M. Hellingrath.[82] The authors in turn roundly criticized their Soviet colleague M. O. Reichel, the editor of a volume on Soviet federalism for comparing the form of Soviet federalism with that of federal bourgeois states.[83] What is most notable about the scholarship on Soviet federalism was the extent to which the authors stressed that all centralization proposals (including the 1929 amendment to the constitution to

75 John N. Hazard , *Soviet Law and Western Legal Systems: a Manual for Comparison* 12–13, 14 (Parker School, 1970).

76 *See* Margolis, *supra*, at 102–110, 103.

77 *See* Margolis, *supra*, at 110 (*citing* SCHUMAN, SOVIET POLITICS AT HOME AND ABROAD).

78 The literature on Soviet federalism is vast and covers all periods of the Soviet state. For further reading on Soviet federalism, *see* Philip G. Roeder, "*Soviet Federalism and Ethnic Mobilization,*" 43:2 *World Politics* 192 (1991); Grey Hodnett, "*The Debate Over Soviet Federalism,*" 18:4 *Soviet Studies* 458 (1967).

79 А. Алымов, С. Студеникин, *Советский Федерализм и Демократический Централизм*, 1–2 советское государство 13 (1933) [A. Alymov, S. Studenikin, *Soviet Federalism and Democratic Centralism*, 1–2 SOVETSKOE GOSUDARSTVO 13 (1933)].

80 *Id.* at 13.

81 *Id.* at 15.

82 Id. at 16 (*citing* K.M. HELLINGRATH, DER SOWIETSTAAT 108 (1930)).

83 *Id.*

create a unified central land ministry) were instigated at the request of the federal republics and the minority populations themselves.[84] This proposition is dubious but needs further scholarly attention to disprove.

The Declaration of the Formation of the USSR provided the right of joinder into the union: "accession into the Union is open to all socialist soviet republics now existing, as well as all potential future socialist soviet republics."[85] This invitation was genuinely believed to be the vehicle by which future states from around the world would go on to join the communist enterprise. Soviet efforts to lead regional integration have been discussed elsewhere (especially in the post-WWII period)[86] and are outside of the scope of this chapter, although the legal aspects of the integration during the interwar period have been understudied.

The most striking aspect of Soviet regional integration policy was the efforts to consolidate Central Asian republics into political units across ethnic lines. The first such effort was the formation of the Transcaucasian SSR (1917–1936), composed of Armenia, Azerbaijan, and Georgia and acting as one of the first constituent republics of the Soviet Union. The key question for Soviet theorists was whether the Transcaucasian SSR could successfully transcend long-standing historical, economic, and tribal divisions. Levin, writing in 1934, argued that the experience of the first decade of the Soviet Union answered this question in the affirmative.[87] His evidence for the "blending of nations" was anecdotal – that industrialization required workers from disparate tribes to work together side by side, destroying ancestral pre-capitalist allegiances.[88] That destruction of tribal and ethnic identity should be seen as a sign of progress may be shocking to current observers, but to Soviet theorists, this represented an objective step forward.[89] As with all previously discussed legal forms, the national (ethnic) state was seen as an *interim measure* designed to

84 *Id.* at 18.

85 Декларация об Образовании Союза Советских Социалистических Республик [Declaration on Formation of the USSR (adopted July 6, 1923), *available at* www.hist.msu.ru/ER/Etext/cnst1924.htm#i (last accessed July 7, 2008).

86 *See, e.g.*, Michael Cismarescu, "*Rumania and the Legal Integration within COMECON*," 2 *Rev. Socialist L.* 103 (1976) (discussion diffusion and reception of Soviet law into Eastern bloc countries in the post-WWII period as well as resistance to "imitation" of Soviet law among the Romanian leadership).

87 И. Левин, *Средняя Азия—Пример консолидации наций в условиях диктатуры пролитариятa*, 6 советское государство 74 (1934) [I. Levin, *Central Asia—Example of Consolidation of Nations Under Conditions of the Proletarian Dictatorship*, 6 Sovetskoe Gosudarstvo 74 (1934)].

88 *Id.* at 74–75.

89 *Id.* at 75 (portraying ethnic consolidation as a "historically and objectively determinate process").

aid this progress toward greater assimilation and cultural, economic, and political consolidation within the Soviet Union.[90] Soviet federalism was claimed to support the national form with a view toward its eventual elimination.

Levin's evidence for consolidation between other Central Asian states was spurious.[91] Writing about the unification of Turkmenistan and Uzbekistan, Levin pointed out that before the Bolshevik revolution, they were divided into competing Khanates and principalities, whereas immediately following the revolution, nascent proletarian movements realized the wisdom of joining forces with the proletarian Soviet state.[92] Levin boasted that the Bolsheviks had "found the key to the deepest desires of the masses," pointing out that whereas it took a "long series of wars to unite Poland, it took merely several months of discussions to unite Turkmenistan and Uzbekistan."[93] Of course, the reality was quite different. The policy on the national question formulated by Stalin in 1924 did end up creating states along ethnic lines. When Turkmenistan and Uzbekistan joined the Soviet Union in 1925 as autonomous republics, this was the culmination of intense bureaucratization and infiltration of the internal political machines of the two states. Reading Levin, one gets a sense that the narrative begins to resemble a Soviet progress story: "Whereas before, Turkmenistan was dominated by patriarchal blood lines, Russian [imperial] power represented a mechanical imposition of a serfdom bureaucracy on top of the feudal organization that destroyed these bonds."[94] But Imperial Russia maintained the states as ethnic enclaves.

"With time," writes Levin, "the dictatorship of the proletariat overthrew the Russian empire, freeing the masses from dependence, exploitation and plunder."[95] The land reforms of 1921–1922 abolished the colonial land regime. With further Sovietization and industrialization, the Central Asian states were able to free themselves economically, "raising the levels of their cultural and socio-political involvement."[96] Tellingly, Levin denies that the Soviet interest in Central Asia had geopolitical or strategic motives, pointing to the centralization of the economic planning bureaus by 1930 as evidence for the interest in the union from the national minorities themselves.[97] This claim seems

90 *Id.* at 76.

91 Иосиф Давыдович Левин (1901–1984) should not be confused with Давид Бенционович Левин (1903–1990), no known relation, another Soviet international lawyer.

92 *Id.* at 77.

93 *Id.*

94 *Id.* at 77.

95 *Id.* at 77.

96 *Id.* at 77.

97 *Id.* at 80.

suspicious (at least in the case of Uzbekistan), as by Levin's own admission, the percentage of workers during the period 1923–1933 who were of indigenous descent was less than half.[98] Future research exploring national resistance movements during the 1920s and 1930s in Central Asia will likely further expose the reality of Soviet quasi-imperialism during this period. Until then, Levin's narrative can be accepted as typifying Soviet international law scholarship on regional integration throughout the interwar period.

In essence, the early Soviet position on the territory of the former Tsarist Empire was not only ambivalent, but outright imperialistic. The cession of vast tracts of territory pursuant to the Brest-Litovsk treaty did not arouse nationalist or imperial sentiments in the early Soviet legal literature. With respect to far flung regions, the Soviet Union argued for strict conceptions of territoriality, except in cases where it was beneficial to argue the opposite position. Thus, for example, the USSR advocated for a new interpretation of territorial accession, arguing that monitoring of territories from the air was a sufficient exercise of control over new territories, particularly those in the Arctic.[99] In this regard, Soviet theory and practice resembled exactly that "imperialist international law" that Soviet jurists criticized and defined themselves in opposition to.

The Russian President is tasked with "defending [Russian] sovereignty" (Охрана суверенитета).[100] The President acts as the guarantor of Russian sovereignty. Defense of sovereignty is also a core part of the Russian presidential oath.[101] "The unlimited nature of sovereignty in terms of political content does not mean that it is bound by moral and political norms, but only their priority over the legal form of sovereignty."[102]

98 *Id.* at 82 (there were 6,017 industrial "workers" in 1923, rising to 36,916 in 1933).

99 Letter from John N. Hazard, p. 21(3) (January 13, 1935) ("[. . .] Based on the International Convention Regulating Transport by Air, [. . .] the Soviet Government has added a new idea to international law when they advocate the use of the airplane to periodically visit and control islands in the polar area discovered and claimed by the Soviet Union. Heretofore discovery was not enough to establish a claim to land, there must also be occupation and control. Coupled with the idea that the polar area belongs to the littoral states, the use of airplanes to control practically makes of the major part of the polar area a Soviet Territory.").

100 Охрана суверенитета

101 Art. 82, Constitution of the Russian Federation; see also Присяга Президента России, http://kremlin.ru/structure/president ("Клянусь при осуществлении полномочий Президента Российской Федерации уважать и охранять права и свободы человека и гражданина, соблюдать и защищать Конституцию Российской Федерации, защищать суверенитет и независимость, безопасность и целостность государства, верно служить народу.")

102 И. Д. Левин, Суверенитет (1948; 2003); *Printsip suvereniteta v sovetskom i meidunarodnom prave* (Moscow, 1947)

17.3 SOVEREIGN ANXIETY BETWEEN SOVEREIGNTY AND суверенность

Cloaked in the doctrinal patchwork of ever-evolving legal and political sovereignty rights and obligations (derivative/corollary rights and obligations), the wannabe sovereign cannot help but feel anxious about their real and imagined – nominal and true – sovereignty profile. Michael Dillon describes this anxiety as an "impossible condition":

> [S]overeigns cannot in fact do, or be, what the modern conception of sovereignty demands that they must do and be. Sovereign decision making can, therefore, only ever simulate and dissimulate what it can never actualise."[103]

As we have seen in our comparative analysis of sovereignty in two nominally opposed legal traditions (Western v. Soviet/Russian), this anxiety manifests in several non-exclusive ways: (1) as conscious awareness of doctrinal incongruity and incoherence, (2) the need to acknowledge the circularity, multiplicity, and incompleteness of formal legal definitions of sovereignty while (3) simultaneously backstopping the incoherence with fiat assertions (express or implied) that indeterminacy is a feature in the system, not a bug.

For Dillon, the way sovereigns manage their sovereign anxiety is by engaging in elaborate forms of political theater, placing increasing emphasis on the performative effects of sovereignty versus strictly legal and/or martial and/or material economic assertions of sovereignty rights.[104] Because sovereigns' rights are always counterbalanced by competing sovereigns' rights, sovereign states never have as much effective sovereign power as they think they do, or may want to possess.[105]

Force ultimately decides outcomes between equal [sovereignty] rights, but total war is a hellish and unpredictable way to resolve sovereignty disputes. Furthermore, polities are rightfully war-averse and sovereigns who treat their people as cannon fodder may face revolt from more popular sovereigns. International law allows sovereigns to wage their wars via ostensibly nonviolent means, appeasing polities, affirming sovereign prerogatives, while still letting sovereigns keep their trigger fingers on their various nuclear options. "That is why spectacle and show [...] is essential to the exercise of sovereign power relations."[106] The spectacle and show of international law can

[103] Michael Dillon, "Sovereign Anxiety and Baroque Politics," in *Politics of Anxiety* (Emmy Eklundh, Andreja Zevnik, Emmanuel-Pierre Guittet, eds., 2017), 193.
[104] Dillon, 193.
[105] Dillon, 193.
[106] Dillon, 193.

help reduce sovereign anxiety, thereby lowering the existential risks of war. Sovereigns are incentivized to play their roles in good faith because rival disenchanted anxious sovereigntists are always in the wings of the world's Ford's Theater.[107]

With this stage set, how does the management of sovereign anxiety play out in international law? Who are the managers?

One of the best contemporary accounts of the diffused, fragmented, and compound nature of sovereignty – and especially sovereignty spectacles, claims, and rites – is Lauren Benton's A *Search for Sovereignty*.[108] Like Levin's observation that we cannot understand the law without stepping outside of the bounds of law, the main insight of Benton's work is that we cannot understand the law of sovereignty without deconstructing the violent contests for narrative primacy over space and time, upon which and against which sovereignty claims are superimposed. Narrative control covers a broad field, from doctrinal primacy all the way to symbolic gestures: the planting of flags, the carving of *lasting* sovereignty claims into stones, the erection of *durable* fortifications. The scenery is integral to the narrative.

The performative rites described above may seem trivial or anachronistic until we recall that the very same rituals survive to the present day in state practice relating to territorial claims, erection of diplomatic compounds (under the cloud of sovereign immunity), space exploration and so forth.[109] So too with evidentiary dimensions of sovereignty – the export of stories, maps, durable artefacts (and, tragically, even people) over vast distances and times. An actor's or agent's ability to preserve "*authentic*" records of sovereignty claims over time, and/or to reconstruct "*authentic*" evidentiary narratives in the absence of tangible evidence, is itself a complex sovereignty ritual intended to serve multiple functions, often simultaneously: (1) substantiate some inchoate or allegedly existing sovereignty claim(s); (2) permit proliferation of competing sovereignty rites, claims, and forms; (3) affirm the role of sovereign as arbiter of the authenticity of these rites, and the legitimacy of said sovereignty claims. At the highest level of abstraction, a sovereign's ability to accommodate multiple competing claims (performed in multiple ritual forms) – including claims that potentially encroach upon a sovereign's *own*

[107] William Shakespeare, *As You Like It* (1623) ("All the world's a stage, and all the men and women merely players.").

[108] Lauren Benton, *A Search for Sovereignty: Law and Geography in European Empires, 1400–1900* (Cambridge University Press 2010), 236–237 (describing various sovereignty classification continuums).

[109] The controversy around Russia's televised spectacle of a submersible planting a Russian flag below on the seabed of the North Pole is a striking recent example.

sovereignty claim(s) – is in many ways, itself a ritualistic projection of *true sovereignty*, a desire to signal the absence of sovereign anxiety.

Benton's search for sovereignty reveals how divisions and tensions between and within political spaces and physical spaces, produce layered and divided conceptions of sovereignty.[110] Narrative command over space and time gives powerful actors measures of control over these divided (and oft-contradictory) conceptions of sovereignty, allowing them to proliferate, collide and transform into mercurial "variegated legal spaces of empire, zones that emerged as legal practices responded to inter-imperial rivalries, intra-imperial politics, and local conflicts, and that combined with selective elements of geographic discourse."[111] This raises a key question (promoted by but unanswered in Benton's *Search*): when sovereigns like Russia retreat from pluralism and begin to exhibit preference for dogmatic, "settled," universal conceptions of sovereignty, is this a mark of growing sovereign anxiety? In mercantile terms, is this posture akin to a desire to lock-in sovereignty gains under a ruleset the anxious sovereign knows is slipping away without its consent and control?

Viewed over a long durée, the evolution of sovereignty claims (legal disputes), rituals (marking, mapping, and storytelling), and material modes of contestation over physical spaces (e.g., territories and extra/inter-territorial spaces like rivers, natural boundaries, and seas) shows that political spaces are axiomatically pluralistic spaces. Building on Benton's account, true sovereigns recognized that sovereign anxiety and/or anxiety about pluralism undermined their sovereign prerogative: conversely, an openness to doctrinal/ substantive pluralism, ritualistic/procedural pluralism, and evidentiary pluralism served to affirm sovereign power by recognizing the sovereign's right to decide the scope of a given sovereignty claim. In contrast to reductionist and teleological stories regarding the progressive development of the international law of sovereignty,[112] Benton's search shows how doctrinal fragmentation aids and abets the sovereigns who otherwise would seem to profit from conceptual convergence around *their* desired form of sovereignty.

Read alongside seminal work by Anghie and other theorists within and outside the legal tradition, one starts to see how plural sovereignty is an extremely effective mechanism for carrying out brutal imperial/hegemonic aims,[113] with subtle but

[110] Benton, 280.
[111] Benton, 281.
[112] This may extend to different legal harmonization/convergence narratives, including "general principles" and even customary international law jurisprudence regarding sovereignty as a type of common knowledge socio-legal form or bundle of rights/obligations.
[113] Dillon (2017) 207 ("The modern baroque sovereignty of which Schmitt speaks is a fractured compound composed of heterogeneous terms. That very heterogeneity must be construed as

potent ideological and normative loads. Bestowing legal sovereignty rights on indigenous populations may sound benevolent and progressive at first. But this simultaneously serves as a forceful denial of sovereignty, from multiple perspectives: from the point of view of the populations being colonized *by* the proponents of quasi-sovereignty; from the point of view of other polities whose range of political possibilities is now constrained by the quasi-sovereign "rights" of the new colony; from the point of view of the colonizer, who gets to determine the scope of quasi-sovereignty; from the point of view of other aspiring colonizers, who must find a new *modus vivendi* with every other actor affected by the new quasi-sovereign regime.

Drawing a contemporary parallel to, say, Great States, regional hegemons, and developing states, we can ask whether this ongoing fragmentation and proliferation of sovereignties, sovereigns, and sovereign claims/arbiters are proof of the liberal mantra of a conflictual, yet durable, legal and political pluralism? Or, does the apparent pluralism actually conceal the presence of just several *true sovereigns*[114] – or worse still, *just one true sovereign*, free of all sovereign anxiety, reigning over us all? How could we measure *true sovereignty*?

For theorists like Levin, sovereignty is both indivisible, yet also often qualified and localised. A military occupation can disrupt the true sovereignty of the occupied state, yet that state nevertheless retains "potential sovereignty."[115] For Levin, it is impossible to determine the presence or absence of sovereignty through strictly formal analysis: a consummate realist, Levin stresses the need for deeper substantive analysis, taking into account relevant "on the ground" facts and circumstances. This is consistent with Levin's propertarian theory of sovereignty that prioritizes manifestations of control over defined territories. It is also in full concordance with the long list of "effective control" tests in mainstream Anglophone and contemporary Russian international law discourse. International lawyers, like all lawyers, prefer objective-sounding standards, elements, factors – and different doctrinal measures of "effective [territorial] control" allow analysts and arbiters with specialized toolkits to showcase their relative expertise, sophistication, and effectiveness, while highlighting the importance and indispensability of the fact-finding process, as a whole, with the international lawyers in the very

an originary state of emergency, the violent resolution of which is always already in play before any sovereign gets started on its mortal counterparts.").

114 Levin, at 52 ("Is it not more accurate to say that under conditions of imperialism, it is possible to speak only of the sovereignty of several great, economically and politically, independent states?").

115 *Id.*

middle of that process. When asked to provide a measure of effective control, the international lawyer cannot but provide measures (plural), because an actual objective measure would render the lawyer superfluous (at least for that task).

As Benton makes clear, although there is something primal and enduring about material conceptions of sovereignty *as* territorial control;[116] instead of observing the emergence of clearer "bright-line" rules for the delineation of sovereignty claims, "we instead see processes generating new sources of spatial and legal differentiation."[117] Today, we observe even more fragmentation of sovereignty forms within increasingly localized and abstracted political spaces. This is readily apparent in ongoing doctrinal innovation with respect to evolving doctrines of jurisdiction (long-arm/extraterritorial, protective, and universal), artificial islands, 'great' Internet firewalls and *cyber-sovereignty*, *crypto-monetary sovereignty*, and so on.[118] Normatively, this type of fragmentation seems tolerable insofar as it helps de-fetishize supposedly comprehensive and universal notions of sovereignty. On the other hand, we need to be careful with sovereignty stories (like Levin's, for instance) that describe the form and underlying phenomenon as an endlessly fractal dynamic dialectical process. There is certainly a theoretical and empirical basis for this view, but we need to pay as much attention to *who* tells sovereignty stories, and *how*, precisely, these sovereignty stories are told. "The identity between empire and exception can lead us to replace investigations of the legal politics and spatial history of empire [normative analysis] with interpretations of metropolitan discourses about empire [descriptive analysis]."[119]

As we saw with Levin's not-so-subtle Russification politics, backgrounding normative commitments may affirm center/periphery divides by subconsciously preferring and naturalizing the center over the periphery.[120] As Benton reminds us, the "paradoxical effect of privileging something called

116 Benton, 281 ("the idea of sovereignty defined first and foremost by territorial control continues to exert influence.").

117 Benton, 282.

118 Joint Statement of Bundesministerium der Finanzen (Germany) and Ministère de l'Économie et des Finances (France) on Libra, September 13, 2019, available at: www.bundesfinanzministerium.de/Content/EN/Standardartikel/Topics/Financial_markets/Articles/2019-09-17-Libra.html ("We believe that no private entity can claim monetary power, which is inherent to the sovereignty of Nations.")

119 Benton, 285 ("For example, accounts about the effects of the denigration of rights in empire on the body politic of the metropole might be substituted for an analysis of variants of rights regimes in empire.").

120 Benton, 284–285 (deconstructing Schmitt/Agamben conceptions of sovereignty as narratives of "historical progression" … a "gradual movement toward naturalizing the exception as a property of sovereignty.").

modern state sovereignty as the outcome of a long historical sequence is to preserve certain assumptions about state sovereignty that tie it to imagined Westphalian competencies," such as the very idea of that effective control over territory is a prerequisite for state sovereignty. We see this in the way the Soviets appropriated, restated and expanded Imperial Russian sovereignty claims over the territories of the Russian near-abroad, and the way that post-Soviet Russia has sought to appropriate, restate, and expand Soviet sovereignty claims over the near-abroad. By asserting and defending Westphalian territorial conceptions of sovereignty, Russian policymakers and international lawyers affirm the innateness and centrality of imperial modes of legal thought. Even when Soviet or Russian international lawyers decry European or American aggression as illegal (violating others' sovereignty), the instrumentalization of "bourgeois" or "Western" sovereignty forms is meant to signal Russia's own status as an imperial actor (even while stridently denying imperial ambition).

Russia's invocation of Westphalian sovereignty naturalizes its own imperial expansion in several distinct, yet related, ways. It grounds Russian sovereign rights as historically constituted, the product of previous "epochs" of martial expansion that are, unsurprisingly, not attributable to any contemporary sovereign that seeks to "merely defend" the conditions of "territorial integrity" in which it now finds itself. From the perspective of Russia as Euro-imperial sovereign, *sovereignty as historical right* not only expunges culpability by operation of time, but also makes the purported sovereignty rights more durable, more ossified, and more permanent. Adoption of Westphalian sovereignty is also recognition of competing Euro-American imperial sovereign claims and rights, strengthening Russia's standing in inter-imperial relations. Adoption of Westphalian sovereignty also projects the naturalness of Russian primacy to Russian and non-Russian constituents within the Russian Empire,[121] formalizing and affirming the power of "gentle Russian civilisers" in the peripheral republics (intra-imperial relations), as well as "naturalising" "great"-Russian supremacy over non-Russian people.

[121] Broadly construed, "Russian Empire" describes the millennial Russian state-building project, including the USSR as the apotheosis of the Russian Empire, and the post-Soviet Russian Federation as a continuator of this millennial "civilizing mission." Regardless of ideological gloss at specific historical moments (eg, Soviet claim that it was objectively impossible for a socialist state to be an imperial state), there are obvious continuities in patterns of Russian imperial rule through the present day: continuous outward territorial expansion along Eurasian corridors; martial conquest and martial defense of "martially acquired" territories; outright overseas *terra nullius*-based colonialism (eg, Russian Alaska); global projection of hard and soft power through military confrontations (eg, Cold War; UNSC; etc.); Space Race, regional economic/monetary integration, and so on.

One of Benton's key insights into the nature of sovereignty claims is *how* variegated sovereignty claims and proffered doctrinal innovations actually strengthened the Westphalian doctrine of territorial sovereignty, even as more pluralism and fragmentation reduced the overall coherence of the doctrinal mesh. Benton explains this by recalling Bodin's conception of sovereignty as "spatially elastic," a juridical construction with "properties that could simultaneously cohere and travel."[122] But even the most exotic and portable versions of sovereignty – those without a conceptual tie to territory or a geographic tie to *a* territory – were always travelling, intellectually, with legal baggage tags that had to be somehow recognizable *as* sovereignty across time and space. Otherwise, there was no need for the baggage. Precisely because they defied easy categorization, such variations were imaginatively rendered in discourses about geography and reference in elaborate practices of legal posturing.[123]

These practices and postures served important substantive and procedural functions. Substantively, when novel quasi-sovereignty rights and various derivative sovereignty forms were asserted as outgrowths, corollaries, and "lawgical" inferences from a more foundational sovereignty right, they affirmed the rule as foundational, even when nominally styled as exceptions or challenges to the rule.[124] In procedural terms, the sovereignty "renderings," "discourses" and "practices" helped to re-center and channel sovereignty claimants and disputants toward institutional sites of contestation under the political and/or intellectual control of the most sovereign of sovereigns: those telling sovereignty stories without the slightest hint of sovereign anxiety.[125]

These sovereign performances play out over time. And the sovereign who controls time ultimately controls the story. Stated another way, spatial/conceptual elasticity, fragmentation, and mutability are powerful doctrinal tools – but in the end, narrative control (just like effective control over territory, or the doctrine of trial by ordeal) is a function of time. Theorists help us understand processes, but it is ultimately historians who make history. Translated into the language of procedure and posture, sovereignty rights only really start to matter when they are asserted as claims: when the rights are translated into legal rites, and when the aspiring sovereigns can exert influence on the time keepers of international law (the court clerks and legislative whips, if you will) to be able

122 Benton, 288–289.
123 Benton, 287.
124 Benton, 280–287.
125 Benton, 279 ("Sovereignty is often more myth than reality, more a story that polities tell about their own power than a definite quality they possess.")

to tell their sovereignty stories. The keepers of time determine whether the claims will be heard, and by whom.

17.4 SELF-SOVEREIGNTY

So who are "we" in this story? Are we the storytellers? The keepers of time? Are we an audience of arbiters of others' sovereignty claims or are we disenfranchised spectators, watching a gruesome sovereignty series every time and everywhere we look around? If the latter, how would we know? Particularly if the greatest myth of sovereignty is the one we tell ourselves about our own innate sovereignty as individuals, or beings, or legal persons of some sort . . . If we are an audience of arbiters, how can we keep up? Doctrinal fragmentation, temporality, and spatiality serve as wrenching plot-twists and cliffhangers, evolving day-after-day into different sub-plots that introduce new actors, without end. Intuitively, we may feel that the more sovereign the audience, the more compelling and consequential the sovereignty stories; the bigger the audience, the higher the likelihood of a "good faith hearing on the merits." But we have no way of telling whether anyone else in this zoomy amphitheater audience really cares.

Or are *we* the sovereigns here? Volunteers, consciously conscripted to reflect on supposed disciplinary "tipping points" through a prism of one's *personal* choice, but in reality, performing scripted roles in an undertaking which by its very nature must be collective. Are you still uncomfortable with the "we"? Do you want a more individualistic conception of sovereignty (echoing Unger's *The Self-Awakened*), one that feels genuinely liberating: *true sovereignty*!? Hope is not lost. We know that ideas like *self-sovereignty* or *self-[referential]-sovereignty* are unstable.[126] They are as oxymoronic as 'self-enforcing contracts' – a legally absurd postulate that lawgically requires the introduction of an outside actor to recognize, or at minimum, hear the sovereignty claim(s) at issue. But if one steps out of the theater and thinks oneself as sovereign, shedding sovereign anxiety is as easy as going for a walk. *I* can alter *my* state, declare myself *sovereign*, occupy a slice of *personal* property that will be *mine*. I can say confidently that Russia has no true sovereignty but that Chukchi people are sovereign, and have been for thousands of years. I can be a state; you can be a state; we can be a state . . . together!

[126] Insofar as *self-sovereignty* is still asserted as a type of sovereignty, it presupposes the existence of, and relation to, an elaborate body of norms and laws that structure said sovereignty discourse. See, e.g., Benton, 291 ("structures and practices of imperial sovereignty depended on conflicts organized around alternative positions about the relation of multiple authorities and of overlapping regulatory frameworks.").

Perhaps this is what Haskell means when he invites us to act "slightly out of professional legal character," or when David Kennedy encourages us to tinker with the aperture: keep walking and searching and reading until "we" can practice a politics of sovereignty that will "ensure a certain political outcome conforms to our broader understanding of truth, justice, the 'good'." But I am not so sure, anymore, whether "our" broader understanding of justice is possible (in any genuinely collective group sense), if "our" default modes of thinking and our most critical moves ultimately reproduce patterns of gross injustice and violence.

These two choices – (1) withdrawal and (2) (in)voluntary conscription – are non-starters. Withdrawal is ultimately futile because we are social beings; and self-sovereignty means next to nothing if you care about others and empathize with their sovereign anxiety. Their sovereign anxiety becomes your sovereign anxiety. (In)voluntary conscription does not work for multiple reasons, including the fact that it requires submission on/to time, by which is meant, somebody else's time. When someone else keeps time, you are on the clock. And sovereign anxiety soars when your change agenda does not fit the conscriptors' timeline or time horizons.

Between these two choices, lies a third: reclaiming time.

18

Systems

David J. Gerber

Relationships among states and substate actors are now interactive and adaptive, but discussions of these relationships often fail to grasp that changed reality. Instead, the language of treaties and international organizations continues to shape most thinking about international law. States and other formal institutions play the primary roles in creating, enacting and giving force to these texts, so they obviously carry some form of authority or decisional weight. As a result, these formal "products" are the natural focus of attention, and they are used as reference points by all involved with the issues they treat. But this perspective obscures increasingly important influences that mold decisions everywhere, and this narrowness inevitably biases international law norms.

A perspective that does not "see" these influences and their consequences cannot be adequate for understanding transnational normative relationships. Moreover, it misses and distorts much that is important in the relationships that international law seeks to regulate. Wealth and power typically steer formal institutions, so a focus on those institutions and their products recognizes and tends to valorize the interests of those with more of those resources and marginalize the interests of those who have less.

Formal institutions and the texts they generate remain important, but they are now embedded in a context of interactions and adaptations. In this new context they form only part of a larger set of relationships that constitutes the normative landscape. Spurred by the revolutions in digital technology, that landscape has evolved into a "global adaptive system." Recognizing and understanding this system makes its dynamics visible! It allows us to see more clearly what is happening and to analyze more effectively the normative relationships among all actors in the global arena. This, in turn, provides the basis for decisions and policies that are made firmly grounded in the realities of the international situation. Above all, it emphasizes the need to recognize and valorize the interests of all – states, substate actors, private institutions and individuals, especially those with limited wealth and power. This system is generating a new dimension in the operation of international law.

This brief essay identifies the basic elements of this changed framework for transnational normative relations. It explains what the global adaptive system of international law is and how it functions, and it explores some of its consequences.

18.1 THE INSTITUTIONAL SYSTEM

Current conceptions of international law in much of the world focus on agreements and institutions.[1] How should the language of a treaty be interpreted? How do international organizations such as the UN function and how can we apply and assess the norms they articulate? The system is a product of a specific history that initially centered on Europe and then absorbed the US and other parts of the world.

Although agreements among political communities, including states, have long been central to relationships among them,[2] modern conceptions of international law are rooted in relations among European states. They are usually traced to the Treaty of Westphalia in 1648, which ended decades of trans-European wars.[3] Intense concern in Europe with these formal documents has given additional depth and richness to the basic idea that agreements among states can control the discretion and power of the individual states and thereby reduce the likelihood of conflict. Concepts the Europeans developed have been continually embellished and refined since then in many parts of the world.

Institutions became a major factor in international law after the First World War. The League of Nations was established in the hope that a durable institution could provide a more effective means giving normative structure to international relations. The founders hoped it would be the basis for establishing a durable peace and for regenerating the devastated world economy.[4] The

1 For a review, see Kal Raustiala, Refining the Limits of International Law, 34 *Ga. J. Int'l & Comp. L.* 423, 426–427 (2006).

2 See, e.g., Eric Posner and Jack L. Goldsmith, International Agreements: A Rational Choice Approach, 44 *Va. J. Int'l L.* 113, 114–115 (2013) (discussing the role of treaties in international law).

3 See Michael J. Kelly, Pulling at the Threads of Westphalia: "Involuntary Sovereignty Waiver"? Revolutionary International Legal Theory or Return to Rule by the Great Powers? 10 *UCLA J. Int'l L. & For. Aff.* 361, 373–374 (2005) (discussing the Treaty of Westphalia's impact as "the basis for the growth of public international law" in addition to other effects it had on international law).

4 See F. S. Northedge, *The League of Nations: Its Life and Times, 1920–1946* 1 (Holmes & Meier, 1986) (discussing how the League of Nations was formed mainly to keep the peace but also for other purposes such as orderly management of economic affairs). For the context of flailing

"failure" of the League to prevent war and devastation led to the creation, after the Second World War, of even more elaborate institutions such as the World Bank and the International Monetary Fund.[5] More nations participated in the growing network of institutions, and they generally were given increasing intellectual, political and economic support.[6]

Universal principles – primarily relating to human rights – also became significant elements of international law after the Second World War.[7] They proclaimed that some principles of international law – for example, freedom from slavery and forced labor – were so fundamental that they applied everywhere and required no implementation. The elaboration and interpretation of these principles provide a further dimension of the international law picture. They add significantly to its content. Even here, however, discussions often focus on incorporating these principles into institutions and agreements.

The discourse of this international system of institutions is largely formal, procedural and focused on the outcome of these procedures – typically, the texts that the institutions produce. They are the products of the procedures and agreements. The procedures and their products also govern the language of international law. They provide the lens that is used in thinking about what is relevant. The lens also shapes what those involved see when they look at the legal dimension of international relations and what is generally considered important.

Yet this formal lens necessarily also limits the visual field of those who use it. It generally fails to capture the new elements that have entered, transformed and reoriented the institution based system. These new forces generate their own dynamics, and, as a result, they subsume the traditional framework within a broader and very different system.

18.2 TOWARD AN ADAPTIVE SYSTEM

The various forms of globalization and the digitalization of communications have added a new dimension to transborder normative relations. There are now more players of more types, from more places interacting in more ways.

hope that surrounded the League, see Zara Steiner, *The Lights that Failed: European International History: 1919–1933* (Oxford, 2005).

5 See, e.g., Benn Steil et al., *The Battle of Bretton Woods: John Maynard Keynes, Harry Dexter White and the Making of a New World Order* (Princeton, 2013).

6 See O. C. Isaac Igwe, History of the International Economy: The Bretton Woods System and its Impact on the Economic Development of Developing Countries, 4 *Athens J. L.* 105, 111 (2018).

7 See, e.g., Debra L. Delaet, *The Global Struggle for Human Rights: Universal Principles in World Politics* (Cengage Learning, 2d ed., 2015).

Crucially, they are also increasingly interdependent. Each can normatively influence others – sometimes directly, in important and obvious ways, sometimes indirectly and in less important and less obvious ways. In competition law, for example, the US and EU directly influence many others by supporting them with resources and training, but they also influence them through the status positions they hold in transnational conferences.

Many more players participate in relations across political borders. States and international organizations remain central players, but the number of states that interact with other players has expanded. Smaller jurisdictions that previously had little or no normative role are increasingly in a position to elicit responses from larger states of players. They often do this by informally joining together to influence discussions and decisions in transnational organizations. This is highly visible in the context of the United Nations Organizations, but it occurs in other contexts as well.

The field of institutions that exercise this type of influence has expanded in many directions. I mention here only a few of the important ones. Sub-units of states such as provinces (e.g. China) often play significant roles in relation to regulatory matters.[8] Non-governmental organizations (e.g., Amnesty International) exert influence and pressure on many governments.[9] Large business corporations such as Google pay very large sums to lobbyists to exercise pressure on governments. Similarly, large globally structured law firms (e.g., Baker and McKenzie) and business consulting firms often pay significant attention to influencing government decisions. These players exercise normative influence through frequent communications, rapid responses, presentation and sometimes manipulation of information on digital media. In short, they have created a highly interactive normative matrix that has its own dynamics and also influences the way traditional international elements function.

These connections, influences and causal relationships are frequently only visible when the viewer has some sense of the whole of which they are part. Just as a map allows the viewer to see the relationship among locations and to judge distances between them, a sense of the whole allows the various communications, institutions and players that are part of the normative field to be viewed

[8] See Ping Lin, The evolution of competition law in East Asia, 28 (In E. M. Medalla ed., Competition policy in East Asia 2005) ("By 2000 more than twenty [Chinese] provinces and cities had enacted their own unfair competition laws or regulations.").

[9] See, e.g., Jude Fernando and Alan W. Heston, The Role of NGOs: Charity and Empowerment: Introduction: NGOs between States, Markets, and Civil Society, 554 *Annals* 8, 12–13 (1997) (discussing the impact of NGOs in exerting pressure on governments to change their policies).

in relation to each other. This enables the viewer to see previously unknown or unexpected connections, judge the relevance of specific situations, trace potential causal relationships and predict future consequences.

Many are aware of at least some of these changes. They are generally seen, however, as random events and interactions, and this is the crux of the problem. The lenses currently used in looking at these events, relationships and influences do not reveal the connections among them. Yet seeing these connections is critically important for grasping what shapes normative decisions across political boundaries. Viewing them through traditional lenses misses or obscures much in this normative field.

18.3 INTERNATIONAL LAW AS A GLOBAL NORMATIVE SYSTEM

18.3.1 *The Contours of an Adaptive System*

Recognizing that the transborder normative field is developing into a global adaptive system makes these dynamics visible. It allows the viewer to interpret and assess more effectively the many and various pieces of information about transnational relations that are continually presented to them. Most who use the term "global system" think of it as merely a vague repository concept applying to things "foreign." Some recognize the institution-based system sketched here. A smaller group has recognized for decades the limitations of the traditional perception of what we mean by a "system" and sought to develop a more refined concept of system to respond to those limitations.[10] We can now recognize that these relationships and events are part of a new type of system with very different dimensions and dynamics than those of the past. They have evolved into a "global adaptive system."

But first we need to briefly review the adaptive system concept, because it is not well known among those who deal with international law. Scientists, scholars and officials in many areas are using it to make sense out of contexts with many and seemingly random pieces of data.[11] They use it to more effectively grasp the relationships among diverse but interrelated elements in a variety of situations and thereby to produce insights into these areas that earlier forms of analysis were unable to generate. Much of the initial work that

10 See, e.g., Myres S. McDougal and W. Michael Riesman (eds.) *International Law Essays* (Foundation Press, 1981).

11 *See e.g.*, Murray Gell-Man, Complexity and Complex Adaptive Systems, in *The Evolution of Human Languages* (M. Gell-Mann, J. A. Hawkins eds. 1992).

identified "complex adaptive systems" was done in the natural sciences, but since the 1990s, its use has spread widely through the social sciences.[12]

In its simplest form, an adaptive system is a space or field of activity in which diverse, interdependent agents (or participants) interact with each other.[13] Each influences others and responds to the claims and decisions of others. Such a system has its own internal dynamics. It channels information flow among the agents and it creates incentives and pressures that influence how agents respond to each other. The interactions within the system are also shaped by the external environments within which they take place. Individual agents respond to information, incentives and pressures from the internal and external environment, and in so doing they also alter the interactions in and outside the system. The interactions are, therefore, continually adapting to both internal and external influences and pressures, which are in turn producing consequences that shape the environment for future interactions. In the literature of adaptive systems, these are referred to as "emergent properties." The better we internalize and understand these internal and external patterned interactions, the greater the potential for foreseeing systemic consequences.

A frequently used example of such a system in the natural sciences is a pond.[14] A pond usually contains aquatic creatures such as amphibian life, fish and a variety of plants. Interactions among these agents generate the most obvious dynamics of the system. But each agent also depends on the water and nutrients in the pond, drawing resources from it for its own use and producing effects on other agents as well as on the water in the pond. How agents interact depends on their own needs and capacities as well as on the environment surrounding the pond (e.g., the temperature of air and water and the introduction of contaminants into the water). Viewing the animals, plants and water in the pond individually, or only focusing on the most visible "actors" without seeing them as integral parts of an adaptive system would miss much that influences what happens within the pond. Each is an agent that interacts

[12] Roy J. Eidelson, Complex Adaptive Systems in the Behavior and Social Sciences, 1 *Rev. Gen. Psychol.* 42, 42 (1997) ("Over the past decade, investigators in many fields have increasingly directed their attention toward the dynamic processes and global patterns that emerge from the collective interactions of a system's individual components.").

[13] For foundational presentations, see John H. Miller and Scott E. Page, Complex Adaptive Systems (2009) and Ang Yang, Intelligent Complex Adaptive Systems (2008).

[14] A classic example is cells, which make up organisms, which in turn make up an ecosystem. Rebecca Dodder & Robert Dare, *Complex Adaptive Systems and Complexity Theory: Interrelated Knowledge Domains*, Research Seminar in Engineering Systems MIT (October 31, 2000), http://web.mit.edu/esd.83/www/notebook/ComplexityKD.PDF; Mitchell M. Waldrop, Complexity: The Emerging Science at the Edge of Order and Chaos, 9 (1992).

with other agents in the system, and their interactions constitute the system. And this system of interactions adapts to changing situations. For example, a change in the temperature of the air or water feeding into the pond can cause some species to weaken and others strengthen, changing the relationships and interactions between them.

The analysis defines the field of relationships (e.g., the pond example above). It proceeds by identifying the agents or actors in the field (e.g., algae, fish, plants and water). It then unravels the interactions, notes their characteristics and identifies the results produced by the system. This opens windows into the dynamics of the system. Some changes are caused internally – for instance, a species of fish in the pond may die out. Others arise externally; for example, where local farmers begin to use a form of fertiliser that changes important chemical reactions within the pond. Changes in the environment may or may not be due to the actors within the environment, and all autonomous events and actors are in fact interactional, related, bound up together. If we view the animals, plants and water in the pond individually, we do not perceive the multiplicity of interactions that represent the dynamics of life in the pond. Recognizing them as components of an adaptive system enables us to see more clearly what is happening and to analyze more effectively the web of relationships among the agents that provide its life and the outcomes it produces.

18.3.2 *International Law as a Global Normative System*

This analysis can be fruitfully applied to law.[15] Our focus here is on a particular area of law – transnational law. Global normative relations now operate as an adaptive system, and recognizing this development provides not only a basis for better analyzing and understanding the forces at work, but also for making sounder and more inclusive decisions. I sketch below the elements and the structure of this normative system: the field of relationships, the agents or actors in the field, their relationships and the forms of interaction among them.

Field: The field of interaction for these purposes includes all decisions that influence normative relations across state borders. Major political encounters are part of the picture, but it also includes specific areas of the field such as, economic regulation (particularly competition law, international trade law

[15] See, e.g., Steven Lierman, Law as a Complex Adaptive System: The Importance of Convergence in a Multi-Layered Legal Order, 21 *Maastricht J. Eur. & Comp. L.* 611 (2014) (broadly examining the law through a complex adaptive system lens).

and securities law) and human rights law. In each of these areas, decisions by one player are likely to have many consequences for other players, and players everywhere find that their success relies on paying attention to decisions of all other players in the area.

Players: States are particularly prominent players in this field, not only because they have long been and remain the central focus of international law in the institutional component of the system, but also because their decisions directly affect those subject to their jurisdiction. Transnational organizations remain an important part of the picture, particularly because they provide platforms for the dissemination of ideas and influences. In this adaptive system, however, many other organizations also participate in the system. For example, major global corporations often have significant influence on normative relations among other players. The influence of Big Data firms such as Google, Amazon and Facebook is often prominent. The field also includes nongovernmental organizations (NGOs) as well as many large private law, accounting and economic consulting firms.

Relationships: These institutions stand in frequent and often intense reciprocal relationships with other players. The relationships are also interdependent, as each relationship tends to have consequences for other relationships. The players are interdependent in a variety of ways. Some may need support from others; others need to influence others in order to effectively pursue their own policies.

Interactions: Interactions can be formal or highly informal. Formal interactions are generally visible to others. Often they are specific exchanges relating to a particular theme or decision in the context of treaty-making or interpretation, or in the context of transnational organizations. In these cases, the interaction is clearly defined and publicly known at least in its broad outlines. Similarly, when players – states, expert advisers or lobbyists seek to influence decisions within transnational organizations, interactions are formally structured. These types of interactions are familiar to those involved in international law, but now we know much more about them.

In this adaptive system, informal interactions are equally important. In the institutional system of international law, there were sometimes discussions of the influences on formal decisions, but the focus was on the formal decisions themselves – that is, the conclusion of a treaty or a policy decision of a transnational organization. With the advent of that system, however, informal influences become a focus of attention. Before the evolution of the adaptive system, there was also much less information about informal influences. In this context, the main issue is the flow of influences within the system. Formal decisions are, as we know, important, but now they are seen in context. The informal influences join them at center stage. Informal influences include, as mentioned, personal communications and power relationships, and now they also include the realm of social media. Messages on the Internet, in blogs, on Facebook and on twitter are critically important in shaping relationships and decisions.

Adapting: The global adaptive system adapts to changes from the outside as well as from the inside. New technologies and their uses change the outcomes it produces. For example, the availability of social media creates new power relationships among states, but also gives non-state players greater opportunities to influence events.

18.3.3 *Examples: Competition Law and Human Rights Law*

Examples from two specific areas illustrate some of these contours and dynamics.

Competition law is a particularly useful example.[16] Virtually everyone is affected by the way global markets are regulated. This leads to high levels of interdependence among the states, significant attention from transnational organizations, and often intense activity by lobbyists and others to influence other players. The field of interaction includes, therefore, all decisions relating to the regulation of global markets.

The players are in virtually constant interaction. Each creating new material and responding in one way or another to the decisions others make. For example, if the European Union decides to impose a heavy fine on Google and bases its decision on a new form of reasoning, all will know about and react to it. If a powerful competition law official in a small African country convinces another official in a similar position in another African country to respond to the EU's decision in a particular way, this may lead to cooperation between the two and perhaps others about a way to respond. Recognizing this global adaptive system of competition law illustrates the way that system functions and provides insights into the kinds of outcomes it produces.

Human rights law operates differently, but it now also constitutes an adaptive system.[17] There is widespread interest across the globe in issues of

[16] For background and context, see David J. Gerber, *Global Competition: Law, Markets and Globalization* (Oxford, 2010). For a specific application of complex systems analysis to competition law, see David J. Gerber, A *Global Guide to Competition Law and Antitrust* (forthcoming, Oxford, 2020).

[17] David J. Gerber, "A Global Adaptive System for Supporting Human Rights?" in Nicolás Etcheverry Estrázulas and Diego P. Fernández Arroyo (eds.): *Enforcement and Effectiveness of the Law – La mise en oeuvre et l'effectivité du droit* 45–56 (Paris, 2018).

human rights, so this again leads to frequent and often intense interaction among states, transnational organizations and NGOs. States are central, because they enunciate and sometimes implement laws relating to human rights. In taking decisions or positions in this area states influence each other. If a major state enacts or decides not to enact a recommendation relating to human rights, for example, other states will often know about it and plan their own policies accordingly. Decisions by transnational human rights organizations, particularly courts, become focal points of interest and relationships within this field. NGOs seek to influence the individual decisions of states and often use decisions by other states and organizations to create pressures and/or incentives that support their policies. The effectiveness of one state's decisions in the area may also depend on reactions by other states, NGOs, etcetera. Each player in the field is aware of what many other players are doing with respect to human rights.

An important additional factor within this adaptive system is the universal character of human rights issues. Players seek to influence each other but they also seek to influence in one way or another, principles which all understand to be universal. Universal principles are often at the center of efforts to influence others because all draw on interpretations of these principles. Each player can draw on other experiences to justify their actions.

18.4 COMMITMENTS AND OPPORTUNITIES

My central objectives in this brief essay have been to highlight a fundamental change in normative relations and to suggest some of the potential benefits of recognizing this change and pursuing the opportunities it presents. Recognizing the existence and role of this system makes visible a major change in the frame of reference for decision-making and restructures incentives for specific decisions. As a result, it leads to a much broader view of transnational normative space and the factors that operate in it.

The traditional focal points of international law – especially, institutions and agreements – remain important, but they are now only part of the picture. An interactive adaptive system has developed around these formal elements, informing them, penetrating them, and relating them. Recognizing the system and its basic operations reveals much about how decisions are made in the institutions and in the creation, interpretation and effectuation of agreements. These insights into the global normative system can and will be greatly expanded as awareness and understanding of the system increase.

This awareness also has important practical and political impacts. It will automatically lead decision-makers to consider a wider range of factors in decision-making and to take into account consequences they may not see from the more traditional perspectives of international law. This can provide a firmer basis for policy and implementation decisions.

Moreover, in an institution-based system, the institutions tend not only to provide the focus of attention, but also the framework for thinking about what is relevant, and those who have the most power within the institutions tend, therefore, to control both. An interaction-based system removes both the focus and the control. It leads decision-makers to consider the consequences of policies and decisions throughout the system. It forces the decision-makers to be aware of consequences they may have intentionally or unintentionally ignored.

This also makes the normative domain more inclusive. All participants in the system – from the most powerful to the least powerful and from the wealthiest to the poorest – influence each other. As a result, smaller or weaker players who may have no weight in traditional institutions can make their needs and concerns known to all others. This can then encourage those who share those concerns to join with them to generate pressure on more powerful decision-makers who might in a more traditional institutional context be unaware of these needs and concerns or of the extent of support for them.

Recognition of this reorientation of international law will not happen quickly, and many of the positive consequences may never be fully realized. Recognizing a fundamental change in "the way things work" is always met with resistance. In general, what has been used as a framework will continue to be used unless and until there are sufficient incentives to change the point of reference. Sometimes decision-makers intentionally combat a change in perspective that can undermine their power or reduce the value of their expertise. Often, however, the resistance is primarily cognitive. We simply don't see what we haven't seen before. Tools for operating within an interactive system have only begun to be developed, so stay tuned.

In the meantime, I hope I've convinced you of the potential value of looking at the field of international law through a broader lens that makes visible the various interacting elements that generate normative decisions at the global level. It not only provides the basis for better grounded decisions, but also emphasizes the need to include all interests and perspectives in making those decisions.

19

Territory

Ralf Michaels

In the spring of 2020, globalization came to a halt, seemingly. In view of the spread of a new kind of Coronavirus, countries worldwide closed their borders. Populations were confined to their own states, sometimes their own districts, or their own apartments. Legal regulations were enacted at the state and substate level, and their enforcement was strictly confined. International organizations, the World Health Organization, proved incapable of bringing the world together and fell into crisis;[1] at the time of finalizing this essay, the US President has announced his plan to withdraw from it. Territory mattered again.

Pandemics originate from tipping points. While the math is complex,[2] its application is intuitive: there is a moment in the spread of a virus when it can no longer be contained, and when policies against it move from containment to mitigation, from individual tracing to mass restrictions. Law is a central element in our responses to such pandemics,[3] and it follows this tipping point – from laissez-faire to lockdown in a few days. Have we seen a tipping point in law, then, too, from globalization to territoriality? Or is reality more complicated? After all, we had already been beyond the stories from the 1980s and 1990s, when talk of globalization accompanied claims for a decline of the territorial state, of borders, and of territory, based on increased trade and communication.[4] Since the 2000s, we have learned that these death stories

[1] Armin von Bogdandy/Pedro Villarreal, "Critical Features of International Authority in Pandemic Response: The WHO in the COVID-19 Crisis, Human Rights and the Changing World Order," *Max Planck Institute for Comparative Public Law & International Law (MPIL) Research Paper* No. 2020–2018, (2020). SSRN: https://ssrn.com/abstract=3600058.

[2] See, e.g., François Louchet, "A Brief Theory of Epidemic Kinetics," *Biology* 9 (2020) 134.

[3] See Ralf Michaels, "Rechtliches Wissen in der Krise," *Kritische Justiz* 53 (2020) 375.

[4] Sabino Cassese, "The Rise and Decline of the Notion of State," *Int'l Pol. Sc. Rev.* 7 (1986) 120–130; Masao Miyoshi, "A Borderless World? From Colonialism to Transnationalism and the

were premature, that the territorial state is alive and kicking and just transmogrifying. The internet, once an idealized space outside of territoriality and of state control,[5] has become reterritorialized through GPS software and server control.[6] Likewise, it would be inaccurate to view the global responses to the new virus as a mere return to territoriality. The closing of borders was accompanied by a frenzied worldwide competition for protective gear, with agents of different countries fighting on foreign airports over the routing of supply flights. While physical travel was and continues to be severely hampered, global communication through the internet greatly expanded the higher education universe: virtual conferences now brings together people from all across the globe and online learning enables students to attend the same school regardless of where they are situated. Legal problems ensue. What we are seeing, in other words, is not some simple trend toward deterritorialization, but rather a complex shift, an adaptation in global governance. The virus can be fought by closing borders, but our bigger threat, climate change, cannot.[7]

All of this suggests two things. First, the relation between territoriality and deterritorialization of law is more complex than a mere story of rise and fall. Deterritorialization and reterritorialization of law seem to go hand in hand. Territory does not lose its importance; it just changes its role within the law. True deterritorialization of law seems far away. Would it even be possible? Could law ever be nonterritorial?

This changing role leads to the second insight. Discussions about territoriality and deterritorialization regularly assume territory to be a mere object. The question is what is done with territory, but not what it is. Consequently, when we theorize, we mostly speak not of territory but of territoriality and its counterpart extraterritoriality,[8] or of territorialization and its alleged counterpart deterritorialization. We tell stories of territorialization through the rise of the state and deterritorialization through globalization, and perhaps reterritorialization through backlash to globalization. But our discussions are confused, and for good reason.[9] We think (or rather: we do not think, we unwittingly

Decline of the Nation-State," *Crit. Inq.* 19 (1993) 726; Martin van Creveld, *The Rise and Decline of the State* (Cambridge University Press 1999). The idea of decline is older.

5 John Perry Barlow, A Declaration of the Independence of Cyberspace (1996), www.eff.org/de/cyberspace-independence.

6 Jack Goldsmith /Tim Wu, *Who Controls the Internet? Illusions of a Borderless World* (Oxford University Press 2006).

7 See Sara L. Sack, "Moving beyond the e-word in the Anthropocene"; in *The Extraterritoriality of Law – History, Theory, Politics*, eds. Daniel S. Margolies et al. (2019), 49–66.

8 Daniel S. Margolies, et al. (eds.), *The Extraterritoriality of Law – History, Theory, Politics* (2019).

9 Stuart Elden, "Missing the Point: Globalization, Deterritorialisation and the Space of the World," *Transactions of the Institute of British Geographers* 30 (2015): 8–19.

presume) that territoriality and territorialization are somehow about territory and its importance, and extraterritoriality and deterritorialization are about a decline of that importance. In order to be able to draw such distinctions meaningfully, however, we would of course have to have a concept of territory. Because we do not, territoriality and deterritorialization are unclear concepts, bound to create misunderstandings.[10] And the fact that different authors can, at the same time, recognize both territoriality and deterritorialization suggests a lack of clarity over concepts.

This assumption of territory as a mere fact – shared widely by proponents of both territoriality and deterritorialization – conceals the degree to which territory is actually constructed. Territory is not merely "there," to be appropriated by those who find it, to be transferred, occupied, or seceded. Rather, territory is the result of specific techniques – agricultural techniques of land, geographical techniques of borders, and, most importantly for international law legal techniques. Territory is both the object of legal regulations and its result: it is created by law, and it in turn creates law.[11]

19.1 CATEGORIES

Territory is a central building block of international law.[12] It appears at multiple places, and creates tensions everywhere. Territory is one of the three traditional elements of the state – and thus, it is difficult to categorize nonterritorial powers within the discipline. Sovereignty is territorial, but actual power is not. Doctrines exist for its acquisition – traditionally cession, secession, and occupation – though scholars today reject the talk of acquisition of territory and prefer to talk of title, a sign of conceptual difficulties.[13] Territorial integrity is protected (except when it is not).[14] Jurisdiction is

10 The difficulty to distinguish has been realised before; see, e.g., Ralf Michaels, "Territorial Jurisdiction After Territoriality," *MICH.J.INT'L L* 27 (2006): 1003; Péter D. Szigeti, "In the middle of nowhere: the futile quest to distinguish territoriality from extraterritoriality," in *The Extraterritoriality of Law – History, Theory, Politics*, eds. Daniel S. Margolies, et al. (2019), 30–48.

11 Ralf Michaels and Annelise Riles, "Law As Technique," in *Oxford Handbook of Law and Anthropology* (Marie- Claire Foblets, Mark Goodale, Maria Sapignoli, and Olaf Zenker eds., forthcoming)

12 See Malcolm N. Shaw, "Territory in International Law," *Neth. Yb. Int'l. L.* 13 (1982): 61–91; Martin Kuijer, "The Changing Nature of Territoriality in International Law," *Neth. Yb. Int'l L.* 47 (2016).

13 See, e.g., Marcelo Kohen and Mamadou Hébié, Territory, Acquisition, in *MPIL Encyclopedia* (2011) no 3.

14 Christian Marxsen, "Territorial Integrity in International Law – Its Concept and Implications for Crimea," *Heidelberg Journal of International Law* 75 (2015): 7–26.

(seemingly) unproblematic when territorially bound and (seemingly) problematic when territorially untethered.[15] Territory is equally an important connecting factor in private international law.[16]

Given that central role, we should expect international law to have a well-elaborated concept of territory, as it does of other central categories like that of "state" or "customary law". Remarkably, it does not. Territory is also a blindspot of international law. Despite, or perhaps because of, its central role in international law, what it actually is rarely gets discussed.[17] Territory itself is under-theorized in international law, almost as if territory was a mere fact to be found in the world.

Even works dedicated to territoriality rarely take time to discuss what territory means. Two examples should suffice. Kohen and Hébié, in their excellent book on territorial conflicts, define territory as follows: "The area in which sovereignty exists or may exist is essentially land and is generally referred to as 'territory'."[18] This is in part circular: territory is defined through the presence or the potential of sovereignty, although sovereignty itself is traditionally defined through territory. And in part it is unclear as to the relation between "land" and "territory": are those the same? (Elsewhere, the authors suggest that "[t]he territory is essentially constituted by land, but not exclusively.")[19] Is territory land plus (potential) sovereignty? Is there any land where sovereignty may not exist? And what makes the shift from land to territory?

15 Ralf Michaels, "Territorial Jurisdiction After Territoriality," in *globalisation and jurisdiction* 105 (Piet Jan Slot & Mielle Bulterman eds., 2004); Hannah L. Buxbaum, "Territory, Territoriality, and the Resolution of Jurisdictional Conflict," *Am. J. Comp. L.* 57 (2009): 631; Cedric Ryngaert, "Territory in the Law of Jurisdiction: Imagining Alternatives," *Neth. Yb. Int'l L.* 47 (2016) 49–82.

16 Andrew Dickinson, "Territory in the Rome I and Rome II Regulations," *Lloyd's Maritime and Commercial Law Quarterly* (2013): 86–132; Toshiyuki Kono, "Territoriality," in *Elgar Encyclopedia of Private International Law* 2 (2017), 1702–09.

17 The same is true in political philosophy. For example, political philosopher Anna Stilz's recent "philosophical exploration" of territorial sovereignty discusses at length the why and the how far of territorial sovereignty, but hardly what is meant by territorial, and not what by territory. Anna Stilz, *Territorial Sovereignty – A Philosophical Exploration* (Oxford University Press 2019). Margaret Moore's "political theory of territory" does include a conceptual analysis in its second chapter. Margaret More, *A Political Theory of Territory* (Oxford University Press 2017) 15–33. She defines territory as "a political concept, referring to the geographical domain of a political entity, typically the state" (p. 15).

18 Marcelo G. Kohen & Mamadou Hébié, "Territorial conflicts and their international framework," in id./id. (eds.), *Research Handbook on Territorial Disputes in International Law* (2018) 5, 5.

19 Ibid., p. 9.

A second example comes from Malcolm Shaw, one international lawyer who has dealt with territory more than most others: "The ideas of territory and sovereignty are closely linked in international law, since the concept of territory itself is concerned with those geographical areas over which sovereignty or sovereign rights may be exercised."[20] The wiggle words in the sentence – "closely linked," "concerned with" – demonstrate how much conceptual unclarity exists here. Three concepts are involved – territory, sovereignty, and geography – but it remains unclear which of them have primacy, which of them are defined by the others. Does primacy belong to geography? Then territory would be defined as those geographical areas over which sovereignty exists. Or does primacy belong to territory? Then sovereignty would be defined as the legitimate power over those geographical areas that are defined as territory. Or does primacy belong to sovereignty? Then it would be sovereignty that turns geographical areas into territory.

Shaw defers responsibility to another discipline, geography: "Territory is, of course, itself a geographical conception relating to physical areas of the globe."[21] The hope, in other words, is that geography can help here. But alas, geography for a long time did not thematize it either. Until recently, territory was a neglected topic for geographers, too.[22] Jean Gottman, a French geographer of Jewish-Ukrainian origins with strong links to US scholarship presented an influential study called "The Significance of Territory" in 1973,[23] a text that Shaw used (albeit incompletely). Some recent textbooks also exist.[24] But only recently, it seems, interest has risen.[25] And the hope we lawyers may harbor that geography can provide us with a clear concept is soon disappointed, because geographers themselves give the ball back to lawyers. Gottmans defines territory as "a material, spatial notion establishing essential links between politics, people, and the natural setting."[26] Worse, he adds yet another element to the mix: "the relationship between sovereignty and territory is built upon a connecting link: the people in the territory or, if it is devoid

20 Shaw, *supra*, note 12, at 73.

21 Ibid., p. 62. "Territorial sovereignty is, therefore, centred upon the rights and powers coincident upon territory in the geographical sense."

22 Stuart Elden, *The Birth of Territory* (University of Chicago Press, 2013) 3, with further references in fn 9.

23 Jean Gottman, *The Significance of Territory* (1973); see already ibid., La politique des états et leur géographie (Armand Colin 1951); ibid., The Evolution of the concept of territory, *Soc. Sci. inform.* 14 (1975) 29–47. On Gottman see also Stuart Elden, *The Significance of Territory, Geogr. Helv.* 68 (2013) 65–68.

24 David Storey, *Territories: The Claiming of Space* 2nd ed. (Routledge, 2012); David Delaney, *Territory – A Short Introduction* (Blackwell, 2005).

25 I rely especially on the work of Stuart Elden. See especially Stuart Elden, *Terror and Territory – The Spatial Extent of Sovereignty* (University of Minnesota Press 2009).

26 Ibid., at ix.

of permanent settlement, at least the activities of people within the territory."[27] Similarly, Elden's definition of territory as "a bounded space under the control of a group of people, with fixed boundaries, exclusive internal sovereignty, and equal external status"[28] demonstrates the interplay of (at least) geography, politics, and law. The title of a relatively young journal – Territory, Politics, Governance – suggests the same.[29] Each discipline passes off the existential questions about territory to another expert community, content to work the concept in traditional unreconstructed fashions.

19.2 ORIGINS

In our usual stories of international law, modern international law and territoriality of law originate in 1648, in what is called the Westphalian paradigm. Like almost all such stories, this one is not entirely wrong, but the way in which it is correct needs to be scrutinized. After all, the effectiveness of law had been geographically confined before, and in that unspecific way, law had been territorialized before. Nonetheless, it is true that something shifted – not in one moment, but over time between the fourteenth and the seventeenth century – that made it possible to speak not only of territorialized law, but also of law. Or, put differently, territory did not precede the territoriality of law, but instead, it was a territorial understanding of law that created territory.

The word territory is older, of course. But its meaning was never simple. Naively, we may think that it derives directly from *terra*, land, and that this is what it depicts – a piece of land. But even the Romans themselves disputed the etymology, and the intuitive etymological link to *terra*, earth, is unclear.[30] What is clear is that territorium did not merely mean land.[31] Territorium was the land around a town, but it had specific qualities. In the Corpus Iuris Civilis, Pomponius defined it as *universitas agrorum intra fines cuiusque civitatis*,[32] the

27 Ibid., at 4. Shaw seemingly adopts this notion, but for him territory, not the people, does the linking: "Territory . . . is the link between a people, its identity as a state and its international role." Shaw 63.

28 Elden (n) 22.

29 See the editorial to the inaugural issue by political geographer John A. Agnew, "Territory, Politics, Governance," *Territory, Politics, Governance* 1 (2013) 1–4.

30 Michiel de Vaan, *Etymological Dictionary of Latin and the other Italic Languages* (Leiden: Brill, 2008), 616. See also ibid. 251.f.

31 Twelve different meanings are distinguished in J. F. Niermeyer, *Mediae Latinitatis Lexicon Minus* 1024–25 (Leiden: Brill, 1967).

32 Dig. 50.16.239.8. On Pomponius' method, see Dieter Nörr, Pomponius oder "Zum Geschichtsverständnis der römischen Juristen" in *Aufstieg und Fall der Römischen Welt* ed. *Hildegard Temporini* 15 (1976) 497, 520 f.

ensemble of acres inside the borders of a city. Territory was thus linked to fixed borders; it was bounded space. And territory was linked to the culturation of the land as acre: land was worked-upon space. Territory thus had an internal and an external aspect: internally, it was land made fruitful, and externally, it was protected. Moreover, these internal and external aspects were connected: harvesting the land was possible because it was protected, and protection of the land was necessary because the land was valuable.

This is not all. Pomponius added another factor when he linked the word, etymologically, with *terrere*, to frighten.[33] Grotius would later approve of this explanation, tellingly in a chapter on the right to the things taken in war.[34] Territory was then not only protected defensively; it was also the land from which people were warned off. Understood in this sense, territory was linked to terror.[35] Barry Hindess uses this link to coin a new (and unattractive) term, terrortory, in order to explain that terror is not confined to terrorists as non-state actors: terreur was at first a strategy of the (French revolutionary) state under Robespierre, and still today most terror is committed by and in the name of state.[36] Stuart Elden expands on the connection in his book on the aftermath of 9/11.[37]

We find here then, already an understanding of territory as marked land and land that relates to power. Territory was land marked by borders and work, and territory was land over which someone (who remains unnamed) has (internal and external) power. Power and marking go hand in hand – it is in large part because of the borders that strangers can be frightened away. And it thereby had an easy connection to jurisdiction and law. Moreover, we already find the element of violence, which later would become connected to the state with its monopoly of violence, and to the international law principle of territorial integrity, which states are allowed to protect with violence.

And yet, the combination of these elements did not yet have a specific legal connotation. Territorium was factually defined; it did not create a jurisdictional entity. The boundaries of the city defined the limits of the sovereign's factual powers, but not in that sense legal boundaries. Territory was not yet a jurisdiction.

33 Dig. 50.16.239.8.

34 Hugo Grotius, *De Iure Belli ac Pacis*, Book Three, 6.4.2. More etymological discussion is found in Barbeyrac's comments; see Richard Tuck (ed.), Hugo Grotius – *The Rights of War and Peace* (2005) 1322–1323.

35 William Connolly, *The Ethos of Pluralization* xxii (1995).

36 Barry Hindess, "Terrortory," *Alternatives: Global, Local, Political* 31 (2006) 243–257.

37 Stuart Elden, *Terror and Territory – The Spatial Extent of Sovereignty* (2009).

A specifically legal concept of territoriality came later.[38] In the fourteenth century, Bartolus had to address the then novel question of conflicts of laws, including the question of the scope of existing laws.[39] The question had not arisen as such in Rome, because Roman law was essentially thought to govern all over the Empire, but it arose now in view of the existence of multiple kingdoms. Until the Middle Ages, law had been understood as personal, which made sense: the law applicable to a person was, almost by necessity, the law of his or her tribe, community.[40] Of course, a leader was able to apply his law within the borders of his city. But that was a consequence of factual ability, not normative consequences.

Bartolus, perhaps the first to do so, discussed territory as a basis of jurisdiction. Jurisdiction, he suggested, applies to a territory, though he hastened to add that it is a quality not of the territory but of the person holding the jurisdiction. Thereby, territory became an object of law. Moreover, Bartolus adopted the old definition of territory as terror and applied it not only outward but also inward: the ability of an army to terrify and dictate in a place enabled it to enforce its laws there. This new, territorial definition of law came, unsurprisingly, with the rise of secular power. Bartolus took pains distinguishing the pope's and the Emperor's territory as separate jurisdictional spaces. In this sense, the rise of territory had to do with secularization. Religious affiliations can be imagined regardless of territory, and indeed, in spiritual matters the canon law was universal. A Christian is governed by Christian laws in life and in death. Secular law, by contrast, is factually limited by borders, and therefore its normative power is also confined within these boundaries.

This was not yet a legal concept of territory, but it made one possible. Such a legal concept was introduced by Bartolus' student Baldus who equated ordinary jurisdiction and its limits with territory and its limits, and also defined the population as territorial.[41] The consequence was that territory had now become a legal concept. "Territory is thus not just the limit of the jurisdiction but its very definition."[42] And in this sense, territory and jurisdiction became almost synonymous, as can be seen in scholarly works on territorial sovereignty of the early modern period.[43] Jurisdiction was territorial, but territory in turn

38 Discussed in Elden(n 22) 218 ff.

39 Nikitas Hatzimihail, "Bartolus and the Conflict of Laws," *Revue hellénique de droit international* 60 (2007) 12–79.

40 Karl Neumayer, *Die gemeinrechtliche Entwicklung des internationalen Privat- und Strafrechts* (1901/1916).

41 See Walter Hamel, *Das Wesen des Staatsgebietes* (1933) 21ff.

42 Elden (n 22) 232.

43 Dietmar Willoweit, *Rechtsgrundlagen der Territorialgewalt: Landesobrigkeit, Herrschaftsrechte und Territorium in der Rechtswissenschaft der Neuzeit* (1975).

was jurisdictional: territory was defined as the area within which the lord could rule, and vice versa. Territory was not just land; it was juridified land.

19.3 SOVEREIGNTY

What is it then that happened in or around 1648? What exactly does the so-called Westphalian system signify? In common parlance, the Westphalian paradigm signifies the settling of sovereignty as the foundation of both domestic and international governance. Territorial states became sovereign both internally and externally: they achieved the monopoly of power within their own territory, and they became formally equal actors in the anarchic system of international relations. Today we know this to be a myth in two ways – the Westphalian peace did not establish a clear break with the past,[44] and both internal and external sovereignty are little more than organized hypocrisy, to use Stephen Krasner's terminology.[45] Given the myth's impact on our thinking, it is all the more important to take it seriously.

We saw earlier that the idea of territory can be traced back to the fourteenth century. The idea of sovereignty is found prior to the Westphalian Peace Treaties in the works of Jean Bodin. The shift from personal to territorial affiliation is presaged in the Peace of Augsburg 1555, with its principle of *cuius regio eius religio* "In a (prince's) country, the (prince's) religion." What is notable is how territory plays into these personal and territorial aspects.

Bodin's work was, as Laura Benton observes, long "notable for its utter lack of attention, and even mention, of territory."[46] Sara Miglietti has recently countered this view.[47] In the famous Book 1 of his Six Livres, Bodin, unlike Bartolus, did distinguish a spatial concept of the city from a juridical concept, and thus seemed to suggest that sovereignty as a juridical concept was personal, not territorial. But while a territory played no definitional role, it did play an operational role; states had to be big enough to host their populations, and given the expansion of populations, it became necessary for territories to expand, if necessary by colonization. This was not experienced as a paradigmatic change, but

44 Andreas Osiander, "Sovereignty, International Relations, and the Westphalian Myth," *Int'l Org.* 55 (2001) 251–287.
45 Stephen Krasner, *Sovereignty-Organized Hypocrisy* (1999).
46 Lauren Benton, A *Search for Sovereignty: Law and Geography in European Empires,* 1400–1900 (Cambridge: Cambridge University Press, 2010), p. 287.
47 Sara Miglietti, "Sovereignty, Territory, and Population in Jean Bodin's République," *French Studies* 72 (2018) 17–34.

rather a more gradual shift toward – as Botero would later suggest – making territory a definitional element of the state.[48]

As for the principle of *cuius regio eius religio*, it did indeed establish territorial grounds for religious affiliation and, by extension, law. Remarkably, this territorialization was achieved through a shift in religious affiliation. In other words, the treaty did not establish territorial jurisdiction over citizens no matter their affiliation; it defined the affiliation of citizens within one region in order to justify that jurisdiction. But once established, the rule could be stripped from its theological background and turned into one of sovereignty only: *qui in territorio meo est, etiam meus subditus est.*[49]

The establishment of territorial sovereignty – sovereignty based on territory – was therefore first and foremost a secularization shift. Personal relations were replaced, after countless religious battles in Europe and in order to overcome those, with territorial connections. Those territorial orientations at first subsumed religious relations (*cuius regio eius religio* meant that personal–relational ties were created through territorial relations), and later replaced them as a central dynamic of the sovereign state. In this sense at least, the territorial state is also the secular state – God's kingdom is not, after all, of this world (John 18:36), and it took the secular (and territorial) state to overcome religious factions.

But the shift to territorial sovereignty depicted also the shift toward the definition of territory as a juridical concept. Boundaries were now no longer physical limitations of actual power; they were normative limits of jurisdictional power. And territory was no longer the physical space within which a prince could actively rule; it was the very space that created the foundation of his rulership. If then today we understand sovereignty as territorial,[50] we must recognize that territory is not merely land, and it is not merely power over land. Territory may today serve as the foundation of sovereignty, but historically it is the other way round: sovereignty creates territory. Its symbols are territorial – the stakes laid, the flags planted. The consequence is legitimacy: territorialization, the making of territory, turns factual power into legitimate sovereignty. For actual power to turn into sovereignty, for land to turn into territory, it has to be given a legal status of legitimacy. And that in turn requires working on the land – the old basis in acres still exists today.

48 Miglietti at 32-33. On Botero see Romain Descendre, "Territorialisation de la politique," in *L'Etat du monde: Giovanni Botero entre raison d'état et géopolitique* (Geneva: Droz, 2009), pp.213–244.

49 Kelsen, *Principles of International Law* 216. See already Kreittmayer, *Staatsrecht* I (1769) 71.

50 E.g. James Crawford, *Brownlie's Principles of Public International Law*, 9th ed. (2019), 191ff.

Sovereignty, then, is a dual imposition on land, of power and of law. Sovereignty is justified power over land, but that justification itself emerges from sovereignty, in a strange loop. (Organized hypocrisy was Krasner's term.)[51] Mere possession of land does not create sovereignty, but neither does it create territory. It is territorialization that creates both sovereignty and territory and creates the link between them that legitimates both.

19.4 STATE

These considerations matter also for our definition of the state. Here is political philosopher David Miller's attempt at a definition: "A natural way to think about territory is to see it as involving a triangular relationship between first, a piece of land, second, a group of people who live on that land and, third, the political institutions that govern those people in that place."[52] At first sight it seems that this triangle reverse-engineers the three elements of the state as found in the work of Jellinek and codified in the Montevideo Convention: a permanent population, a defined territory, and government.[53] Indeed, territory has been called an indispensable element of the state. Malcolm Shaw calls its necessity "self-evident" and cites Lassa Oppenheim's famous quote, that "a State without a territory is not possible."[54] Gottman agrees: "On ne conçoit pas un État, une institution politique, sans sa définition spatiale, donc territoriale" (we do not conceive of a state, a political institution, without a spatial and therefore territorial definition).[55]

But the three elements of the state are by no means symmetric. The need of a government, or an administration, may indeed be self-evident in an analytical sense – indeed, state and government are often used synonymously, and a nation without a government is just a nation and not a state.[56] The need of a population is somewhat less self-evident, but plausible: a government without a governed has no role; laws and normativity exist between people. The need of a territory, by contrast, is less obvious. Governance does not require a territory. Max Weber's famous definition of the state as "a human

[51] Stephen Krasner, *Sovereignty: Organized Hypocrisy* (1999).

[52] David Miller, "Territorial Rights: Concept and Justification," in *Political Studies* 60 (2012) 252, 253. Cf. Moore (n 17) 8; Elden (n 22) 206.

[53] Georg Jellinek, *General Theory of the State* (1900), 250–258.

[54] Shaw (n. 11) 61, citing to Lassa Oppenheim, *International Law*, 8th ed. (1955) 451 ("a State without a territory is not possible").

[55] Gottman, Géographie 71.

[56] It is in this sense that Kelsen equated law and state.

community that (successfully) claims the monopoly of the legitimate use of physical force within a given territory" is deeply unclear. What does it mean to say that a territory is given? Who gives territory? And what is it that is given here?

Take another look at Miller's quote: he thinks of territory not as one element on the same level of others, but rather the triangular relation that brings all three elements together. Just as Kelsen equates state and law, so Miller equates state and territory. A state does not have territory, it is territory.[57] And so the role of territory with regard to the state is ambiguous. If territory is a necessary element, does that mean we should deny statehood to organizations without a territory? Or should we expand our notion of territory to account for modern states? Is Oppenheim making an analytical or an empirical claim? And is Shaw correct that this is "self-evident"? Or does it suggest something more sinister – that we discuss, through the notion of territory, what is and is not legitimate?

The shift to territory was not, after all, merely a way to create peace among warring Christian factions. It was also a technique of governance, with winners and losers. If territory is a necessary element of the state, then those without territory cannot have a state, and thus no control over their affairs. Within Europe, the shift came at the expense, most visibly, of Jews. The nation state may seemingly have been grounded in the nation, but it was open only to nations that could establish territory. In the rush of European nations to found nation states, the Jewish nation was left stateless because it had no territory, and it was unable to have a territory in part because Jews were not, in many countries, allowed to own land. When a Jewish territorial state was finally founded, belatedly after World War II, that foundation was viewed as a colonial act of war by its neighbors, and a seemingly endless fight over territory ensued.

The same was true outside of Europe. If some factual impact on land was necessary to turn it into territory and thereby provide sovereignty, then those who do not impose such impact cannot be sovereign. This is how colonization could be justified: land was possessed by locals, but they had no sovereignty.[58]

[57] Cf. Michel Foucault, Security, Territory, Population: Lectures at the College de France, 1977 – 78 (2007) p. 11: "…sovereignty is basically inscribed and functions within a territory, and that the idea of sovereignty over an unpopulated territory is not only a juridically and politically acceptable idea, but one that is absolutely accepted and primary…."

[58] See Mamadou Hébié, "The acquisition of original title of territorial sovereignty in the law and practice of European colonial expansions," in *Territorial Disputes* (n 18) 36–86. The acquisition of derivative title of territorial sovereignty in the law and practice of European colonial expansions, ibid. 87–144. Very instructive is also Henry Jones, "Property, Territory, and Colonialism: An International Legal History of Enclosure," *Leg. Stud.* 39 (2019) 187–203.

In the Americas, influential European scholars insisted that natives had some kind of title to land – Bartolomé de Las Casas spoke of *ius ad rem*, as opposed to *ius in re*[59] – that made it necessary to acquire the land in some fashion, through purchase (Manhattan) or through formalized occupation (Latin America). But the right of the locals was never conceived as complete. "The Indians occupied but did not possess the land," wrote Tocqueville in his book on America, "It is by agriculture that man wins the soil."[60] Locke developed his labor theory of property against this colonial background: the vast American lands were appropriated only through the labor of the European settlers.

In this context, the idea of *terra nullius* was also an idea about territory. Australia was *terra nullius* not because nobody lived there but because the people who did live there had not made the land their own, had not turned it into territory. The concept of terra nullius itself was likely a post facto justification established in the nineteenth century to justify colonization.[61] But the idea that Australia's original inhabitants did not have sovereignty over their land because they had not turned it into territory, had not territorialized it, informed already the early justifications of appropriation.

And later, the idea of territory as a sufficient element enables the postcolonial world to treat former colonies as formally sovereign states, even if they are not economically sovereign.[62] Territory may have originated with ownership over land: the king's territory was also his land (as is still the fiction in English land law). In former colonies, the public/private distinction has undermined this. (Remarkably, Malcolm Shaw first developed his concept of territory with a view to Africa). Postcolonial states that have territorial sovereignty but lack economic sovereignty have the shell without the substance. And, of course, territorial integrity – internal sovereignty – is never complete; it stands under the proviso of compliance with certain supranational, universal, deterritorialized norms.

59 See Kenneth Pennington, "Bartolome de Las Casas," in *Great Christian Jurists in Spanish History*, eds. Rafael Domingo and Javier Martínez-Torrín (Cambridge: Cambridge University Press, 2018), 98, 105.

60 Alexis de Tocqueville, *Democracy in America* 30 (1969), Cf. William Connolly, "Tocqueville, Territory, and Violence," *Theory, Culture and Society* 11 (1994): 19–40, 24–29.

61 Andrew Fitzmaurice, "The Genealogy of Terra Nullius," *Austral. Hist. Stud.* 129 (2007) 1–15.

62 Christopher Clapham, "Sovereignty and the Third World State," *Political Studies* (1999), XLVII, 522–537; Jody Emel, Matthew T. Huber, Madoshi H.Makenea, "Extracting Sovereignty: Capital, Territory, and Gold Mining in Tanzania," *Political Economy* 30 (2017) 70.

In this regard, 9/11 is a good example for the complex link between territory and terror. The United States was attacked by an actor that was neither a state, nor a person (but a network, al-Qaeda) and not territorial. The response was twofold. On the one hand, US President George Bush argued that the "war on terror" was "a new type of war" with a "new enemy," and his legal adviser uses this to argue that traditional limitations on the right to wage war no longer apply.[63] On the other hand, Bush reterritorialized the conflict, to make it manageable. The new war, Bush said, was waged not only against terrorists themselves but also "those who harbor them and finance them and feet them." And thus the US responded by identifying an oppositional state (Afghanistan, which harbored al-Qaeda at the time), a targeted person (Osama bin-Laden), and a territory that could be, and was, bombed. At the same time, the US distinguished the territorial and thus legitimate state from the deterritorialized and thus illegitimate state, despite many existing parallels in discourse.[64] And Islamist terrorism regroups under the name of the state – Da-Esh, or the Islamic State – that goes on to try and occupy territory. This did not turn it into a state in the view of international lawyers, and of course it was not recognized by other states.[65]

All of this makes doubtful recent proposals that territory should be removed as a necessary element of the state.[66] Jain has argued that territory should be understood as a precondition for the creation of states but not necessary for their continued statehood.[67] Territory is here given a mere functional role, and as such could be replaced by functional equivalents. The role that territory plays for the law is not, however, functional but definitional. Territorial integrity can be overcome; territory can be redefined to suit different interests. The problem then is not that territory would be necessary in an ontological sense, that a state could not physically exist without a territory just as a human could not physically exist without a body. Rather, the reason is that

63 Michael Byers, "A New Type of War: Blair's and Bush's attempt to change international law," in *London Review of Books* (6 May 2004).

64 On these see the work of Lena Salaymeh.

65 Christian Tomuschat, The Status of the "Islamic State" under International Law, 90 Die Friedens-Warte 223–244, 229 (2015); 19–20; Deon Geldenhuys, The Islamic State (IS): An Exceptional Contested State, 6 Austral 9–35, 18–20 see also the debate between Ralph Janik, Is the Islamic State a State? Völkerrechtsblog (10 June 2016), https://voelkerrechtsblog.org/is-the-islamic-state-a-state/, and Sinthiou Buszewski, "A Response to 'Is the Islamic State a State?'", Völkerrechtsblog, 10 June 2016, https://voelkerrechtsblog.org/a-response-to-is-the-islamic-state-a-state/.

66 Veronika Bílková, "A State Without Territory?", in *Neth. Yb. Int'l L.* (2016), 19–47.

67 Abhimanyu George Jain "The Twenty-First Century Atlantis: The International Law of Statehood and Climate Change-Induced Loss of Territory." *Stanford Journal of International Law* 50 (2014) 1–50.

the state is a social construct itself, which is coexistent with an idea of territory. It might be possible to redefine territory in ways that do not describe physical spaces, but that would be a very different move.

19.5 JURISDICTION

A similar malleability exists in the law of extraterritoriality for jurisdiction. In a simple analysis, we find, in the twentieth century, a move from a strict ban on extraterritorial jurisdiction to a greater permission of such jurisdiction. Put differently, jurisdiction is now permitted more liberally outside of a state's territory, keeping the definition of territory intact.

In reality, the shift is somewhat more complicated. In the early twentieth century, jurisdiction was relatively strictly confined within a state's territorial borders. That can be and was often explained through territorial sovereignty. At the same time, it was related to a restraint from regulation altogether. American Banana, the famous case in which a US court refused to assert jurisdiction over the activities of a US company abroad, was remarkable not because it left US consumers unprotected from anticompetitive conduct enacted outside of US borders, but directed within them. It is remarkable also because it meant that US authorities had to leave US corporations without regulation in what were literally banana republics – Latin American states whose economies relied largely on the exportation of fruits, and whose governments were too weak (or too corrupt) to properly regulate foreign corporations. If the US prides itself that it was not a colonial power, this is historically wrong even in the literal sense of colonization (think of the Philippines and Hawaii). But more importantly, the exercise of US power over lands outside its borders rests on allowing economic domination without providing the protection of US law.[68] This may be called territoriality insofar as jurisdiction ends at the borders. But it could also be called deterritorialization in the way in which it creates, effectively, areas without law, non-territories.

This changed with the shift to the effects doctrine as a permitted basis of jurisdiction – first in the United States (and against the protest of European countries), later worldwide. Under the effects doctrine, states can exercise jurisdiction over conduct outside of their territories, as long as such conduct has intended effects within their territories. That such jurisdiction is called

[68] Ralf Michaels, "Empagran's Empire International Law and Statutory Interpretation in the US Supreme Court of the Twenty-First Century," in *International Law in the US Supreme Court*, eds. David L. Sloss, Michael D. Ramsey & William S. Dodge (Cambridge University Press, 2011), 533–546; James Thuo Gathii, "Imperialism, Colonialism, and International Law," *Buff. L. Rev.* 54 (2007) 1013, 1062–1063.

extraterritorial is odd, given that an important connecting factor, namely the effects, is clearly situated within the territory. In this sense, the effects doctrine is also a territorial doctrine. It correlates with a shift in the understanding of law – from a liberal laissez faire to a regulatory state model focusing on the protection of consumers. And it still does not allow the regulation of conduct abroad that has no such impact, meaning that foreign countries without strong regulatory powers and agencies are still not able to protect themselves against the conduct of US and European corporations. The idea of lending Western laws and enforcement agencies to the protection of such countries may smack of imperialism.[69] It does so only, however, because we think of such jurisdiction as violating principles of territoriality.

Today, we are seeing a withdrawal from so-called extraterritorial jurisdiction. The US Supreme Court in particular has revived a "presumption against extraterritoriality" and used it to restrict the scope of US regulatory laws. Such restrictions are often justified with respect for foreign sovereigns and their territorial sovereignty, though that is often doubtful. When South African plaintiffs brought reparations claims for apartheid injustices before US courts, such claims were dismissed because they might interfere with the South African government's own preference for a truth and reconciliation process – even though the government itself was not opposed to such reparation claims. When plaintiffs worldwide brought claims against a vitamins cartel in US court, their claims were dismissed with a view to whistleblowing procedures in Europe, even though many of these plaintiffs came from countries where no procedures existed that US enforcement could interfere with. In such situations, it appears that what is meant with territory is not actual bordered land and more a justification not to have to interfere.

In this context, a recent decision by the German Constitutional Court is worth mentioning.[70] The Court decided that rights under the German Constitution bind the State, in this case its intelligence service, even when the State acts outside German borders against foreigners. The decision has been heavily criticized as undue interference with the ability of intelligence services to perform their duties. Insofar as such criticism goes to what services must be able to do, it is a matter of balancing. The real criticism is more fundamental: intelligence services must be able to work without constraints when they act abroad. That seems unwarranted.

69 Ralf Michaels, "Supplanting Foreign Antitrust," *Law and Contemporary Problems* 79 (2016) 223–247.

70 German Const. Court 19 May 2020, 1 BvR 2835/17, www.buerfg.de/ers20200519_1bvr283517en.html; English press release at: www.buerfg.de/ers20200519_1bvr283517en.html.

19.6 CONCLUSION

If there was a tipping point for territory, it happened not in the 1980s with territorialization, and not in 2020 with deterritorialization. The tipping point – and it was a process more than a point – happened between the fourteenth and the seventeenth century, with secularization and the contemporaneous rise of ideas of territorial sovereignty. For this purpose, physical boundaries were turned into normative limits, and physical space was turned into jurisdiction. The territorial state replaced the religious community.

This has implications for the role of territory today. First, it helps understand what territory is. Is territory really just land – an object of the law, a connecting factor, to be derived from the expertise of geographers, measured with boundaries, and fed into the law? Or is it a project of the law itself – endlessly malleable, distanced from land and physicality, subject to limitless discretion of those in power? The answer is, arguably, in between these two extremes. Territory remains related to physical land. It is different in this sense from the much more ephemeral notion of space, which can be territorial, social, or all kinds of other things. But territory is never unmarked land. Territory is not found, it is produced.[71] Territory is juridified land – land turned into territory through legal techniques. Territory, then, has constant and changing aspects to it. Land as a physical entity remains mostly constant (though of course not even that is true, in view of land-winning techniques in the Netherlands or in the South Chinese Sea). Similarly, territory as an element of legal argument remains relatively constant.

But more importantly, territory always remains a malleable concept. Territory is always defined by the specific relation between land and territory mediated through law, and as that law changes, so territory changes as well.

It has implications for the understanding of law as well. It seems easy to imagine an "end of territory," in favor of law based on community affiliation alone, regardless of territory[72] or some "end of geography" that would signify a loss in importance of physical spaces.[73] But communities are, in the end, different kinds of territories. Modern law and territory are mutually

[71] David Storey, *Territories: The Claiming of Space* 1, 2nd ed. (2012).

[72] Cedric Ryngaert & Mark Zoetekouw, "The End of Territory? The Re-Emergence of Community as a Principle of Jurisdictional Order in the Internet Era," in *The Net and the Nation State*, ed. Uta Kohl (2017), 185–201. See also Adeno Addis, "Community and Jurisdictional Authority," in *Beyond Territoriality – Transnational Legal Authority in an Age of Globalization*, eds. Günther Hand et al. (2012) 13–33.

[73] Daniel Bethlehem, "The End of Geography: The Changing Nature of the International System and the Challenge to International Law," *EJIL* 25 (2014) 9–24; see especially the list of six "challenges" on p. 18.

constitutive: law constitutes territory, but territory in turn constitutes law, is a foundation of the way we think law. Just as Bentham said that "property and law are born together, and die together"[74] so we can say that territory and (modern) law are born together and die together. Another conception of law would have to go back before secularization and sovereignty, would have to provide foundations other than the presumed universality of Christianity and the special limitation of territory. We see some such attempts in the inauguration of human rights as a secularized renewal of catholicity and natural law, others in the turn to markets and social norms as similarly detached guides of action. Maybe they will prevail, and law without territory will be possible. Or, of course, law will just disappear.[75]

This helps, finally, to understand the territoriality of law, too. Territoriality has not declined, it has shifted.[76] Territoriality must be understood as a specific way of thinking about law as intrinsically limited by the boundaries of territory: the extraterritorial is indeed of special justification, the infra-territorial seemingly not. By shifting the conceptual boundaries of territory, we shift the boundaries between what needs special justification and what does not, between what is and is not considered anomal. But we do not change the nature of law as being an order of inclusion and exclusion, which Hans Lindahl has argued as being intrinsic to ideas of law and authority.[77] If we wanted to overcome territoriality, we would have to overcome not merely the link of law and physical space – this itself a quite implausible project. We would have to imagine law as overcoming boundaries altogether.

[74] Jeremy Bentham, *Theory of Legislation*, 2nd ed. (1871) 113.

[75] Niklas Luhmann, *Law as a Social System* (2004) 490.

[76] See, e.g., Martin Kuijer, Wouter Werner, "The Paradoxical Place of Territory in International Law," in *Neth, Yb. Int'l L.* 47 (2016) 3–17. And see, more fundamentally, Gilles Deleuze/Felix Guattari, *A Thousand Plateaus* (1987).

[77] Hans Lindahl, *Authority and the Globalisation of Inclusion and Exclusion* (2018).

20

United Nations

Martin Wählisch

In a world that is equally interconnected and divided, the United Nations is under enormous pressure to unite the international community. The aim of the UN Charter to maintain international peace and security while promoting economic and social advancement of all peoples has been praised as the foundation of global constitutionalism, but unilateralist tendencies have been eroding the spirit of universalism in recent times. In this context, the utopia vested into the UN as an ideal for collective security, world governance, and global solidarity increasingly risks to be falling short of reality.

The UN's leadership has been quite vocal about the erosion of multilateralism and the resulting negative impact on the effectiveness the organization. In May 2019, the outgoing High Commissioner for Human Rights Zeid Ra'ad al-Hussein warned of a possible "collapse" of the UN, mindful of the paralysis in cases such as Syria and Yemen.[1] In June 2019, UN Secretary-General António Guterres stressed to the Fifth Committee of the General Assembly in charge for the organization's budget that the financial situation of the UN is at a "tipping point."[2] The organization faced the largest cash crisis in nearly a decade due to unpaid membership contributions. Meetings scheduled after regular working hours or on the weekend were canceled, interpretation services to the Security Council were cut down, provisions of individual water pitchers for Council members curtailed, and even the UN headquarters

I sincerely thank the editors John Haskell and Jean d'Aspremont for their helpful and constructive comments throughout this exciting book project. The views expressed herein are those of the author and do not necessarily reflect the views of the United Nations.

1 Zeid Ra'ad Al Hussein, I Will Not Stay Silent. Our Leaders Are Failing Human Rights, The New York Times, May 6, 2019.

2 António Guterres, Remarks to the Fifth Committee on "Improving the Financial Situation of the Organization", June 4, 2019.

fountain was shut off to save money.[3] As some diplomats put it mildly, the UN is certainly no longer at its heyday of love and care. However, the organization remains the center of gravity for the international community, although its force is questioned. Debates in the Security Council on multilateralism and the role of the United Nations are a reflection of this trend. As the Secretary-General put it "multilateral efforts are under immense stress" given the anxiety, uncertainty, and unpredictability across the world, which should be a wakeup call to commit to the "ideals of collective action while pursuing a new generation of approaches and architecture capable of responding."[4]

This chapter provides a critical reflection on the contemporary challenges and opportunities of the UN as the world's key international organization. It looks at the evolution of the UN system and socio-legal incentives of the international community to jointly address issues of global concern. In this context, the chapter analyzes the status quo of multilateralism based on qualitative and quantitative aspects, weighing recent policy and codification initiatives under the UN banner. The chapter concludes with the consideration of parameters indicative for approaching tipping points that shape the future of the United Nations, multilateralism and the international community.

While the purpose and effectiveness of the United Nations has been called into question by some in the recent past, this chapter argues that the organization remains an indispensable cornerstone of international law and its creation, even if the tectonics of the world's order are in flux with moving boundaries of law and politics. The UN continues to be a key part of the global law and policy machinery, because it is unique in its universal approach, including its all-encompassing values, and programmed constant striving for progress. It enables the organization to cope with and respond to recurrent new fault lines in international affairs. Although exclusive international summits for world leaders of advanced economies à la G7 and G20 might be increasingly in the spotlight of international attention for global decision-making, the UN's inclusive responsibility for human rights, development, and peace and security is without equivalent alternative. Although there is the feeling that international law is in crisis, the UN stands symbol for the commitment to a global community with shared responsibilities and the

3 Colum Lynch, On the Wagon: UN Cuts Back on Liquor, Interpreters, and Water Pitchers, Foreign Policy, October 18, 2019.

4 António Guterres, Remarks at Security Council Open Debate on "Strengthening Multilateralism and the Role of the United Nations," November 19, 2018.

common sense of unity, albeit serious misbeliefs in multilateral solutions and attempts to break the existing rules-based international order apart.

20.1 THE CRITIQUE: OVER SEVEN DECADES OF HIGHS AND LOWS OF INTERNATIONAL COOPERATION

The creation of the UN as a safeguard mechanism for international peace was itself a turning point in the shadow of the Second World War. It is the inherent impetus of the organization's mission to "save succeeding generations from the scourge of war, which twice in our lifetime has brought untold sorrow to mankind" as unprecedented tipping points to humanity.[5] US President Truman called the adoption of the Charter of the United Nations the moment toward building "a better world."[6] He stressed that the Charter is neither final nor a perfect instrument, acknowledging that "changing world conditions will require readjustments."[7] The UN was seen as an ideal and the beginning of a new world order built on the wreckage of the old.

Since its foundation, the UN has not been short of criticism. Critique has circled around its composition and institutional setup, ability to live up to its promises because of challenges to accountability and limited enforceability of global rules, and the perceived moral relativism because of underlying political choices and ideological bias. Described by some as the "tower of babble" with an "overwhelming bureaucracy and underwhelming leadership," the organization has seen both admiration and skepticism.[8]

First, a challenge has been the construction of and limitations to the exercise of global authority through the UN. The distinctive balance of power in the organization engineered around the veto of the "Big Five" of the Security Council has already been a major point of disagreement since the San Francisco Conference and adoption of the UN Charter in 1945. While it is intended as a safeguard mechanism for multilateral action, the veto power is seen by other UN Member States as outdated and unjust, even more so now given changed geopolitical circumstances.[9]

5 UN Charter Preamble.

6 Harry S. Truman, Speech at the Closing of the San Francisco Conference, June 26, 1945.

7 Ibid.

8 Dore Gold, *Tower of Babble: How the United Nations Has Fueled Global Chaos* (Crown Forum 2005); Thomas G. Weiss, *What's Wrong with the United Nations and How to Fix it* (Polity Press 2012).

9 Member States Call for Removing Veto Power, Expanding the Security Council to Include New Permanent Seats, as General Assembly Debates Reform Plans for 15-Member Organ, UN Doc. GA/12091, November 20, 2018, www.un.org/press/en/2018/ga12091.doc.htm, accessed on October 28, 2019.

A key argument for reform is that a balanced expansion of the Council would better reflect current global political and economic realities and ensure increased representation of developing countries, including permanent and non-permanent seats for Africa.[10] The hope is that this would allow to keep the oath to "we the peoples of the United Nations" as postulated in the Preamble in the UN Charter.

The UN remains criticized for its seemingly Western-centric orientation with translucent post-colonial attitudes that conserve the last century's structures of authority instead of revolutionizing the global space of wealth, dependence and justice. Scholars have even provocatively raised whether UN peacekeeping and peacebuilding is a new form of imperialism in disguise.[11] Some might argue that the whole mantra of progress in the UN is largely an illusion, and that the UN just reflects great power politics disposition.[12] At the same time, the anti-internationalization front tends to question why any powerful nation-state should concede governance at all to a global level. For them, the future does not belong to globalists but to patriots.[13] It seems as if the UN is for some not enough and for the others too much – a conundrum that is difficult to solve in an international community with inherently different voices.

Second, the mechanics for collective security for world peace have indeed seen occasions of malfunction. During the Korean War (1950–1953), the UN's dream of the eternal peace quickly met the reality of the Cold War with new alliances and bloc-thinking that turned Truman himself away from the internationalist vision. The "Uniting for Peace" resolution of the General Assembly, initiated by the US to circumvent a dead-locked Security Council, stands symbol for the powerlessness of the world's quasi-government. In other cases, the promise for collective security of humanity was seemingly not strong enough to prevent catastrophes of human suffering, including the genocide in Rwanda (1994) or the massacre of Srebrenica (1995). Srebrenica was the worst mass killing on European soil since World War II. At the commemoration of the twentieth anniversary of the Rwandan genocide, UN chief Ban Ki-moon emphasized that the "shame still clings, a generation

10 Ibid.

11 David N. Gibbs, "Is Peacekeeping a New Form of Imperialism?," *International Peacekeeping* 4.1(1997): 122–128; Constanze Schellhaas and Annette Seegers, "Peacebuilding: Imperialism's New Disguise?," *African Security Studies* 18.2(2009): 1–15.

12 This issue has been of debate since the creation of the United Nations, see Herbert W. Briggs, "Power Politics and International Organization," *American Journal of International Law* 39.4 (1945): 664–679.

13 For the debate, see: Amitav Acharya and Dan Plesch, "The United Nations: Managing and Reshaping a Changing World Order," *Global Governance* 26.2(2020): 221–235.

after the events."[14] In more recent times, the handling of the armed conflict in Syria has been in the sharp focus questioning the Council's ability to respond effectively to grave humanitarian situations.[15] Ban Ki-moon shared in March 2015 that he has "only shame and deep anger and frustration at the international community's impotence to stop the war" seeing how "year, after year, after year, the world has watched Syria being torn apart."[16] His words reflect the eagerness of the institution to do good while facing the realism of global Realpolitik.

Third, the constituted rules-based international order under the UN banner has faced inconsistencies. There have been cases where norms of international law and principles of the UN Charter were simply ignored by those who themselves are supposedly in charge of protecting them. The US military action in Iraq in 2003 is seen as one of those examples. UN Secretary-General Kofi Annan stressed at the time that the intervention of the US was nothing but "illegal."[17] In more recent instances, unilateral moves by a permanent member of the Security Council were decried by the other Council members but could not be stopped, such as when Russia annexed Crimea in 2014 or when the US recognized Israel's sovereignty over the Syrian Golan in March 2019.[18]

The point here is that those instances of inconsistency erode the rules-based international order. Critics rightfully highlight that there seems to be "double standards" of international law, if not even a two-class system of perceived privileges in the UN family.[19] Optimists would say that those circumstances

[14] Remarks at the commemoration of the 20th anniversary of the Rwandan genocide, UN Secretary-General, April 7, 2014, www.un.org/sg/en/content/sg/statement/2014-04-07/remarks-commemoration-20th-anniversary-rwandan-genocide-english-and, accessed on October 28, 2019.

[15] Graham Melling and Anne Dennett, "The Security Council Veto and Syria: Responding to Mass Atrocities Through the 'Uniting for Peace' Resolution," *Indian Journal of International Law* 57.3–4(2017): 285–307.

[16] In Syria, "'Best Humanitarian Solution Is a Political Solution to End the War," Secretary-General Tells Pledging Conference, UN Doc. SG/SM/16634-IHA/1363, March 31, 2015, www.un.org/press/en/2015/sgsm16634.doc.htm, accessed on October 28, 2019.

[17] "Lessons of Iraq War Underscore Importance of UN Charter – Annan," UN News, September 16, 2004, https://news.un.org/en/story/2004/09/115352-lessons-iraq-war-underscore-importance-un-charter-annan, accessed on October 28, 2019.

[18] Security Council Members Regret Decision by the United States to Recognize Israel's Sovereignty over Occupied Syrian Golan, UN Doc. SC/13753, March 27, 2019; Security Council Fails to Adopt Text Urging Member States Not to Recognize Planned 16 March Referendum in Ukraine's Crimea Region, UN Doc. SC/11319, March 15, 2014, www.un.org/press/en/2014/sc11319.doc.htm, accessed on October 28, 2019.

[19] See, e.g., Thomas M. Franck, "Of Gnats and Camels: Is there a Double Standard at the United Nations?," *The American Journal of International Law* 78.4(1984): 811–833; Carlos Ortiz, "Does a Double Standard Exist at the United Nations: A Focus on Iraq, Israel

have been exceptional, but they perpetuate the primacy of the powerful over the right of the truthful in a system where supposedly compliance is deemed to be the norm.[20] This also creates some sense of "organised hypocrisy" when the UN is not acting when it should or stays silent went it should not because of conflicting political pressures.[21] From a game theory perspective, those occasions of misbehavior are indeed destabilizing.[22] However, at least, they will not ignite an implosion of the international order as transgressions are to be expected, although they are not acceptable.

Fourth, there have been contradictions regarding the do-no-harm premise which obliges the UN as an organization to prevent and mitigate any negative impact of its actions on affected populations. Some dark chapters are cases of sexual exploitation and abuse by United Nations personnel, for instance by peacekeepers in the Democratic Republic of the Congo, the Central African Republic, and other places. The UN has taken special protection measures, including prioritizing the rights and dignity of victims, ending impunity, engaging with Member States, civil society and external partners, and improving strategic communication for education and transparency, but challenges remain.[23] Another prominent case is the cholera epidemic in Haiti in 2010 that was believed to be imported by United Nations peacekeepers.[24] The UN admitted that it has "a moral responsibility to the victims of the cholera epidemic" while upholding the immunity of the organization from any legal proceedings.[25] A more recent case has been the accusation that the UN failed victims that lived in UN-run camps contaminated by lead from a nearby industrial mine for more than

and the Influence of the United States on the UN," *Wisconsin International Law Journal* 22 (2004): 393–415.

20 See also James N. Rosenau, "Powerful Tendencies, Enduring Tensions and Glaring Contradictions: The United Nations in a Turbulent World," in: Albert J. Paolini, Anthony P. Jarvis, and Christian Reus-Smit (eds.), *Between Sovereignty and Global Governance: The United Nations, the State and Civil Society* (Palgrave Macmillan 1998) 252–273.

21 Michael Lipson, "Peacekeeping: Organized Hypocrisy?," *European Journal of International Relations* 13.1(2007): 5–34.

22 See also Kenneth W. Abbott, "Enriching Rational Choice Institutionalism for the Study of International Law," *University of Illinois Law Review* 1(2008): 5–46.

23 Report of the Secretary-General on Special Measures for Protection from Sexual Exploitation and Abuse, UN Doc. A/73/744, February 14, 2019, https://undocs.org/en/A/73/744, accessed on October 28, 2019.

24 Thomas G. Bode, "Cholera in Haiti: United Nations Immunity and Accountability," *Georgetown Journal of International Law* 47(2015): 759–791.

25 Noting Court Decision Upholding United Nations Immunity in Haiti Cholera Case, Secretary-General Urges Member States to Boost Support for Overcoming Epidemic, UN Press Release, UN Doc. SG/SM/17991, August 19, 2016, www.un.org/press/en/2016/sgsm17991.doc.htm, accessed on October 28, 2019.

a decade in Kosovo after the 1998–1999 war.[26] On one side, the UN acts as a "good Samaritan" while on the other side it has shielded itself from responsibility of any accused wrongdoing.[27]

Fifth, some have raised that the UN is in a crisis of relevance given many other international venues for multilateral cooperation.[28] Groups like the G7 and G20 have taken on global governance to advance economic, political, and security issues. These "multilateral steering groups" have been initially fora for macroeconomic coordination but now also cover matters of "high politics."[29] They are seen to be more flexible and adaptable institutions to maintain peace among the great powers and secure their prosperity.[30] Member States like France argue, for instance, that the G7 does not stand against the United Nations, but rather in support of it.[31] They say that the G7 is a "driving force and a space where new solutions can be tested, before being promoted in other forums such as the United Nations and multilateral technical or financial institutions."[32] Nonetheless, the proliferating and fluctuating set of new intergovernmental arrangements have certainly changed the dynamics of multilateralism.[33] Those "clubs" have expanded the pluralistic pattern of global order and challenge the universal approach of the UN.[34]

20.2 THE COMMITMENT: GEARING UP FOR SYSTEMIC CHALLENGES OF THE INTERNATIONAL COMMUNITY IN THE TWENTY-FIRST CENTURY

The UN's second Secretary-General Dag Hammarskjöld is often quoted for having said that the organization "was not created to take mankind to heaven,

26 Katharina Rall, UN Criticized for Failing to Live Up to Its Own Values in Kosovo, Human Rights Watch, October 25, 2019, www.hrw.org/news/2019/10/25/un-criticized-failing-live-its-own-values-kosovo, accessed on October 28, 2019.

27 Kristen E. Boon, "The United Nations as Good Samaritan: Immunity and Responsibility," *Chicago Journal of International Law* 16.2(2015): 341–385.

28 William W. Burke-White, "Power Shifts in International Law: Structural Realignment and Substantive Pluralism," *Harvard International Law Journal* 56(2015): 1–79.

29 Stewart M. Patrick, The G8 Proves Its Relevance, Council on Foreign Relations, May 27, 2011.

30 Peter I. Hajnal, *The G7/G8 System Evolution, Role and Documentation* (Routledge 1999) 1.

31 The G7: Frequently Asked Questions, France Diplomatie, www.diplomatie.gouv.fr/en/french-foreign-policy/french-g7-presidency/the-g7-frequently-asked-questions/, accessed on October 28, 2019.

32 Ibid.

33 Shepard Forman and Derk Segaar, "New Coalitions for Global Governance: The Changing Dynamics of Multilateralism," *Global Governance* 12.2(2006): 205–228.

34 Deborah Welch Larson, "New Perspectives on Rising Powers and Global Governance: Status and Clubs," *International Studies Review* 2.2(2018): 247–254.

but to save humanity from hell."[35] What he foresaw was probably that despite some faults, the UN is indispensable. We do not live in an ideal world, which makes organizations such as the UN imperfect but also imperative because of its well-intended aim to maintain peace, promote development, and protect human rights for the common good. The very ideal and cooperative purpose of the United Nations is "inescapable," more than "hopelessly utopian," at a time where global challenges are evidently transnational.[36]

Despite the systemic flaws and mentioned deficiencies, the track-record of the UN regarding its positive contributions and benefits seems unbeatable as a commitment to humanity. Rationally, the organization provides various important functions, including as a global service provider, engine of the global law and policy machinery, and vision for global idealism. All this makes the UN the global counterweight to unilateral propositions and untamed hegemonic power.

Since its inception, the United Nations has been spearheading efforts to maintain peace and security, through blue helmet peacekeeping, peace mediation initiatives, and other means. The UN's work is credited as a major factor for the 40-per cent decline in conflict around the world since the 1990s, having brokered over 170 peace settlements and assisting about 50 countries per year with their elections.[37] The organization's conflict prevention initiatives are often invisible but contribute significantly to defuse diplomatic tensions in one way or the other.[38] On the development and humanitarian side, the UN provides food to over 90 million people, delivers humanitarian aid in over 40 countries, makes sure that about 58 percent of children in the world are vaccinated, and assists more than 34 million refugees.[39] The UN World Health Organization (WHO) and UN partners have led the global effort to eradicate smallpox, decreased polio by more than 99 percent, and fought the outbreak of the Ebola virus.[40] If requested, the UN responds to rapidly to

35 Secretary-General's remarks at Dag Hammarskjöld lecture: "Evolving Threats, Timeless Values: The United Nations In A Changing Global Landscape," March 30, 2016, www.un.org/sg/en/content/sg/statement/2016-03-30/secretary-generals-remarks-dag-hammarskj%C3%B6ld-lecture-%E2%80%9Cevolving, accessed on October 28, 2019.

36 Joseph E. Schwartzberg, *Transforming the United Nations System: Designs for a Workable World* (United Nations University 2013) vii.

37 Douglas Roche, *The United Nations in the 21st Century: Grappling with the World's Most Challenging Issues: Militarism, the Environment, Human Rights, Inequality* (Lorimer 2015) 29.

38 Bertrand G. Ramcharan, *Preventive Diplomacy at the UN* (Indiana University Press 2008) 209.

39 UN, *The Essential UN* (United Nations 2018) 1.

40 World Health Statistics 2018: Monitoring health for the SDGs, WHO 2018, https://apps.who.int/iris/bitstream/handle/10665/272596/9789241565585-eng.pdf?ua=1, accessed on October 28, 2019.

emergencies caused by natural disasters such as floods and hurricanes.[41] Despite marginal critique by some, these achievements of the UN are largely acknowledged.

As the international community's global policy engine, the UN has codified a panoply of international law, including international human rights law, environmental law, international criminal law, international trade law, the sea law of treaties, space law, and other key areas. Following the expiration of the Millennium Development Goals (MDGs) in 2015, the Sustainable Development Goals (SDGs) promoted by the UN provided a common and global blueprint for all Member States to reach a world of dignity for all by 2030. In 2016, the Paris Agreement on addressing climate change was signed by the largest amount of countries ever in a single day, exemplifying the force of international consensus. The UN remains the go-to place to discuss future issues of universal concern, including rising challenges of international security and the emergence of Artificial Intelligence (AI), cyber-governance, biotechnology, and other frontier domains.[42] These policy artefacts indicate that the UN continues to be a venue of choice for multilateral diplomacy disregard its insufficiencies and the emergence of multiple new fora that complement the international policy discourse.

Eventually, the most powerful asset of the UN is its function as a vault for hope and dreams of the international community and its people of a "better world." Empirical studies have shown that public support of the UN is closely linked to the extent to which citizens believe that nation-states fail to properly address pressing global political matters.[43] In other words, international organizations like the UN are perceived as better alternatives to synthesize international affairs. As surveys of the last decade show, publics around the world continue to have a positive impression of the UN.[44] The real leverage of

[41] "Tropical Cyclone Idai Affects 1.5 Million Across Mozambique and Malawi, as UN Ramps Up Response," UN News, March 15, 2019, https://news.un.org/en/story/2019/03/1034741, accessed on October 28, 2019.

[42] Artificial intelligence summit focuses on fighting hunger, climate crisis and transition to "smart sustainable cities," UN News, May 28, 2019, https://news.un.org/en/story/2019/05/1039311, accessed on October 28, 2019. See also CEB Survey on Frontier Issues, Secretariat of the Chief Executives Board for Coordination (CEB), October 27, 2017, www.unsceb.org/CEBPublicFiles/FINAL%20Summary%20of%20responses%20to%20CEB%20survey%20on%20frontier%20issues%202017-10-27.pdf, accessed on October 28, 2019.

[43] Matthias Ecker-Ehrhardt, "Why Do Citizens Want the UN to Decide? Cosmopolitan Ideas, Particularism and Global Authority," *International Political Science Review* 37.1(2016): 99–114.

[44] Moira Fagan and Christine Huang, United Nations gets mostly positive marks from people around the world, Pew Research Center, September 23, 2019, www.pewresearch.org/fact-tank/2019/09/23/united-nations-gets-mostly-positive-marks-from-people-around-the-world/, accessed on October 28, 2019.

authority left to the UN is its powers of moral and political persuasion to frame ideas as global references. The UN is not just a "talk shop"; it wields authority because it represents the "collective sentiment" of the international community.[45] This inherent utopian dream embodied by the organization is a normative one with regard to the reliance on international law as a factor of global order but also a practical one as an aspirational dream to ultimately achieve the goals of the UN Charter.[46]

20.3 CONCLUSION

"More than ever before in human history, we share a common destiny. We can master it only if we face it together. And that, my friends, is why we have the United Nations," said UN Secretary-General Kofi Annan with confidence a few weeks before the beginning of the new millennium.[47] Indeed, anyone scrutinizing the United Nations "cannot fail to see both promise and disillusionment" as it "mirrors humankind with all its failings and all its potential."[48] As others have highlighted, the organization "does not exist in isolation from the world that it is attempting to serve."[49] Against this oscillating background, the UN is a seismograph for tipping points in international law and international relations, for the ups and downs of international commitment and unresolved global problems.

In 2020, the United Nations is celebrating its 75th anniversary. Following the Zeitgeist of mega announcements, the UN promised to have the "biggest-ever global conversation" about the future of the planet.[50] The objective of the

45 Ian Hurd, *After Anarchy: Legitimacy and Power in the United Nations Security Council* (Princeton University Press 2017) 6.

46 See also Rossana Deplan, "Building Pragmatic Utopias: The 'Other' Security Council, International Law, and the United Nations Dream," *German Yearbook of International Law* 60(2017): 608; Martti Koskenniemi, *From Apology to Utopia: The Structure of International Legal Argument* (Cambridge University Press 2006).

47 Secretary-General Emphasizes Important Role of the United Nations for the New Millennium, UN Press Release, UN Doc. SG/SM/7262, December 15, 1999, www.un.org/press/en/1999/19991215.sgsm7262.doc.html, accessed on October 28, 2019.

48 Horst Koehler, "The End of Humankind's Dream?: The United Nations in the 21st Century," Address given at the official ceremony hosted by the United Nations Association of Germany to mark the 70th anniversary of the founding of the United Nations (Translated from the original German), Berlin, Germany, October 21, 2015, www.horstkoehler.de/en/speeches-texts/the-end-of-humankinds-dream-the-united-nations-in-the-21st-century/, accessed on October 28, 2019.

49 Thomas G. Weiss and Sam Daws, "World Politics: Continuity and Change Since 1945," in: idem, *The Oxford Handbook on the United Nations* (Oxford University Press 2007, 1st ed.) 4.

50 We need to talk: UN gears up for 75th anniversary with Global Conversations, UN News, October 24, 2019, https://news.un.org/en/story/2019/10/1049961, accessed on October 28, 2019.

dialogues would be "to listen to the hopes and fears of a wide range of people, to learn from their experiences, and spark discussion on ways to build a better world for all."[51] "We need to talk" has been a slogan for the celebrations. This call emphasizes the essential of the pressing urgency to reconnect the organization, its Member States and "we the peoples" as noted in the UN Charter. The recurrent aim in this endeavor is to keep the United Nations relevant to those its promises and serves.

Against the backdrop of COVID-19, the attempt to increase trust of people in public institutions is important more than ever before. At a time of mis- and disinformation aggravating fears and concerns about the global mess, State interventions and the benefits of multilateral responds are measured by their deeds. Words of global commitment remain honorable but vanish quickly from a local perspective if they remain without tangible action. The pandemic showed that the UN remains both a token for joint action and punch bag depending on what seems more advantageous for domestic politics and needs. In all of this, the organization plays a delicate function that justifies and protects its existence. For the spirit of utopia to survive, the UN needs to deliver on its potential.

Reflecting about the central theme of this edited volume, it appears that it might not be the lack of commitment to universal norms at large that has brought us into this real or perceived crisis of international law, but rather the unavoidable compromises international affairs entail and the moments in history when they peak. There seem to be at least two consequences: eyes shut and keep going; or lower the bar of commitment to be more accurately judged against one's self-obliged promises. Eventually, the latter is what is silently happening when the commitments miss matching their deeds and this recalibrated vow becomes the new normalcy.

Indeed, new challenges to the global law and international policy machinery will constantly test past commitments and make future apologies for noncompliance sound almost like a mockery. For the UN there is nothing left but the exceptional choice to conserve its institutional core of values, principles, and beliefs, while constantly reinventing parts of itself through thematic expansion, celebrating innovation, and manoeuvring through the messy real-world realities. Eventually, the UN is a policy, law and dream machine at the same time for which "value for money" cannot be mechanically defined in this transactional era.

Political advisers of the highest UN leadership have pointed out that profound change of the "fraught global landscape" is confronting the UN;

[51] Ibid.

while "precisely when it is most needed," an "international order based on cooperation is no longer guaranteed."[52] Others have suggested that the UN and multilateralism are seemingly "under siege" at a time when pulling out of multilateral arrangements in favor of making bilateral deals is in vogue, and called for a "great reawakening of the United Nations."[53] The calls for a "Second Generation" of United Nations, restructured and back in shape so that it can rise to its challenges, stand as a symbol for the desire to make the organization instead of decommissioning and replacing it.[54]

Secretary-General Guterres has made proposals to reform the United Nations since the beginning of his term in January 2017 to pursue sweeping changes in the areas of the UN development system, the management of the organization, concerning the peace and security pillar. He has highlighted that the goal of reform is a twenty-first century United Nations "focused more on people and less on process," "more on delivery and less on bureaucracy."[55] "We know that the true test of reform will not be measured in words in New York or world capitals. It will be measured through tangible results in the lives of the people we serve – and the trust of those who support our work through their hard-earned resources. Value for money while advancing shared values – that is our common goal," Guterres emphasized.[56] In this spirit, it needs eternal perseverance, belief and steadiness to keep the critique and commitment of the United Nations in balance. The UN is far from perfect, but without it, the world would be a far more disconnected and divided place.

52 Michèle Griffin, "The UN's Role in a Changing Global Landscape," in: Thomas G. Weiss and Sam Daws (eds.), *The Oxford Handbook on the United Nations* (Oxford University Press 2018, 2nd ed.) 823.

53 Thomas G. Weiss, "The UN and Multilateralism under Siege in the 'Age of Trump'," *Global Summitry* 4.1(2018): 1–17.

54 Michael Bartolo, *Second Generation United Nations* (Routledge 2019). See also Hitakshi Joshi and Maherbaanali Sheliya, "The Efficacy of the United Nations in a New World Order," *Journal of Advances in Humanities and Social Sciences* 4.6(2018): 279–286; Yves Beigbeder, *The Internal Management of United Nations Organizations* (Palgrave 2017); John Allphin Moore and Jr., Jerry Pubantz, *The New United Nations: International Organization in the Twenty-First Century* (Routledge 2017).

55 António Guterres Remarks at UN Reform Event, UN Headquarters, September 18, 2017, www.un.org/sg/en/content/sg/speeches/2017-09-18/secretary-generals-reform-remarks.

56 Ibid.

21

Universalism

M. N. S. Sellers

International law purports to be universal, applicable everywhere and binding on all people and states. This "law of nations" begins, as Henry Wheaton famously insisted, with "those rules of conduct which reason deduces as consonant to justice, from the nature of the society existing among independent nations."[1] Thus international law transcends, claims to transcend, or at least *should* transcend culture, religion, and all other transient elements of human difference to protect our shared humanity,[2] and all of this would be true, as Hugo Grotius persuasively observed, even if we were to concede (*etiamsi daremus*) that there is no divine sanction for these universal truths.[3] The very concepts of international law, the law of humanity, and the law of nations assume and require recognition that "the inherent dignity" and "the equal and inalienable rights of all members of the human family" are indeed "the foundation of freedom, justice and peace in the world."[4] International law asserts itself as our universal entitlement, "without distinction of any kind, such as race, colour, sex, language, religion, political or other opinion, national or social origin, property, birth, or other status."[5] If it did not, it would not be worthy of our attention or respect.

How then can one speak of "tipping points" or engage in a "critique" of international law, whose only source and purpose is universal justice, and the

1 Henry Wheaton, *Elements of International Law* (Philadelphia, 1836) at §11, p. 46. Cf. James Madison, *An Examination of the British Doctrine Which Subjects to Capture a Neutral Trade Not Open in Time of Peace* (London, 1806) at p. 41.

2 *See* M. N .S. Sellers, *Parochialism, Cosmopolitanism, and the Foundations of International Law* (Cambridge, 2012).

3 Hugo Grotius, *De Iure Belli ac Pacis libri tres: In quibus Ius Naturae et Gentium item iuris publici praecipua explicantur* (Frankfurt, 1626) at prolegomena, p. vi: "Et haec quidem quae iam diximus, locum haberent etiamsi daremus, quod sine summo scelere dare nequit, non esse Deum, aut non curare ab eo negotia humana."

4 *Universal Declaration of Human Rights* (December 10, 1948) Preamble.

5 *Ibid.*, Article 2.

common good of all human beings?[6] The concept of the "tipping point" is useful for international law in at least two legal contexts; first, in the foundational battle for transnational legality itself, and second, for the subsidiary task of delimiting international law's particular jurisdiction, with regard to other sources of law or authority.[7] Note the conflict between the concept of "tipping points" in law and the concept of a "critique" of law. To make a "critique" of law is to evaluate the law as it actually is (κρίνω, κρίνειν), whereas to identify a "tipping point" of law is merely to identify the point at which law becomes sociologically salient and widely taken into account.[8] To make a "critique" is to engage with the actual substantive value of law as a normative science. To discover the "tipping point" at which certain laws become effective is to engage in a sociological study. Put another way: "critiques" concern the *substance* of normative truth, while "tipping points" concern the *processes* through which ideas gain currency, whether they have any normative value (or not).

The distinction between criticism and the study of tipping points mirrors the distinction between philosophy and rhetoric, which also marks the difference between the legitimacy and the effectiveness of law. International law seeks both. Without legitimacy, law has no value, but without effectiveness, law has no influence on public affairs. To make a critique of the law is to make the argument for a better understanding of the law. Critics seek to propagate a particular point of view. They also seek to precipitate a tipping point, after which their perceptions will become canonical. This requires not only truth, but persuasiveness, not just accuracy, but guile. Precisely because international law lacks the decisive legislative, executive, and judicial institutions of most national legal systems, the power of publicists and public opinion is magnified. International law may indeed be "those rules of conduct which reason deduces, as consonant to justice, from the nature of the society existing among independent nations,"[9] but the requirements of reason can be opaque, which opens the possibility that tipping points in the public perception of international law may be separate from – or even unrelated to – a reasoned understanding of what international law actually requires us to do.

6 *Cf.* Hugo Grotius, *De Iure Belli ac Pacis* (Frankfurt, 1626) at prolegomena, pp. iv–v: "Haec vero quam rudi modo iam expressimus societatis custodia humano intellectui conveniens, fons est eius iuris, quod proprie tali nomine apellatur."; John Rawls, *The Law of Peoples: With The Idea of Public Reason Revisited* (Cambridge, Massachusetts, 1999) p. 67: "a common good idea of justice that takes in account . . . everyone in society."

7 On "Tipping Points," see Malcolm Gladwell, *The Tipping Point: How Little Things Can Make a Big Difference* (Boston, 2000). Gladwell stressed the importance of "connectors," "mavens," and "salesmen" in getting ideas to be more widely accepted by society at large.

8 *See* Thomas Schelling, *Micromotives and Macrobehavior* (New York, 1978).

9 *See* Henry Wheaton, *Elements of International Law* (Philadelphia, 1836) at §11, p. 46.

21.1 JUSTICE AGAINST POWER

The first and most significant tipping point to consider in the discourse of international law is the balance between justice and power, between the rule of law and arbitrary assertions of unwarranted authority. Emer de Vattel observed that the fundamental content and requirements of the law of nations are "necessary."[10] International law is "necessary" because it arises from the realities of human nature and the necessary requirements of a just society. The law of nations is the science of the rights and duties that govern nations and states – and their peoples or subjects.[11] But there has always been a rival point of view, attributed by Hugo Grotius to Carneades, that all men and nations seek only their own advantage, to the detriment of everyone else, and that it would be foolish to pretend otherwise.[12] Thomas Hobbes clearly stated this pernicious doctrine when he wrote that the natural state of all men and nations is perpetual "Warre,"[13] in which there is "no Law," no "Justice or Injustice" and "Force and Fraud" are "the two Cardinell vertues,"[14] so that "every man has a Right to every thing; even to one another's body."[15] This doctrine is antithetical to the very concept of international law.[16]

The foundational conflict between international law, which seeks to establish a more just world on the basis of reason and humanity, and the doctrines of Carneades and Hobbes, which seek personal advantage at the expense of all others, will never be entirely resolved. Cicero and Grotius found the first foundations of law in human sociability which leads us to co-operate and consider the welfare of other human beings,[17] but if we are honest we will admit that there is also a strong natural human propensity for injustice,

[10] Emer de Vattel, *Le Droit des Gens, ou prinçipes de la Loi Naturelle, Appliqués à la conduite et aux affaires des Nations et des Souverains* (London, 1758) at préliminaires, §7, p. 4: "Nous apellons *Droit des Gens nécessaire* celui qui consiste dans l'application du Droit Naturel aux Nations. Il est *nécessaire*, parceque les Nations sont absolument obligées à l'observer."

[11] *Ibid.*, §3 p. 1.

[12] Hugo Grotius, *De Iure Belli ac Pacis* (Frankfurt, 1626) at prolegomena, p. iii.

[13] Thomas Hobbes, *Leviathian, or The Matter, Forme, and Power of a Commonwealth Ecclesiasticall and Civil* (London, 1651) at chapter XIII, p. 62.

[14] *Ibid.*, p. 63.

[15] *Ibid.*, at chapter XIV, p. 64.

[16] See *e.g.* John Bolton, National Security Advisor of the United States, *Speech to the Federalist Society*, September 10, 2018: "the hard men of history are not deterred by fantasies of international law."

[17] Hugo Grotius, *De Iure Belli ac Pacis* (Frankfurt, 1626) at prolegomena, p. iv: "Inter haec autem quae homini sunt propria, est appetitus societatis, id est communitatis, non qualiscunque, sed tranquillae et pro sui intellectus modo ordinatae cum his qui sui sunt generis." *Cf.* Marcus Tullius Cicero, *de legibus*, I.v.16: "quae sit coniunctio hominum, quae naturalis societas inter ipsos; his enim explicatis fons legum et iuris inveniri potest." *See also*, I. xv. 42–43.

drawing us to unite into self-interested factions, which violate the rights of other people and nations.[18] Publicists seeking to develop and clarify the doctrines of international law have often been mistaken in their perceptions of international justice, and most such mistakes have favoured the publicist himself, or the publicist's co-nationals, to the detriment of justice and the common good.[19]

The very fact that the only proper basis, purpose, and source of international law is universal justice and the common good of all humanity invites critique when the law as it is applied and understood in practice fails to meet these unattainable standards.[20] The first tipping point to be considered in evaluating international law must be the threshold question whether the international legal system, taken as a whole, makes international relations and international society more just than they would otherwise have been, or not. If international law, taken as a whole or in relevant part, bends the arc of the moral universe towards justice,[21] then it is worthy of our support. If not, it should be made to do so. The same is true of every particular doctrine, custom, and practice of international law. We have a duty to undertake a critique of international law in the light of its purposes, and to make the law function as it always ought to have done, in the service of justice and peace.[22]

21.2 UNIVERSAL TRUTH

The first principle of international law – that all members of the human family have inherent dignity, and therefore equal and inalienable rights – supplies the standard against which we must measure our existing doctrines and institutions.[23] This universalism, which is at the heart of international law,

18 Thus, even Hugo Grotius may be seen to have shaped his interpretation of international law for the benefit of Dutch commerce. *See* Hugo Grotius, *Mare Liberum: sive de jure quod Batavis competit ad Indicana commercia dissertatio* (Leiden, 1609).

19 On this phenomenon *see (e.g.)* Antony Anghie, *Imperialism, Sovereignty, and the Making of International Law* (Cambridge, 2004).

20 *See* M. N. S. Sellers, "The Purpose of International Law is to Advance Justice – and International Law Has No Value Unless It Does So" in *Proceedings of the ASIL Annual Meeting* vol. 111 (2017) p. 301.

21 *Cf.* Theodore Parker, *Ten Sermons of Religion*, 2nd ed. (Boston, 1861) pp. 84–85. *Cf.* the many references to this quotation by Martin Luther King, Jr. and Barack Obama, among others.

22 Thus the doctrine "Inter Gentes Jus et Pax," motto of the American Society of International Law (1906).

23 *Cf.* Emer de Vattel, *Le Droit des Gens* (London, 1758) at §15, p. 9: "Les Nations étant libres et indépendantes les unes des autres, puisque les hommes sont naturellement libres et indépendans . . . La Société naturelle des Nations ne peut subsister, si les Droits que chacune a reçus de la Nature n'y sont pas respectés."

does not preclude the possibility of difference, or the necessity of protecting difference, when difference and the protection of difference are themselves among the requirements of a just society.[24] This introduces the second significant tipping point in international law, which arises in making the distinction between those human concerns that are universal, global, or transnational, and therefore properly the subject of international law, and those human concerns that are parochial, cultural, or private and therefore not properly the subject of international law, but rather of national or local concern, or rightly beyond the reach of any legal authority.

The tipping point between the universal and the particular, or between what is properly cosmopolitan and what ought to be parochial, hinges on the nature of the subject matter.[25] Some concerns, such as human rights, environmental protection, and peace are inherently transnational and universal,[26] while other matters, such as culture and democracy, are more properly national and local.[27] The more homogenous, unified, and culturally distinct a political community becomes, the more likely the dominant faction will oppress minorities and impose its will on the rest,[28] requiring transnational guarantees (for example) that no state shall deprive any person of life, liberty, or property, without due process of law.[29] States, on the other hand, should not relinquish control when the objectives of the proposed action are best achieved at the regional or local level.[30] Local solidarity, shared experience, and parochial projects supply much that is sweetest in life, in pursuit of civic ceremonies and other community enterprises.[31]

Drawing the line between what is or properly ought to be transnational and universal and what is or ought to be local and particular constitutes one of the central purposes and therefore the second great tipping point of international law, governing the legitimacy of the enterprise itself. International law loses legitimacy and normative force when it invades what ought to have been the domestic jurisdiction of states. International law equally loses legitimacy and

[24] *See* M. N. S. Sellers (ed.), *Parochialism, Cosmopolitanism, and the Foundations of International Law* (Cambridge, 2012).

[25] *See e.g.*, G. A. Bermann, "Taking Subsidiarity Seriously: Subsidiarity in the European Community and in the United States" in *Columbia Law Review* vol. 94 (1994) at p. 331.

[26] *See e.g.*, *Charter of the United Nations* (1945) Preamble.

[27] *Ibid.*, Article 2 § 7.

[28] *See* "Publius" James Madison, *The Federalist: A Collection of Essays Written in Favour of the New Constitution* (New York, 1788) no. 10, in volume 1, p. 5, on "The Utility of the Union as a Safeguard against Domestic Faction and Insurrection."

[29] *Cf. Constitution of the United States*, Amendment V (1791) and Amendment XIV (1868).

[30] *Cf. Treaty on European Union*, Article 5.

[31] *Cf. International Covenant on Economic, Social, and Cultural Rights* (1966) Article I.

normative force when it fails to control and govern states where it ought to have done so. Thus, the legitimacy of the international legal system as a whole turns on two axes. One axis concerns the line between justice and arbitrary power. The second concerns the balance between universal and parochial concerns. These are the two most important "tipping points" of international law.

21.3 LEGITIMACY

The first "tipping point" to be considered in evaluating international law is whether the international legal system taken as a whole, or any particular proposed rule of international law, is legitimate or not. By "legitimate" I mean actually legitimate, which is to say conforming to the standards and principles that justify the practice in question.[32] The standard of legitimacy for all law and legal systems, including international law and the international legal system, is justice and the common good of humanity.[33] This doctrine of Aristotle[34] and Cicero[35] became the basis on which Hugo Grotius,[36] Emer de Vattel,[37] and Henry Wheaton[38] built the modern science of international law, which they justified as necessary for a just society of independent states.[39] Without legitimacy, international law loses its authority to be obeyed. Without legitimacy, there can be no normative force.

The legitimacy of law or any other social practice is a matter of degree. Law can be more (or less) legitimate, more (or less) worthy of our respect or obedience. Thus, the relevance of the concept of "tipping points" to the study of international law. At what point does the system of international law as it actually exists gain sufficient legitimacy to deserve our deference? This can hinge on many factors, but first among them should be the universal value of human well-being. To earn legitimacy, most legal systems claim to "establish justice," or "insure domestic tranquility," or "promote the general welfare," or "secure the blessings of liberty" for those they presume to rule.[40]

32 *See* M. N. S. Sellers (ed.), *Law, Reason, and Emotion* (Cambridge, 2017) at p. 26.
33 *See* M. N. S. Sellers, "Some Thoughts on the Value and Purpose of Law" in Joshua Kassner and Colin Starger (eds.) *The Value and Purpose of Law* (Stuttgart, 2019) at p. 256.
34 Aristoteles, *Politika* at III.vii.1; 13.
35 Marcus Tullius Cicero, *de officiis*, at III.vi.26.
36 Hugo Grotius, *De jure Belli ac Pacis* (Frankfurt, 1626).
37 Emer de Vattel, *Le Droit des Gens* (London, 1758).
38 Henry Wheaton, *Elements of International Law; with a Sketch of the History of the Science* (Philadelphia, 1836).
39 *See supra*, note 1.
40 *See e.g. Constitution of the United States* (1787) Preamble.

Applied to international law this requires maintaining international peace and security, suppressing acts of aggression, implementing the principles of justice, and promoting respect for human rights and fundamental freedoms for all.[41]

Legal systems and those who promote legal systems or regimes make constant reference to the standards of legitimacy that justify the law, not only because they may in some cases sincerely seek justice, liberty, and the public welfare, but also because they do not. Powerful and self-interested actors seeking to impose their authority on others will be more effective if they employ law as the instrument of their oppression. This legal technique works best when the law's subjects accept, respect, and conform to the law's demands. This guides even the most cynical, corrupt, and oppressive rulers to speak in the name of justice, to claim justice as their purpose, and even (when it costs them little), to act justly. The law is more effective when it is just, because justice invites obedience and co-operation. All legal regimes claim justice, because justice confers legitimacy, and even spurious claims of justice can bolster authority, when they are believed.

21.4 EFFECTIVENESS

Law is only useful when it is effective, and all law seeks to be effective, whether it is legitimate or not. This leads to a second tipping point in international law, as in every other legal system. Law can be legitimate or not, and some legal systems may be more legitimate than others. The same is true of effectiveness. Some legal systems are more effective than others. And the less effective legal systems are, the less useful they will be, even if they are otherwise legitimate – or would have been legitimate, if they were more effective. This makes effectiveness itself an element of legitimacy. Legal systems are useless if they have no effect, which may alter the nature of what ought to be the law in practice. This interrelationship between legitimacy and effectiveness is particularly acute in the case of international law, which lacks strong enforcement mechanisms. The law's effectiveness depends upon its legitimacy, and vice versa.

The science of law, like all other social and normative sciences, requires two distinct and complementary approaches: philosophy and rhetoric. Philosophy is the study of truth, in this case the truth about international law. Rhetoric is the art of persuasion.[42] The legitimacy of international law is primarily

[41] *Charter of the United Nations* (1945) at Chapter I, Article 1.

[42] Aristoteles, *Rhetoriké*, I.2, 1355b. 26f.

a philosophical question, concerning the requirements of a just society of states.[43] But the effectiveness of international law is primarily a question of rhetoric, concerning the presentation and structuring of international law to secure the obedience, the deference, and perhaps even the allegiance of those whom law seeks to guide and control. Philosophy and law begin as theoretical and normative inquiries, but they must become practical and rhetorical to be effective, since law must be effective to be fully legitimate, which complicates the equation.

The universal authority, universal validity, and universal value of international law (the "*droit nécessaire*") arise from universal human nature, which dictates certain rights and duties, necessary for a just society of states.[44] But securing the effectiveness of international law depends on the actual power of existing states, the actual prejudices of existing cultures, the actual needs of existing peoples, and any number of considerations that may or may not directly reflect the requirements of justice, or the necessary principles of international law applied to a society of sovereign and independent nations. Peace and security (for example) may have different requirements than justice, yet there will be no justice without peace and security (and vice versa), so they must be taken into account.[45]

21.5 TIPPING POINTS

The metaphor of "tipping points" is useful in understanding universal international law because it illustrates and makes vivid the primary truths on which the whole system depends. First, the legitimacy (and therefore the normative authority) of international law must reach a certain level (or "tipping point") before the law becomes valid for its subjects. Second, the effectiveness (and therefore the practical authority) of international law must reach a certain level (or "tipping point") before the law becomes binding in fact. The first inquiry corresponds to an ideal theory of international law – the law as it ought to be, without reference to the constraints and corruption of existing reality. The second inquiry reflects the actual non-ideal situation in which we live, taking the power and corruption of the existing order more fully into account. This second tipping point considers how much justice and legitimacy must be

43 *See* M. N. S. Sellers, *Republican Principles in International Law, The Fundamental Requirements of a Just World Order* (Basingstoke, 2006).

44 Emer de Vattel, *Droit des Gens* (London, 1758) at préliminaires, §7, p. 4.

45 *See Charter of the United Nations* (1945), Preamble and Article I.

sacrificed in practice, in order to secure a more effective international legal regime.

The point at which the established international legal regime or any other institution tips towards actual legitimacy depends on the standard that justifies the practice.[46] In the case of international law, the standard of legitimacy is global justice and the establishment of a just international legal order. Global justice, in turn, requires the proper structure of rights and duties, benefits and liabilities, restrictions and liberties in global society, so that a worthwhile and fulfilling life is as much as possible available to all, taking everyone into account and disregarding no one. This is the "common good" conception of justice advanced by Aristotle, Cicero, Grotius, Vattel, Wheaton, and all those who established and developed the practice of international law.[47] Achieving global justice requires the gradual and progressive development of international law and institutions,[48] taking into account the barriers and limitations that stand between universal justice and the corrupt reality of our existing world. Some price in legitimacy must always be paid to achieve effective law. But there is a tipping point beyond which the price for effectiveness becomes too steep, and the whole construct falls.

The final vital tipping point in international law occurs when some human need or interest becomes so implicated in international society that it tips into the jurisdiction of international law. Like the tipping point between justice and power, this tipping point between parochial and global concerns may shift as international society becomes more integrated and advanced – or perhaps more disorganised and chaotic. In this respect, international society as a whole may be illuminated by the emergence and development of multinational federations, such as the European Union or the United States of America. First, such obviously transnational concerns as taxation, commerce, currency, science, and international peace and security can be seen to require the jurisdiction of some federal authority.[49] Later, human and procedural rights demand transnational enforcement.[50] Finally, the financial[51] and environmental[52] needs of international society cannot be fulfilled without recourse to international laws and jurisdiction. Each step towards

46 *See* M. N. S. Sellers (ed.), *Law, Reason, and Emotion* (Cambridge, 2017) pp 26ff. on "Legitimacy."

47 *See supra*, notes 5, 17, and 34.

48 *Charter of the United Nations* (1945) Article 13 (1) (a).

49 *See e.g. Constitution of the United States of America* (1787) Article I §8.

50 *Ibid.*, Amendment XIV (1868).

51 *See e.g. Marrakesh Agreement Establishing the World Trade Organization* (1995).

52 *See e.g.* the *Paris Agreement* (2015) of the parties to the *United Nations Framework Convention on Climate Change* (1992).

international institutions makes necessary co-ordination more possible, where it was not possible before.

21.6 CRITIQUE

While the study of tipping points is sociological and pragmatic, the practice of critique is normative and decisive. And although the tipping point between effective and ineffective law may be discovered by observation, the tipping point between legitimate and illegitimate law requires criticism. Determining whether the law or legal system is legitimate or not invites a critique – and the critique must take place in the light of the universal standards that justify (or ought to justify) the law. This brings the inquiry back to the fundamental principles of global justice, and above all that "all human beings are born free and equal in dignity and rights," and being "endowed with reason," should "act towards one another in a spirit of brotherhood."[53] This makes the universal rights of humanity "a common standard" for all peoples and all nations, and the necessary foundation for all "freedom, justice, and peace in the world."[54]

To make an effective critique of international law, and establish the "tipping point" at which international law secures its legitimate authority, would-be critics must make clear and respect the simple and easily understood standards that justify the law of nations. "Those rules of conduct which reason deduces as consonant to justice from the nature of the society existing among independent states"[55] rest in turn on recognition of "the inherent dignity and of the equal and inalienable rights of all members of the human family."[56] The first task and organising principle of all criticism of international law must always be to secure and protect (through the rule of law) the human rights and mutual obligations that arise from the "dignity and worth of the human person and the equal rights of men and women" everywhere.[57]

All those who would make a critique of international law, or pursue a study of the "tipping point" at which international law achieves legitimate authority, must bear in mind the simple standards of dignity, equality, and fraternity that justify the enterprise. The clear, uncomplicated, and easily understood standards of Grotius, Wheaton, and the *Universal Declaration of Human Rights* provide the yardstick against which all proposed laws and legal standards may

53 *Universal Declaration of Human Rights* (December 10, 1948) Article I.
54 *Ibid.*, Preamble.
55 *See supra*, note 9.
56 *Universal Declaration of Human Rights* (December 10, 1048) Preamble.
57 *Ibid.*

be measured and criticised. Too often scholars and practitioners of international law forget its universal foundations and slip into fantasies of unexplained, unsupported, and therefore ultimately unconvincing doctrine, which makes the whole legal system less effective, by bringing it into disrepute. All criticism of international law on any basis other than its justice or injustice, its legitimacy, or its effectiveness will necessarily fail. Only universal values can support the law that claims to regulate humanity.

21.7 CONCLUSION

International law is universal and must be universal, if it is to govern the world. The universal standards that justify the enterprise arise from the inherent dignity and equal and inalienable rights of all members of the human family. To deny these principles is to destroy international law. The tipping point at which international law achieves legitimate authority is the point at which international law sufficiently recognises and secures the dignity and worth of all human beings and the equal rights of men and women everywhere, through the international rule of law. This underlying standard of justification requires that all critique of international law begin with these principles, or fail, by losing its putative legitimacy. To achieve international jurisdiction, international law must rest on universal truths, which it finds in the universal dignity of the human person, and equal worth of every human being.

International law asserts the claims of justice against arbitrary power. This makes the law of nations both "necessary" and universal, because it rests on human nature, and the nature of human society. There is a temptation in speaking of "tipping points" to consider only the point at which laws become effective, which is significant, and important, but not sufficient to understand what matters most in the international legal regime. International law is a normative science and therefore requires not only observation, but also critique. We must be able to explain why universal laws are legitimate, and justified, or they will cease to be effective, because they will be unworthy of our consideration, of our obedience, or our respect. International law arises from universal truths. Forget or undermine these foundations, and the whole edifice will fall to the ground.

Index

For EU product safety concerns, contact us at Calle de José Abascal, 56–1°,
28003 Madrid, Spain or eugpsr@cambridge.org.

www.ingramcontent.com/pod-product-compliance
Lightning Source LLC
LaVergne TN
LVHW010341220926
848484LV00004BB/1025